MW01088925

The Afterlife of *Little Women*

The Afterlife of *Little Women*

BEVERLY LYON CLARK

Johns Hopkins University Press

Baltimore

© 2014 Johns Hopkins University Press
All rights reserved. Published 2014
Printed in the United States of America on acid-free paper

2 4 6 8 9 7 5 3 1

Johns Hopkins University Press
2715 North Charles Street
Baltimore, Maryland 21218-4363
www.press.jhu.edu

Cataloging-in-Publication Data is available from the Library of Congress.

A catalog record for this book is available from the British Library.

ISBN-13: 978-1-4214-1558-1 (hardcover: acid-free paper)
ISBN-10: 1-4214-1558-5 (hardcover: acid-free paper)
ISBN-13: 978-1-4214-1559-8 (electronic)
ISBN-10: 1-4214-1559-3 (electronic)

Special discounts are available for bulk purchases of this book.
For more information, please contact Special Sales at 410-516-6936 or
specialsales@press.jhu.edu.

Johns Hopkins University Press uses environmentally friendly book
materials, including recycled text paper that is composed of at least
30 percent post-consumer waste, whenever possible.

For Roger, Adam, Wendy, Kristina, and Matthew,
and in memory of Norma and Maurice Lyon

Contents

Acknowledgments   *ix*

Introduction   1

1 Becoming Everyone's Aunt, 1868–1900   8

2 Waxing Nostalgic, 1900–1930   42

3 Outwitting Poverty and War, 1930–1960   102

4 Celebrating Sisterhood and Passion since 1960   138

Notes   201
Index   259

Acknowledgments

I am grateful to the colleagues who, over the years, have shared Alcott materials and enthusiasm for Alcott, including Jan Alberghene, Hilary Crew, Chris Doyle, Greg Eiselein, Linnea Hendrickson, Joel Myerson, Anne Phillips, Lauren Rizzuto, Daniel Shealy, Mary Shelden, Betsey Shirley, Laureen Tedesco, and Roberta Trites. And to friends, family, and colleagues who have offered insights into various chapters, including Roger Clark (always my best first reader), Cécile Danehy, Susan Dearing, Tommasina Gabriele, Ed Gallagher, Marah Gubar, Lori Kenschaft, Tessa Lee, Kim Miller, Paul Sorrentino, Sue Standing, Josh Stenger, Maureen Taylor, and Mary Beth Tierney-Tello. Participants in the meetings of the Children's Literature Association, the American Literature Association, the Foxboro Monday Club, and the Illustration, Comics, and Animation Conference have provided invaluable feedback. Kim Guarino of the Wheaton College Library creatively tracked down hard-to-find titles through interlibrary loan. Ken Davignon found brilliant ways to reproduce images from dusty tomes, as did Megan Wheaton-Book and Zephorene Stickney. Paula Smith-MacDonald captured the scarf with flair. A number of students and former students have done invaluable research into Alcott-related matters over the years, including Iris Doubleday, Haley Fisher, Rachel Kapelle, Erin Kole, Courtney LaBrie, Fiona McQuade, and Karen Mlyniec. Many thanks to the Mars Fellowship Program, the Mellon Faculty/Student Research Grants, and the Wheaton College Student/Faculty Research Partners program for funding that enabled the students to undertake this work. Finally, I'm deeply grateful to Matt McAdam at Johns Hopkins University Press and an anonymous reviewer.

Among the many studies of book history and especially of reception and of authors' legacies that have informed my thinking, I am particularly indebted to Barbara Hochman's *"Uncle Tom's Cabin" and the Reading Revolution: Race, Lit-*

eracy, Childhood, and Fiction, 1851–1911 (2011) and Barbara Sicherman's *Well-Read Lives: How Books Inspired a Generation of American Women* (2010). I am also deeply indebted to the dedicated and pioneering work of Joel Myerson, Daniel Shealy, and Madeleine Stern in making Alcott letters, journals, and publishing data readily accessible.

Brief portions of chapters 1, 2, 3, and 4 appeared in different form in *Kiddie Lit: The Cultural Construction of Children's Literature in America* (Johns Hopkins University Press, 2003) and in the introduction to *"Little Women" and the Feminist Imagination*, ed. Janice M. Alberghene and Beverly Lyon Clark (Garland, 1999). A couple of paragraphs in chapter 2 echo portions of my *"Little Women* Acted: Responding to H.T.P.'s Response," *Lion and the Unicorn* 36 (2012): 174–92. I am grateful to the Taylor & Francis Group for permission to reprint portions of the Garland introduction. I am likewise grateful to David M. Bader for permission to reprint his *Little Women* haiku from *Haiku U.: From Aristotle to Zola, 100 Great Books in 17 Syllables* (Gotham Books, 2006), 26; and to the Houghton Library at Harvard University for permission to reprint excerpts from letters and clippings in the Alcott collections.

The Afterlife of *Little Women*

Introduction

> Readings are not controlled by the text or by any one regime of
> reading. The task of reception history is in the first place to describe
> those readings in all their wildness.
>
> —John Frow

I hold my childhood copy of *Little Women*. A solid, tangible object. Unchanging,
it would seem, except for the yellowing of its pages and the peeling of its lami-
nated cover. Unchanged, I assumed when I first read it, from what Louisa May
Alcott had originally written—or at least I had assumed a kind of authenticity. Yet
what appears to be solid and unchanged is not.

For what I read was abridged—"A Modern Abridged Edition," it says on the
title page. But back then I didn't scrutinize title pages. Several chapters that appear in unabridged versions are missing ("Burdens," "The P.C. and P.O.," among
others), eliminating some of the incorporated stories and some of the moralizing.
And parts 1 and 2 of the novel are combined, unremarked, without page break or
discontinuity in chapter numbering.

As for what makes the abridgment "modern": On the cover a young woman
reclines on a sofa, in a room whose unfinished wooden walls and sloping ceiling
signal that she is in an attic. She is reading, not writing. She may represent the
novel's Jo March; she might represent the reader of the novel. The book she holds
appears to be leatherbound, with gilt trim. Thus does the Whitman Publishing
Company image the value of an item in its Famous Classics series, even if its own
product lacks the leather and gilt. The young woman wears a long green skirt,
a white blouse, and black flats. Her look is slightly old fashioned, in this 1955

edition, although maybe only by a decade or so: her blouse resembles one in a Simplicity pattern book of the 1940s. She is not dressed like a young woman of the 1860s.

The title on the cover is in pink, above the young girl, and casts a thin lavender shadow. The font carries Western associations for me; indeed, online I can find similar fonts labeled Saloon Girl, Cowboy Western, and Outlaw. My adult self is tempted to think that if the colors signal the traditionally feminine, the font hints at the passionate, outlawed subtexts of the novel. The author's name does not appear on the cover.

Inside, "Louisa May Alcott" appears on the title page, and the book claims to be newly illustrated. These illustrations, black and white with pale pink or green washes, are less anachronistic than the image on the cover. Or at least the clothing is. The image opposite the first page of text shows the four March sisters as cozily overlapping figures, facing what must be a fireplace in profile on the right, its light casting shadows behind them. Yet for readers unfamiliar with fireplace screens and pokers and with an uncertain sense of history, it could be a television set encased in shelving. Jo and Amy gaze at it intently. The words and cameo portraits on the page to the right become the story and images that they gaze at.

Little Women is a mutable text. The words aren't always the same. The illustrations and packaging vary widely. The social context in which we encounter the text varies too, and what we already "know" about the book before we read it colors what we read. I don't remember how old I was when I first read *Little Women*, nor do I remember who introduced me to it. But I do know that I read it independently, not as assigned reading for school, nor had I previously seen a film version. I doubt that I'd heard the book dismissed as sentimental subliterature. Nor did I find the title off-putting, demeaning.

The novel speaks differently to different readers, and differently to the same reader at different times. When I read *Little Women* as a child, Jo was the character who most spoke to me. It was her rambunctiousness that attracted me. It was her reading and writing. It was also, I think, her ability to negotiate all this in a close-knit family, although that was not uppermost in my conscious mind. I felt empowered by her, this Jo who could run and talk slang (not that those actions seemed very daring to me), this Jo who liked to read and write. It didn't matter that she eventually married; my enthusiasm didn't have to be controlled by the ending of the book. Or maybe it mattered a little. I'd wanted Jo to marry Laurie, but not passionately so (yet maybe that dispassion is a latter-day projection). Still, it probably seemed appropriate to me that she marry; I hadn't yet encountered many models of unmarried womanhood. (There was my second-grade teacher,

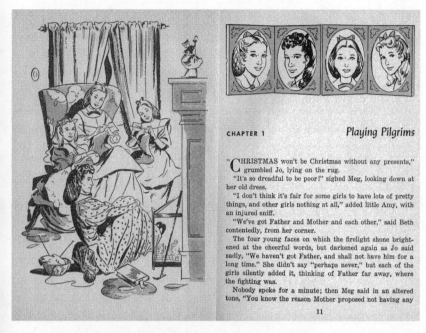

Facing the text and basking in its glow
Illustration by Jill Elgin for *Little Women* (Racine, WI: Whitman, 1955).

whom we called Missy. I don't now remember anyone else.) And I didn't really think that work and family were incompatible for a woman; Jo may have given up her public writing, for a while at least, in *Little Men*, but she still had work. *Little Women* and its sequels made it possible for a girl growing up in the 1950s to dream of having it all—family and career—even though I didn't know many actual women who did. It probably isn't accidental that the motto I chose for my high-school yearbook, wanting "to work, to love, to give," sounds as though it comes out of an Alcott novel. I can think of no other author that I'd read who speaks so cogently to all three desires.

And of course I'm working now from my memories of my early engagement with *Little Women*. Critics of literature for the young have long puzzled over the relationship between childhood and memory, given that those who produce such literature and those who publish comments on it are almost always adults, remembering. The influential early theoretical exploration of children's literature, Jacqueline Rose's *The Case of Peter Pan, or the Impossibility of Children's Fiction* (1984, rev. 1993), examines the adult construction of childhood as "a pure point of origin," a fantasy that grounds and mediates our relationship to language and to the past. Thanks in part to the realism of *Little Women*, especially its semi-autobiographical nature, its readers have always engaged in such looking back-ward—to the Civil War period of the book's setting and to the time of publication shortly afterwards, to portrayals of childhood and to an adult's childhood reading. Like *The Tale of Peter Rabbit*, it is what Valerie Krips, in *The Presence of the Past* (2000), calls a "nostalgic icon," embodying both a specifically literary and a more diffuse cultural value. It functions as a focus for collective memory but also, as Carolyn Steedman has noted of the child figure more generally, is able to "express the depths of historicity within individuals."[1]

In any case, I had gone on, when young, to read *Little Men* and *Jo's Boys*—but it was the lively Jo of *Little Women*, especially the first part of *Little Women*, that mattered most. I identified with Jo, but not with all aspects of her as they played out through the series. Barbara Sicherman has suggested that for young women of an earlier era, at the turn of the previous century, reading was both "an esteemed cultural practice" and "a wellspring of aspiration"; indeed, "at once study and play, a source of knowledge and pleasure, public performance and private dreaming, reading opened up space unlike any other."[2] I can see now that, with the exception of public performance, reading *Little Women* played the same roles for me.

And even the other ways in which the novel gives play to desire, ways that I couldn't have articulated back then, made it seem as if one could have it all. As Kathryn Kent argues, this novel and others by Alcott underscore the instability of gender and desire and of the boundaries between identification and desire. Does one want to be Jo or to have her? Kent states that "Alcott's novels query, 'Are you my teacher or my mother? Are you my sister or my lover? Are you my daughter or my pupil?' (And what it means to be a daughter, because Jo is more of a 'son' than a daughter to Marmee, destabilizes even these categories.)" Kent later cites Jo saying, with respect to lovers, "I'd like to try all kinds," thus signaling "a proliferation of identifications and desires within the family" and beyond.[3] Again, with Alcott, I could dream of having—and being—it all.

Few of my students in the last decade or two had been enthralled by *Little Women* as children—unlike a number of students in the 1980s, as I note in chapter 4. A few recent students recall being urged by their mothers to read the book but not being engaged by it. When they read it now as undergraduates, as an assigned text, some find themselves pleasantly surprised by the novel; some, dismayed by the preachiness. Most seem to identify with Jo: when I ask which character students like best, most say something like wanting to be Jo. A few students prefer Meg or Amy. One student liked Beth best for being like her own mother. A number of men students who prefer Jo say they would like to have her as a friend. Thus some students don't so much identify directly with a character as want to "be with" one. Theorists posit that identification during reading is shifting and unstable, and indeed "the 'identification' which the reader . . . makes is not necessarily with the hero/heroine . . . but with the story. It is the anticipation of satisfaction from the story/fantasy that holds our attention, not some identification with a particular character."[4] Young readers interviewed by Holly Blackford often seemed to identify more with a storytelling narrator than with characters; they seemed to feel they were "seeing rather than participating (as a human embodied being) in the social relations of the text."[5]

The students in my class were, furthermore, responding to a teacher who had assigned the book as required reading. So their responses would be tempered by their sense of what I might want to hear and of how comfortably they could disagree with me. Some of the men might also feel uncomfortable about admitting, in a class of fifty, to identifying directly with a female character: their claim to wanting to "be with" Jo might be as much a cover as a direct insight into the ways in which readers engage with texts. Records of response are always proximate. Even a student speaking up in class a day after first reading a novel, speaking as honestly as she can, is speaking from memory, tapping only her conscious responses and framing those responses with the vocabulary and within the frameworks that are available to her.

In her lifetime Alcott received hundreds of fan letters, although most have not survived. Like my students' comments, such a letter is complexly engendered. It may aptly reflect the writer's response as well as he or she can record it. But it is also shaped by the writer's sense of self, as well as his or her perception of the author as audience, whether the writer is hoping to receive a response—and perhaps collect an author's autograph?—or to affect the outcome of a projected sequel. (Please make Jo marry Laurie, fans wrote soon after part 1 was published.) A child writer, in particular, would likely have additional audiences to propitiate or defy: a hovering parent, a commanding teacher. (Only the propitiating ones are likely to be forwarded to the author.)

In the chapters that follow, I trace the afterlife of *Little Women* primarily by examining written commentaries, including letters, autobiographies, and occasionally diaries, although, like fan letters, these must be used with caution. Such responses derive from a narrow spectrum of those who could write and had access to the means to do so. And not only are letters shaped to fit the needs of their recipients but published letters have been chosen by editors and sometimes shaped by them too. Even diaries were not strictly private in the nineteenth century.

Alcott wrote her own childhood journal knowing that her parents would read the entries, and often she recorded her attempts to live as they would like. Sometimes, in short, one can look at direct responses to *Little Women*, but even those are shaped by the needs and desires of the writer and of any perceived reader.

Other sources of response must be treated cautiously as well. Sometimes one can get indirect reports, as when Alcott comments on the fans who besiege her. Sales figures from the publisher and circulation figures from libraries are suggestive, although one can't be sure that a purchased or borrowed book will actually be read (perhaps obtained just for show? to be in on the latest trend or to assure a mentor that one is reading something "wholesome"?), or whether it will have a single reader or multiple ones.

Published reviews may reflect a broader pattern of response than that of any given individual, the reviewers acting as "informed agents" of their readers even as they model how to respond.[6] Such a reviewer's stance reflects his or her own response but is also colored by perceptions of audience, including the editors of the periodical as well as its readers. Maybe generating a little controversy with some iconoclasm will be a good thing, or, more likely, the reviewer tries to anticipate the responses of the readership, while guiding its members in their choices and also shaping their responses. But reviewers of works whose audience includes children are almost always at some distance from that part of the audience. They are rarely children themselves, and they may differ with respect to class and race as well. They choose a stance toward their projected audience, maybe one of condescending superiority, maybe one of nostalgia as they remember their own childhood experience of reading, maybe one colored by recent encounters with children, fond or otherwise. And they may be responding to a cultural image of the book or author. (A common refrain, upon a modern adult's reading of *Little Women*, is how much better it was than expected, how unsentimental it was, given how sentimental he or she expected it to be.)

But it says something when the one item a child saves while fleeing the Chicago fire in 1871 is a copy of *Little Women*. Or when a producer labors for eight years to obtain permission to mount a stage production of *Little Women*, a century ago, and then labors to find a theater manager willing to host it—and the result is a hit Broadway show. Or when a producer similarly labors to persuade film executives, two decades ago, until she becomes one herself and produces a successful film version. That says something about the passion of the producer and about her sense of an untapped potential audience. It says something about the audience that made the production a hit, whether it was moved by nostalgia and sentiment or by a sense of being empowered or, ambivalently, both.

Such a production both enacts its creators' response to *Little Women* and mediates the response of others—as do other imitations, adaptations, translations, illustrations. Often readers have tried to enact *Little Women*, whether they try to follow a model of behavior outlined in it, or form a Little Women club whose members write stories—or create a formal adaptation performed on stage or screen, or sketch illustrations, or write a novel that modernizes the book or pursues a tangent unexplored in the original, or write a biography that plays the facts of Alcott's life against those in her autobiographical novel. Sometimes these responses extend the world of the novel, metonymically, perhaps imagining the experiences of Mr. March while he is away from the scene of the novel; sometimes they are metaphoric translations, perhaps imagining what might constitute a modern Jo.

And often these responses engender additional responses. Thus I scrutinize reviews of adaptations, broadly defined, to gauge response not just to the adaptation itself but to Alcott's novel, or to the public image of the novel. Even if adaptation theorists tell us that we should judge a presumed adaptation as a work in its own right, as I note in subsequent chapters, audience members still connect it intertextually, to some degree, with the presumed original.

The chapters that follow track the afterlife of *Little Women* in all these modes, devoting attention both to responses that had a significant impact at the time or are representative and to those that are symptomatically interesting for the ways in which they configure or reconfigure the novel. In chapter 1 I examine the responses of reviewers and other readers from the publication of part 1 in 1868 until the end of the century, a time span when Alcott willingly took on the persona of Aunt Jo, as "the children's friend," and was also held in some esteem by cultural gatekeepers. During the next three decades, addressed in chapter 2, Alcott was increasingly dismissed by the arbiters of high culture but had a strong popular following; a key year was 1912, when Orchard House was officially opened to the public and the first authorized full-length dramatization was a success on Broadway. Chapter 3 addresses the next three decades: Alcott's critical reputation was still at a low point, but *Little Women* continued to be popular, speaking both to audiences struggling during the Depression and to those experiencing postwar prosperity—especially through the vehicles of the 1933 and 1949 Hollywood films, respectively. The final chapter addresses how Alcott's standing has changed since 1960, in the wake of the feminist movement and of the publication of Alcott's lost thrillers: adaptations—verbal, visual, musical, and material—have proliferated, from picture-book versions to adult retellings, from anime to opera.

CHAPTER 1

Becoming Everyone's Aunt, 1868–1900

> Miss Alcott['s] name has already become a household word among
> little people.
>
> —New York Times, 1871

> This lady took the public heart by storm six years ago by the publi-
> cation of *Little Women*, and has since been established as a prime
> favorite with old and young. . . . Not Miss Burney, not Mrs. Stowe,
> not Bret Harte, after the appearance of the *Heathen Chinee*, ever
> received the adulation that has been poured out at Miss Alcott's feet
> by a host of enthusiastic juveniles. And the seniors are not much
> more moderate.
>
> —Harper's Monthly, 1875

> Grave merchants and lawyers meeting on their way down town in
> the morning said to each other, "Have you read 'Little Women'";
> and laughed as they said it. The clerks in my office read it, so also
> did the civil engineer, and the boy in the elevator. It was the rage in
> '69 as "Pinafore" was in '78.
>
> —*Frank Preston Stearns, 1895*

Louisa May Alcott had been notoriously reluctant to write the novel that became *Little Women*. She'd had some success with *Hospital Sketches* (1863), a
fictionalized account of her experiences as a Civil War nurse, and the editor
Thomas Niles invited her "to write a girls book." She said she'd try, and she
"began at once" in September 1867, although she "didn't like" it.[1] In the press of

other projects, she put it aside, even though Niles inquired about it the following February. It wasn't until May 1868, after Niles nixed the idea of a fairy book and urged her again to write the girls' story, that she worked on *Little Women* in earnest. Modeling the family in the story on her own, she noted ambivalently in her journal, "Marmee, Anna, and May all approve my plan. So I plod away, though I don't enjoy this sort of thing. Never liked girls or knew many, except my sisters, but our queer plays and experiences may prove interesting, though I doubt it" (*J* 165–66). The following month she and Niles both found the first twelve chapters dull. In August, though, when she read proof for the book, she decided that "it reads better than I expected. Not a bit sensational, but simple and true, for we really lived most of it, and if it succeeds that will be the reason of it. Mr. N. likes it better now, and says some girls who have read the manuscripts say it is 'splendid!' As it is for them, they are the best critics, so I should be satisfied" (*J* 166). These early readers were positive, even if Alcott herself remained reluctantly so. Then in November, inspired by the success of part 1—"Pleasant notices and letters arrive, and much interest in my little women" (30 October 1868, *J* 167)—Alcott wrote a chapter a day of part 2.

Within the novel Alcott staged several scenes of reading—and storytelling—and thereby modeled readers' responses to her own work.[2] The first is Marmee's reading of a letter from her husband, away at war. He provides straightforward advice to his four daughters, to "do their duty faithfully," and the sisters model straightforward response, each resolving to do better, "to be all that father hoped to find her" when he returned.[3] All is as convention would have it: the patriarch rules, speaking through the matriarch; the daughters will try to submit to his rules. Thereafter, however, response to readings and to stories becomes more complex.

There is, for instance, the staging of Jo's play, "The Witch's Curse." Jo and her sisters are absorbed in the play, but as Meg is about to leap from a tower the train of her gown snags, and the scenery collapses. The seating for the audience collapses too. No one is hurt; all laugh. The theatrics are undercut by humor. But are we also being cautioned against absorption, a common fear at the time regarding fiction,[4] or perhaps against absorption in sensational dramas? If the former, then a counterexample appears two chapters later, when Jo recounts her day's adventure of reading to her wealthy Aunt March, who has insisted on a course of Belsham's essays. When Jo is caught reading fiction, *The Vicar of Wakefield*, and Aunt March wants to hear what has so entranced her niece, the older woman herself becomes enthralled, as Jo verifies when she later glimpses her aunt rapt in the book. Jo tacks a moral onto her anecdote—that riches don't guarantee happiness—a gloss that Marmee reinforces. Yet this gloss seems a bit artificial, not exactly what the story communicated in the telling: its other moral would seem to endorse the pleasures of subverting adults' strictures and of reveling in the glory of fiction.[5] We're given access to two different readings, and although the one advocating the insufficiency of wealth attempts to contain the other one, the pleasures of the anecdote itself are not entirely erased. One could read the imposed gloss as endorsing an adult's perception of how she might want a story like *Little Women* to be read, as inculcating wholesome values. Jo's enthusiasm in the telling, however, exceeds and overflows the attempted strictures, and readers' subsequent enthusiasm for *Little Women* echoes Jo's response to Goldsmith's novel. The text sets up two models for reading: readers have generally followed Jo's enthusiastic example for their own reading, even if they may endorse the moralizing model when they imagine how reading *Little Women* should affect others, especially when those others are young.

Later scenes in the novel further play out the possibilities for both modes of reading. The sisters enact *Pilgrim's Progress* by trying to live according to the precepts of Bunyan's book—and also those of the New Testament, which their mother gives them and which they read from daily.[6] Yet Alcott endorses the pleasures of fictional reading as well, as when Jo ensconces herself in her garret, fortified with apples, to devour both them and *The Heir of Redclyffe*.

In any case, sales of part 1 of *Little Women* were brisk in 1868 but truly took off—as Frank Preston Stearns indicates in the third epigraph to this chapter—in 1869. Alcott's works became wildly popular, and she herself became a celebrity. Critical esteem soon matched the popularity but trailed off about a decade later. Sales dipped in the late 1870s too but then—unlike critical esteem—surged and accelerated in the 1880s. This diverging response to Alcott's work marks the early stages of an overall divergence, in the latter part of the nineteenth century, between popular and esteemed fiction.

⌇

The popularity of *Little Women* reflects the positioning of literature for the young in the mid-nineteenth century, before the market sharply segregated literature for young and old, and for boys and girls. The novel signaled a departure from previous moralizing in juvenile literature—the kind in which all the naughty boys were "eaten by bears, or tossed by mad bulls, because they did not go to a particular Sabbath-school," and "all the good infants who did go" were of course "rewarded by every kind of bliss, from gilded gingerbread to escorts of angels, when they departed this life, with psalms or sermons on their lisping tongues," to quote *Little Women* itself (281)—even if to a latter-day reader the book may still seem rather preachy. It can be seen as inaugurating a new genre for children, as it melded some aspects of the sentimental novel popular in the 1860s—the emphasis on sisterliness, perhaps the importance of motherhood—with the domestic fiction long a staple of juvenile literature. It was perhaps the first American book explicitly directed to girls as an audience, offering four models of girlhood, at a time when children's literature was only starting to undergo gender segmentation. *Little Women* also provided a taste of the intelligentsia's Concord for the American middle class, a concrete, even spirited taste: as Van Wyck Brooks later suggested, Alcott "invested the Concord scheme of life with the gaiety and romance of a Robin Hood ballad."[7] In any case, the book was popular with boys as well as girls, and also with men and women: it struck a chord in the nineteenth-century U.S. imagination, as sales figures, library circulation records, fan letters, and personal testimony attest.

With respect to sales, within a month of publication Roberts Brothers had printed three thousand copies of part 1 of *Little Women*, and the publisher encouraged Alcott to write a continuation. In the succeeding months Alcott's popularity grew exponentially. Part 2 of *Little Women* (also known as *Good Wives* or *Little Women Wedded* and now often packaged with part 1) appeared six months later; within a month of issuing it, Roberts Brothers needed to print an additional seven thousand copies.[8] Within a month of publication in 1870, the firm needed thirty thousand copies of Alcott's *An Old-Fashioned Girl*; within a month of issuing *Little Men* in 1871, forty thousand. Sales of *Little Women* fell off in the late 1870s but surged again—and then accelerated—after Roberts Brothers published a newly illustrated edition combining parts 1 and 2 in 1880. In the mid-twentieth century Frank Luther Mott listed *Little Men* as one of the three best sellers of 1871—and *Little Women* as one of the twenty-one best sellers in U.S. history.[9]

The sequels that Alcott wrote in response to Niles's urging, *Little Men* and finally *Jo's Boys* (1886), both renewed interest in *Little Women* and attested to the depth of their predecessor's popularity. So did the Roberts Brothers ploy of sometimes advertising five Alcott novels that were not about the Marches as part of the Little Women series. Further attestation of the popularity of *Little Women* comes from the subsequent publication and popularity of similar series, family stories that feature a feisty girl, by such authors as Susan Coolidge (Sarah Chauncey Woolsey) and L. M. Montgomery.

Additional indicators of Alcott's popularity in the nineteenth century appear in the occasional listing of the most circulated books in libraries. In 1871 *Little Women* and *An Old-Fashioned Girl* were among the most popular recent books in the New York Mercantile Library, the largest U.S. lending library; in 1886 its librarian reported needing to purchase five hundred copies of *Little Women*, the second highest number for a single book; in 1893 *Little Women* may have been the twelfth most circulated novel, but Alcott was apparently second only to Dickens as the most popular novelist in U.S. public libraries.[10] And these were in general library holdings, not just juvenile collections, where Alcott was even more dominant. In 1893, for instance, *Little Women* headed a list of books that librarians considered children's favorites.[11] In an 1894 poll of popular books in the Sunday school library, in an era when some Sunday school librarians were dubious about *Little Women*, the novel nevertheless came in fifth.[12] By 1880, according to the *New York Times*, Alcott was "generally regarded as the most popular and successful literary woman in America."[13]

The most detailed and accessible data for a single library appear on the website What Middletown Read. The site codifies public library records for Muncie, Indiana, between 1891 and 1892 and between 1894 and 1902. Alcott may have been only the seventh most popular author in Muncie's library during this period, but her *Under the Lilacs* (1878) was the most frequently borrowed of all titles, with 478 transactions; *An Old-Fashioned Girl* and *Little Men* were also in the top twenty, at fourteenth and twentieth.[14] *Little Women* registered 272 transactions, trailing *Little Men* by 23. Anne Trubek suggests that *Little Men* was more popular in Muncie "perhaps because it was checked out by boys, too."[15] And there is at least some evidence for that hypothesis in the data. It's hard to be certain whether the person checking out a book was the primary reader: a seventeen-year-old messenger boy may have been borrowing *Little Women* for himself, but might the forty-three-year-old civil engineer, married for twenty-one years, have been checking it out for his wife or offspring? Still, about 27 percent of the listed patrons of *Little Women* whose gender can be determined were male, compared with 33 percent for *Little Men* and 38 percent for *Under the Lilacs* (46 percent of the library's patrons overall were male). Gender aside, it's possible that *Little Women* was borrowed less because more families owned the book. Trubek reports that blue-collar readers were somewhat more likely than white-collar readers to borrow works of classic literature; perhaps white-collar readers owned copies of works by Shakespeare and other classic authors.[16] In any case, it's not clear why *Under the Lilacs* was so popular at this library. Certainly there can be a good deal of variation among libraries, depending on the population served and the recommendations of individual librarians; the popularity of this novel in Muncie is not reflected in the other data on library usage that I have consulted, and national sales data suggest the preeminent popularity of *Little Women*, among Alcott titles, during this decade.[17] Nevertheless, *Little Women* was popular with all classes of readers in Muncie, from the nine-year-old son of an undertaker to a seventy-three-year-old widow, from a thirty-two-year-old divorcee to a thirty-three-year-old unmarried day laborer, from a sixteen-year-old stenographer to a forty-five-year-old physician. One can also get some sense of *Little Women*'s popularity from the direct responses of readers. One should be cautious, as Jonathan Rose points out, since fan letters "over-represent enthusiasts and under-represent disgusted or lukewarm readers."[18] So perhaps one shouldn't put too much stock in gushing enthusiasm. Yet one can read the surviving fan mail to Alcott symptomatically, as indicating an attempt to achieve intimacy with the author as a person, someone very like if not the same as her young character Jo or an older Aunt Jo, and often an attempt to be directive, to influence the future directions of the fiction. In 1871 Alcott wrote that letters forwarded from her publisher "were very gushing from Nellie and Dollie and Sallie Somebody asking for pictures, autographs, family history, and several new books right away"; more generally, she noted having received "over a hundred letters from boys & girls, & many from teachers & parents," these last often "us[ing] my books as helps for themselves."[19] A decade later she wrote, "Autograph letters I do not answer, nor half the requests for money and advice upon every subject from 'Who shall I marry' to 'Ought I to wear a bustle?' "[20] She told an interviewer of receiving "religious advice," "reams of poetry," and "matrimonial advances."[21] In 1873 she alluded to "frequently recieving [*sic*] letters from English people" about her books; in 1875, to receiving several from admirers in Holland.[22] An obituarist wrote that "probably no writer ever received so many letters from those who only knew her by her books, but who felt that they could freely address her either to thank her for the pleasure they had derived from her writings or to ask advice about their own little affairs."[23] She had become everyone's aunt.

Most of the letters have not survived, although an occasional one appeared in print and a few linger in archives. One from a teacher, for instance, was reprinted in the *Christian Union* in 1884: his or her schoolchildren are unanimous that "Aunt Jo's" "are the *best* books that they have ever heard," and the teacher adds, "I think I can understand boys and girls better now."[24] In archived letters from Indiana, apparently instigated by a teacher, a schoolgirl wrote, "We all love you very much because you have given us so much pleasure by writing those nice books"; a boy chimed in, "Our class have read Little Men and Little Women. We all like them first rate."[25] According to an advertisement in an edition of *Little Men*, a girl named Nelly conflated Alcott and Jo and claimed, "We were all so disappointed about your not marrying Laurie; I cried over that part,—I could not help it."[26] The disposition of the Marches' neighbor Laurie was a contested issue for contemporary girl readers: a *Boston Herald* article, noting that Alcott wrote part 2 of *Little Women* in response to letters urging "her to continue the story," quotes a girl as writing, "If you do not write another volume of 'Little Women,' and tell us more about Jo, and make Laurie marry Beth, I will never read another of your books as long as I live. Yours most respectfully,/MAMIE BROWN."[27] More commonly readers wanted Laurie to marry Jo. As for other responses, a boy living in the West apparently made a table that he sent to Alcott as a tribute, one she described as having a "delicious wiggliness"; a girl in the West wrote the publisher, at the time of Alcott's death, that she'd like to donate the dollar she'd received at Christmas to a monument for the author; a woman living in Turkey wrote a Chicago newspaper suggesting something similar, via nickel subscriptions from rich and poor.[28]

Letters likewise appeared in periodicals that invited children to write to the editor. In publications ranging from the *Maine Farmer* to the *Christian Union* to the children's magazine *St. Nicholas*, children frequently note having read *Little Women*, often declaring it a favorite. Satie S. claimed that it "is a book that I can read over and over again and every time it seems as interesting as if it were a new book."[29] When Alcott died in 1888, hundreds of children wrote to *St. Nicholas* to "attest their dear love for the author."[30] In a high-school graduation essay in 1898, Anna Thaner declared of *Little Women*, "Many a girl ha[s] been stimulated by it to higher ambitions and better principles."[31] It's not clear whether the ambitions were worldly or moral.

Satie and Anna were hardly alone. The historian Barbara Sicherman catalogs a host of notable women who grew up in the nineteenth century and for whom *Little Women* was a foundational childhood text. Edith Wharton's upper-class family may have disdained the book's "bad English," and working-class young women may have preferred more escapist fiction.[32] But Jane Addams read and reread *Little Women*; Carey Thomas, future president of Bryn Mawr College, took on the persona of Jo to her cousin's Laurie; Jo was the physician S. Josephine Baker's favorite fictional character.[33] Other readers include the Chicagoan Martha Freeman Esmond and her daughter: in 1888 Esmond wrote a friend that Alcott's "death, three days ago, touched me greatly, for I read and loved her books in my youth. So did Martha Jr., who came yesterday, wet eyed, to show me her copy of 'Little Women.' She was reading it at the time of the Chicago fire and it was the sole piece of property she saved from the flames. Today she treasures it."[34]

Helen Keller "loved 'Little Women' because it gave me a sense of kinship with girls and boys who could see and hear."[35] Harriet Beecher Stowe, who was an adult when the novel appeared, told Alcott's editor, "There have been no books of the kind equal to Miss Alcott's since Maria Edgeworth's."[36] The gossip columnist Louella Parsons "read the Alcott books over and over again."[37] For Marian de Forest, author of a 1912 dramatization, Alcott's "work anticipates the thoughts of the modern writer. No wonder the book lives. I was brought up on it, but the play has made me love it better than ever and I find new beauties in every page."[38] Other women growing up in the latter part of the nineteenth century who loved Alcott's books include such writers as Edna Ferber, Sara Teasdale, Bess Streeter Aldrich, and Lucy Lillie, who remembered "the wild delight with which 'we girls' read, imitated, rehearsed, laughed, and cried over" *Little Women*.[39] The African Americans Ida B. Wells and Mary Church Terrell were more measured in their responses, but Terrell implied that she had read Alcott's works with enthusiasm.[40] Men too, like future President Theodore Roosevelt, "worshipped" the book.[41] It was likewise a favorite of the future drama critic and man about town Alexander Woollcott: a friend would later teasingly call him Louisa M. Woollcott, a remark that says something about Alcott's influence but also hints at what would later become dismissal of her work.[42]

British fans included the writers Charlotte Yonge and Constance Smedley and the actress Ellen Terry, who told an autograph seeker at a luncheon, "My ambition is gratified; I sit at the same table and behold with my own eyes, the authoress of 'Little Women.'"[43] The novelist Frank Swinnerton acknowledged Alcott—before whom "I abase myself," he claimed—as the most important influence on his writing.[44] Rudyard Kipling, while visiting a small town in Pennsylvania, spoke admiringly of "meeting in the flesh, even as Miss Louisa Alcott drew them, Meg and Joe and Beth and Amy," and an unnamed Englishman appears to have inspired the later movement to restore the Alcott family's Orchard House: the president of the Concord Woman's Club took this "great admirer of Miss Alcott's stories" to see the house and felt shame at its dereliction.[45] Recent British critics have suggested that American girls' books such as Alcott's were more popular imports in England than British books were in the United States, proffering as they did a girlhood relatively liberated with respect to propriety and physical freedom.[46]

The Americanness of Alcott's books—a feature stressed by British critics, as I discuss later—may have hindered their popularity somewhat outside the United States. But not by much. In 1871 the American publisher's representative wrote Alcott from London that "there are few American authors who are as popular here as yourself."[47] In 1873 a journalist described *Little Women* as having obtained "a universal welcome in English households"; in 1889 the London *Daily News* claimed that "Miss Alcott's books were and are to the full as popular in this country as in her own" and the *Saturday Review* called Aunt Jo "everybody's Jo"; in 1890 the London *Guardian* declared that "there are probably few in England whose childhood, or love of children's books, dates from 1865 who have not read her 'Little Women.'"[48] Nevertheless, in the most comprehensive survey that I have located, Alcott was popular in Britain but hardly preeminent. In an 1884 poll of two thousand young people aged eleven to nineteen, Alcott does not register among boys' favorites, yet she ranks twenty-fourth among girls' favorite authors and *Little Women* ranks seventh among their favorite books.[49]

Little Women also gained popularity elsewhere in Europe in the nineteenth century; it was translated into German, Dutch, French, Swedish, Danish, Greek, as well as, apparently, Russian and Japanese. The first German translation appeared in 1873 or 1876.[50] The first Dutch one appeared in 1876: the title given to part 1 translates as "Under mother's wings" (*Onder moeders vleugels*), a title that has been retained for subsequent translations. Dutch reviewers noted that Alcott's "books are generally recognized to be a treasure for children" and that indeed "never from her hand appeared a book that did not excel [*sic*] by its contents and form."[51] The translation also spurred the Dutch to create their own girls' fiction.[52]

The first French translation appeared in Switzerland, under a title that is a direct translation of the English one: *Petites femmes* (1872). It was positively received by critics. One French reviewer claimed that only English and American writers—including Alcott—"write well for children"; another, that the four sisters "are more original, more *spirituel* and amiable than those one generally finds in Europe. They are true Americans."[53] A Chicago paper reported that the translation was "fast becoming a great favorite with the French demoiselles."[54]

Yet it was the 1880 translation that provided the iconic title and the most influential version in France: *Les quatre filles du docteur Marsch* (The four daughters of Doctor Marsch), translated by P.-J. Stahl (Pierre-Jules Hetzel), deemed by a reviewer "a rare book, that appeals to the imagination and the heart, and is agreeable and healthy food for young minds."[55] *Marsch* might subsequently be regularized to *March*, but the title has otherwise been the same ever since for translations, abridgments, and subtitled or dubbed films, especially when the audience has included juveniles. In 1981 in Manitoba, for instance, one could watch the 1978 TV movie starring Susan Dey under the title *Les quatre filles du docteur March*.[56] Even now the French Wikipedia (fr.wikipedia.org) lists the book under this title, although it also notes a new, "faithful" 2010 translation appearing under the title *Les quatre filles du pasteur March*; being faithful seems to require fidelity not to the English title but to a modification of the familiar French one. The need to name the father in the various iterations of the title is, of course, one of its curiosities. Another is that, for the French, in early translations Mr. March was not a clergyman but a doctor, a transformation apparently deemed necessary in nineteenth-century Catholic France, where readers might be uncomfortable with the idea of a married clergyman; references to the Protestant *Pilgrim's*

Progress were deleted as well.[57] But it's less clear why, in the 1880 translation, Jo does what many readers elsewhere have longed for her to do: she marries Laurie. In any case, even in subsequent French translations in which the text has been realigned with Alcott's, the title has stayed the same—which speaks to the extent to which *Little Women* became a cultural phenomenon in France, linked to a single, highly recognized title. In the 1990s alone there were at least nine versions published under this title (49).

In the United States some young fans created clubs based on *Little Women*. One early group called itself the Little Men and Little Women; it's not clear what activities the members engaged in.[58] Some groups were formed "for philanthropic purposes."[59] Others pursued literary endeavors: one set of girls called themselves the Alcott Reading Club; in another the members read papers at weekly meetings, but lacking time to write their own stories, they copied many from *St. Nicholas*; another did their own writing, including stories "in which Italian princesses and English dukes played a prominent part."[60] An African American novel for girls casually refers to a girl in college writing an essay as a member of the Alcott Literary Club.[61] Particularly enterprising were the five Lukens sisters, who lived in a small town in Pennsylvania: inspired by the March sisters' *Pickwick Portfolio*, the girls created a family newspaper in 1871 that eventually had a thousand subscribers across the country before it wound down three years later.[62] And Vassar undergraduates took names from *Little Women*, calling themselves not just by the sisters' names but also Pa March, Marmee, and even the Twins (one person), nicknames that they retained into adulthood.[63]

Although most fans don't specify what they loved about Alcott's work, many appear to have especially appreciated her characters. One wrote that the novel "is so real, the characters are so real and sweet."[64] Another, self-identifying as Jo, felt that "Miss Alcott must have seen us four girls before she wrote the story."[65] A British woman appreciated Alcott's valuing of the ordinary, her loving attention to the sisters' "grand aspirations, homely duties, mistakes, troubles, and 'good times,'" not to mention the detailed attention to clothing, to making do with little, as with Meg's "many-times-pressed-and-mended white tarlatan."[66] Readers also appreciated Alcott's attention to moral behavior. One teacher reported that, like the adult Jo at Plumfield School in *Little Men*, she kept "a 'Conscience Book,' and it did much good," and overall, "the children are better and happier for hearing" *Little Women* and *Little Men*.[67] But children too claimed—maybe especially when writing for or to adults—that "this story has helped me a very great deal in leading a better and a happier life" or "it shows us how to persevere."[68] An astute reviewer for the *Springfield Daily Republican* duly noted Alcott's keen observation and vivacity but also pointed to her access to both elite and ordinary experiences: she had "a life which has no parallel on earth—that of a young woman in New England who shares the fortunes of the people, while she has access also to the culture and opportunities of wealth."[69]

Yet the reading public did not embrace *Little Women* altogether uncritically. The gap between parts 1 and 2 enabled direct response from the audience. Thomas Niles had encouraged Alcott to add a chapter to what would become part 1 "in which allusions might be made to something in the future."[70] She complied, ending the volume by suggesting that the curtain might rise again on the Marches, "depend[ing] upon the reception given to the first act" (185).

Readers responded to the invitation. Alcott reported that "enthusiastic young ladies" wrote her "clamorously demanding that [Jo] should marry Laurie, or somebody."[71] Alcott humorously claimed that she "didnt dare to refuse & out of perversity went & made a funny match for her."[72] Which is to say, Alcott married Jo not to the romantic young Laurie but to the older and less physically attractive Professor Bhaer. This decision not to marry Jo to Laurie elicited a "general groan of dismay among the young women of America."[73] Mrs. Henry Ward Beecher claimed to know "one grave lady [who took] Jo's refusal of Laurie more to heart than that young gentleman, for he got over it, and our young friend has not yet ceased grumbling!"[74] As another contemporary reader remembered of her childhood reading, "the crowning disappointment was that Laurie did not marry Jo. . . . They might have quarreled, but how interesting the disputes would have been, how piquant the making-up! Jo should have consoled her boy instead of falling in love with the tedious Mr. Bhaer."[75] A British reader noted her initial dismay with Jo's choice of Bhaer and speculated that "any love affair at all, in connection with Jo, was forced upon Miss Alcott by external pressure, and not naturally evolved from her 'inner consciousness.'"[76] Yet this reader also attested to Alcott's remarkable power in "winning over" the reader, even to the point of leading one to admire Bhaer. Still, the dismay that readers have felt, then and now, probably only augments the power of the book—"the lack of satisfying closure helping to keep the story alive," as Sicherman argues, adding that subversion of the expected love plot may have made it easier for some readers to ignore the ending and to focus on Jo's questing individuality.[77]

Certainly readers cared deeply about the book. And they lionized Alcott. In 1875 she was besieged for autographs and kisses at the Woman's Congress in Syracuse; two months later, at Vassar, she was importuned for a speech but consented instead to "place herself in a prominent position and turn around slowly" so all could see.[78] That same year her father, Bronson, lecturing at a "Young Ladies College" in Wisconsin, noted that when he asked how many students had read *Little Women*, 150 young women rose and raised their hands, and afterwards "scores of hands were stretched, arm over arm, by the gathered group, to take that of the papa.' And then as many autographs were inscribe[d] in Albums and little slips extemporized at the moment."[79] Declining a request from a potential visitor that year, Alcott noted that she and her family entertained "over a hundred a month, most of them strangers. A whole school came without warning last week & Concord people bring all their company to see us."[80] Clara Gowing, a family friend, noted that a disgruntled Alcott had once told some boys, "Whatever you do, don't do anything to get fame."[81] Another family friend, Lydia Maria Child, noted in 1876 that the Alcott family had "a Christian hatred of lionizing."[82] Christian because forgiving? Or reminiscent of stories of early Christians fed to lions—and thus a justified hatred? But hatred, in any case.

Alcott was especially forthright in her journals about the "impertinent curiosity" of the "sight-seeing fiend" (July and August 1872, J 183). At times she could be pleased "to see so much innocent enthusiasm even about so poor a thing as a used up old woman," as when thirty women students from Boston University visited in 1880 (May 1880, J 225). But in 1872 she noted that she might "skip out of the back window when ordered out for inspection by the inquisitive public," or, when her sister May wasn't available to act as hostess, "say 'No,' and shut the door. People *must* learn that authors have some rights; I can't entertain a dozen a day, and write the tales they demand also" (July and August 1872, J 183). She added, "Reporters sit on the wall and take notes; artists sketch me as I pick pears in the garden; and strange women interview Johnny [her nephew] as he plays in the orchard" (August 1872, J 183).

Alcott satirized such lionizing in verse and fiction. In the humorous "The Lay of a Golden Goose," written in 1870, published in 1886, she addresses response to her work before and after *Little Women*—or rather before and after an allegorical goose lays a golden egg. The cock, for instance, advises her to keep her "proper sphere," but after she lays golden eggs, it "give[s]/A patronizing crow." And the "News-hunting turkeys" run "with all their legs/To gather facts and fictions of/The goose with golden eggs."[83]

In *Jo's Boys*, the final volume in the March family trilogy, Alcott devotes a chapter to what she calls "Jo's Last Scrape." The character representing Alcott, Jo March Bhaer, has achieved fame after writing a "hastily scribbled . . . little story describing a few scenes and adventures in the lives of herself and sisters."[84] She starts an account of a single day—"a true tale" (49), the narrator avers—by sorting through her mail. The day's haul includes requests from at least a dozen people seeking autographs; a letter from a southern woman requesting a donation "to purchase a new communion-service for our church"; one from an aspiring author asking Jo to put her name to the first edition of his novel, after which he'd change it to his own (request denied); one from a sick girl asking for a book (she gets it); a brief one from a young boy calling Jo's books "first-rate"; letters from a mother seeking advice on careers for her seven young daughters and from a young man on "what sort of a girl he shall marry"; an admiring poem in an "incoherent style" (an effusion the narrator calls "a true one"); a request to change a published tale to "make it end good"; and "another from an irate boy denied an autograph, who darkly foretold financial ruin and loss of favor if she did not send him and all other fellows who asked autographs, photographs, and autobiographical sketches" (51–53). The rest of the day brings an artist to the outside of Jo's house to sketch it; an importunate reporter barging inside; a similarly importunate mother and her three daughters from Oshkosh, who are not fooled by Jo's attempts to pass herself off as a housemaid; young ladies from a seminary; young men from a Christian Union, enthusiastically tramping mud inside the house; and an admirer catching a grasshopper in the garden, to add to a collection of "grasshoppers from the grounds of several famous folks" (63).

An early-twentieth-century biographer declared that Alcott "seems to have felt the annoyances of glory more than most authors."[85] But it seems likely that she was besieged more than most. *Little Women* sold more copies than almost any other American novel published in the nineteenth century. Alcott was also a woman: she would have seemed more approachable than a "great man" would, and although her sisters could provide some interference, she had no wife or personal assistant to protect her. As an author whose works targeted children (as well as adults), she must have seemed more approachable still. Finally, given how autobiographical her Little Women series was, and given her willingness to call herself Aunt Jo, readers who felt intimate with the fictional Jo March seem to have felt intimate with Alcott. As an obituarist noted, "She wrote so much of her own life into books that she was nearer to the public than most writers."[86]

In *Little Women* Jo dreams of fame as part of her castle in the air; in *Jo's Boys* she regrets its appurtenances. One could see her as simply not having understood in the first book, the realities of fame. Then again, Katherine Adams points to the shifting associations with privacy during this time: at midcentury the desire for privacy struck many as antidemocratic; by the time Alcott was writing *Jo's Boys* such a desire was often seen as progressive and hence acceptable.[87] Jo's differing responses in the two novels could thus reflect cultural shifts. Yet her later response is, as Adams details, complex and multilayered: when Jo says, "Time is money," as a justification for her annoyance, she is accepting market forces—she presumably wants to continue to write and to sell what she writes—and thus, "even as Jo calls for a protected space that precedes market relations, Alcott suggests that no such place exists and begins to subvert the natural rights defense of privacy" (161). Further, by stressing that the anecdotes she relates are true, Alcott is again offering the public a glimpse of her private self even as she asks this public to leave her alone.

Her public life was imbricated in her private life: the fictional realm that brought her public fame centered on her slightly fictionalized private domesticity. Fans so confounded Alcott and Jo that they were sometimes disappointed that the person they glimpsed or the figure in the photograph they viewed was so much older than the fifteen-year-old Jo of the beginning of *Little Women*.[88] As someone for whom "media interest . . . is transferred from reporting on [her] public role"—in her case, as an author—"to investigating the details of [her] private [life],"[89] Alcott was a celebrity. More precisely, she enacted what Joseph Roach has called the "public intimacy" of celebrity, offering the promise of availability and familiarity.[90]

Contributing to the confounding of public and private at this time was a cultural shift in approaches to reading and to authors. As Barbara Hochman has argued, nineteenth-century readers often read to "get at the author": early in the century they wanted to know the author through his or her works, assuming an "imaginative unity of author and text"; later, when Alcott was writing, authors had become personalities, even celebrities, and readers increasingly wanted to learn personal details.[91] In keeping with the first line of thinking was a claim by a British writer that "to know her books is to know Miss Alcott."[92] As for the second, it was an open secret that the fictional Marches were based on the Alcotts, and Roberts Brothers assiduously marketed Alcott's life. The firm stressed the connection between Alcott and the fictional Jo by marketing her as Aunt Jo, the presumed author of the short stories in the six volumes of Alcott's *Aunt Jo's Scrap-Bag* (1872–82). Alcott herself sometimes referred to the Alcotts as the Marches, May as Amy, Anna as Meg.[93] The publisher likewise made sure that Alcott sat for frequent photographs to distribute and that information on what she was working on or the state of her health or when she was sailing to or from Europe was available to newspapers for their Literary News columns. In a single month and a half in 1873 Alcott's name appeared in at least eleven items in the *New York Evening Post*.[94] Readers' hunger for personal news also gave rise to misinformation, such as that Alcott had died in 1871 (she lived till 1888), or that she "will have nothing to do with those people who used to snub her when she was a factory girl" (working in a factory was one employment that she did not essay), or that she had published "an ardent protest against woman suffrage" (she was a suffragist).[95]

Curiously, one of the ways in which Alcott was able to guard against some invasions of her privacy was through enacting tropes of Romanticism. As the person who became the primary breadwinner for her family, she was attentive to her income: she was a professional writer. In many ways she anticipated the professionalism of those who would be writing a few decades later, the realists who mirrored common life and relied on "skills of observation, a knowledge of manners and customs, and an adeptness at mimicking speech."[96] She was a realist of the nursery who was adept at capturing dialogue, individualizing the speech of her characters. Taking on the breadwinner role gave her an excuse for writing, and some space, although it didn't provide full protection. So whereas the later realists consciously turned away from Romantic ideas of genius, Alcott instead borrowed their tropes—the artist in the attic, writing as if possessed—a move that, paradoxically, enabled a woman to be professional. She wrote in a garret in her early years and could get caught up in what she called a vortex of writing: she would write for hours at a stretch over a period of weeks, sleeping little, and her family would allow her to escape the quotidian round of women's chores, instead serving her, bringing apples and tea and cider to her attic.[97] She thus freed herself from the interruptions that a nineteenth-century woman living in a family would be subject to—and from the interruptions of curiosity seekers.

The illustrations of nineteenth-century editions of *Little Women* further reinforce the autobiographical connections, making the private public. Those for the first edition of part 1 were by May Alcott, Louisa's youngest sister, the one corresponding to the artistic Amy in the novel. As Susan Gannon astutely observes, these amateurish illustrations are sometimes allegorical (Meg facing temptation at Vanity Fair, for instance) but also interestingly at odds with the text: in the much-reprinted first rendition of the scene that would become an iconic image of family togetherness, with the four sisters clustered around Marmee, the five figures are oddly separate, their gazes askew, despite the overlapping mandala-like clustering of their bodies; the most vigorously active figure in May's three separate images of the sisters is Beth, the least active of the sisters in the novel; and in the exciting scene in which Jo's anger almost leads to Amy's drowning after falling through thin ice, we simply see a mature young woman serenely skating, a superficial fashion plate.[98] In this last it's as if May were rewriting the story to diminish the danger to her fictional self and to foreground her fashionable desires; in the process she also minimized the anger and jealousy that animated the novel. May

"Keep near the shore; it isn't safe in the middle." Jo heard, but Amy was just struggling to her feet, and did not catch a word. —

Amy—and May—skate the surface
Illustration by May Alcott for *Little Women* (Boston: Roberts, 1868).
Courtesy of Marion B. Gebbie Archives and Special Collections, Wheaton College.

served as both a reader of the novel and an interpreter for others; certainly some readers paid attention to the minutiae of dress in the novel, as May did, and later illustrators felt a similar urge to showcase fashion.

In 1869 and 1870 Hammatt Billings created illustrations for part 2 and also part 1, but the images that more fully underscore the autobiographical connections are those for the 1880 revised edition.[99] Alcott's publisher, perhaps in response to the market, perhaps as a way to renew the copyright, tinkered with the language in *Little Women*: the characters now conform somewhat more to gender ideals (Marmee becomes "tall" instead of "stout," and "noble-looking" rather than not "particularly handsome," while Laurie becomes taller than Jo rather than about the same height), and the language is less colloquial and regional ("ain't" becomes "are not"; "quinny-dingles" becomes "notions"), even as the visual aspects of the book make it more regional and less generic.[100] Frank Merrill's visual images of the March family, for instance, echo features of the Alcott family.[101]

Furthermore, in some print runs of this edition, the frontispiece features one of the houses where the Alcotts had lived in Concord, Massachusetts (the town is not named in the novel); in other runs, this image is moved to the middle, between parts 1 and 2, and the frontispiece is either a portrait of Alcott or an image of the four sisters and Marmee reading a letter from Father (a fragment is reproduced on the cover of this book). The caption for the house image reads, "Home of the Little Women"—whether "home" is to refer to the setting of the novel or the place where it was written. In any case, Edmund H. Garrett's image is of the Alcotts' Orchard House. To a modern eye accustomed to deciphering Google doodles, the shapes in the fence, starting with the round gate, almost spell out "Orchard House." (This fence appears to originate with Garrett: it does not resemble the woodland fence and gate fashioned by Alcott's father, Bronson, as sketched by May Alcott.)[102] Fictional and real families coalesce in an image of a house whose leafy framing both distances the building from the viewer and memorializes the image as a keepsake. Framed by trees, festooned with vines, the house also merges with its natural setting, in accord with Bronson's design principles. The physical monument of the house (although it wouldn't officially become a monument till after the turn of the century) speaks to the monumentality of the book even as it hints that the book is domestic. The later substitution of the image of the iconic fivesome as the frontispiece suggests a shift in the positioning of the book as well, its association with a more interior and relational domesticity.

Paradoxically, this localized specificity of the visual images gives the book a national significance. The effect anticipates some of what Amy Kaplan would find characteristic of late-nineteenth-century local-color fiction, which embodies both

Home of the Little Women.

Housing the Alcotts and the Marches
Illustration by E. H. Garrett for *Little Women* (Boston: Roberts, 1880).
Courtesy of Yale Collection of American Literature, Beinecke Rare
Book and Manuscript Library, Yale University.

a point of origin and a contrast with urban development, "solidifying national centrality by reimagining a distended industrial nation as an extended clan sharing a 'common inheritance,' in its imagined rural [in this case, village] origins."[103] Yet the 1880 edition of *Little Women* also tied the novel to elite culture, to a Transcendental family and the Concord that had come to represent the country's elite literary achievements, a pedigree reinforced when the Transcendentalist Bronson billed himself, on his lecture tours, as the "father of the Little Women." (Clara Gowing pointedly suggests that it was after *Little Women* became famous that his tours became profitable.)[104] In a couple of Merrill's illustrations Jo happily interacts with children, providing yet another emblem of the positioning of Alcott in the national imagination, as the "children's friend."

Indeed, *Little Women* could very much be considered a national novel. The Civil War is the reason for Mr. March's absence, as a chaplain, and the girls knit quantities of blue socks, presumably in support of the Union effort, even if the novel engages little with the physical fighting of the war. Amy's experiences at school humorously recapitulate the Civil War: the teacher, Mr. Davis, has banished gum "after a long and stormy war" and has "made a bonfire of . . . confiscated novels and newspapers" in his efforts to keep order among fifty "rebellious girls"; the pickled limes that Amy smuggles to school have been declared "a contraband article" (58). The argument between Jo and Amy—Amy burns Jo's manuscript out of pique over not being included on an outing—may not be between brother and brother, but it does model how civil strife can be resolved: Jo must conquer her anger, must learn to control her passions. Published in the immediate wake of the war, *Little Women* portrayed the reunification of a family stressed by war and also metaphorically represented the reunification of the country as a whole, no longer a house divided against itself: it was "about a house conflicted but not divided, a family that offered an analogy and possibly a corrective to America."[105] These resonances probably contributed to the book's popularity in the United States.

The novel was also very American in being about a nuclear family at a time when virtue and affect were increasingly vested in this family configuration. As the historian Stephanie Coontz notes, the ideology of domesticity had earlier embraced engagement in the public sphere, but after the Civil War it retreated to the confines of the nuclear family.[106] *Little Women* offers a metaphor for the war even as it provides a privatized retreat; it further bridges the periods before and after the war by combining a prewar emphasis on "passionate female bonds that frequently took precedence over relations within the nuclear family" (65) with the postwar emphasis on the nuclear family.

The "Camp Laurence" chapter, in which Laurie and the March girls entertain British visitors, proclaims the book's American qualities in another register,
playfully reenacting the War of Independence. The British visitor Kate conde-
scends to Meg when the latter admits to working as a governess; Laurie's tutor,
Mr. Brooke, whom Meg will eventually marry, quickly asserts, "Young ladies in
America love independence as much as their ancestors did, and are admired and
respected for supporting themselves" (110). Laurie and the Marches, inspired by
"the spirit of '76," happily defeat the British visitors at croquet even though one
of the British boys cheats. Yet even as the British are here defeated, Kate becomes
a partial proxy for the British reader, teaching such a reader how America differs
from Britain but also, with her condescension, how not to read the novel.

In part 2 as well, themes of American independence undergird the book's
meanings. When Amy and Jo make a call on Aunt March, Jo is aware of her
tendency "to burst out with some particularly blunt speech or revolutionary sentiment" before her aunt (235). During a discussion of a charity fair to benefit the
freedmen, she sits "with her nose in the air, and a revolutionary aspect," and
declares, "I don't like favors; they oppress and make me feel like a slave; I'd rather
do everything for myself, and be perfectly independent" (236). Thus the sister
chosen as a companion for a European tour is not Jo but Amy—the sister who
"possessed that reverence for titles which haunts the best of us, . . . which . . . still
has something to do with the love the young country bears the old,—like that of a
big son for an imperious little mother, who held him while she could, and let him
go with a farewell scolding when he rebelled" (233). She's the March girl least
likely to rebel, as it were, even if she did smuggle pickled limes into school. The
choice of Amy is unfortunate, from Jo's perspective, but the American context
that Alcott provides makes Jo's actions positively rebellious. At the same time,
the invocation of slavery and freedmen conflates the Revolutionary and Civil
Wars. The translation from Revolutionary to Civil War—from a war often imaged as a child breaking free of a parent to one imaged as brother striving against
brother—underscores the sibling rivalry between Jo and Amy, perhaps also the
need to overcome such rivalries. But in the process, race is submerged to gain a
victory for middle-class womanhood. In refusing to act like a slave, Jo declines to
help former slaves, and only someone who had never herself been a slave could
say that social obligations "make me feel like a slave."

Whatever the subliminal messages of *Little Women*, whatever the reasons for
its popularity, there's no denying that it was immensely popular. Certainly children loved Alcott. It may have been from an adult perspective that she earned
her nineteenth-century sobriquet "the children's friend." The *Overland Monthly*

associates the phrase with her as early as 1875,[107] and its currency was reinforced when Ednah Cheney called her first biography of Alcott *Louisa May Alcott, the Children's Friend* (1888) — an association enhanced by the book's frontispiece, in which Alcott is reading to a varied throng of children, including some who seem to wear European national dress.[108] But children, especially girls, simply loved Alcott's books. In 1888 the fiction writer Harriet Prescott Spofford referred to Alcott as "the writer better loved by the children of America than Shakspere himself."[109] And Alcott's work appealed to adults as well as children; the immense sales figures alone imply that it wasn't just being read by the young. "Meg, Jo, Beth, and Amy," wrote the editors of *Godey's Lady's Book* in 1870, "are friends in every nursery and school-room; and even in the parlor and office they are not unknown."[110]

ᴄ∼

It's not always easy to distinguish popular from critical reception in the nineteenth century. Popularity was not yet seen as divergent from critical esteem. Still, one can gain some sense of elite esteem, if not indeed critical esteem, by examining recommendations, reviews, and essays in literary and other periodicals, and also, I will argue, by examining biographies.

In the nineteenth century, most critics judged literature on the basis of its aesthetic qualities but also its ennobling effect. When Horace Scudder became editor of the *Atlantic Monthly* in 1890, he noted in his diary that his "heart beats quicker at the thought of serving God in this cause of high, pure literature."[111] *Pure,* for him, meant not just aesthetic but moral purity: he rejected essays or fictions that he found skeptical or nihilistic (225–26). Those who focused on the ennobling qualities were often concerned about the effect of literature on the young.

By the end of the nineteenth century, *Little Women* was a fixture on lists of recommended reading for children. The British Edward Salmon found Alcott "conspicuous in the front rank" among writers for girls and added, "Her power of interesting one in quite ordinary events is exquisite and worthy of Jane Austen herself."[112] In the United States in the 1890s, *Little Women* was prominently recommended for children by the Pratt Institute; for girls and women by the American Library Association; for a girl's library by Thomas Wentworth Higginson.[113] It was likewise recommended for school libraries, for rural traveling libraries, and for village libraries.[114] Earlier, in a list for libraries in general prepared by the librarian Frederic Beecher Perkins, ten of Alcott's works appear, and she is on his A-list (not an inferior "b" or "c"), along with Andersen, Austen, Boccaccio, and Charlotte Brontë (whereas Anne and Emily are "b" authors).[115] At the end of the century *Little Women* was one of "the twenty best books for boys" named by "an

Reading "Louise" reading
Illustration by Lizbeth B. Comins for Ednah D. Cheney, *Louisa May Alcott, the Children's Friend* (Boston: Prang, 1888). Courtesy of Yale Collection of American Literature, Beinecke Rare Book and Manuscript Library, Yale University.

American writer"—it being "one of the few 'girls' books' that all boys will read, even if they do it on the sly or in a corner."[116] Not just for the young, it figured as well on a bookseller's list of what were commonly agreed to be the hundred best works of European and American fiction and on Walter Pulitzer's list of "Fifty Best American Novels."[117]

Yet some of those concerned about the moral qualities of literature did not approve of the book, especially for Sunday school libraries. Although the Universalist *Ladies' Repository* (Boston) approved of *Little Women* in 1868—"Our Sabbath Schools will all want it"—the Methodist periodical with the same name (published in Cincinnati) did not: it was "not a good book for the Sunday school library," because "not a Christian book. It is religion without spirituality, and salvation without Christ."[118] Niles wrote to Alcott in October that the March sisters' staging of a play in the opening chapter barred the book from Sunday school libraries.[119] In 1882 *Little Women* was not on the interdenominational *Christian Union's* list of recommended Sunday school titles; the editors did recommend it in 1887, but as a work "not specially intended for the Sunday-school."[120] In 1888, in an obituary, a writer for the Methodist *Christian Advocate* said of Alcott's works, "Though not religious, they are entertaining, often instructive, and a moderate installment, well selected, in the family life, and counterbalanced by works with a deeper purpose, will help the young people to form a love for reading, and recall to the elder the thoughts and scenes of youth."[121]

Beyond the caveats of the guardians of religion, there were the concerns of the literary elite. Esteem and popularity intersected complexly in the nineteenth century, not yet seen as intrinsically opposed: popularity could enable critical recognition, which could then foster additional popularity. At midcentury, Charles Dickens's works were both popular and esteemed. By the end of the century, however, critical esteem for Dickens had waned, and the highly esteemed works of Henry James did not have much popularity with a general public.[122]

Alcott's work was esteemed enough to be included in high-school and college curricula. John S. Hart's *Manual of American Literature: A Text-Book for Schools and Colleges* (1873) devoted a page to her, and he also gave her some attention in his more comprehensive *Short Course in Literature, English and American* (1877). Overall, discussions of Alcott appear briefly but frequently in nineteenth-century manuals, histories, and compendia of American literature.[123]

During this century the most prestigious magazines took children's literature—including Alcott's—seriously enough to review it. The *Atlantic Monthly* reviewed five of her works; the *Critic*, eight; *Harper's Monthly*, fifteen; the *Nation*, nine; *Literary World*, twenty. Reviews appeared as well in such varied periodicals as the *Youth's Companion*, *Godey's Lady's Book*, the *Journal of Health*, and *Catholic World*. In 1889 a writer claimed in *Cosmopolitan*, "About twenty years ago a million or more men, women and children enjoyed the most delightful literary surprise which native wit had devised within the century"—namely, *Little Women*.[124]

With respect to the content of the reviews, part 1 of *Little Women* was positively received: reviewers found it "capital" and indeed suitable for young and old. But it wasn't until part 2 appeared in 1869 that reviewers fully appreciated what had become a best-selling phenomenon. Alcott's writing was now described repeatedly as "fresh" and "natural." Many would agree with the reviewer for the *Hartford Daily Courant*: "She is brilliant, witty, has remarkable descriptive powers, and is as eminently successful in collating the sympathies of the reader as almost any writer that we now have."[125] Despite what he or she called the "limited field" of this novel's genre, the reviewer in the *Eclectic Magazine* nevertheless designated *Little Women* "the very best of books to reach the hearts of the young of any age from six to sixty."[126]

Alcott's reputation continued to grow during the next few years, even if not all commentators were wildly enthusiastic. In contrast with Sunday school librarians, an occasional literary commentator might be generally dismissive of women's writing: Alcott might be classed with other women authors, and, "in general, what they have written lacks the solidity and the higher qualities of sustained artistic style attained by the masculine authors."[127]

Some criticized her lack of what critics conceived of as a plot, yet as one reviewer noted, Alcott "has shown the rare faculty of connecting a series of matter-of-fact incidents that may and actually do occur, without any of the monotony that attaches to the best and liveliest of social or domestic circles."[128] Indeed, another noted of a later novel that "plots too often have a well-rounded completeness that suggests unreality, whereas Miss Alcott's stories are too life-like to have smooth sailing throughout the voyage."[129]

Other reviewers criticized Alcott's use of the vernacular, finding her language too ungrammatical or slangy. One reviewing *An Old-Fashioned Girl* (1870) in the *Eastern Argus* complained of Alcott's faulty pronoun reference, her use of *who* to refer to a bird, and her use of *laid* instead of *lay* and *who* instead of *whom*.[130] Alcott was, admittedly, a fast and somewhat careless writer. But language was also one of the few markers of class in a nation that thought of itself as democratic and virtually classless. So it's not surprising that the elite *Atlantic* and various British journals faulted Alcott's language. So did that high-toned women's journal *Godey's Lady's Book*, whose editors disparaged the frequent use of *ain't*, which gave Alcott's work "a *faux air* of vulgarity," even as they lamented, with respect to characters in *An Old-Fashioned Girl*, "a dash of vulgarity as well as hardness in their lives that makes us fear that Miss Alcott has been unfortunate in her experience of Boston life."[131] (Some respectable young women in the novel are gainfully employed.) The librarian Samuel Green politely sneered that "immature minds and uncultured persons" might find Alcott's work attractive, yet "many of the most careful mothers prefer, in the case of several of her writings, that their children should not read them when young."[132] Thomas Wentworth Higginson, a frequent champion of women writers, now best remembered for his patronage of Emily Dickinson, was also critical. In the 1888 edition of his *Short Studies of American Authors*, Higginson devoted one of eight chapters to Alcott, yet he concluded that "the instinct of art she never had. It is difficult to imagine her as pondering a situation deeply, still less as concerning herself about phrase or diction"; he added that Alcott might be a moral model, but if young writers wished to achieve something lasting, "they must look beyond her to greater and more permanent models."[133]

The best contemporary response to disparagement of Alcott's language—criticism of her slang if not her artlessness—appeared in *Scribner's Monthly* in 1876. This writer noted that Alcott was often accused of "a certain literary crudeness," yet "she is unquestionably one of the few women who can make not merely small children but even college Sophomores talk with something of the raciness of real life." The reviewer added that condemnation had been especially loud in England: "One would think that a child a hundred years old might be entitled to some voice in arranging his own vocabulary; but the theory seems still to prevail in some quarters, that all new Americanisms, however indispensable, are slang, and all new Anglicisms, however uncouth, are classic."[134] Certainly a similar argument—the need to create an American vernacular for fiction—contributed to establishing Mark Twain as a classically American author among the cultural elite a few decades later.[135] Such claims were rarely made for Alcott.

As the *Scribner's* critic suggested, Alcott's language was a crux for British commentators. At the end of the century a story circulated that a British publisher intended to publish an edition of *Little Women* "from which all expressions distinctly American are to be eliminated" in order to "make the book more suitable for reading in English class-rooms."[136] The story is apparently apocryphal, but it does capture a British attitude. A review of part 2 of *Little Women* in the *Athenaeum* suggested that "there is no lack of quaint Transatlantic expressions," especially by Jo, and thus it is no wonder that Laurie eventually chooses Amy instead.[137] Another British reviewer found *Little Women* entertaining but regretted that the girls "all speak after a fashion most inferior to their education and training"; he or she particularly faulted Amy for saying, "She cried quarts, I know she did."[138] In 1890 an Englishwoman admitted to having felt, as a girl, "a little restless discomfort to be overcome in regard to phrases and idioms which struck unfamiliarly upon our ears," but "all the greater, therefore, must the magic have been which captivated us so completely."[139] Another noted of fictional American girls, including Alcott's, that "if to our ears some of their phraseology is a little awkward, we must acknowledge that they themselves are not *gauche*"; indeed, "the heroines of Miss Alcott's novels talk extremely well."[140]

Overall, responses to *Little Women* in British periodicals were positive, but they were also likely to stress how American the book was. One reviewer found in Alcott's works, along with those by other American women, a distinctive "household idealism, quaintness, and piety, not easy to describe, but unmistakably to be recognized."[141] Another suggested that British "women will find here portrayed a state of society to which they are utterly unaccustomed," even if the "touches of human nature and traits of character . . . are common to all the world."[142]

Some Britons noted a kind of precociousness in an American little woman such as Alcott's, someone who "has begun life, wears long dresses, looks after the morals of her boy acquaintances, and takes a foremost place in the drama of life, when her European contemporary is leading a humdrum life in the schoolroom, and knows herself to be a person of no moment to any one beyond her parents and governess": "she has already entered and is an actor on that world of emotion and excitement which begins some five or six years later with us."[143] Another reviewer, who called *Little Women* "the most delightful book either *of* or *for* children that has yet been produced," found American young people "more precocious" than those in England and thus "old-fashioned"—and "hence, no doubt, the expression 'little women' as applicable to girls."[144] The phrase *little women* was indeed frequently used in the United States at this time to refer to girls, whereas the singular form of the phrase as used in Britain, in, say, *Bleak House* to apply to Esther Summerson, was likely to be a diminutive for a grown woman.[145]

Americans, nowadays at least, may be particularly aware of the gendering of *Little Women*, how it seems to speak especially to girls and women. But what has seemed to strike readers outside the United States from the beginning is how representative it is of America. Alcott's obituary in the London *Times* concludes, "In her stories she has done for New England, in kind though not in degree, what Miss Edgeworth did for Ireland."[146] And writers for or about girls in other countries, whether or not they modeled their works closely on *Little Women*, are often seen as having created books that did for their country what *Little Women* did for the United States. In 1940 the publisher of the twenty-seventh edition of Ethel Turner's *Seven Little Australians* (first published in 1894) noted that the book was considered "comparable to that world famous book 'Little Women' and Miss Turner became known everywhere as Miss Alcott's true successor."[147]

What British and American reviewers most frequently invoked as the reason for the success of Alcott's works, however, was "the thorough reality of her characters," her "power of intense realization and portraiture," "her thorough genuineness and steady adherence to the real," her being "truer to nature than a veritable narrative of actual events."[148] In the words of the Cuban poet José Martí, who found Alcott's work healthy and vigorous, "Allí chispea la vida" (Life sparkles there).[149] Enthusiasm for the lifelikeness of Alcott's works had its dangers: it could readily lead to dismissal of her writing as artless, a mere transcription of reality. And many reviews of a biography published the year after Alcott's death concluded that her life had been better than her art. It has been hard for some critics to recognize the life in her art. Few reviewers were as astute as one writing for *Scribner's* in 1871, addressing Alcott's "absolute fidelity to real life": "She is entitled to greater praise as an artist than has been bestowed upon her; ultimately she will be recognized as the very best painter, *en genre*, of the American domestic life in the middle classes; the very faithfulness, the aliveness—there *ought* to be that word—of her pictures prevents their having full justice done them at once."[150]

Alcott's realism appealed to young and old. I've already noted her popularity with both; such popularity was possible in part because children's literature was not yet sharply segmented from that for adults. In the twenty-first century we're accustomed to a segregation between literature for adults and that for children, and we're likely to associate Alcott with the latter. Yet in the nineteenth century children were likely to dip into the pages of "the best American magazines for adults, the *Atlantic, Harper's Magazine,* the *Century"*; as late as the 1890s the editor of *Harper's* claimed to print nothing "that could not be read aloud in the family circle."[151]

Indeed, the age classifications we now try to impose on Alcott's varied works often diverge from those in the nineteenth century. We now consider *Hospital Sketches,* a slightly fictionalized account of her experience as a Civil War nurse, a book for adults. Yet early reviewers considered it part of a "youths' library" or stated that it "will be sure to go" into the hands of those who had read *Little Women*; the pioneering children's librarian Caroline Hewins recommended it as a book "for the young" in 1882; a thirteen-year-old writing to *St. Nicholas* in 1878 had as a matter of course read not just *Little Women* and *Eight Cousins* (1875) but also *Hospital Sketches*.[152] On the other hand, in 1885 the Indianapolis Public Library classified all of Alcott's books as adult fiction.[153] A year later Alcott herself declared that *Jo's Boys,* the final book in the March family series, was "not a child's book, as the lads are nearly all over twenty" (and unlike the avowedly juvenile books, it was published without illustrations)—although then and now others have generally classed it with her literature for children.[154] After the turn of the twentieth century, Alcott was pigeonholed as a writer for juveniles, and the crossover book *Hospital Sketches* largely disappeared from view: it was not on lists of books recommended for children even when Alcott was represented by half a dozen titles, and none of Alcott's works that we now associate with a more adult audience, such as *Moods* (1865; rev. 1882), figured on any lists a century ago, for children or adults. But from a nineteenth-century perspective, Alcott wrote "of all the phases of youth—of bridals and of schools and of 'little men' and of young mothers."[155] In 1893 I find a sorting that starts to resemble modern ones:

the *Catalogue of* "A.L.A." *Library* lists *Hospital Sketches* as for adults and then six Alcott titles as for juveniles. In 1904 the updated A.L.A. *Catalog* of eight thousand volumes recommended for popular libraries even more fully anticipates recent sortings: Alcott's *Work* (1873) joins *Hospital Sketches* as adult fiction, and there are nine juvenile titles. Nineteenth-century experts simply didn't agree on how to separate Alcott's *oeuvre* into juvenile and adult categories; rather, the categories bled into each other. In the twentieth century the categories congealed.

The market for books for children and adolescents was also less gender segregated in the nineteenth century than it subsequently became. Alcott's work had considerable appeal to males—remember those lawyers and merchants, that civil engineer and that elevator "boy," whom Frank Preston Stearns recorded as having thrilled to *Little Women*. I might also point to an 1880 comment in the *New York Times*: "There is a tenderness, a sweetness, a peculiar gentleness about Miss Alcott's works which we really think no one else has. There runs no vein of over-sentimentalism in her books, for, with a rare insight into a boy's nature, she rather likes to describe him as having strong masculine traits."[156] In consciously writing for girls, at a time when the ideals of masculinity were not completely dominated by those of the self-made man or the masculine primitive, Alcott was not necessarily excluding boys or men. It was still possible, in some quarters, to admire the ideals of the Christian gentleman, dedicated to service, self-discipline, and generosity, rather than competitive individualism.[157] Many nineteenth-century reviewers assumed that both males and females would enjoy Alcott's work: a reviewer for the *Atlantic* might, in fact, make a passing reference to an audience that included "young people just getting to be young ladies and gentlemen."[158] By the turn of the century the winds had shifted enough that Teddy Roosevelt could feel self-conscious about having enjoyed girls' books: "At the cost of being deemed effeminate, I will add that . . . I worshiped 'Little Men' and 'Little Women' and 'An Old-Fashioned Girl.'"[159] Yet despite Alcott's appeal across genders, if a work seemed addressed largely to girls, the nineteenth-century cultural elite was likely to consider it as having a less broad appeal, as being less serious, than a book for boys.

It's true that when some elite reviewers addressed Alcott's work, they did try to police a boundary between literature for children and that for adults.[160] But the most frequently invoked marker was what might nowadays mark a boundary between novels for young adult boys and young adult girls: the absence or presence of romance, what reviewers called love-making. The marker has remained, but what it demarcates has shifted from age to gender. In 1881, for instance, Horace Scudder did not "altogether find satisfaction in the suppressed love-making of these young people" in Alcott's *Jack and Jill*, and in 1882 a British reviewer figured that Alcott's collection *Proverb Stories* wasn't really "for children, at least not for English children; for there is a great deal of love-making."[161] Lyman Abbott, who happily suggested that children would read *Little Men* with interest, while their parents would read it with profit, nevertheless noted the marriages in part 2 of *Little Women* and remarked that it "is a rather mature book for the little women, but a capital one for their elders."[162] Alcott had directly challenged such a perspective in the opening paragraph of part 2: "If any of the elders think there is too much 'lovering' in the story, as I fear they may (I'm not afraid the young folks will make that objection), I can only say with Mrs. March, 'What *can* you expect when I have four gay girls in the house and a dashing young neighbor over the way?'" (190). Elite critics were likely to feel some discomfort with children's literature that overstepped their sense of romantic propriety—and indeed with children's literature itself, unless the literature seemed to be primarily for boys.

At times the discomfort felt by an *Atlantic* reviewer could engender a Jamesian circumlocution, a backhanded disavowal of the absence of "adventure and sensation": "If we said that Miss Alcott, as a writer for young people just getting to be young ladies and gentlemen, deserved the great good luck that has attended her books, we should be using an unprofessional frankness and putting in print something we might be sorry for after the story of the 'Old-fashioned Girl' had grown colder in our minds."[163] With less circumlocution, Henry James himself, hoping to put children in their place—the better to create a fictional niche for adults only—castigated Alcott for being "vastly popular with infant readers," for catering to their views "at the expense of their pastors and masters," for not writing the charming kind of tale that Lyman Abbott's father, Jacob, had written for a previous generation, with the aunts "all wise and wonderful," the nephews and nieces never "under the necessity of teaching [the adults] their place."[164] (One child is reported as having responded to James's review, "I don't want to know the man who wrote that.")[165]

James wasn't the only nineteenth-century adult who felt uncomfortable with the prominence given to children and their views in Alcott's works. Such discomfort was echoed by socially conservative reviewers in, say, *Catholic World* and also by Agnes Repplier in the *Atlantic*. Like James, Repplier focused on Alcott's *Eight Cousins*, where the heroine Rose "is of the utmost importance to all the grown-up people in the book, most of whom it must be acknowledged, are extremely silly and incapable." For Repplier the touchstone juvenile writer of the past was Maria Edgeworth, whose Rosamond has opinions that "do not carry much weight, and she is never called on to act as an especial providence to any one."[166] The British

Walter Lewin tellingly responded to Repplier that perhaps "the little people of the past, like the women of the past, were only suppressed, and, essentially, were always very much what (now that they have liberty to grow according to nature) we discover them to be."[167]

Certainly the reviewers for the *Atlantic*, the most prestigious literary journal of the day, were uneasy about Alcott's work. They were far more receptive to boys' books than to ones considered suitable for girls. After all, the two men who edited the journal between 1871 and 1890, William Dean Howells and Thomas Bailey Aldrich, themselves wrote classic boys' books. Howells also wrote long, positive reviews of Aldrich's *Story of a Bad Boy* (1870), Twain's *Adventures of Tom Sawyer* (1876), and Charles Dudley Warner's *Being a Boy* (1896) for the magazine. In contrast, the reviews of Alcott's work were relatively short, and the *Atlantic* reviewed only five of them. Its first, as if in response to the popularity of *Little Women*, was the Jamesian one of *An Old-Fashioned Girl* in 1870, quoted above. After the initial circumlocution, the reviewer complained about "some poor writing, and some bad grammar" but found the "little book" pleasing, "almost inexplicably pleasing," given its "plain material." The reviewer of *Jack and Jill*, in 1881, also seemed puzzled, although the befuddlement was more rhetorical. After objecting to "the suppressed love-making," Scudder faulted Alcott for a self-consciousness that impaired the book's simplicity and concluded, "We are, no doubt, unreasonable readers; we object to the blood-and-thunder literature, and when in place of it we have the milk-and-sugar we object again. What do we want?"[168] In a review of an 1889 book about Alcott's life, an *Atlantic* writer acknowledged that there was "much that is both winning and repelling in her stories" and then lamented that "great possibilities were lost in Miss Alcott's career."[169] Such possibilities were not realized when a woman wrote for children.

Although Alcott published several stories and a poem in the *Atlantic* early in her career, she did not do so after 1863. As Richard Brodhead argues, in the pivotal 1860s, when high and low culture were separating, Alcott still had access to all levels—to the high culture being cultivated by the *Atlantic*; to the low culture being created by such story papers as *Frank Leslie's Illustrated Newspaper*, whose readership still overlapped with that for domestic fiction; and to an older strand of culture that affirmed a "domestic-tutelary model of writing."[170] Alcott could choose her market depending on her needs; for her, prestige was fine, but money was more important. In a letter to Aldrich, then editor of the *Atlantic*, she mentions that her publisher "once told me that you 'hated' me because my little works sold well."[171] Aldrich apparently went on to regale the Radical Club, which Alcott herself had attended, with a flippant verse in which he situated Alcott's "Rose in

Bloom on a silk divan" amid "fumes of sandalwood," sipping wine with her Arab lover.[172] So much for the homely pieties with which Rose and other Alcott characters became associated.

The journal the *Critic* provides yet another window onto Alcott's reputation in the final decades of the century. In its 1893 readers' poll of "best" American books, *Little Women* came in twenty-fifth, one of only four books by women in the top forty.[173] The relatively elite readers of the *Critic* had not fully sifted children's literature out of the canon, as increasingly happened in the late nineteenth and early twentieth centuries. The editors themselves, however, were further along in the process and were less willing to countenance Alcott. In 1886, of a hundred or so American authors "worthiest of being read," they named Emerson and Hawthorne, of course, and also Frances Hodgson Burnett, Mark Twain, Henry James, and the then relatively forgotten Herman Melville.[174] They did not, however, include Alcott. Her work might be good for children, as reviews in the *Critic* repeatedly iterated, but for professional critics it did not count as great literature.

Overall, Alcott's works were critically esteemed, especially before about 1875; they were regularly reviewed in the leading U.S. literary journals and in major British ones. But by about 1875, and certainly by the time of her death in 1888, whatever elite enthusiasm there had been had ebbed. American obituaries were often a bit measured about her literary accomplishments. That in the *Boston Post* referred to Alcott as "a facile and clever writer" with a "graceful if slender artistic faculty."[175] The obituarist in the *Critic* noted, "Miss Alcott's claims to popularity as a writer do not rest upon the literary merit of her books. She had great faults of style, and her characters were not always the most admirable."[176] And in the *Independent*: "She was not a great authoress, even in juvenile literature; she was more — a great, at one time a wonderfully great influence."[177] The conjunction of her death with her father's only a couple of days earlier might inspire an attempt to link the two, and thus to link Alcott to the high culture of Transcendentalism, but she is seen as purveying it in practical terms: "The father reached the few and the daughter the many, and excepting the writings of Emerson the Transcendental movement has found in no others such a setting forth of its fundamental ideas and such a practical exhibition of its ethical influence in the sphere of home."[178] In general, the obituaries stress the popularity or moral benefit of Alcott's work over its literary merit, although an occasional writer predicted that "much of loftier pretensions will die, while the world is calling for new editions of 'Little Women.'"[179] Obituaries in England tended to be more positive: in the *Academy* we are told, "Few writers are more popular, and none more deservedly so"; in the *Athenaeum* Alcott is called a "distinguished author," her *Hospital Sketches* are "brilliant," and *Moods* "never attracted the attention it merited"; in the London *Times* she is attributed with "a forcible style, with considerable humour and a keen eye for character."[180]

Another marker of esteem is attention to Alcott's biography. In the final decades of the century, several brief accounts of Alcott's life appeared, and in the decades after her death in 1888 a number of people published reminiscences.[181] Biographical dictionaries and collections with titles like *Stories of Our Authors* (1898, American, for a juvenile audience) and *Celebrities of the Century* (1887, British, for a more mature one) were bound to include some discussion of her. After her death, after Roberts Brothers was no longer circulating copy about Alcott's current activities, newspapers still printed bits of filler about her life. Particularly popular was an anecdote, reported with varying embellishments, about a librarian enthusiastically recommending *Little Women* to a patron only to be rebuffed, and learning shortly afterward that the patron was Alcott.[182] Such an anecdote was of interest in part because of the rising cult of celebrity. But, as I've noted earlier, nineteenth-century readers also sought the author in the text: as Janet Zehr has suggested with respect to critics who focused on the ennobling qualities of literature, "Knowledge of an author's essential character seems to have been, for some critics, the true end of reading."[183] An author's biography could be central to readers' understanding of and relationship to a text. Indeed, what constituted criticism and appreciation at the time included a good deal of what many literary scholars would now dismiss as mere biography.

The most influential biographical account of Alcott in the nineteenth century, and for decades afterwards, was by Ednah D. Cheney, a friend of the Alcott family active in reform movements. Cheney published a brief book about Alcott's life for juveniles, called *Louisa May Alcott, the Children's Friend* (1888), and another, for adults, *Louisa May Alcott: Her Life, Letters, and Journals* (1889), a collation of Alcott's letters and journals, interspersed with commentary. Both accounts are fully in accord with the nineteenth-century norm, in biographies of famous figures, of proffering virtuous role models.[184] Cheney's juvenile biography emphasizes childhood incidents, detailing some of the family's poverty. It was probably not controversial, more than two decades after the Civil War, to mention that the family had hidden a fugitive slave; but somewhat more daring, three decades before women gained the right to vote in the United States, to mention that Alcott "was an ardent advocate of Woman's Suffrage and other plans for the advancement of women."[185] It's interesting, then, to see how Cheney treats Alcott's adult distaste for living in Concord, in Orchard House, blaming it on the "harrowing visions" she had suffered there when recuperating from "fever of the brain" after serving as a nurse during the war.[186] In fact, Alcott found it hard to write in what became the family home because there were so many demands on her time, domestic and familial. Only when staying in her married sister Anna's house in Concord, not Orchard House, did Alcott feel "free from the cares always so burdensome to me."[187] Anna could attend to those cares. But a desire to escape womanly duties is not readily reconcilable with what Cheney wanted to stress in both biographical accounts, namely, Alcott's devotion to duty, to serving her family.[188]

The 1889 volume was widely reviewed and especially influential. In it Cheney praised Alcott's writing for children but was mildly critical of the writing addressed to a more adult audience. And Cheney was extremely laudatory of Alcott's life, stressing her sacrifices for family members, emphasizing her father's sobriquet for her, "Duty's faithful child."[189] Most readers of the two biographies have remembered the devotion to family. Cheney's net effect was thus to domesticate Alcott, downplaying her individualism and the complexity of her relationship to her family, making her more traditional than she actually was—and her work more traditional and domestic too. Indeed, contemporary readers were likely to find Alcott's life story "far more eloquent and fascinating than any of her bright stories."[190] Cheney's praise of the juvenile works, emphasizing their moral value; her belittling of such works as *A Modern Mephistopheles* (1877); and her great enthusiasm for Alcott's life helped set the tone for critical response for decades. Well into the twentieth century newspapers would run filler gleaned, directly or secondhand, from Cheney. One anecdote, recounting the Prince of Wales winking at a young girl in Alcott's party when he and his retinue were in Boston, had a particularly long life. Many elided the young girl with Alcott and shifted the point of the story from the humanity of the prince, as in Cheney's rendition, to the coyness of a flirtatious middle-aged Alcott.[191] In any case, as critical trends shifted, and providing uplift and role modeling was no longer a criterion for literary greatness, Cheney's terms defined a reason why Alcott's stature declined, a decline only augmented by the tale of the inappropriate flirtation.

∽

Alcott, then, consciously wrote a book for girls in 1868 and thereby found her publishing niche, becoming the "children's friend." Still, during the nineteenth century her work was read and appreciated by adults as well as children, by males as well as females. If *Little Women* was especially appreciated by young people, it was not confined to the nursery. As children's literature became increasingly segregated from literature for adults, however, Alcott was increasingly identified with the former and lost favor with the critical establishment—an identification and loss that some boys' books, at least, seemed to evade. In general, the more a journal or critic was oriented to the concerns of adults, especially males, of a certain class standing and with a certain pretension to cultural elitism, the more likely it or he or she was to sneer politely at Alcott. And the less likely it or he or she was to take children's literature—the field with which Alcott's name became increasingly synonymous—seriously.

In 1896 excerpts from *Little Women* were reprinted in the editor-novelist-critic Charles Dudley Warner's thirty-volume *Library of the World's Best Literature*. Yet almost all of the hundreds of books and articles addressing Alcott at the end of this century and the beginning of the next appeared in popular venues. (Then again, ventures like Warner's sought to be popular too.)[192] Alcott's popularity with the general public remained strong. In March 1888 notices about her death appeared on the front pages of newspapers across the country, including that of the *New York Times*. And by the end of the century, accounts of literary pilgrimages to New England would be incomplete if they didn't include stops at Orchard House, other houses where the Alcotts had lived, and the Alcott gravesite in Sleepy Hollow Cemetery,[193] thus contributing to a growing wave of nostalgia, a wave that would continue to build during the next decades.

CHAPTER 2

Waxing Nostalgic, 1900–1930

"What would you think about a play of *Little Women*?"

"I love the book," said Grace George, "but I doubt if the boys and girls of today would. They're so sophisticated."

Bill Jr. and Alice were both present and they at once began to protest.

"Why I love it!" said Alice. "I almost know the book by heart. Pop could I play one of the girls?"

"Sure, I read it too," said Bill Jr. "And *Little Men*. They'd make a good play and I'd like to see it."

— *Jessie Bonstelle, quoting the family of William Brady*

In the first decade of the twentieth century *Little Women* enjoyed an extraordinary popularity, but one that was in many ways under the radar. Some commentators claimed that the novel was read less than it had been by a previous generation, yet book sales and library holdings suggest that it was at the peak of its popularity. The dialogue that I have quoted in the epigraph, between William Brady, who went on to produce the successful Broadway play in 1912, and his family, hints at the positioning of *Little Women* at the beginning of the century. An adult generation thinks that the book might be too old-fashioned, but a younger male and female protest that they have read and liked, if not loved, *Little Women* (although the male has to mention *Little Men* too, as if to disinfect associations with the too distinctly feminine). The young Alice Brady did go on to play one of the girls in the production, specifically Meg, at the start of her very successful acting career.

The popularity of *Little Women* at the beginning of the century culminated in 1912 with the opening of Orchard House and the successful Broadway run of the first authorized dramatization. Yet at a time when many women were striving for independence, including the vote, what *Little Women* seemed to represent was the joys of the domesticity of yesteryear. *Little Women* was most popular, in short, when it was most domestic.

୰

Alcott's novel was not, however, receiving much attention from the gatekeepers of the academy. Around the turn of the century, scholars still made some acknowledgment of Alcott; texts with titles like *A Manual of American Literature* (1905, 1909) might still devote a paragraph to her. And the author of the entry on Alcott for the 1911 *Encyclopaedia Britannica* found "unfailing humour, freshness and lifelikeness" in *Little Women* even if her later works dwindled in value.[1]

A benchmark for criticism early in the century was the four-volume *Cambridge History of American Literature* (1917–21). American literature did not yet have an assured position in the academy, a situation that the publication of the *Cambridge History* helped to remedy. The American canon was also shifting: the collection devotes chapters both to authors in the process of being demoted (Longfellow, Whittier, Lowell) and to those being elevated (Thoreau, Twain). Academics were likewise starting to reconceptualize American literature. Later in the century an aesthetic focus on individual works and a tendency to limit attention to a restricted range of masterpieces would dominate. But in the early decades of the twentieth century a historical focus on literature as an expression of national life still held sway in the academy and in the *Cambridge History*. As the editors announce in their preface to the first volume, the collection is "a survey of the life of the American people as expressed in their writings rather than a history of *belles-lettres* alone."[2] Thus the contributors attend to works that aesthetic purists might not, strictly speaking, consider literature, "such as travels, oratory, memoirs, which have lain somewhat out of the main tradition of literary history but which may be, as they are in the United States, highly significant of the national temper" (1:xi). Chapters are devoted to historians, orators, magazine writers, journalists, educational and philosophical writers—and writers of children's literature. The chapter "Books for Children" is striking both because it exists in this scholarly history, even as the discourse was professionalizing and the canon was narrowing, and because it provides insight into how the academy—specifically the chapter author, Algernon Tassin of Columbia University—viewed and categorized children's literature.

Consider the way Tassin classifies certain nineteenth-century novels as children's literature, novels that have in recent decades been resurrected as important women's literature, which is to say, literature for adults. He may somewhat self-consciously note that Harriet Beecher Stowe's *Uncle Tom's Cabin* "is now almost exclusively a juvenile" (2:401), yet he never indicates that Susan Warner's *Wide, Wide World* was ever anything else. What Tassin marks, in effect, is the passage of these works, earlier or later, out of the canons of adult culture, leaving works of such power, for lack of anywhere else to go, in the nursery. As for *Little Women*, Tassin acknowledges its "abiding charm" and grants it a "most assured position" (2:402) among books for children.

His comments also reveal how the premises of the *Cambridge History* open the door to inclusion of children's literature. He argues that "American literature for children has reached a comparative eminence which it shows in no other department" (2:409). More importantly, he claims that "one can get more of American life from the juvenile than from adult fiction of the period" (2:406). One might therefore conclude that the most characteristically American achievement of American literature is its literature for children, that no other literature so distills the "national temper" that the editors of the *Cambridge History* wanted to capture. Yet other contributors to the volume are rather dismissive of children's literature, disparaging, for instance, Hawthorne's works for children and more generally ignoring works for the young.

Elsewhere in the academy the position of *Little Women* was less assured. In a 1908 text for high schools and colleges, Clayton Hamilton claimed, "The characters of 'Little Women' may be worth the while of children; and it is not an adverse criticism of Louisa M. Alcott to say that they are not worth the while of mature men and women."[3] But of course it is an adverse criticism. Hamilton's sentence drew this response in *Life* magazine: "NONSENSE. Mr. Hamilton may be a very clever writer about the drama and literature, but he knows little of children or human beings when he says that. We know mature and hard-headed and prosaic gentlemen who read 'Little Women' over and over every year or so with unfailing delight."[4] It's characteristic that this rebuttal of both the adverse criticism and the preferences of the mature appears in a popular magazine, not a scholarly one.

Emblematic of scholarly reaction by the 1920s is that of the polymath Lewis Mumford, who asserted that "the daughter of the philosopher reverted on a lower level to the Yankee peddler: she became a hack writer, purveying lollypops and chocolate cordials to the middle-class market."[5] Class and age here define each other, whether directly or metaphorically, even as peddling and the saccharine negatively define literary quality. And even in a popular venue shortly after the turn of the century one can find discomfort with the accolades heaped on Alcott, trying to deflect them to her father: a journalist in upstate New York lamented the emphasis a biographer placed on Alcott's early poverty as a disadvantage, for her improvident father's high ideals made him "in part the author of his daughter's splendid work"; in time he "will take his true place."[6]

◦⌣

Outside the academy the positioning of Little Women was, for the most part, very different, as attested by sales and circulation figures, polls, anecdotal accounts, reissues, spinoffs, and other adaptations. Enthusiasm seems to have peaked in the first decade and a half of the century.

One can't necessarily trust an offhand estimate in a 1913 drama review "that every fifth person of reading age in the United States has read 'Little Women,'"[7] yet the publisher's records indicate not only the continuing U.S. sales of Alcott's work but also a trend of increased popularity by the end of the first decade of the century. In the 1880s Roberts Brothers had printed about 107,000 copies of Little Women (parts 1 and 2 separately or the two together in one volume); in the 1890s, about 127,000; but in the first decade of the twentieth century, the last one for which figures are available, the number of copies printed more than doubled, reaching about 303,000.[8] The first decade of the new century accounted for more than half of the total of about 598,000 in the four decades since publication. In comparison, about 178,000 copies of Little Men, or 40 percent of its total of about 411,000, were printed in that decade. The relatively frequent mention of Little Men by commentators in this decade, sometimes before Little Women,[9] may hint not so much at its actual popularity vis-à-vis the latter as at an increasing anxiety that it demeans men and boys to read a book called Little Women. Interest in Alcott's novel may have been spurred, in part, by the publication of a new edition in 1902 with illustrations by Alice Stephens, but Little Women was, quite simply, popular.

Such a claim is supported by reports from booksellers. There was nothing quite as systematic as the New York Times bestseller list in the early twentieth century, but for several years the Bookman published a monthly report of the books most in demand at bookstores in various U.S. cities. Between April 1909 and September 1913 Little Women was frequently one of the top three best-selling juvenile books in reporting bookstores in such cities as Memphis, Cleveland, Atlanta, San Francisco, Washington, Kansas City, and Des Moines.[10]

Before 1900 the novel had often appeared on lists of the most popular or most circulated books, one of the top ten, perhaps, or maybe in fourth place. In the first decade or so of the twentieth century it was often first. In a weekly listing in the New York Times of the books that were most in demand in the New York

Public Library, *Little Women* was frequently one of the three most popular juvenile titles; in 1909 it was apparently the most popular book overall for juveniles in New York.[11] Alcott's works, especially *Little Women*, head the lists of juvenile books most frequently borrowed in communities ranging from Boston in 1902 to Cape Girardeau, Missouri, in 1919.[12] In 1912 in Cleveland "there were 325 copies of 'Little Women' on the shelves of the public library or, to be exact, never on the shelves, for the demand is constantly in excess of the supply, and Jo and Amy and Beth never get a chance to rest."[13] According to the Main Street Public Library database, five midwestern small-town libraries acquired at least twenty-three copies of *Little Women* during the first three decades of the century (outpacing the perennially popular *Uncle Tom's Cabin*, at seventeen).[14]

In polls and contests, too, Alcott often heads the list of young people's favorites. In a Chicago professor's 1905 survey of three thousand children, *Little Women* ranks first among the books most enjoyed, as it does in a 1901 survey of about two thousand North American young people.[15] Contests are less reliable gauges than polls, given that children may choose to write on a topic likely to meet with the approval of the judges. Yet Alcott figures frequently in prize-winning essays on a child's favorite book or fictional character. She may have been second to Dickens when it came to the number of children's essays on favorite characters in fiction in Minneapolis in 1901, but in a 1903 contest inviting children to submit essays on "favorite characters in fiction" to the children's magazine *St. Nicholas*, "the admirers of Jo outnumbered those of any other more than two to one."[16] When in 1907 New York teachers submitted four thousand children's reviews of their favorite books to the librarian of the New York Board of Education, *Little Women* was the most reviewed book.[17] In a 1923 contest sponsored by the *Bookman*, children wrote on "Books I Like to Read," and *Little Women* was again the most popular title.[18]

The novel also appeared frequently in children's individual accounts of favorites. Newspapers frequently published letters on a children's page and often encouraged children to name their favorite books. *Little Women* figures frequently in such letters and also appears in the less common letters to Santa, whether girls in Georgia wanted a copy along with a doll or bicycle, or a boy in Iowa wanted an air gun too.[19]

When asked why they liked *Little Women*, children might respond that her stories were "more natural" or "more real" than others or, according to a boy, "she tells of merry hearts in the house."[20] In 1903 a sixteen-year-old wrote that she had "laughed heartily over the writings by the members of the 'Pickwick Club,' and enjoyed immensely the contributions of 'Augustus Snodgrass'"; in 1907 a thirteen-year-old liked the "very delightful, homey feeling" of the book; in 1909 a child found the characters "so real that we wouldn't be surprised to see them step out of the book and shake hands like old friends"; in 1912 a fourteen-year-old claimed, "No one could call the book 'preachy,' and yet it contains many lessons in self-denial"; in 1924 a girl claimed the book "is true to life, humorous, and shows a living helpful spirit."[21]

The novel wasn't just read by children, whether a Chicago preacher called it "one of the best of all books" in 1903 or a Providence librarian claimed in 1913 that adults enjoyed it as much as children did.[22] Some men simply assumed that "it interests daughters and mothers rather than fathers and sons," but sometimes a man casually, nondefensively, mentioned having read *Little Women*: "As a boy I read it when it was too dark to go swimming or play baseball."[23] Well, maybe not altogether nondefensively: the writer needed to note that he read Alcott's novel only when it wasn't feasible to undertake more boyish pursuits. A similarly defensive boy might read his sister's copy, but he still read it: "Of course, when you were a youngster you read Miss Alcott's 'Little Women.' Girls found it on the Christmas tree or Santa Claus brought it to them. Boys read their sisters' copy on a rainy day, when there was nothing else to read, or borrowed it from the public library after a surfeit of the Optic, Alger and Henty books."[24] The novel was a favorite of a Colonel Gaston of North Carolina, who "held Louisa Alcott and her books in fond memory" after a teacher read it aloud when he was "a lad of perhaps 10."[25] The immigrant Leo Lerman, suggesting a role the novel played for other immigrants as well, loved the book: "It was all so American, so full of a life I did not know but desperately hoped to be part of, an America full of promises, hopes, optimisms."[26] A New Zealander noted, starting with a disclaimer, " 'Little Women' is not a boy's book, but I suppose I can be enrolled in a great army of men and women, boys and youths, who join with girls and young ladies in admiring Louisa M. Alcott's vivacity and naturalness."[27]

Nevertheless, from a masculine perspective *Little Women* was becoming a catchword, a target. Ring Lardner Jr. read the novel in the latter part of this period and later remembered it fondly, yet he also remembered his more famous father saying, solemnly, that he himself "liked Beth best, . . . because she died."[28] An Englishman claimed, "No self-respecting boy would read any book which his sisters praised so highly as Louisa Alcott's 'Little Women.' "[29] Lavinia Russ writes of being told by Ernest Hemingway in the 1920s, " 'You're so full of young sweetness and light you ought to be carrying *Little Women*.' (He had never read it.)"[30]

Women were generally more positive. The actress Mary Astor, who played

Marmee in the 1949 film version, claimed that she was "of the generation that read and loved *Little Women, Jo's Boys* and *Little Men*"[31]—adumbrating a recurring refrain, then as now, that one belonged to the last generation that truly loved Alcott's works. The African American writer Ann Petry "felt as though I was part of Jo and she was part of me."[32] A film reviewer in the thirties remembered the book—"one of our sweetest and earliest memories"—as having "a lyric wistfulness which hurts with its beauty."[33] Alcott could also inspire domesticity, maybe especially in one who would go on to write about it: the home economist Florence La Ganke developed her interest in cooking "the day she read about Daisy's kitchen in 'Little Men.'"[34] In the 1920s *Little Women* was named as a favorite by the social reformer Mary McDowell, the judge Mary Bartelme, and Mrs. B. F. Langworthy, later the national president of the Parent Teachers Association.[35] The writer Walter Prichard Eaton later stated that he hadn't much cared for the novel as a boy but that when he had encouraged his wife to replace her copy, so tattered that it had become unreadable, she "hugged it to her bosom" and refused, saying that she didn't need to read it again because "I know it by heart"; Eaton closed his essay by musing that *Little Women* had become a classic.[36]

Outside North America *Little Women* was still popular, even if its popularity didn't reach the peak it attained in the United States. In a London readers' poll of the "Best Hundred Books for Children" in 1900, *Little Women* came in seventh—to the consternation of a journalist in Sheffield who called it "a charming tale, no doubt, but surely out of its place."[37] (Some boys' books were lower on the list.) Only two girls out of two hundred surveyed in British secondary schools mentioned it as a favorite in 1906, but they may have felt they'd outgrown it; in a poll of comparable girls elsewhere in the empire Alcott was the second favorite author.[38] In 1904 Jo March was the "favourite girl-character in fiction . . . by an overwhelming majority" in a *Girl's Realm* poll of more than three thousand girls; in 1905 the novel was the second most popular book among eleven- and twelve-year-old girls in a London elementary school; in 1909 and 1910 it was the seventh and sixth most popular prize book among elementary-school boys and girls in London.[39] In 1919 several working-class women in Sheffield reported having been fond of it.[40] G. K. Chesterton was astonished to discover, as an adult, that Alcott's books "were extremely good"; he later claimed to "know few women in England, from the most revolutionary Suffragette to the most carefully preserved Early Victorian, who will not confess to having passed a happy childhood with the *Little Women* of Miss Alcott."[41] A reviewer of a biography could even attribute to Alcott "a genius of which Shakespeare would not have been ashamed."[42] Still, the reputation of the novel as a domestic idyl or moralizing text was taking on a life of its own: the British educator Lilian M. Faithfull classed it disdainfully as an evangelical book,[43] when in fact it contains very little overt Christianity (Christmas is celebrated as a secular holiday, an occasion for giving, it is true, but not one for going to church).

Part 1 of the book had been translated into Japanese by 1906: in the interest of retaining the purity of girl readers, the romantic love between Meg and John Brooke was omitted, as were references to the girls' growth, although Jo (here named Takashi), more mannish than in the original, was allowed the ambition of becoming a professional writer—and indeed influenced a number of Japanese women to become writers.[44] In 1910 a New Zealand journal reported on a literary lecturer who claimed, with respect to Bronson Alcott, that "perhaps the most important service that he rendered the world was becoming the father of Louisa May Alcott."[45] The following year, when girls at a literary meeting in Christchurch were asked if they'd read *Little Women*, "every hand was promptly raised."[46] In France a few years later the future existentialist Simone de Beauvoir "identified myself passionately with Jo."[47] In a 1924 poll of the favorite books of two hundred children in Australia, *Little Women* came in fourth.[48] An Australian journalist of the time reminisced that "we all loved Jo," and a few years later one recalled, "When I was young 'Little Women' was a household word in every schoolroom. . . . Put me on, even now, at any page, and I think I could tell you, in Miss Alcott's very words, paragraph after paragraph, of the girls' adventures."[49] According to a 1920s report on Moscow's libraries, *Little Women* was one of the most popular books, adults keeping it so much in circulation that "children have scarcely any chance to read it."[50] The author E. M. Almedingen remembers seeing much-loved, tattered copies of the novel, soon after the turn of the century, in a Russian abbey and a village school, and her psychology instructor in St. Petersburg assigned it as well.[51]

The popularity of *Little Women* seems to have abated somewhat by the 1920s, at least in the United States. It is difficult to gauge sales at this time (especially since the novel had entered the public domain), and figures reported in the media vary widely. Still, searches of online newspaper archives suggest that *Little Women* figured less frequently in the media in the 1920s than it had in the previous two decades, and responses that disparaged the book as too sweet were appearing with greater frequency. When Jessie Bonstelle's stock company performed *Little Women* in Rhode Island in 1922, the reviewer praised the director and the company for the success of the play, despite the "Polly-Anna-like trash" of the novel: "None but Bonstelle could mould so successful a drama on such rot and it is doubtful if another set of players could make the four acts bearable, not only bearable, actually a pleasure. The excellent play last night came as a shock."[52] In 1924 a writer for the *Washington Post*, commenting on books one might want to have on a desert island, claimed, " 'Little Men' and 'Little Women' and all the rest of Miss Alcott's operas, can go down with the ship for all me."[53] Yet he added, curiously, that he might possibly try to smuggle in as an eleventh book Alcott's *Lulu's Library* (1886–89), a three-volume collection that most readers, then as now, have deemed less worthy than Alcott's better-known works; indeed, her (and Anna Alcott's) *Comic Tragedies* (1893) was one of his original ten, representing drama.

Still, *Little Women* was getting some play in consumer culture, even if it didn't yet have the material presence it would gain in later decades. It figured, for instance, in department-store displays. In 1915 in Boston, Jordan Marsh displayed copies of the book, manuscript pages, a portrait, and dolls dressed as the Little Women.[54] In 1919, when Marshall Field in Chicago held a book-fair exhibit on the "making of American Books," the first items it advertised as on display were Alcottiana: Anna's ("Meg's") "wedding bonnet," Alcott doll clothing, and the copper tea kettle that Alcott used while a nurse during the Civil War.[55]

Alcott's books continued to be popular in libraries in the 1920s. One small-town newspaper reported in 1926 that a "big city" library might find *Little Women* and works by Twain falling out of favor, but not here, where the thirty-one copies of Alcott's book were constantly checked out and there was often a waiting list.[56] As for the big cities, in 1927 *Little Women* was still the book requested most by teenaged girls in the New York Public Library.[57]

In polls, by the 1920s Alcott's novel was somewhat less likely to appear as the top children's favorite overall, but it might be the top favorite for girls at this time when more systematic surveying (not just lists compiled from self-selected respondents) was coming into vogue. In the first decade or so of the twentieth century, in scores of media references, *Little Men* had often been mentioned in the same breath as *Little Women*, if not indeed named first; now the other Alcott work most likely to be mentioned was one that didn't include *men* or *boys* in its title: *An Old-Fashioned Girl*. Alcott's work now seemed to be more exclusively associated with females. In a 1919 survey of a Minnesota junior and senior high school, *Little Women* was the fourth favorite overall but tied as the top favorite for girls.[58] In a 1928 survey of the voluntary reading of late-elementary-school students in several schools in Illinois, *Little Women* was the most popular choice, but only because it was such an overwhelming favorite with girls; no boys indicated having read it.[59] In a national survey of 36,750 children conducted in 1924–25, *Little Women* came in second for seventh graders, according to the authors' idiosyncratic popularity index.[60] In a survey of about two thousand children at about the same time, Lewis

Terman (best known for inventing the Stanford-Binet IQ test) and Margaret Lima found *Little Women* heading the list of books liked by girls, although it did not appear in the boys' top twenty.[61]

Librarians and other educators, however, favored *Little Women* throughout the period. Alcott may have been excluded from the academic canon, but she was a lively presence in the library and education canons.[62] One can't necessarily trust a 1912 media report that the book was "one of the standard classics in all high school courses," especially when such reports were part of the hype for the 1912 dramatization.[63] More trustworthy is a 1913 report in an education journal that the book appeared on eighteen of fifty elementary-school course lists.[64] *Little Women* was, in any case, a staple on librarians' and others' lists of recommended reading for the young throughout the period and beyond—in New Jersey in 1901, California in 1910, Wisconsin in 1914, New York in 1919, Missouri in 1919 (for libraries serving African Americans), Washington State in 1922, Minnesota in 1925, and Alberta in 1926, among many others.[65] It featured prominently on lists in periodicals as varied as the *Ladies' Home Journal*, the children's magazine *St. Nicholas*, the literary journal the *Bookman*, the NAACP's *Crisis*, and the *Jewish Daily News*.[66] It was the first book purchased for the Los Angeles County Library in 1912.[67] If the novel was often specifically recommended for girls, it wasn't altogether omitted in recommendations for boys, appearing, for instance, on a list of books "that all boys should read" created by the librarian of the Chicago Public Library.[68] It headed a 1924 list, published by the Bureau of Education, of forty books that children should read before age sixteen.[69] Most significantly, in 1922 *Little Women* led the list of twenty-five books—a two-foot shelf of books—recommended by a joint meeting of the American Library Association and the National Education Association for use in the first through eighth grades.[70] This list, and *Little Women's* position on it, was widely reported across the country in both newspapers and professional journals. At least one journalist suggested that the report had renewed interest in Alcott.[71]

School-focused materials from early in the period often foregrounded *Little Men* more than *Little Women*. An article in the *School Journal* describing how to celebrate a Miss Alcott Day (on her birthday) with essays and dramatizations and stressing that Alcott "was more interesting and heroic than any of her story-book people") included a twelve-year-old's script for a scene from *Little Men*.[72] A school reader edited by Fanny Coe, *The Louisa Alcott Story Book* (1910), includes a biographical sketch and nine stories from Alcott's various short-story collections, together with an excerpt from *Little Men*. Indeed, the preface to the collection foregrounds *Little Men*: "The selections for this book have been made from 'Little Men' and the other best known books by Miss Alcott with a view to furnishing to the schools a supplementary reader which should furnish instruction in ethics."[73] The only mentions of *Little Women* appear in the biographical sketch and the back matter. The omission may reflect the prominence of *Little Men* at this time and may also be an attempt to "appeal to boys and girls in equal measure" (iii), though, curiously, the excerpt from *Little Men* portrays not a pillow fight or Dan's wild scrapes but girls learning to cook.

Among other commemorations by educators, in 1913 a school in Baltimore was named the Louisa May Alcott Elementary School.[74] In June 1912 a grammar school in San Francisco celebrated a Louisa Alcott Day, with costumes, songs, and a play, perhaps celebrating the eightieth anniversary of Alcott's birth (albeit not in November, Alcott's birth month). It called forth the following in an editorial:

> It is customary for schools to celebrate the anniversaries of great and patriotic men, and the reason for such observance and homage is to instill in the hearts of the children the virtue of patriotism and to inspire them to emulate the heroes in devotion to country and duty. To include the name of Louisa Alcott among those whom the children should honor in gratitude and emulate in achievement is wise and edifying. If the practice would contribute to juvenile literature some other such gracious books as "Little Men" and "Little Women," the children to come would have a rich legacy of delight.[75]

Alcott is to be emulated not just for being dutiful and domestic (common associations with her at this time, as I will go on to discuss) but for her achievement as a writer.

Elsewhere too her book was frequently recommended, appearing in a London poll of recommendations in 1900, for instance.[76] In 1928 British admirers honored Alcott by creating a memorial Little Women bed in the Royal Free Hospital in London.[77] A Canadian journalist, noting the British educator Lilian Faithfull's dismissal of *Little Women*, found the memorial "more like a just English appreciation."[78] The novel has been one of the few books recommended in all editions of the Toronto Public Library's *Books for Boys and Girls*, first published in 1927.[7]

As in the previous century, the publication of accounts of Alcott's life played out continuing interest in and response to *Little Women*, often giving some insight into how it was read. Although reminiscences and brief accounts appeared in anthologies and periodicals, only one full-length biography appeared during these three decades.[80] Belle Moses's *Louisa May Alcott, Dreamer and Worker: A Story of Achievement* (1909) is primarily a recycling of materials in Ednah

Cheney's 1889 biographical study. Moses's book appears to have been marketed to a juvenile audience, if one judges from its back matter, although its content seems no more juvenile than Cheney's compilation, despite a rather breathless ("Poor Louisa!") style.[81] It may promise, in its title, to focus on Alcott's work and achievements, and Moses does indeed discuss the work, but she also plays up the Alcotts' domestic pieties—"Never did parents have their children's welfare more wholly and unselfishly at heart"[82]—as well as possibilities for romance. "But the chapters that really please us most are those that deal with the 'Laurence Boy,'" she notes of *Little Women*. "About one million two hundred and fifty thousand, nine hundred and ninety-nine girl-readers, from ten to fifteen years of age, have been in love with *Laurie* during the last forty years, and probably as many more faithful 'loveresses' will rise up and adore him in the years to come. But for *Laurie*, indeed, it is doubtful if Miss Alcott herself could have written the book" (196–97). As for Alcott's own life, "No doubt, being a true woman, had a great love come to her, she would have obeyed its call," and "we find ourselves wondering if she would not have been happier with a home, a husband, and little children of her own" (76, 289). Moses marks a turn at about the turn of the century toward favoring the domestic and the heterosexually romantic in responses to *Little Women* even while gesturing toward work and independence.

Representative of such a turn is the brief biographical sketch of Alcott that appears in the first edition of the Girl Scout handbook, *Scouting for Girls* (1920). Alcott here is an early adumbration of a Scout, someone who effectively "earned half a dozen merit badges by her knowledge of home economics and her clever writing!" Yet her writing gets short shrift in this two-page discussion headed "The Homemaker," as we learn of Alcott trimming hats, papering the walls, darning stockings, and "drop[ping] the pen, often and often, for the needle, the dishcloth and the broom." Thus should "every Scout who finds housework dull" benefit from Alcott's example.[83]

The most interesting of the shorter biographical accounts that appeared during this period bucks this domesticating trend. Gamaliel Bradford was one of the innovative biographers of the time, following the lead of Lytton Strachey, whose approach was less celebratory than that of Victorian biographers and more irreverent and psychologically probing. In "Portrait of Louisa May Alcott," which appeared in the prestigious *North American Review* and in his *Portraits of American Women* in 1919, Bradford is not particularly interested in Alcott's love life (although he does find eroticism in her work) and suggests that she may have been influenced more by a "conscientious sense of duty" than by family affection.[84] He focuses on exploring the extent to which Alcott was an artist. He argues that she was, that she didn't write just out of financial necessity nor to preach, despite the moralizing in her stories. He concludes that her work, "if not great or original, was sane and genuine" (403). "The worshipers of art for art's sake may sneer at her," he adds, but the great poets don't necessarily "deserve much more of our gratitude than those who make our souls forget by telling charming stories" (403).

Of course another gauge of popularity is the number of reissues of the novel, of various sorts. Abridgments wouldn't really take off for several decades, but in 1919 *Little Women* was one of the hundred condensed novels, or "Ten Minute Novels," serialized in newspapers across the country, along with other works we might now deem children's literature but also novels by Dickens, Eliot, and Hardy—"Boiled Down So Everyone Will Have Time to Read."[85] Instant gratification, instant culture.

A more notable retelling appeared in 1923: Nora Archibald Smith published an eight-page condensation that commented on Alcott's story as well as summarized it, noting its fame, including its popularity among recent immigrants. "Why is this book so beloved," the narrator asks, answering that, no, the girls aren't rich, nor do they "have thrilling adventures," nor do they win fame: "only one of them has any idea of a career, and she does not 'career' very long."[86] Smith notes that at the beginning "there is but one hero to four heroines," yet then "other heroes mysteriously appear, as they are likely to do when princesses are sufficiently attractive" (11). She favors romance over career. Significant events in part 1 are then mentioned, though not the opening Christmas scene and the sacrifice of the family's breakfast, and when we are told of Amy burning Jo's manuscript there is no discussion of learning to overcome one's anger. An idealized "bond of love" is stressed (15), not self-sacrifice. Most of part 2 is condensed to a paragraph, in which the narrator notes that "we are not sure that we altogether approve of Friedrich B[h]aer, the German professor, with whom our headlong heroine finally tumbled into love" (17).

The color plate that accompanies the story, showing the four girls clustered around a book, is a new one by Jessie Willcox Smith. The critic Edward Nudelman has aptly praised the compositional balance of the image, including the framing of the four figures.[87] What's striking in this image compared with others of the foursome is that Smith provides not the static clustering common during the book's first century (of the sort that she'd provided for an edition of the full book eight years earlier) but a looser one, the figures more spread out, the sisters somewhat independent of one another even as their overlapping forms hint at togetherness. Beth would appear to be standing to the left (her hair is down, as one of the younger sisters), her back to the audience, her head turned toward and

Not the usual Jessie Willcox Smith
Illustration by Jessie Willcox Smith for Nora Archibald Smith, *Boys and Girls of Bookland* (New York: McKay, 1923).

gazing down at the rest. Jo is seated in the middle, leaning forward and absorbed in a book, possibly reading it aloud. Meg is seated to the right, gazing down at blonde Amy, whom she partly embraces. Amy sits on the floor, leaning on Meg's knee, gazing up at Jo, her mouth open as if talking. Jo is at the center, Beth and Amy gazing at her from upper left and lower right. The picture captures the special relationship between Meg and Amy and also Jo's centrality and her bookishness. The blue of Jo's and Amy's dresses, contrasting with the red tones dominant elsewhere in the image, may hint at the similarities between the two headstrong sisters. Beth's standing, though, slightly apart from the rest, puts her in what could be read as a position of power—but it could also hint at her inclination to leave the rest, departing upward.

Other newly illustrated reissues during these decades include one published in the United States in 1902, illustrated by Alice Barber Stephens; the 1913 Player's Edition, with photographs of scenes from the 1912 Broadway play; two editions from 1915, one illustrated by Smith, the other by Richard Jones; two from 1926, one by Clara Burd, the other by Percy Tarrant; and one from 1929 illustrated by Frances Brundage. In England as well numerous artists tackled *Little Women*, beginning with Jessie T. Mitchell in 1897 and including Adolf Thiede, H. M. Brock, M. V. Wheelhouse, Norman Little, Harold Copping, G. Ridout, and M. E. Gray.[88] The illustrations from this period are decorative, decorous, and domestic. The artists attend to dress, for instance, but more to their decorative effect and old-fashioned quaintness than to their authenticity. I'll discuss images by several artists in some detail.

One of Stephens's fifteen graytone plates focuses on Amy feeding peacocks near Nice while Laurie watches. One peacock has fanned its tail behind her and five others cluster in front, their tail feathers arrayed like Amy's own graceful draperies. Thus perhaps does Stephens include some indirect commentary—Amy as vain as a peacock?—a subtext reinforced by the compositional similarity of this image to an earlier one of a young Amy playing dress-up at Aunt March's. There Amy consciously preens in front of a mirror, with a turban and impossibly flounced and flowing draperies. In both images, one or more birds look on (in the first it's a mocking parrot), and Laurie gazes from the right.

Jessie Willcox Smith likewise appreciates the draperies, and her eight color plates also tend to foreground romance,[89] and also Jo, who appears in six images. Like Stephens, Smith provides an image of Amy and Laurie at Nice, this time at Valrosa. Her Amy does not blend into the decorative framing but contrasts with it, the pale pinks of the luxuriant rose bushes in the upper half of the image contrasting with the sky in the background and the light blue of Amy's dress. The paleness of her dress contrasts with Laurie's black jacket, though her dress is also coordinated with it by being accented with black trimming, and he wears what appears to be a rosebud over his heart.[90] The net effect is romantically decorative, as is that of Smith's other illustrations and indeed Stephens's. Valrosa is not a scene that resonates with my own memories of the book, but it did seem memorable for early-twentieth-century women.[91] Smith is also responsible for one of the most reproduced images of the four sisters clustered in overlapping togetherness, the frontispiece of the 1915 edition. Her romanticized images well capture the nostalgia with which *Little Women* had become associated.

Among the other editions, no longer was *Little Women* deemed unsuitable for the Sunday school library. The British Sunday School Union had published a

version illustrated by Jessie T. Mitchell as early as 1897. In none of the eight illustrations does Mitchell feature a religious connection; even the obligatory death
scene does not show the bedside of an angelic ailing Beth but instead a sitting
Beth lamenting the death of her pet bird. Many of the illustrations function as
fashion plates, as Jo and Meg contemplate what to wear to the Gardiners' dance,
Amy provides the final touches to her table at a fair, and Jo at the end prepares
to set out on a walk, where she may happen to meet the Professor—the sisters
variously sporting large hats or muttonchop sleeves or capes fashionable in the
1890s. Still, the frontispiece, the only image showing all four sisters, features Jo
announcing that she is the author of a published story: it is the only frontispiece
of the iconic foursome that I have found that foregrounds Jo's writing.

By 1913 the Religious Tract Society was publishing secular works with a high
moral tone;[92] the preface to *Little Women* makes no reference to religion. Instead
Flora Klickmann traces "the book's longevity" to its focus on "the everyday happenings in a normal home, the love of parents and children, the strength of home
ties, the 'give and take' of family life," and adds that not only did Alcott care for
her family but "she is a standing example of the way pluck and determination and
love can enable a woman to triumph over a weak, frail body and delicate constitution."[93] Klickmann herself, the editor of the *Girl's Own Paper*, published by the
society, had struggled with illness, having shifted from a career in music to jour-
nalism as a result.[94] For her, *Little Women* featured domesticity but also pluck.

As for other paratextual contexts provided by the Religious Tract Society, the
cover of my edition features three sisters quietly playing pilgrims, reenacting
John Bunyan's *Pilgrim's Progress*, a pilgrim staff clearly visible. Harold Copping's
frontispiece is more playful: Amy is playing dress-up (a favorite scene for artists
inclined toward the decorative), with Aunt March's parrot commenting, "Ain't
we fine? Get along, you fright! . . ." The image pokes gentle fun at Amy's love of
finery but also, I would argue, invites admiration. The seven other color plates
feature images of the sisters—and also Miss Crocker. A very minor character,
she's the unexpected visitor who dines with the family when Jo serves her ill-fated
dinner of too-young lobster, too-old asparagus, and salted strawberries. There's
no picture of the dinner itself; instead—a fashion plate. Overall, only two images
portray more than one sister: the cover image and one of Meg preparing for Vanity Fair. Instead of the iconic clustering of the four sisters, or of the four sisters
gathered around Marmee to hear a letter from Father, this scene is the one that
images the family in the novel: the grouping of the sisters forms a circular cluster
not unlike that in the iconic images, even if the directions of their gazes all diverge
(and with Beth perhaps already outside the charmed circle). Yet because of the

girls' implied activity, the image does make domesticity relatively active. The featured object here is not a letter but a trunk, and it's not at the center but part of the circular composition: it hints not at the absent presence of the father but at worldly delights and indeed the opportunity to leave the domestic circle, even as it anticipates the "four little chests" of the sisters' keepsakes that Jo will later commemorate. Most of Copping's illustrations foreground dress—like the other illustrations from this period, and indeed much as the *Girl's Own Paper* had increasingly done under Klickmann's editorship. The only visual hint of something religious is the pilgrim's staff on the cover. *Little Women* was now a fashionable secular novel.

っ

Various adaptations of *Little Women* in the early decades of the twentieth century testify to its prominence as an influential text and give insight into how it was being read, while in turn influencing how it was read. In the past, critics of adaptations, as well as ordinary readers and spectators, have placed great store in the concept of fidelity to an "original" work. In his foundational *Novels into Film*, however, George Bluestone stresses the autonomy of film adaptations, how such a film "will inevitably become a different artistic entity from the novel on which it is based."[95] A later theorist such as Linda Hutcheon, who examines adaptation among various media, stresses the dialogic relationship between and among versions of a text, acknowledging the creativity of interpretive choices (rather than adherence to or divergence from a so-called source) but also how the audience too engages in a dialogic interpretation, one that negotiates between knowledge of a named source and the adaptation.[96] Key adaptations of *Little Women* during this period were fictional spinoffs and a Broadway play—and perhaps, if one considers adaptation more broadly, the staging of Orchard House.

One striking trend a century ago was the appearance of juvenile books that I call spinoffs, conscious responses to *Little Women*—not books by authors who created their own family stories about the Katy who Did or the Anne who went to Green Gables (although the novel did indeed influence these authors) but rather reworkings of specific Alcott characters and incidents. It's as if at a time of changing expectations for women it was important to try to reimagine *Little Women* for modern girls, whether to encourage them to be more old-fashioned or to be more modern. If "publishers complain of the scarcity of good books for girls, and their readers say that no successor to Louisa Alcott has yet come to view,"[97] then one approach was to reframe *Little Women*. Between 1890 and 1930 there were at least four such independent titles and one series: the Australian Ethel Turner's *Seven Little Australians* (1894), the British Mrs. George de Horne Vaizey's (Jessie

MEG GOES TO VANITY FAIR.

Departing from the domestic circle
Illustration by Harold Copping for *Little Women* (London: Religious
Tract Society, 1913).

Mansergh's) *Sisters Three* (1900), and, in the United States, Marion Ames Tag-gart's *The Little Women Club* (1905), May Hollis Barton's *Four Little Women of Roxby, or The Queer Old Lady Who Lost Her Way* (1926), and the four books in Gabrielle E. Jackson's Three Little Women series (1908–14).[98]

In Turner's *Seven Little Australians* six siblings, including both boys and girls, still have a father but their mother has died; their young stepmother also has a baby. The oldest of the Woolcot children, Meg, is sweet and domestic, tempted by a friend to be fashionable and seek a sweetheart, but she soon overcomes the temptation. The next oldest girl, called Judy though her given name is Helen, is wild and rambunctious and the child that most puzzles her father. We are told that her "restless fire . . . would either make a noble, daring, brilliant woman of her, or else she would be shipwrecked on rocks the others would never come to, and it would flame up higher and higher and consume her."[99] Near the end of the story, the siblings are on a picnic in the bush, and Judy has pledged to look after the youngest, the baby, with her life. Foreshadowing portends that something dire will occur, and when Judy is temporarily distracted, the baby toddles off. A rotten tree topples—is about to crush the baby—and Judy rushes forward. The baby is saved, but Judy dies rescuing him. In short, it's not a Beth-like angel in the house who dies but an impetuous Jo-like character. In this touchstone of Australian literature—"No other Australian children's book rivals the lasting popularity of *Seven Little Australians*," according to Clare Bradford—the unruly female dies. Bradford judiciously suggests that "through this drastic closure Turner solves the narrative problem of a female character who resists the gendered expectations of the world of the novel but for whom there exists no alternative model of female subjectivity."[100] And Joel Myerson rightly points out that the character receiving the most focus in Turner's novel is really Meg and, furthermore, that by the end of *Little Women* the original Jo effectively dies too.[101] To a less judicious reader, though, the drastic closure afforded Judy may simply seem like punishment for female independence.

In the British *Sisters Three*, three teenage sisters live in the country with their author father and a little sister they call Mouse; their two brothers are mostly away at school. It's not the father who is absent but the mother, and it's the father who is an author, indeed a highly regarded one, not one of the daughters. And there's no Beth equivalent, unless one counts the use of the nickname Mouse. The oldest sister is attracted to finery, like Alcott's Meg. But she settles down without much fuss to housekeeping and ends up engaged to a promising young author whose physical disability will require some care and attention. The middle sister, the pretty one, wants to please others and, like Amy, is invited to spend several years away from the family, in her case in London. Finally, the artistic and somewhat boyish one is Norah, a talented violinist. More adventurous than the other sisters, she explores an underground passage with the (almost) neighboring Rex—and unlike Jo and her Laurie, she will wait, at the end, for him. She finally plays her violin not in public but for the entertainment of her family and Rex, remaining within the domestic sphere. The novel emphasizes courtship more than *Little Women* does.

As for American works, one spinoff tells the story of a Little Women Club in which girls consciously reenact Alcott's novel. In real life, Alcott-related clubs have taken a variety of forms. In the previous chapter I noted some of the spontaneous clubs set up by nineteenth-century girls. In the first decade of the twentieth century, even as some girls continued to create Alcott-inspired clubs spontaneously, adults were increasingly taking control and setting up clubs for the young: Little Women Clubs were proposed to raise funds for the preservation of Orchard House, and settlement workers set up a Louisa M. Alcott Club, aimed "at instructing small girls in all branches of housekeeping."[102] In Taggart's *The Little Women Club* the club is created by the young. Then again, it's an adult who writes the book, creating a model for her young readers. In any case, the novel's four friends, aged eleven to thirteen, decide to enact Alcott's novel, drawing in an older girl, Phoebe, as Laurie (whom one of the four loves intensely, presumably a schoolgirl crush), and a new neighbor, Mr. Acre, as Mr. Lawrence (as the name is spelled in the book). The girls refer to such elements of Alcott's novel as Jo meeting Apollyon and the little books that Marmee gave each daughter; like the Marches, they set up an informal post office and undertake charity to a poor family, Irish instead of German. *Little Women* plays the role of predecessor text that *Pilgrim's Progress* does for Alcott's novel, but as if the dailiness of middle-class girls' lives is not enough, the plot is leavened with the Fauntleroyesque sensationalism of discovering that Mr. Acre is Phoebe's long-lost wealthy grandfather.

As for Barton's *Four Little Women of Roxby, or The Queer Old Lady Who Lost Her Way*, four sisters, aged twelve to eighteen, are orphaned, living on their own in a small town, trying to make ends meet. The oldest takes in sewing and has primary responsibility for tending to the home; the next, "the only real business girl of the family," works for a milliner until work falls off and she is laid off; the third, Alice, tries to help out by making candy to sell; Bab, the youngest, is ill with "lingering pleurisy" during much of the volume.[103] And the queer old lady of the subtitle? She wanders into town, leaving a train that has been stopped by snow, and is taken in by the sisters. Unfortunately, the woman can't remember the married name of the half-sister she was on her way to visit, but fortunately, she is an excellent nurse and helps Bab through a crisis. The elderly woman eventually finds the piece of paper on which she'd written the name, and her brother-in-law turns out to be—what else—the four little women's long-lost uncle. So the girls no longer need to be poverty stricken. Alice may, like Jo, find a creative way to cover a burned spot on the shabby dress she has to wear to a party, but no one is befriended by or tempted to emulate the snobbish girl in town. Alice and another sister will eventually marry, we learn at the end. The sister with millinery skills ends up co-owner of the store and may some time marry too, but her future is left open. And the Beth figure, Bab, the one who had a long-drawn-out fever and nearly died, goes to college. Death and grieving and powerful emotions are evaded, as opportunities for women are evoked.

But the most interesting of the spinoffs—most interesting in how it addresses the cultural moment even as it attests to the continuing significance of *Little Women*—is the Three Little Women series, and I will discuss it at some length. For it harbors inconsistencies that speak to cultural contradictions at the beginning of the century, especially those associated with the occupational opportunities available to the New Woman and the continuing expectations of domesticity, at a time when Alcott might be called "one of the finest of pioneer American business girls."[104] These four books were sufficiently well regarded that *Youth's Companion* offered them as premiums to subscribers, listing them right after the "Louisa Alcott Library."[105] Gabrielle Jackson contributed frequently to *St. Nicholas* and wrote at least thirty-nine juvenile titles. She also wrote a couple of advice books, including *The Dawn of Womanhood* (1908), published the same year as the first of her Three Little Women books. In it she advises young women how to be, in effect, genteel: don't be a flirt, dress and eat in moderation, and think of the needs of others. Although she doesn't proscribe it, Jackson is wary of young women going to college, since college women tend not to marry till after age thirty and a woman should really become a mother before twenty-five, she claims.[106] In a chapter on historical young women, she addresses the life of Alcott, who "for more than thirty years . . . worked and hoped, doing cheerfully whatever her hand found to do, meeting with many disappointments, overcoming many obstacles"; her life provides a model, as does *Little Women*, "which has helped many more little women than the modest author ever dreamed it could" (205). Although many fields are now open to women (no excuse, in short, for being idle), "the noblest sphere for woman"—for the "peace and tranquillity of the nation"—is "at the head of her own home as wife and mother" (229–30, 254).

The three sisters in Jackson's fiction series are Eleanor, about seventeen in the first volume, bookish and academic; Constance, fifteen, the most domestic of the three; and the madcap ten-year-old Jean. As in *Little Women*, the family has declined in wealth because the father endorsed a loan to a friend who then defaulted; and like Mr. March in part 1 of Alcott's novel, Mr. Carruth is absent from the family circle, but in this case because he has died. There is likewise a strong-willed aunt who, like Aunt March, scolds but provides financial help, and there is a friendly, wealthy young man nearby, not unlike Laurie.

Yet there are also significant differences. For one thing, the mother may provide a sentimental center for the girls, but the center is only sentimental. As Constance tells her when Mrs. Carruth threatens to try to find a way to help earn money, "You represent *home* to us girls. Without you it would be the harp without its strings, the organ without its pipes. It would disintegrate. Keep it for us. Try to feel that you are doing far more in our busy hive by just being our Queen Bee than you ever could by going abroad in the land to gather the honey. Let *us* do that."[107] Yet Mrs. Carruth is not a source of strength and power in the family. She takes an active role in mothering only with a working-class girl who, in the second volume, needs counsel after some morally dubious but not irretrievable behavior with a young man. We don't see such mothering with her own daughters; instead they try to protect her. We are told that Mrs. Carruth "moved serenely and quietly through life, ruling and guiding more by example and innate force than by any special activities or spoken words,"[108] but we don't witness such example or force. The narrator goes on to say, "Her daughters were her companions, her friends, who went to her as naturally with the various questions and problems which came into their lives as they would have gone to each other" (*Work* 263). And thus she is not like Alcott's Marmee, whose daughters are likely to turn to her before they turn to their sisters. The servant Mammy Malviny later states, "She's *all* mother, an' ain' fitten ter be nothin' else. *Her* place is right hyer in de home wid her chillern, an' if *I* kin help it she ain' never a-gwine to go out ob it. She's de *haid*, she is, an' de *mistis*" (*Work* 296). Mammy may be intending to say that Mrs. Carruth shouldn't have to be anything else, but it's tempting to read her as saying that the woman isn't fit to be anything but a mother. Mammy may be married by this point, yet it's acceptable for her to work outside her home. Not Mrs. Carruth, though.

Mrs. Carruth is further infantilized when we are told she has a religious "faith which made doubt impossible; the faith which makes the little child turn to God and ask for a new dolly. . . . A simple faith which greater souls might do well to emulate" (*Work* 284). That claim sounds rather like a romanticized nineteenth-century account of faith—think of Beth's dying—except for the request for a new doll. Perhaps this crassness is simply an extension of the March girls' being materially rewarded for the selflessness of giving away Christmas breakfast with an astonishing feast sent over by Mr. Laurence. But seriously, we're to emulate praying for a toy? Religious nostalgia collides and colludes with the emerging consumer culture.[109]

The real source of strength, the moral center of the family, especially early on, appears to be Mammy. Born in slavery, she moved north when the southern-born Mrs. Carruth married—and embodying the stereotype of the faithful retainer, Mammy refuses to leave when the Carruths can no longer pay her and even lends the family money. She tends to the household chores but also enables the girls' various projects, whether she takes over the care of a neglected horse befriended by Jean or transports and sells the candies that Constance decides to make to help the family's finances. At times Mammy is played for comic relief, especially in the later volumes, but her judgments of character are always sound: the estimable young man Hadyn Stuyvesant, for instance, is indeed "de very cream ob all creation," and the perfect Constance is "a pearl o' price" (*Success* 299). And if an outsider tries to swindle her beloved family, she is the one who gets to the bottom of it.

Also different here is the constellation of the sisters. Jean may get into pickles, even if not pickled limes, but her adventures provide action and humor. None of the sisters seems to have Meg's fascination with the fashionable world, although all are as class-conscious as she or Amy. Jo's traits are spread among the sisters: bookishness to Eleanor, strength of purpose and narrative centrality to Constance, tomboyishness and sacrificing one's hair for money to Jean. But it's not the bookish girl who rescues the family in a crisis. Indeed, thanks to careless experimenting with acids, Eleanor actually causes the fire that destroys the family home—and hence the family resources, since the insurance company denies payment because of the presence of the chemicals.

Instead it's domestic Constance to the rescue. In the first book we learn that she

> was the domestic body of the household; prettiest of the three, sunshiny, happy, resourceful, she faced the family's altered position bravely, giving up the advantages and delights of the seminary without a murmur and contributing to her mother's peace of mind to a degree she little guessed by taking the most optimistic view of the situation and meeting altered conditions with a laugh and a song, and the assurance that "*some* day she was going to make her fortune and set 'em all up in fine shape once more."[110]

It's as if Alcott's Beth has become an earthly savior instead of a heavenly one, and the selfless domesticity that she represents, too unworldly to survive in Alcott's world, has been redeemed. After the fire, when rent is added to the family's expenses, Constance starts making fudge and other candy to sell. This modest little angel in the house turns out to have the acumen of a self-made man. Independence is reduced to the merely financial, and even that is cloaked with a celebration of domesticity, the candy-making an extension of housewifely activities.

As for the past gentility of the Carruths, it's defined by descent not from Boston elites but from southern planters. Perhaps New England did not provide a sufficiently romanticized past for suggesting the true inner worth of a family that might otherwise seem merely middle class. This one "sports the refinement of generations of ancestors whose positions in the great social world, and the world of culture, had never been questioned" (*Work* 24). Yet other cultural meanings are at play as well. Alcott's 1868 *Little Women* provided a reunited family that could hint at the reunification of the nation after the Civil War. Forty years later, Jackson's, exalting the aristocracy of the middle class—Mrs. Carruth reigning as "essentially a Southern housewife,"[111] a princess more than a housewife—enacts a different deployment of region, race, class, and gender.

The historian Nina Silber has noted the ways in which literature of the late nineteenth century by northerners enacted national reunion: the loudest proponents of sectionalism, the advocates of the Confederacy, are powerless and hence nonthreatening black slaves and white women; white southern men are likely to be weak and ineffectual; and a masterful white northern man ends up carrying off the southern belle. His doing so restores order to a socially and economically fractured society and confirms northern white masculine dominance. The belle ends up not seeking regional or personal independence but happily reverts to domesticity.[112] In Jackson's series the white man with southern roots is the faintly ridiculous schoolmaster who courts Eleanor. And Jackson overwrites the Alcotts' commitment to emancipation with nostalgia for a slave-owning past: "Alas for the days of such ties and such devotion!" (*Three* 65), the narrator declaims in the first book, nostalgic for a time when, presumably, slaves behaved like the devoted Mammy.

As for social class, I've already noted that in the nineteenth century Alcott was at times criticized for vulgarity, especially in her language, although sometimes the criticism extended to other gaffes. Early in the twentieth century the Harvard professor Barrett Wendell noted that *Little Women's* "personages display that rude self-assertion which has generally tainted the lower middle class of English-speaking countries."[113] Amy Lowell and the influential children's librarian Anne Carroll Moore subsequently joined Edith Wharton in disparaging the "very bad English."[114] Katharine Fullerton Gerould provided the fullest indictment, writing in the *Atlantic Monthly* in 1911. She noted, for instance, that Jo's lack of the subjunctive—"Don't talk about 'labelling' Pa, as if he was a pickle-bottle!"—might be explicable because Jo is "a willful freak"; but even "exquisite Amy" writes, "Don't that sound sort of elegant and rich?"[115] (I'm not entirely sure whether it's the subject-verb agreement—possibly aping the vernacular of the British upper classes?—that is objectionable or the intrusion of "sort of.") Alcott is also guilty of allowing her heroines to be unchaperoned, Gerould noted, and the household lacks "the greater and lesser amenities of life," which is to say, "you know that their furniture was bad—and that they did not know it."[116] Jackson would seem to address the occasional complaints about Alcott's language—for being at times ungrammatical and vulgar—with what might strike a modern reader as hyper-refinement. Jo's slang—"pegging away" instead of "studying hard"[117]—was part of her liveliness, her pushing of boundaries, not, within her book, reason for disdain. Similar behavior in Jackson's books evokes the latter. A young woman who works for Constance and whose tastes she tries to elevate says, "Well, you're the boss! Oh, I beg your pardon, Miss Constance, I didn't mean that! I mean you're—." Constance replies, "I'll make believe I didn't hear" (*Success* 52). So much for calling a boss a boss.[118]

Jackson's characters also exhibit snobbery. Alcott's works weren't devoid of it: she looked down on the immigrant Irish, and so did Amy and her schoolmates. Yet the snobbery we find in Jackson's work, as in Gerould's essay, is closer to that of the socially elite Gardiners and Moffatts in Alcott's world, for whom "taste" and conspicuous—or conspicuously inconspicuous—display are "commy la fo" (88), as the "exquisite" Amy might say. Eleanor's "instincts," for example, "shrank from any member of her family launching upon a business enterprise" such as Constance's candy-making (*Three* 138). Still, the first novel in the series ends with a celebratory accounting of the income the girls are providing—how many boxes of candy sold, for how much money, how many students tutored by Eleanor, for how much, ditto. Jackson concludes with a kind of vulgar display to the reader, tallying the profits of a commodity culture based on market competition, even while paying lip service to an older domestic economy whose byword is honor. The tension is encapsulated by the way in which Constance's candy is sold. She never sullies her hands with direct selling (sullying said hands in the kitchen apparently does not endanger her class standing): her candy is sold through a booth in an office building, where sales are on an honor system. Thus is the family freed from direct selling to strangers. No shopgirls they. Yet in an impersonal building where anyone is free to come and go, no one raids the candy or the cash box—at least not until a key point in the second volume, but that mishap is soon resolved.

In the next paragraph after the celebratory accounting, Constance announces that she's "going to be a genuine business woman, see if I'm not" (*Three* 312). And she does become one, not fully confined to the private sphere, in an impersonal market economy that yet upholds an older standard of honor. No robbers here, and certainly no robber barons.

Several years later, in the third volume, *Three Little Women's Success*, Constance's financial success is assured; she now employs three young women, but we hear little of day-to-day operations. Nor is much celebratory attention paid to Eleanor's graduation from college at a time when only 3 percent of women aged eighteen to twenty-one even attended such an institution.[119] Instead it's time to turn to what Alcott would call the "lovering." Eleanor is wooed and won by a teacher who "consummat[es] his dreams" by founding a boys' school, but unlike in the school founded by Jo and her Professor, the woman plays no active role, and the school itself caters only to "affluent youths" (*Success* 294, 293)—Alcott's wild Dan and meek Nat would not be welcome. As for Constance, she survives the machinations of an insurance agent. Yet his desire to marry her seems evil primarily because of his class status: when, for instance, she turns from him, he sneers, "Workin' for her livin' an' tryin' ter play the big-bug, too, ain't she?" (*Success* 126). His pointing to her occupation hints that her own class status is at risk, but his sneering, his slang, and his dropped g's put him as firmly in his place for the reader as Constance's turning away does.

In the first chapter of this third book, Eleanor is "resolved to be independent," Constance "would never be happy if dependent upon others," and she aims for "absolute independence for her mother" (*Success* 13, 15, 19)—yet independence means only financial solvency. Still, Constance's wooing at the end of the book suggests a kind of independence, even if the word has disappeared from the text by then. When the horse she is riding is hit by a car, she has the steadiness of nerve to improvise a tourniquet and the strength to hold it till a veterinary ambulance arrives. "My little girl! my little girl!" her companion, the wealthy Hadyn, exclaims. "Dear, dear heart!—so courageous, so brave, so strong! So perfect a woman in your tenderness combined with your strength" (*Success* 311). Despite his lip service to strength and courage, though, she is kept in her place by *little*, a word that appears at least ninety-six times in this volume. Frances Armstrong has noted that for Alcott littleness at times entailed diminishment but at other times was a means to greatness.[120] In Jackson's novels—with their "little girls," "little mothers," "pretty little rooms," "trembling little figures"—diminishment is the rule. Still, the "little" accident precipitates Hadyn's declaration of love. The titular success in this novel might, in the context of the previous novels in the series, seem to refer to financial stability, indeed prosperity, but it finally seems to mean success in the marriage market.

Independence again figures prominently at the beginning of the final novel—Constance providing independence for her family, Eleanor inheriting it from the benevolent crusty aunt—and then again disappears. Constance's flourishing candy business has moved from the home to a factory and has "made her family practically independent" (*Wives* 13). Once she and Hadyn marry, he wants to relieve her of "the burden and responsibility of such a growing enterprise," and after initially objecting, Constance realizes "how strongly he felt, and how it distressed him to have his wife engaged in any active business pursuit when the necessity for it no longer existed," so "she resolved to try playing 'lady of leisure'" (*Wives* 49). Alcott's Jo may marry, but she actively participates in the school at Plumfield, and she eventually writes for publication. Jo deconstructs the separation of public and private spheres. The married Constance may be allowed brief forays outside the home to provide morally uplifting amusement for the working "girls" in the factory dormitory, but aside from the odd charitable endeavor, she's to enact a kind of domesticity without real labor, to live "the life of pleasure and freedom from responsibility" (*Wives* 16), with her protector not, as for her mother, her daughters or a black servant but a white male. The white patriarchal family has been restored, and Constance's independence has become a different kind of freedom—"freedom from responsibility."

The last appearance of the term *independence* is in connection with Jean's defying Mammy's curfew while the rest of the family is away, the girl's years at boarding school having given her "a wider idea of independence" (*Wives* 149). Yet for all that Jean has playfully imagined becoming a strong-minded old maid and maybe even a suffragist, she seems to decide against the latter because of the signature color scheme of yellow and blue: "it wouldn't be becoming, so that alone will deter me from joining my down-trodden sisters" (*Wives* 39). Mammy would approve, for she has earlier dismissed "dese hyer twenty-centuries women . . . wha's spilin' fer ter hike ter de polls an' vote" (*Work* 296). When Jean is then in a car that breaks down and the young driver goes for help and tells her to sit quietly, "perhaps never in her life would Jean be nearer respecting [him], for he was daring to lay down the law to her for the first time" (*Wives* 183). That's apparently what a man should do. Not that Jean obeys. She wanders off in the rain, only to be rescued by another young man, her true knight-errant. So maybe that's what a true man should do. The novel closes with Jean and her knight happily reunited after they dry off, but that's another story—or rather none at all, since, unlike in Alcott's series, the story of each of the Three Little Women pretty much ends once she marries. Wifehood seems to extinguish each as fully as death did Alcott's Beth. The marriage plot here segregates public and private spheres so completely that even the publicity of publication ceases. The impossibility of sustaining domestic entrepreneurialism speaks to the cultural contradictions between women's longings and women's realities at the start of the twentieth century, a time when the United States was emerging as a world power with imperialistic ambitions, Teddy Roosevelt was fighting corporate monopolies, and some women were marching shoulder to shoulder for women's right to vote, a time when domesticity was highly contested. Sally Mitchell writes of contemporary British girls' books that the suddenness of a marriage at the end of a book could be "a wink at its irrationality." She further notes,

> Popular culture . . . mediates, meliorates, makes small steps thinkable, and perhaps moves the mean. To create a socially comfortable role for new girls who would become new women—independent, educated, intelligent, self-fulfilled, economically self-sufficient—it was probably necessary to reassure both girls and their parents that the role was appropriately feminine, with all the complex social and emotional burdens that "feminine" encoded.[121]

Overall, the compulsion "to retell the same story over and over in different ways"[122] in these spinoffs—to keep retelling *Little Women*—hints at the severity of the crisis for the little women of the time, even as the works attempt to mitigate it.

One potential spinoff from this period that is addressed to a more adult audience is F. Scott Fitzgerald's short story "Bernice Bobs Her Hair," which first appeared in the *Saturday Evening Post* in 1920. It is not so much a reimagining of Alcott's overall premise in modern guise—though Susan Beegel makes a case for its close correspondence to *Little Women*—as a rethinking of the cut-hair trope and of society as Vanity Fair. Fitzgerald juxtaposes Alcott's Little Women to the modern Bernice and Marjorie to comment on the jazz-age girl, on trying to be popular, part of "a generation adrift without moral guidance," in Beegel's words.[123] Fitzgerald directly invokes *Little Women* when Marjorie says of Alcott's characters, "What modern girl could live like those inane females?"[124] Acting on a "jealous whim" (45), Marjorie goads her visiting cousin Bernice into the shocking action of cutting her beautiful hair; Bernice retaliates by cutting Marjorie's braids while the latter sleeps. In 1920 a girl doesn't cut hair, her claim to beauty, out of a sense of self-sacrifice for the family, but on a whim and out of spite against a family member, even while making a nod to an emerging fashion. Neither girl comes off well in the story, but it's clear that domesticity and service to the family are now old-fashioned.

Not till the end of the twentieth century, and the second women's movement, do I find a similar spate of retellings, this time in books addressed to adults—but more on them in chapter 4.

᷄

Nineteen twelve was a watershed year. The writer Floyd Dell has noted that women's suffrage activity was then intense; the election of Woodrow Wilson as president signaled reform; and in the arts, Edna St. Vincent Millay published "Renascence," Harriet Monroe founded *Poetry*, Vachel Lindsay published "General Booth Enters Heaven," and Maurice Brown started the Little Theatre in Chicago.[125] That is, little theaters and little magazines were beginning to promote innovative work. Nineteen twelve was a watershed year for Alcott's reputation as well, but in a way that resists the reformist and radical trends championed by Dell. Alcott was publicly commemorated when the first authorized dramatization of *Little Women* opened on Broadway, to great acclaim, and the Orchard House memorial opened in Concord; both events received considerable coverage in the press.

The 1912 Broadway hit wasn't the first dramatization of *Little Women*. There had been amateur theatricals of various sorts, including school and household productions. As early as 1870 Thomas Wentworth Higginson saw an amateur performance by children.[126] In 1873, with Alcott's approval, W. H. Venable published dramatizations of two scenes in a collection called *The School Stage*, possibly the same "Scenes from 'Little Women'" presented by a school's Philocalian Society in Chicago in 1874.[127] In 1875 in Iowa, despite Alcott's disapproval, college women staged a dramatization.[128] In 1900 the *Ladies' Home Journal* published scripts for two-act dramatizations of scenes from *Little Women* and *Little Men*; these versions were frequently performed thereafter (a single performance by amateurs required no permission from the Alcott heirs).[129]

But the 1912 production was the first full-scale authorized dramatization. Jessie Bonstelle, a pioneering woman director (*Little Women* was her "greatest triumph"),[130] had sought permission from the Alcott heirs for eight years, finally outliving one of Alcott's nephews and also outliving the first dramatist who had been approved. She then turned to Marian de Forest, a drama critic and fan, because de Forest "had never written a play" and "would have more appreciation of Miss Alcott's work than she would have desire to build for herself"—or at least she would "be more ready to submit to the corrections of the Alcotts," who retained the right of approval.[131] De Forest wrote the first draft from memory: it was thus "stripped," she reported, "of all unessential, trammeling incidents. Only the high lights remained."[132] Or only the parts that foregrounded romance. She then filled in with dialogue from the book and with lines from other Alcott works.[133]

Certainly Alcott fans expected to hear lines from the novel: decades later May Lamberton Becker recalled going to the Broadway opening, and after the famil- iar first line—"Christmas won't be Christmas without any presents"—"that great audience gave a sort of gasp and then applauded so furiously that they stopped the show."[134] There is, in any case, a freshness in the dialogue, especially where de Forest reproduced Alcott's. One reviewer of the play claimed that "the homely dialogue is actor-proof."[135]

The surviving correspondence between de Forest, Bonstelle, and Alcott's nephew (and adopted son) John Pratt Alcott suggests that John at first wanted the play shaped more like those then popular on Broadway, with more action, much less attention to Beth's death—if any—and greater foregrounding of Jo, thus creat- ing a star vehicle.[136] De Forest and Bonstelle objected, with Bonstelle stating, "I would stake my long experience on the stage that to eliminate the death of Beth and make 'Little Women' all comedy, would be to ruin the play and to entirely lose the spirit of the book."[137] She explained that "the moment we get away from the spirit of the author, we lose the interest of the public. Women and children have always particularly loved the story and have been mainly responsible for its continued popularity. Women and children will make the success of the play, of that I am sure."[138] The two women prevailed, although de Forest later reported that she had inserted more comedy as she revised and that she had reduced the emphasis on Beth's death.[139] As for John Alcott, he later reported approvingly that it was "a play without a big thrill, without a gripping climax, without a star and without a problem."[140] In the words of one drama critic, "Something almost hap- pens, but never exactly does."[141]

The play opens with the girls talking together but visually individualized; their pose at the opening, in an image much reproduced at the time, hints at their inhabiting separate worlds.[142] The sisters go on to enact a few moments from the melodramatic play that Jo is writing, with Jo demonstrating to Amy, for in- stance, the proper way to fall. It's as if de Forest included a glimpse of Jo's play to differentiate the realistic family drama onstage from nineteenth-century-style melodrama. The later crashing of a tower offstage during a rehearsal effectively disposes of the melodrama. Yet perhaps the interweaving of the play within the play, not distinctly marked as a separate production—we don't see the perfor- mance of *The Witch's Curse* or even the rehearsal—hints at continuities between the staged and the stage, continuities that reviewers saw between de Forest's play and its audience.

Bonstelle reported being deluged with letters from fans asking that Beth not be allowed to die, that the Marches get rich immediately, that Meg marry at the

At home on Broadway
Photograph from Broadway production, 1912, in Marian de Forest, *Little Women:
A Comedy in Four Acts* (New York: French, 1921).

beginning, and, of course, that Jo marry Laurie.[143] De Forest did not diverge from
Alcott's plotting in these respects. Some of the changes she did make enabled
compression and the use of only two settings: a reproduction of the family sitting
room and, in the last of the four acts, the Plumfield apple orchard. Thus Jo does
not go to New York, so Professor Bhaer has to live nearby. Laurie proposes to Amy
not in Europe but after they return, as they recall their time at Valrosa.

   Other changes moderate the moral imperatives of the book, especially that of
self-sacrifice. The girls do not spend their Christmas dollars on gifts for Marmee,
nor do they sacrifice their Christmas breakfast to the Hummel family. Jo still
sacrifices her hair but seems to do so as a quirky expression of impulsiveness. It's
as if charitable impulses are encapsulated in Jo's later exclamation, in response
to a reference to the family's kindness to Laurie, "Well, Marmee has always told
us: Cast your bread upon the waters, and after many days it will come back—
Buttered!"[144] This riposte to Ecclesiastes does not appear in the novel but was a
favorite expression of Alcott's mother.[145] The novel essentially enacts the expression when the sisters are rewarded for casting their Christmas breakfast upon the
metaphoric waters with a sumptuous feast provided by Mr. Laurence—ice cream

instead of butter. In the play's apothegm and the book's action, a material reward subtly undermines the self-sacrifice implied by the charitable act.

Or perhaps the charitable impulse is diverted to a more purely religious one. Certainly Beth's death scene is notably different in the play. In the book she leaves Jo with thoughts of service to their parents, saying, "You'll be happier in doing that, than writing splendid books, or seeing all the world, for love is the only thing that we can carry with us when we go, and it makes the end so easy" (327). In the play Beth speaks more religiously and sentimentally: "Dear, happy little mother in that room upstairs," she says of Meg. "I thought of the angel sent to show those little babies the way to this life and— . . . perhaps waiting to show some weary soul the way to—a more perfect life—how strange the coming and the going—and how beautiful—I think I've just been waiting to see Meg's babies" (III, 105). De Forest told a journalist, "I felt that the spirit of Louisa Alcott was helping me to build up the climax of my third act, the death of Beth and the manner in which the March family would meet sorrow. I read page after page of her memoirs, and from her own account of the death of her gentle sister, the real Beth, I wrote this scene."[146] As if anxious about changing the story, de Forest calls on Alcott's spirit for justification and then seems to translate that spirit, in the play, into an angel. Yet in doing so she counters the narrator's disclaimer in the novel that "seldom, except in books, do the dying utter memorable words, see visions, or depart with beatified countenances" (327).

Not only are the moral imperatives tamed in the play, replaced by a more sentimental religiosity, but so are strong emotions. De Forest's Amy doesn't burn Jo's manuscript, nor does Amy fall through the ice because of Jo's failure to give warning, so Jo doesn't need to overcome her dangerous anger. Instead Jo is annoyed—or "cross" (II.i, 50)—that John Brooke has been treasuring Meg's glove and apparently wants to marry Meg. There is verbal sparring between Jo and Amy early in the play, especially in connection with the latter's malapropisms, but no depth in their sibling rivalry, no hint, for instance, that Amy's trip to Europe comes at Jo's expense. And thus no need for Jo to subdue the self quite so strictly.

Most other changes foreground the romances.[147] Unlike in the book, Meg is self-conscious about the arrival of Brooke from the beginning, primping when he is announced—with Jo glaring at her, according to the stage directions, already conscious that "lovering" is in the air. Jo doesn't require later hints from Laurie. The play's Marmee discounts marrying for money, preferring to "see my girls poor men's wives if they were happy and contented" (II.i, 53).[148] But she does not go on to say, as she does in the book, "better be happy old maids than unhappy wives" (84). There would seem to be no desirable alternative to marriage for a girl.

Laurie seems interested in Amy early on—he goes off to skate in the first act not with Jo but with Amy. And unlike in the book, we see the Professor before Laurie proposes to Jo; just after Bhaer leaves, Jo comments to herself on how nice he looked, how "he couldn't have gotten himself up with more care if he'd been going a-wooing" (II.ii, 83), and according to the ever-explanatory stage directions, "*seems confused at her own suggestion.*" The audience is thus not to become too invested in the possibility of a romance between Jo and Laurie—minimizing, I would argue, some of the power of the book.[149] But also, absent hundreds of pages for character development, this shift in chronology more smoothly enables Laurie's change of heart from Jo to Amy. Indeed, one of the reasons that Bonstelle gave for not making "a star part out of Jo" was that greater attention to Jo's interactions with Laurie and less attention to Amy would have made it "difficult to reconcile the audience to her [Jo's] marrying Bhaer."[150]

More emphatically in the play than in the book, Amy is subsumed by her work, becoming a work of art rather than creating one. By the end of the play she is no longer sketching, just mentioning past sketches. She copies a Madonna early on, as in the book, and indeed allusions to the Madonna recur more than in the book, as if to replace Alcott's references to *Pilgrim's Progress*: de Forest replaces a Christianity of journeying and striving with one of maternal caring, thereby reinforcing a sentimental idealization of motherhood. Eventually Amy becomes a Madonna, "hover[ing] over the cradle [of Meg's twins] like a golden-haired Madonna" (III, 91). Laurie soon afterwards greets her by saying, "You're a picture in that gown!" (III, 94), a compliment that makes her a work of art, not a creator of one. In the book Amy admits to Laurie that visiting Rome led her to realize that she was not a genius, but she keeps on sketching, and only much later does Laurie propose. In the play, however, Laurie responds to her admission by saying, "I—I—well, I don't think a career is suited to you, Amy—you belong—" (IV, 117), and then he proposes. The middle-class New Woman of the time found it difficult to reconcile career and marriage. In the play the two are antithetical.

The frequent early hints of Jo's interest in Professor Bhaer culminate in a stagy set piece where he proposes and the two appear under an umbrella, as in the book, or rather a sunshade, given the difficulties at the time of staging rain—and, apparently, the need for tangible rain, if it's presumably raining, in such a "realistic" play. The stage directions indicate that, unlike in the book, all the remaining characters line up to peek at the couple. As for their gendering, the play's Jo is granted a measure of independence when she thinks of having a school at Plumfield before Bhaer proposes, but it's not clear that she ever publishes the book she has been working on. In contrast, he is an established author, unlike in the novel. He has translated Shakespeare into German and, early on, is at work on a translation of Schiller into English; he eventually sends Jo a copy of the latter book, autographed, crediting her as his inspiration. There is some reference to Jo having made a name for herself with her writing, but he's the tangibly, visibly successful author, Jo his feminine muse.

Furthermore, although parental authority is here diluted, authority shifts not to the little women but to their future husbands. Marmee is less a moral authority than a prognosticator of romance, alert early on to Amy's attraction to Laurie and Jo's to Bhaer. Bhaer's echo of a line spoken by the narrator in the novel is emblematic. Alcott's narrator says that "at midsummer there came to Meg a new experience,—the deepest and tenderest of a woman's life" (226), the clichéd "deepest and tenderest" allowing the reader to infer that Meg is pregnant.[151] De Forest gives a related but more overt line to Bhaer: "Motherhood is the deepest and tenderest experience in a woman's life" (III, 101). No need for inference here. Just patriarchal and "wholesome" sententiousness.

When Bonstelle tried to shop the play, theater managers declined it as too wholesome, thus unlikely to attract the public, or as lacking a "big third act" or a leading man or woman and hence a role for a star.[152] She also noted, with some interest, that the managers she spoke to didn't *"know the book!"*[153] But William Brady eventually agreed. He was a showman who produced Broadway shows and prizefights.[154] Prizefights and *Little Women*? Not so big a stretch, really, at a time when Broadway prized spectacle. And a time when middle- and upper-class men were anxious about their masculinity and their interests turned to violent sports, and the complementary move was to confine women to domesticity,[155] for which *Little Women* had become a nostalgic icon. Brady claimed not to have read the book before Bonstelle approached him, indeed never to have heard of it,[156] though as the epigraph to this chapter suggests, the rest of his family seems to have been familiar with it.

Broadway at the time featured musicals, melodramas, extravaganzas, and sentimental romances—plays that many now would consider "artistically trivial," star vehicles that foregrounded "power, passion, sacrifice, romance, salvation," with "climaxes for every act, building up artfully to the peak of suspense."[157] *Little Women* didn't fully follow these tenets. Indeed, it lacked a strongly linear plot with a rising action, a climax, and a dénouement. One critic quipped that it would "probably [be] the most popular play of the season. . . . It is everything that the learned doctors tell us a dramatic work should not be. It has no carefully plumped out plot, no 'big scene,' no theme."[158] Another New York critic noted that it was "as uneventful as the unwinding of a ball of yarn."[159] In the words of a third, someone who enthusiastically praised the casting, the script, and the staging, "there are no smashing 'dramatic' moments; there is no 'emotional' acting; there is no 'grip,' no 'thrill'; there is nothing to stir cheers from the spectators."[160] But the play was nevertheless shaped to suit the norms of sentimental romance.

One or two reports to the contrary, *Little Women* appears to have been very successful in its pre-Broadway run.[161] On January 20, 1912, it premiered in Wilkes-Barre, where the audience "crowded the theatre" despite placards at the entrance warning of a measles epidemic; a local reviewer called the production "one of the theatrical surprises of the season."[162] The following week, in Buffalo, New York, the audience responded with "marked approval" to the opening performance, and ticket sales were very strong.[163] The play was positively reviewed in Detroit and Chicago in February; reviewers were especially appreciative of the acting at Beth's deathbed, going on to say, "Never were there more tears in a theater," or to note "the absence of the merely mawkish."[164] In March in Minneapolis the demand was so great that the theater added an extra matinee performance.[165] In October in Pittsburgh the play was "presented to one of the largest audiences of the season and certainly a most delighted and thoroughly charmed one."[166]

Later in October, in New York, the play "captured the heart of the city" and had "exceeding great success"[167]—and indeed it continued to do so on tours across the country during the next two years. "One of the most substantial hits of the year in New York," it ran for 184 performances.[168] It may not have been the leading box-office draw of the season—*Within the Law* and *Peg o' My Heart* ran for 541 and 503 performances, respectively—but its run was very successful at a time when 100 performances was deemed excellent.[169]

The play appealed not just to the public but also to the press: "The unanimous praise of the New York press burst upon it like a flood and its success with the public is said to have been equally spontaneous and emphatic," a contemporary claimed.[170] New York notices were "extraordinarily good," with critics variously referring to the play's "exquisite charm," its being "well staged," overall "really delightful," "first rate," indeed "the best play we have ever seen of transient sorrows, simple wiles, praise, blame, love, kisses, tears and smiles."[171] Or to cite comments that were reprinted on a theater lobby card, the play "was the realization of a dream," "like a favored glance at a magic edition of Louisa M. Alcott's famous book with all the characters come to life," "as fresh and wholesome as a drink from the old spring," "the best dramatization of a great popular story we have ever seen."[172] The reviewer for the *Brooklyn Eagle* was particularly enthusiastic, concluding, "'Little Women' is an achievement of which the American stage may well be proud. Without depending on the ordinary rules of dramatic construction, ignoring the conventional stage tricks, it makes us live for a few brief hours, the sweet and simple lives of simple folk, to share their sorrows and to delight in their happiness. Art can do no more."[173] In the hyperbolic words of a reviewer in San Antonio, "If it is the last play you ever see—if you have to abandon your business, or neglect your home, or place a mortgage on the old farm to get to it—see 'Little Women.' "[174]

Little Women apparently "attracted more visitors to New York than any play of the season."[175] Matinees, in particular, "always played to packed houses," whether they were accommodating the "hundreds of school children" who came in with their teachers from the suburbs or the elderly "puritanical churchgoers" unaccustomed to going out at night.[176] Or perhaps matinees simply catered primarily to women.[177] In any case, the management added a third, then a fourth, matinee each week, and the play became known as "one of the greatest matinee plays of the day."[178] Notices in 1914 hyped it by claiming, "Today it is regarded as the most valuable theatrical property in America."[179]

A truism of the time was that the theatergoing public was largely female, especially the "matinee girl," who might worship a matinee idol[180]—although the claim that such a group constituted the majority, given that most performances were not matinees, suggests that the stereotype had a life of its own. One drama critic memorably described the group as "the modish, marcelled, be-ratted and polo-coated young women of 16 to 19 from whose high-heeled ranks the modern playhouses draw most of their patronage."[181] He or she was predicting that the proposed dramatization of Little Women would hardly appeal to this audience and would therefore flop. Still, as Marah Gubar points out, at the turn of the century and earlier, Broadway offered an extraordinary mélange of works, including plays appealing to young and old.[182] As indeed Little Women did. Adolph Klauber, of the New York Times, declared, "Amazing, then, to find as grown-ups that the old spell is still potent, that our hearts go out to Jo and Beth and Amy and the rest of them quite as much as they did in the old days when we begged for 'five minutes more to finish the chapter.' "[183] According to the Atlanta Constitution, "Some one said: 'Why, that's a play for children.' A man of forty replied, 'Yes, children from eight to eighty.' "[184]

Little Women was likewise popular on the road, with four companies touring the country during the next couple of years, even though road shows in general were declining.[185] In Washington, DC, "youth with its ebullient enthusiasm could scarcely vie with old age in expressions of appreciation and enjoyment."[186] The first-night audience in Lincoln, Nebraska, may have been "surprisingly small," but the show was popular enough in Philadelphia to require a fourth week of performances.[187] A Boston journalist claimed that "the play holds the absorbed interest even of the man who goes to scoff."[188]

Critics with a nineteenth-century sensibility about the functions of art—to delight but also to uplift—were especially enthusiastic. According to Jackson Haag,

> Once in a great many years the stage fulfills its mission because some genius evolved the kind of play that meets all requirements, being clean and wholesome; telling a sentiment awakening tale in a simple yet effective manner; imparting entertainment without offending our sense of propriety and good taste and yet giving us amusement of a healthful kind and delivering its message of hope and cheer in a way that cannot but impart beneficial thoughts and send us from the theater with a higher opinion of humankind than possibly we had when we entered.[189]

Note the invocation of sentiment ("a sentiment awakening tale"), a contested term. Haag seems to invoke it positively, adding, "I don't know when I have enjoyed myself as I did last evening." But five days later he distanced himself from sentiment: "As a producer of tears in the theater, that surest indication that womankind is 'having a perfectly lovely time,' 'East Lynne' will now have to look to its laurels, for 'Little Women' . . . is going after its record with such determination as to jeopardize its position in the American drama"; the play made its primary appeal to "those who are so chock full of sentiment that it oozes out at the tear ducts."[190] Haag enacts a shift that seems to happen to some intellectuals who enjoy Alcott-related works while immersed in them but later have to realign their responses, perhaps in accordance with how they think they're supposed to feel (remember that circumlocutory critic cited in the previous chapter, the one who feared saying something in print that he might later regret upon cooler reflection). Haag also enacts in microcosm a shift in sensibility that the theater was undergoing at this time.

The shift had to do in part with the evaluation of sentiment. Most critics of the production were neutral to positive about the evocation of sentiment in *Little Women*. An occasional critic might find the play "a trifle saccharine": "To be sure the sentimentality was occasionally laid on with a trowel. The suggestion of harps in the air was just a bit too strong in Beth's dying scene." Yet, this critic went on, the play "never cloys because it is so genuine in its sweetness."[191] Most reviewers were noncommittal about the frequency of tears in the audience. Even "your seasoned opening nighter will . . . get out his handkerchief, blow his nose and slyly wipe his eyes when patient little Beth comes to the end of all things earthly," noted one.[192] "Sedate men and settled women cried over the death scene of Beth," noted another.[193] One critic stated that "a bartender, noted for his rough-and-ready tactics in business hours, came out after the performance with tears streaming down his cheeks, remarking that 'This piece is d——d fine.'"[194] This odd coupling of tears and toughness made manly tears acceptable. But it's notable that responses to the play are here associated with embodiment, with a bodily reaction by the audience, and a reaction that would later be discredited. In a study of the usage of *sentimental* in film criticism of the 1920s, Lea Jacobs notes that it was increasingly used in connection with violations of middle-class decorum, whether bodily or linguistic.[195]

Only a few critics of the play became sardonic, as when Burns Mantle claimed that it "is fast reducing Gotham to a sea of grateful tears. . . . We all cried the first night of 'Little Women.' Mr. Brady cried, and Leander Richardson cried, and Alan Dale cried, and Diamond Jim Brady got his tears so mixed with his pearls that his shirt front looked like the front breadth of a Salome dancing costume."[196] In Alcott's novel, after Amy burns her manuscript, Jo wants to cry but knows "tears were an unmanly weakness" (65), and indeed Jo and Alcott's narrator often disdain sentiment. For all that *Little Women* has been associated with the sentimental in the popular imagination, its relationship with sentiment is complex: sentiment is both sought and disavowed.[197] Manly discomfort with crying had increased by 1912, but critics didn't yet discredit all tears, as they were more likely to do after World War I.

In the eighteenth century the idea of the "man of sentiment" was not an oxymoron but an ideal that many strove to emulate. In the nineteenth century the sentimental was increasingly associated with women and middle-class domesticity and hence devalued.[198] The meanings and connotations of *sentiment* and *sentimental* were still in flux early in the twentieth century. *Sentiment* could simply refer to feelings, especially the feelings associated with courtship, and was still often used neutrally, without negative judgment. *Sentimental* was at times simply the adjectival form of this understanding of sentiment—and thus neutral—although increasingly it carried the negative connotations associated with being excessively emotional, as did *sentimentality*. In the words of a writer in the British *Westminster Review* in 1892, "Sentimentality is very different from sentiment, and a sentimental man quite another being, in general estimation, to a man of sentiment."[199] A 1915 review of a new edition of *Little Women* used *sentimental* neutrally, to refer to the emotions associated with courtship: "Miss Alcott herself was not at all sentimental and apparently never had a love-affair. Her family seem to have filled her heart to the exclusion of an outside affection."[200] The British writer Angela Brazil, however, recognized the negative connotations of *sentimental* and disavowed them in 1922: "There is nothing sentimental about 'Little Women,' though of true sentiment we have tender touches."[201] Another British commentator, noting that "the most successful girls' books have come from America," found *Little Women* "free from the mawkishness which then drove girls of any character to the bookshelf of the boys," and the "fresh romance" in part 2 "untainted with what Mrs. Gaskell aptly called 'pink sentimentality.'"[202]

The shifts in the meanings of *sentimental* and especially *sentimentality* are inadvertently captured by a 1922 writer for the *Chicago Tribune*. The author took exception to an 1889 claim that *Little Women* "contained t[o]o much sentiment," noting instead, "It contains a great deal of sentiment, but it does not run away into sentimentality."[203] The 1889 account actually reads: "But while they [Alcott's books] are characterized by humor, cheerfulness, good morals, and natural action, their healthfulness may be somewhat questionable on account of the sentimentality that is woven into her work and breaks the natural grace of childhood by introducing the romantic element, and a hint of self-importance and independence that tends to create a restless and rebellious spirit."[204] Whatever one makes of the negative commentary on independence, this earlier writer uses *sentimentality* to refer to the introduction of courtship in the novels; by 1922 the term had generally come to mean an excess of sentiment.

Suggestive of the tendency by some to categorize *Little Women* as sentimental is the claim of a Philadelphia reviewer of the play that "those who read the novel of Louis [*sic*] M. Alcott, from which it [the play] was made, might be led to expect something 'goody-goody' or mawkishly sentimental, as the book certainly was in spots. They must be agreeably surprised in the stage production."[205] Someone who found the book more sentimental than the play must not have read the book in a while.

Whatever the connotations of *sentimental*, in the early decades of the century *Little Women* itself was increasingly associated with the treacly—with "glorious sunshine" and "delicious simplicity," with whatever was "bright, clean, joyously, innocent."[206] A sign that the title had become a byword for innocence—even if not quite universally—is a humorous piece in the *Los Angeles Times* in 1926: when applied to for permission to stage the play in the school auditorium, a member of the Long Beach Board of Education asked, "Has that show got a drunken character in it?" The understated response: that "there wasn't a single stagger in the whole story."[207]

Critics often noted that de Forest's dramatization diverged from what was then thought to be necessary in plays, whether for being clean and wholesome or for violating the expected dramatic structure. Henry Taylor Parker, of the *Boston*

Evening Transcript, was unusually insightful in mapping the strengths of the play against expectations for theater at the time, addressing sentiment among other things. He was sometimes called the "dean of American critics" or perhaps "a small and bitter gargoyle above the Brahmin sea" at the theater.[208] H.T.P., as he signed himself—hence his nicknames Hard-to-Please and Hell-to-Pay[209]—noted that one might expect a dramatization of *Little Women* to be essentially "a succession of tableaux vivants, plus the spoken word," since the "tale lacked 'story,' much more what publishers' press-agentry calls 'dramatic encounters.'" Furthermore, "sentiment coats the whole."[210] Parker recognized that sentiment was not altogether approved of, yet those who decried sentiment often "weary all within earshot by the particular and private sentiments—and often sentimentalities— that they happen to cherish. No; it may be doubted whether even the Harvard Socialist Club will ever eliminate sentiment from human nature." Still, the novel "has two qualities that suit it to the present theatre even by the severe standards of the Puritan youth. It is rich in character and it is rich in atmosphere." The characterizations are vivid, the characters' actions "the out-croppings of traits beneath," the young Jo and Amy, especially, evolving with consistency. Parker also seemed to have some recognition of Jo's independence: "No doubt in these days she would be bitten with 'the uplift' and write pamphlets about it, exactly as in those sixties she was bitten with story-writing." As for atmosphere, Parker praised the reconstruction of the setting. Overall, the play "gives many kinds of pleasure to many kinds of spectators," keeping "even the sceptical spectator amused, interested, gently stimulated": indeed, it had many characteristics of highly esteemed Russian plays, fitting the "Muscovite dramatic theory and practice" of reproducing "the variegated and unexpected course of actual life." We have moved here from a nineteenth-century sensibility to a twentieth-century one, from melodrama to European realism, at a time when the Little Theatre movement, which fostered both realism and expressionism, was being launched.[211]

Let me comment more on atmosphere and character. *Atmosphere* could refer to an abstract wholesomeness, as in "the sweetness, the fragrance of that simple, wholesome little community at Concord to which it will always be a pleasure and inspiration to revert."[212] Brady and Bonstelle attended especially to the concrete atmosphere: they sought realism, a kind of surface illusionism, since "atmosphere plays quite as important a part as plot," and the many who had read the novel would "be looking for it."[213] They consulted photographs of the Alcotts' Orchard House in Concord. They spent more than four thousand dollars to create the concluding orchard scene. One reviewer described this scene—"the sun-swept orchard at Plumfield on a golden October afternoon, with real trees in the foreground and a little rustic bridge leading the eye to a vista of fine old trees in the distance"—and suggested that even the robin that chirps to Beth "sings much more like a real robin than most stage birds which warble on Broadway": "It is the careful attention given to such little details as this which has preserved the atmosphere of the book."[214]

Brady and Bonstelle also sought "real" properties for the play (whose use one journalist appreciated as "one of the chief points of interest in the production"): they obtained "real" period costumes, getting donations from throughout the Northeast of "polonaises, double skirts, panniers, long pointed waists, stiff with whalebone," among other items.[215] The advance publicity stressed these attempts at authenticity, yet in a letter to the wife of Alcott's nephew, Bonstelle indicated that the March sisters' dresses had been copied, not from an 1860s source, but from the recently published illustrations by Alice Barber Stephens because the costumes were so "simple and lovely."[216] Indeed, the photo-identification expert Maureen Taylor notes that most of the costumes are not quite right for the 1860s: Jo's and Meg's collars date from the 1850s, Amy's puffed sleeves from the 1830s, Hannah's ruffled dress from the 1870s, and the final costumes for Amy, Laurie, and Brooke are vintage 1912.[217] Even the antimacassared armchair onstage dates from the twentieth century. It was more important simply to invoke the quaintly old-fashioned than to be historically accurate.

Still, the producers claimed authenticity. Then again, it's a question of what one means by authenticity. For some, it can be a matter of evoking genuine emotions, a sense of belonging, connecting one's past and present.[218] For others, it requires historical accuracy. And the producers did make some gestures in this latter direction. There were Alcott artifacts, for instance: the russet boots that Alcott, like Jo, used in family theatricals, the dagger likewise, Anna/Meg's wedding bonnet and her hair trunk and her infant's jacket, a rag doll made by a six-year-old Alcott child, family dishes, an afghan, an escritoire, and even "Mrs. March's gray travelling cloak worn by her when she went on her journey to Washington," a journey her original did not undertake.[219] As de Forest noted in a letter to John Alcott, "For advertising purposes there is great advantage in using the original as far as we can in getting up the costumes and in the scenic production."[220] One viewer particularly attuned to costume, who described Amy's opening dress as "trimmed with the darlingest puffings of cerise silk" (those 1830s sleeves), was quick to notice that she later seemed to wear what Meg had worn, cut down, retrimmed, the attentive audience murmuring in "sympathy and amusement."[22]

A few critics located atmosphere in a latent Transcendentalism. One for the *Springfield Republican* astutely pointed out that "homes in which the enterpris ing daughter kept the family on its feet [and] could affectionately address her father as 'Plato' " were not exactly typical. Yet the reviewer was more intent on emphasizing the extent to which the New England girls portrayed in both play and book derived "no small part of their unconquerable charm [from] the New England atmosphere which they were privileged to inhale at its richest and finest moment," a culture that was "one of the finest flowers of the Anglo-Saxon spirit, and peculiarly our own."[222] And in the *Buffalo Express* Edward Doyle noted, "Brought up in the Transcendental atmosphere of 'plain living and high thinking,' with Emerson, Thoreau and Hawthorne as neighbors and family friends, what wonder that the reader of today is startled by the modern spirit which Miss Alcott, the Jo of the story, has put into her little book!"[223] Doyle had a sense that the March family wasn't typical of its time and attributed the modernity to a pantheon of men—but might it be the portrayal of a woman that was especially modern?

As for the characters, critics stressed that the players seemed not so much to be acting as to have stepped out of real life, as if they "might have come right down among the people in the seats and clasped hands with them as old and much loved friends," or else "one feels half ashamed for peeping into the March homestead unobserved."[224] And many reviews continued a critical tradition that artless Alcott simply transcribed reality. "She did little or no creating. The Alcott family was the story," wrote William Sage in the *Cleveland Leader*.[225] He added, 'Between ourselves it isn't such good literature as if it had been imagined in all its verity, but is far better. It is life itself, and though the things that happened in it could have occurred in no other family, they still impinged so much on the happenings in other families that their appeal was instant and universal." Unusually adroit in addressing how the atypical Alcotts engaged the typical, he went on to attribute the uniqueness of the family to Bronson, whom Sage had once, spellbound, heard speak. Sage gave no indication in the main text of his story that Alcott provided a positive portrayal of an independent woman. The headline writer, though, might have had an inkling, for the piece is entitled "Suffragettes Rejoice."[226] Not everyone in the early twentieth century was unaware of Alcott's support of suffrage, but I have found only two or three mentions in hundreds of announcements and reviews of the play. Instead its "wholesome" mores are likely to be contrasted with the modern "rush of getting rich quick, suffragetting and social climbing."[227]

There is little mention in the reviews of Jo's independence. Or, rather, the adjective *independent* may be applied casually to her—"the independent, loyal, big-hearted Jo"[228]—without acknowledging the politics of her independence.

Feminine independence was reduced to something altogether different when a critic described "the independence of *Meg* in marrying the man she loved."[229] Independence in what respect? Independence from her earlier dream of having a luxurious house and thus of marrying someone rich? Independence from the cantankerous Aunt March, who decries John Brooke? Independence from Jo, who wants to keep Meg in the nuclear family? Certainly not independence from Meg's parents, who favor the match, even if they encourage the two to wait while Brooke earns money to provide a home. And not individual financial or personal independence, at least not as we now view it.

Critics almost seemed to assume a contrary message, that Jo is not particularly independent. Certainly she does end up marrying. A writer for the *Woman's Home Companion* suggested that the young women in the audience, "their minds torn by conflicting, up-to-date theories of individuality, woman's economic position, and marriage, feel that all these vexing problems will be solved when the right 'John' comes along."[230] Alcott was also credited by a critic in Pittsburgh with being "far removed from the modern type of woman," thanks to her "unostentatious self-sacrifice and devotion."[231]

Other commentators stressed the typicality of the characters—relying on language associated with melodrama, the dominant theatrical mode of the previous century, according to which praising actors for their portrayal of types was indeed praise. One reviewer associated types with what we now might call universality, praising the portrayal of Beth's dying as "so refined in thought and so beautifully executed, that the dying girl upon the stage loses mere personality and becomes a type, a kindred grief borne in the hearts of all."[232] Jo, in turn, is "the typical American girl."[233] The audience is transported "to a typical New England home."[234] A reviewer transported by American typicality might even invoke much that never appears in book or play: "The play, like the book, exploits the simpler ideals of life when girls stayed at home; embroidered book marks for Christmas presents, baked cakes and sent valentines unsigned—valentines with crinkled paper adorning them."[235] (Alcott's Marches knit socks for Union soldiers instead of embroidering bookmarks and share pickled limes with friends rather than crinkled-paper Valentines.) One reviewer found the play, "in an essential and ancestral sense American"; another, "essentially an American play, redolent of the soil."[236] And on to more flag-waving: Marmee is "a true reflection of the New England motherhood which has contributed some of the greatest men to the nation"; and "it is essential to the solidarity of our future as a nation that the home shall be kept intact; for is it not from out its doors the young men and women who figure in the affairs of the country come?"[237] In short, according to a slightly later commentator, "the story of Meg, Jo, Beth and Amy, real American girls in the best sort of American home, has exerted a more potent influence than all the lectures that ever were delivered or all the patriotic literature that ever was distributed!"[238] If some American commentators were becoming wary of sentiment, at least as expressed in *Little Women*, sentiment expressed as patriotism did not elicit similar strictures. Associating the novel with the sentiment of patriotism became, in effect, a way of dressing sentiment in acceptable garb.

The play was not as successful in London in 1919, despite the German Professor Bhaer's postbellum translation to the French Professor Barre—and despite enthusiasm for Katharine Cornell as Jo.[239] As the critic for the London *Times* stated, "And does the book give us such a Jo as Miss Katharine Cornell? We can not believe it."[240] Maybe the play was too American for a country of "theatre-goers notoriously indifferent to American plays."[241] Or maybe sentiment was faring less well—both book and play considered "overloaded with sentiment"[242]—after the Great War. The theater ran an advertisement in the *Times* that quoted very positive responses, noting the "enthusiastic reception," the "rapturous applause," for this play based on the book by "a 'Jane Austen' of the schoolroom."[243] The snippets are, of course, cherry-picked, and they tend to emphasize the audience's reception more than the critic's judgment. The ad quotes the reviewer for the *Westminster Gazette*, for instance, as noting, "It was, therefore, to be expected that the play would be extremely good, and it was so, and also full of all kinds of coyness." "Coyness" sounds an odd note, yet the critic seems nevertheless to be calling the play extremely good. But the line in the original review read, "It was, therefore, to be expected that the play would be extremely sweet and extremely good: and it was so, and also full of all kinds of coyness."[244] The inclusion of "extremely sweet" ironizes "goodness" and makes it moral rather than aesthetic. Indeed, the reviewer continued, "There were four young ladies emerging from the school age, and one of them died; and the fact that they did not all die, together with their unutterably spotless father and mother and the kind old gentleman from across the road and the irreproachable young man who loved them, shakes for ever the authority of the proposition that the good die young."

During the next several decades there would be several revivals of de Forest's *Little Women* in the United States. The play ran briefly in New York in 1916, before it went on the road again (critics in Washington and Philadelphia called it the best offering that season at their respective theaters).[245] There were also revivals in the 1930s and 1940s—and in 2006. The play is now a bit dated: a review of the 2006 production faults it for its formal dialogue (praised as true to life a century ago), its focus on "covering lots of plot points" (deemed essential a century ago for Alcott fans) and its minimizing of "some of the grittier, true-to-life aspects of the stories," specifically Beth's death.[246]

Starting in the 1920s, there were, as well, innumerable school and community productions of *Little Women*, whether of de Forest's play or another redaction, in Missouri, Alabama, Ohio, and Utah in 1928; in Texas, California, and Wisconsin in 1929—just to cite notices in one online archive, newspaperarchive.com. Such a production could combine some aspects of the new realism of the Little Theatre movement with significant appeal to a middle-class audience. But whatever local enthusiasm such productions might generate, none created the national excitement of the 1912 Broadway show, an excitement that would, however, be matched by that for at least one of the later film productions, as I will note in the next chapter.

                                                                                               ~

Such excitement did not greet the two silent films of *Little Women*. Both the British one, released in 1917, and the American one, formally released in 1919, are presumed lost. The British version seems not to have found its way to the United States, and I have found little about it in the British press: advance publicity stressed that "its exquisite pathos" was balanced by "real humour"; "great interest is sustained throughout," noted a reviewer in Dundee, and "large audiences" attended this "very human and touching picture play" in Bristol.[247] But there were hundreds of announcements and advertisements—and a few reviews—of the American one. Tracking these notices of a little-noticed film, while attending to the positioning of motion pictures at the time, provides a window on perceptions of *Little Women*.

The American film version had been screened in at least a couple of cities during the two months before it was purchased by the Famous Players–Lasky Corporation and formally released by Paramount-Artcraft in January 1919.[248] Paramount was the first successful distributor of films nationwide, and as part of Famous Players–Lasky it was starting to pioneer the vertical integration of production, distribution, and exhibition that would soon become a hallmark of the film industry. In seeking especially to exploit an urban middle-class audience, Paramount "promoted spectacular, feature-length film adaptations of stage plays starring prestigious Broadway stars"—or in the words of its own promotional materials, "foremost stars, superbly directed, in clean motion pictures."[249] William Brady, who had produced the Broadway play, was the independent producer of this film version. Richard Koszarski credits him with having driven the World Film Corporation into failure a couple of years earlier;[250] subsequently, as an independent producer, Brady seems to have released only two films, one of them

Little Women. At World Film his motion pictures were old-fashioned, Koszarski claims, hewing too closely to the theatrical. It's likely that his *Little Women* drew heavily on the stage version he'd produced seven years earlier.

Critics noted that this motion picture lacked the plotting, climaxes, and melodrama then common in films but praised it for its artistic continuity. It probably had a relatively high ratio of words to images: commentators variously praised it for incorporating so many well-remembered lines or found their frequency distracting. The actresses were "lovely" and the costuming "quaint." Overall the film was praised, though in moderation.

Motion pictures at the time had far less prestige than what was increasingly called the legitimate stage. One way that producers attempted to gain prestige was by filming versions of classic literature, a practice still common for films seeking prestige: one estimate is that two-thirds of Academy Award–winning films have been adaptations.[251] Certainly the titles of such films have name recognition, something that was probably especially important for motion pictures that, like this one, didn't feature a star.[252] Or perhaps the star—the celebrity associated with the film—was Alcott herself. In any case, associations with classic literature carried a certain cachet, proffering cultural capital to those who attended. The producer and director of *Little Women* heightened the classic connections, including connections with the Transcendentalists and a bygone era more generally, by filming on location in Concord and including a much-mentioned glimpse of Emerson's house.[253]

For as with the play, Brady paid special attention to the atmosphere, and advance publicity stressed the authenticity of the setting. In a pre-release interview the director, Harley Knoles, went into detail about researching the setting, going to Concord and examining pictures and records, asking people what episodes they remembered best to determine the most popular ones—and choosing a cast such that the four sisters "look exactly as Louisa M. Alcott made them look in her book."[254] Or perhaps, as subsequent publicity materials suggest, "the players selected had the unqualified approval of several residents of Concord who knew Miss Alcott and the little women of whom she wrote."[255] The exteriors were filmed "at the old Alcott homestead," Orchard House, and the studio sets were "copied from the rooms in the old house."[256]

Costuming was a different matter. A writer for *Variety* casually noted that the actresses wore the "quaint dresses of that period," thus presumably 1863–68.[257] But the costumes were not authentic to the period. Maureen Taylor tells me that Jo's wide V-neck collar in the stills reproduced in newspapers is not, nor is the way the men's ties are tied, among other things.[258] The producers, like those for the earlier play and for subsequent dramatizations, relied instead on a general sense of nostalgia for a bygone age, preferring quaintness to accuracy. *Little Women* was a conduit to an artificially constructed past.

Anne Maxwell received credit for writing the scenario, but it's likely that she drew on de Forest's 1912 dramatization—and not just because of the trend at the time to film successful Broadway plays. The reported highlights of the film reproduce incidents in Alcott's *Little Women*, such as Jo's cutting her hair to provide money for her mother to travel to nurse her father. But in one instance Maxwell seems to replicate the plotting of the Broadway play in preference to Alcott's version. In the book Meg's twins are born, and Beth later dies, and the two events are not explicitly connected. In the play, however, Beth's death is coordinated with their birth: she claims to have been waiting to see the babies.[259] In the film, according to one account, Beth embraces the twins before dying;[260] this convergence would seem to be carried over from the play. In addition, given that a still from the film echoes one from the play, the film's *mise-en-scène* would seem to draw on the play's setting. In the novel Bhaer proposes to Jo in the rain, raising an umbrella as they walk to the March family home, with no tree noted nor fam-

Staging and screening a romance
Photograph from Broadway production, 1912, in Marian de Forest, *Little Women: A Comedy in Four Acts* (New York: French, 1921).

ily members nearby. In the play Bhaer proposes in the Plumfield orchard, and a publicity photograph shows others stagily eavesdropping. The seated lovers, the tree, the eavesdroppers—all are replicated, left-center-right, in a still from the film. A caption suggests that the film's lovers are Meg and Brooke, and indeed the costuming suggests that Jo is not on the left, but the film still seems to be borrowing from the play, with a rather stagy scene—reinforcing the claim that Brady followed theatrical conventions too assiduously. In any case, as I've already argued, the play had foregrounded domesticity, romance, and a manufactured sense of tradition, at the expense of fostering women's independence; no evidence suggests that the film—"one of the most interesting romances ever screened," according to one ad[261]—differed.

Unlike for the play, though, there's little evidence that the film swept the country by storm. It was screened broadly but did not get the kind of press in 1918–20 that the play had in 1912–14. The relative paucity of reviews may say something about the film's quality and popularity. Certainly the reviews that did appear,

Still from 1919 film *Little Women* (Paramount-Artcraft). From the core collection, production files of the Margaret Herrick Library, Academy of Motion Picture Arts and Sciences.

though positive, were less enthusiastic than those for the play, and indeed the title does not appear on a *New York Times* reviewer's list of the best films of 1919.[262] Other factors also affected the relative dearth of newspaper attention, to this and other films, including the accessibility of films, their lower status, and the history of their relationships with newspapers.

Films were relatively accessible. Advertising pages in newspapers indicate that there were numerous motion pictures available in a given week even in small communities, in contrast with a single live road show making a one-night stand. An editor might thus be unwilling to invest in reviewing all the films in town, and indeed films at this time stayed in most theaters just a single night, occasionally two, and local reviewers were rarely provided an advance press screening.[263]

Films also had lower status, both artistically and morally, than the legitimate stage did. Some cultural crusaders were concerned about the influence of films on children and also women. Numerous studies tried to gauge how frequently children indulged and how deleterious the effects were. In 1923 a researcher polled schoolchildren in grades 4–8 in Milwaukee and discovered that 2,791 of the 3,468 polled had attended the movies during the previous week, 742 of them attending more than three times.[264] That same year a national survey of 37,000 high-school students, who were apparently somewhat less likely to attend movies than their younger counterparts, showed that the boys and girls nevertheless had, on average, attended just over one film per week.[265] A 1929 study of Chicago children revealed that 27.2 percent of juvenile delinquents attended between five and seven times a week, compared with only 0.4 percent of Boy Scouts.[266] As is often the case, correlation was assumed to mean causation, and general anxieties about the media were translated into fears for children.

The status of moving pictures was nevertheless in transition. During the second decade of the twentieth century, films were gaining middle-class respectability, overcoming an association with the working-class and immigrant audiences who had predominated at storefront nickelodeons. A sociologist casually noted in 1916 that "nine tenths of the [film] plays are cheap melodramas or vulgar farces," yet he also stated that if six years earlier the primary patrons had been lower middle class, they had now "long been joined by the upper middle class."[267] Exhibitors built opulent picture palaces, and producers chose subject matter that increasingly targeted "respectable" middle-class women, including plots based on classic literary works[268]—Paramount in particular made such choices. And although its valuation by the cultural elite had slipped, as I suggest earlier in this chapter, *Little Women* still had a claim to classic status, and it continued to be valued by middle-class women. The shifting of the status of motion pictures was uneven, though. Many films continued to favor risqué subject matter. In the early teens, for instance, there had been a spate of films about the white slave trade, sensationalizing the dangers to middle-class women of their increasing appearance in public spaces—including theaters. Even in 1919 the films playing opposite *Little Women* included not just *Pollyanna* and *Daddy-Long-Legs* but also *Satan Junior* and *The Unpardonable Sin*. As one newspaper notice proclaimed, "If a sweet and wholesome play—without a touch of syncopated music, a shimmie or bare-knee appeals to you—go and see 'Little Women.' "[269]

An exchange of letters between *Little Women*'s producer and the Alcott heirs suggests the instability of what constituted films at this time, successful films at least. After the 1912 Broadway success, Brady negotiated with John Alcott and his wife, Eunice, about filming *Little Men* and *An Old-Fashioned Girl*, but in 1915 he judged that only "sensational, gripping, thrilling drama" was in demand in motion pictures, and he was not going to go forward with those projects. So Eunice sent him Alcott's Faustian thriller, *A Modern Mephistopheles*. His response? He says he read it but didn't think it offered promise of success, given the demand for "the lurid and melodramatic," and he feared "that anything with the sweet appeal stands no chance."[270] "Lurid and melodramatic" is actually a pretty fair description of the plot of *A Modern Mephistopheles*, with its young poet who passes off as his own the poetry written by an older man, who in turn lusts after the ingénue, plying her with hashish, while she is married to the young poet. Still, whether or not he actually read the novel, Brady's vacillation between the sweet and the luridly melodramatic speaks to the uncertainty and instability of the kind of film that would be successful in this decade.

The history of film advertising and reviewing also had an impact on the presence of reviews in newspapers. Only in the early teens did film advertisements and studio press releases appear with some frequency in the press, and reviews followed later. About 1913, journalists were generally reframing movie stories provided by film distributors or pasting together such pieces with notices in trade papers.[271] By 1918, only two of New York's major daily newspapers, then numbering more than a dozen, carried regular film reviews.[272] Thus the many newspaper announcements of *Little Women* as a coming attraction, in New York and across the country, used very similar language. In countless newspapers we learn that the motion picture "is a lavender scented picture of New England during the days of the Civil War," that it is "filled with humor, pathos and delicate sentiment," and that therefore "this will be an event in which every woman and child in the city, and men, too, for that matter, who have read this immortal story, will be intensely interested."[273]

Yet even if there were few bona fide reviews of the film, there were hundreds of announcements and advertisements. And variations in the tone of the newspaper publicity suggest the anxieties of theater managers at this time of transition, as they played out possible strategies. Some stressed the film's cultural status, the theater itself being "The Home of High-Class Photoplays."[274] The choice of *Little Women* might, one commentator announced, "do more to bring the screen to its proper place than all of the regular program releases which are manufactured with machine-like precision."[275]

Some announcements and advertisements went so far as to claim that the screen version of *Little Women* was "even more impressive than the book" or was "much more wonderful and appealing than the printed word," or, according to a New Zealand working-class newspaper, that the March sisters were "even better on the screen than in the book."[276] Some assumed a middle-class audience already familiar with the book and therefore interested in seeing the film; others, an audience aspiring to the middle class: "no need to read the book now."[277] Despite the divergence in their implied audiences, both claims capitalize on the status of Alcott's novel. And on its familiarity—and hence its market branding. Many visual images also underscore the film's connection to the novel, depicting figures reading the book or characters stepping out of the pages of a book.[278] One ad reproduces both a still in which a male character, probably Brooke, holds a book and an amateurish, uncredited rendering of Jessie Willcox Smith's 1915 frontispiece to the book, thus directly and metaphorically invoking the film's source.[279]

Other advertisements stress the educational or moral value of the film, assuaging the fears of those concerned about what the motion picture was doing to children and women. The *Moving Picture World* encouraged getting school groups to attend, as indeed happened in some communities.[280] In Winnipeg a matron was present at a Saturday morning matinee to take care of unaccompanied children, and schoolchildren were invited to write why *Little Women* was a great story (the prizes to be theater tickets).[281] Other showings across North America benefited Parent Teachers Associations, the Association for the Aid of Crippled Children, war-relief efforts, and the Camp Fire Girls.[282] The worthiness of such benefits might endorse the worthiness of the film. But also such community outreach was common practice for film exhibitors, to promote the theater "not as a site of potential danger but instead as a public vessel for good," as a modern scholar notes.[283] One notice stressed the moral value of the film by proclaiming it "A Picture Play Every Church Minister and Congregation Should See."[284] Another stressed the "great educational value" of the film by pointing not to the value of Alcott's writing or of the pictorial depiction of her home but to the fact that "the home of Ralph Waldo Emerson also is shown";[285] such a reference boosted the film's educational value and tied the film to elite culture. And indeed, in one theater a local dignitary gave short talks on Emerson's house and other notable sites between reels.[286]

Many advertisements connected the film to the successful stage version—not for nothing did some members of the industry call their productions photoplays. An ad in Virginia went further in attempting to connect stage to screen, noting that the stage success had been "translated into the language of the masses— the movies."[287] We're presumably meant to consider such a translation positive, though the fact that this ad is the only one I've found that mentions the idea may suggest that some exhibitors didn't necessarily want to celebrate mass appeal, at least with a film making an appeal to middle-class culture. Indeed, some adver- tisements distanced the film from what presumably appealed to the masses by stressing its divergence from melodramatic "problem" films: one ad read, "They never had a 'triangle' in their family."[288] Then again, a couple of managers did take a more sensational approach. In one Pennsylvania newspaper, one can find the bizarre announcement that

Professor Baer [sic] and Jo had been "going together" so long that the whole town was preparing to celebrate the wedding. But Jo never wore that tell-tale solitaire. Then! One day the Professor came down a curving, shaded road through the trees and CAME UPON JO IN THE ARMS OF ANOTHER! But hold on a minute. It's not as bad as it sounds. The Professor wasn't a quitter and his col- legiate experience told him something that you can find out.[289]

Putting aside the inevitable studio and exhibitor hype, it appears that great things were expected of the film. Grauman's Theater, the first of the iconic Hol- lywood theaters opened by Sid Grauman and the most prominent West Coast theater at the time, offered a pre-release viewing on New Year's Day—a time "new-born of happiness, joy and abounding good cheer. . . . Not a more apropos photoplay than Louisa May Alcott's celebrated 'Little Women' could have been chosen for the occasion."[290] The screening was preceded by a prologue, with the actors from the film appearing on stage—perhaps an effort to stress the con- nection with a play produced on the legitimate stage, though in fact a number of exhibitors preceded their films with live programs at this time, even if such programs weren't usually coordinated, as here, with the contents of the films.[291] An ad in an Arizona paper later reported that "this picture had the most successful run of any picture at Grauman's million dollar theatre in Los Angeles of any picture of the season."[292] Probably studio hype—I didn't find this claim in the *Los Angeles Times* but in a newspaper called the *Mohave County Miner and Our Mineral Wealth.*

Still, the film appears to have been reasonably successful, despite the problems exhibitors were experiencing with attendance because of fears about the influenza pandemic, yet its not being an overt war film was an advantage after the November 1918 armistice.[293] The Arcadia in Philadelphia kept *Little Women* on a second week in January 1919 "in order to accommodate thousands unable to gain admission last week,"[294] and two weeks later the film was playing in eight other theaters in Philadelphia—a sign not just of the emergence of second-run theaters, of hierarchical distribution, but also of the film's ability to continue to draw an audience.[295] In July in Cedar Rapids, Iowa, *Little Women* was declared "exceedingly popular" since the "patrons . . . kept the theater pretty well filled at each performance despite the heat."[296] In October in Wellington, New Zealand, "the initial screenings . . . sufficiently proved to packed houses that Louisa M. Alcott's famous story provides one of the best photo-plays to date," and later in Otago, New Zealand, a final matinee called forth a note that this "picturisation" had "evoked a unanimous chorus of approval from all who witnessed it."[297]

Three newspaper pieces that seem to be reviews rather than boilerplate appeared in the *Chicago Tribune*, the *New York Tribune*, and the *New York Times*. Although two of these are quite favorable, none suggests that the movie had the "phenomenal success" of the play. In Chicago, Mae Tiné gushed about the acting. A more detailed analysis in the *New York Times* praised the atmosphere ("Many of the scenes are charming glimpses of the period"); found the acting satisfactory, if a little too consciously posed at times; criticized the frequent interruptions by subtitles as a minor shortcoming (as if countering, in part, enthusiasm voiced elsewhere for well-remembered quotations); and noted an anachronism: a briefly glimpsed telegram cites Newcomb Carlton as the president of the Western Union, but he wasn't born until 1869. Overall, though, the film was "good," and indeed "yesterday's spectators at the Strand seemed to respond with mirth and quick sympathy as gay scenes and grave were flashed before them."[298]

Four months later, however, Virginia Tracy, writing in the *New York Tribune*, castigated the film as being so "'reverently' produced" that "no breath of life break[s] through the deadly and deadening sweetness of that saccharine glaze."[299] We are given tableaux set in charming interiors and lyrical exteriors, she tells us, but "neither the book's humor nor its strong, homely feeling has been grasped by a scenario which simply droops from deathbed to deathbed as if glad to land at any definite base." (How many deaths were there? I wonder.) As for Jo, "Dorothy Bernard is hopelessly miscast—with her feminine littleness it is hard to tell what she could do with the part except to sentimentalize and conventionalize it as she does."[300] Tracy is castigating the film, I might emphasize, and not the book.

Few reviews of the movie appeared in general-interest periodicals—unlike for the 1912 play—although a number appeared in trade journals and fan magazines. Some of these reviewers commented on how *Little Women* exceeded or diverged from cinematic expectations of the time. One in *Variety* praised the continuity: "The picture runs along with a smoothness which is particularly noticeable and at the same time pleasing."[301] That for the *Moving Picture World* commented on the challenge of filming a story without a linear, suspenseful plot: "All this is difficult to assemble for presentation in an art of expression which ordinarily demands one or another situation of high suspense to hold popular interest, so difficult that courage was needed to undertake it, but the logic and consistency of all that is shown compensates heavily."[302] In *Motion Picture Classic*, Frederick James Smith found the film "a delightful picture—sans vampires, punches, and all the usual 'essentials' of the photodrama."[303] These three writers offered additional praise of the film, finding it variously "a picture out of the ordinary" or "a highly finished product, one of the best of its kind," or else the reviewer claimed, "Even if 'Little Women' doesn't hold a niche in your heart as a novel, it will get you as a picture."[304] The writer for *Variety* also lauded the retention of "those sweet touches of human interest which the authoress knew so well how to portray" and the "good looks and quaint dresses" of the actresses.[305] Now here we may be verging on the "saccharine glaze" that Tracy found so annoying. The attitude parallels that of the reviewer for another journal, *Motion Picture Magazine*, who may have found the film nearly a classic (it just moved a little too slowly), but he or she also reflected the increasing tendency to equate *Little Women* with the saccharine—with, to be precise, "the Polyanna [*sic*] and Elsie Dinsmore philosophy"—and thus to view it as embodying "the simplicity of life before women wanted the vote."[306] Film critics in 1919, like drama critics in 1912, had lost sight of the fact that Alcott was a suffragist.

As some of these reviews hint, *Little Women* was becoming ever more associated with the sentimental at a time when upper-crust critics were growing increasingly disdainful of anything connected with the term. In 1912 drama critics had been almost uniformly positive about the evocation of sentiment, but in 1919 film critics were less so. Notices apparently drawing on studio press copy may have noted, favorably, the "delicate sentiment" of the film, but the critics who invoked Pollyanna and the saccharine were less positive. So, indeed, were drama critics responding to the 1919 London stage revival. One called the play "a solace for the sugar-shortage."[307] Another suggested that the play was "one of those very charming and sentimental pieces which instantly appeal to all classes of play-goers"— framing sentiment not as an intrinsic strength, as critics tended to in 1912, but as enabling broad appeal.[308] For others, it was only Jo and the acting of Katharine Cornell that saved the play from lapsing, in the words of one, into the "merely sugar-plum." This last critic readily admitted to having never read the novel but still proceeded to doubt that the book could "give us such a Jo as Miss Katharine Cornell."[309] Alcott's novel had become an icon of sentiment and didn't require further investigation. Thus the play—and the film—was sentimental too.

Overall, the film was probably more like a stage play than other contemporary films were, even if it interspersed stage sets with a travelogue view of Concord. The acting in a 1919 film, especially one based on a popular stage play, would strike us now as histrionic. Although Dorothy Bernard had previously worked for D. W. Griffith, who was known for training actors to act with immediacy,[310] the acting of hers that I've seen strikes me as similar to the unhand-me-you-foul-fiend style of gesturing that we now associate with nineteenth-century melodrama. I've found no reviews suggesting that the acting in *Little Women* was innovative in following a more modern, understated style; indeed, Brady's inclination toward the theatrical probably influenced the acting style. And scholars have suggested that actors in historical or costume films and in sentimental stories with dignified characters were particularly likely to exhibit the most marked posing.[311] The film probably was not particularly noteworthy artistically, despite its good continuity; it was morally successful; it seems to have been reasonably successful financially. Indeed, a studio historian calls it "a very popular 1919 release."[312]

Let me add a few additional impressionistic and inconclusive musings. The fact that the film is now lost may hint that it was not a significant artistic endeavor, but since only 30 percent of American silent films are still extant in any form, complete or incomplete, its disappearance is not a definitive judgment.[313] More telling, perhaps, is the omission of *Little Women* from the wish lists of the silent films that modern scholars most want to locate.[314] Yet that absence may still reflect the attitudes of such scholars toward Alcott's work, whether or not they've read it.

Finally, consider the afterlives of people associated with the production. The already successful director Harley Knoles would go on to make a dozen more films in the next decade, stopping with the end of the silent film era. The film probably neither helped nor hindered his career. That wasn't the case with Brady. He appears to have produced only one more film, although he continued to be successful on Broadway. Also suggestive is that the film does not appear to have helped launch the careers of any of its young actresses. Not "star vehicles" but more like ensemble productions, significant dramatizations and films of *Little Women* have provided unusually fertile staging grounds for successful careers: for Alice Brady, who played Meg in the 1912 Broadway hit and went on to a very successful stage career; for Katharine Cornell, Jo in the 1919 London revival, later hailed as "The First Lady of the American Stage";[315] and for Katharine Hepburn, Jo in the 1933 film. But the young actresses in the 1919 film did not go on to more wondrous things; none was still acting in films five years later.[316] The two young male actors are a different story: Conrad Nagel, who made his film debut as Laurie, would become a matinee idol, and Henry Hull, John Brooke, became a well-known character actor (most notable, apparently, for playing the lead in 1935's *Werewolf of London*). In contrast, the role of Jo seems to have marked basically the end of the film career of Dorothy Bernard, who had had leading roles in several short Griffith films. After a hiatus of more than thirty years, she would go on to make guest appearances on 1950s television shows.

⌒

Finally, if the early decades of the century foregrounded the domesticity of *Little Women*, it's only fitting that this domesticity became enshrined in a domicile. In the late nineteenth century, no literary pilgrimage to Concord would be complete without a view of one or more of the houses in which the Alcotts, both Bronson and Louisa, had lived, whether it was the house that subsequently came to be known as the Wayside (now more strongly associated with Hawthorne, a subsequent resident); or the Thoreau-Alcott house, still privately owned; or Orchard House. As I noted in chapter 1, a nineteenth-century pilgrim might mention all three, without giving great priority to Orchard House.[317] Even in 1912 a visitor seeking the Alcott home might find himself or herself directed to the Thoreau-Alcott house (where a family member still lived).[318] Orchard House nevertheless became the house most strongly associated with Alcott, even though the family didn't move there till after her younger sister Elizabeth had died and Louisa was twenty-six. Although Alcott stayed there at times, sometimes for several months, it was more precisely her parents' home. Yet she did work on *Little Women* there and also drew on the house for the fictional March family home. As I noted in chapter 1, an image of it was the frontispiece for a nineteenth-century edition of *Little Women*, captioned not "Alcott's Home" but "Home of the Little Women."

As for the disposition of Orchard House, in 1903 the real-estate listings in the *Boston Evening Transcript* advertised it as "Louisa May Alcott's Home in Concord," a "beautiful old estate" with trees planted by Thoreau and Alcott, near the homes of Emerson and Hawthorne and—for those interested in a less literary form of culture—near golf links that "are among the finest in the State."[319] Harriett Lothrop, better known as Margaret Sidney, author of *The Five Little Peppers* (1881), had bought it in 1901 and apparently hoped to sell it to someone seeking to preserve it.[320] It's not entirely clear whether she'd purchased it as a speculative investment or as an act of homage: Alcott's nephew indicated that his family had been unable to persuade her to sell it at a reasonable price; another commentator suggests that it was Lothrop's generosity that finally enabled the purchase by the Concord Woman's Club.[321] In any case, Lothrop claimed that she wanted to preserve "a 'happy home center' where love rather than Bronson's Orphic musings 'prevailed.'"[322]

Pleas for preservation appeared as early as 1902. At first a commentator might simply express a pious wish: "It is to be hoped it will always be occupied by some one who will cherish its history."[323] Later came pleas for donations, for someone to preserve it perhaps as "a *home* once more, breathing peace and rest to weary wielders of the pen," to cite someone who had encountered at least twenty-five fellow pilgrims to the abandoned and decaying shrine one day in 1909.[324] The Concord Woman's Club undertook to preserve the home in 1911, seeking donations by trying "to reach every woman in the state if possible."[325] There were also national pleas, some by the club, some by others: pleas to "American boyhood and girlhood," in the *Youth's Companion* in 1910; to "all lovers of Miss Alcott," in the *Dial* in 1911.[326] On a page of a 1911 issue of the *New York Sun* are separate appeals to temperance supporters and to suffragists.[327] Three months earlier in Illinois, fourth-grade twins had journeyed to Chicago to ask the editors of the *Tribune*, "Don't you think that if a thousand children saved their pennies, . . . we could get enough to buy the house?"[328] The Woman's Club of Concord agreed to purchase the building by July 1911, having received "contributions of from 10 cents to $2 . . . from all sections of the country," starting with "five cents from a little girl, saved from her allowance of two cents a week."[329] Even before the house formally opened in 1912, thousands of people visited annually; by 1924, according to one report, that number had swelled to 23,347—an increase fueled in part, as was the increase in visitors to other house museums, by the rise of the automobile.[330]

As Anne Trubek has recently noted, authors' house museums are "melancholy monuments to death." Visits to them are partly about making sacred pilgrimages, partly about preserving history, partly about using an object to compensate for loss, partly about "the longing created by the fact that words separate writers from readers yet create an ineluctable intimacy between the two": in short, "they ignite and continually frustrate our desire to fuse the material with the immaterial, the writer with the reader."[331] Writers a century ago rarely waxed so theoretical, but a few offered insights into the cultural contexts for the creation of this house museum. One for a Boston paper treated the house as authenticating the novel, as material evidence for the truth of Alcott's story—as "conclusive and definitive proof that, after all, the story was true."[332] One for the Washington, DC, *National Tribune* urged that America, like other countries, give "a distinct and honored place in our history" to "those who have made our literature" by preserving their houses, including that of Alcott—"after all, does not Louisa Alcott belong to the whole Nation, and should not every State have a hand in the preservation of the Alcott home?"[333] This writer documented the functions of house museums as shrines and the implicit link between love of home and love of nation. Shrine, home, nation: the historian Patricia West notes that the function of house museums was shifting at this time, so that they were not just "churchlike 'shrines'" but also "a particular kind of model home," inculcating values viewed as traditional.[334] House museums, writes West, "inspire devotion to a particular version of 'the home' as the mainstay of American identity, thereby creating loyal republican citizens and homogenizing a persistently heterogeneous population."[335]

A visitor in 1912 noted the way in which Orchard House offered a combined tribute to "the highest ideals and the homeliest household tasks," the way "the Alcott family, in all their varied individuality and their deep family unity, filled it with philosophy, private theatricals, and household joys."[336] This visitor captures the duality of house museums, which generally celebrate someone active in the public arena (usually a man) by memorializing the private sphere. West suggests that Orchard House celebrates the novel more than the woman: it is not the house where Alcott grew up but the one that provides an architectural setting for the story.[337] Yet it may be more precise simply to say that the focus of the museum is diffuse: author Louisa, philosopher Bronson, the entire Alcott family, the fictional March family. Even now the Orchard House web page proclaims "Home of 'Little Women,'" while the sign in front of the museum reads "Home of the Alcotts." The museum continues the conflation of author and character— or author's family and fictional family—encouraged by Roberts Brothers in the nineteenth century. And indeed the memorialization of this particular building as the Alcott house, a house that provided a model for the March family home and not one where Alcott herself had spent her childhood, further confounds fictional and actual families. Many commentators, then and now, have assumed that it was the house where Alcott lived when she was growing up.

West has unearthed the politics of the Concord Woman's Club as it raised funds for restoration. The group would shortly split into pro- and antisuffrage factions: the former were inclined to celebrate Alcott the reformer; the latter, "the ostentatiously traditional domesticity envisioned as a source of cultural stability" that *Little Women* could represent; yet both factions could agree on memorializing the novel, with its internal contradictions as to woman's place.[338] An additional contradiction that West notes is that the founders of the museum reinforced the invention of the Alcotts as a typical, traditional family inhabiting "a model single-family suburban home," even though the family had experimented with communal living, Alcott herself lived much of the time in various rooms in Boston, and indeed the family was not emotionally and physically stable.[339]

Further contributing to the contradictions embodied by the museum is the house itself. The nineteenth-century writer Lydia Maria Child recognized some of its disjunctions when she claimed, "It seems as if the spirit of some old architect had brought it from the Middle-Ages and dropped it down in Concord. . . . The whole leaves a general impression of harmony, of a medieval sort, though different parts of the house seem to have stopped in a dance that became confused because some of the party did not keep time."[340] West describes the layout and furnishings as "a curious hybrid of a progressive-era, neo-colonial, single-family suburban home and an idealized nineteenth-century cottage."[341] Indeed, the shabby gentility of the Alcotts, with their battered furniture and relative lack of Victorian ornaments, translated rather smoothly into the early-twentieth-century preference for simplicity, in reaction to ornate Victorian fussiness and miscellaneous bric-a-brac.[342] Furthermore, Bronson had amalgamated one house with another on the property, "turning the back one sideways, and you can see where they join, in the middle of the dining-room floor," a visitor noted in 1912, so it was no wonder that the "house has a large set of hall-stairs coming calmly down one side of its dining-room."[343] The house also embodies the fluidity of separate spheres in New England middle-class homes, as David Watters argues, with no formal parlor but a multipurpose family one, for a family with separate individuals cooperating in interdependent spaces.[344]

Accounts of Orchard House a century ago are slightly more likely to mention individuality—as in the report above of the family's "varied individuality and their deep family unity"—than do other reports of Alcott-related matters. A writer for the *New York Times* in 1911, discussing the house in the context of the "wonderful men who lived in Concord," claimed that "the strongest, stoutest, bravest man among them all was Bronson Alcott's tomboy girl, Louisa": Bronson's schemes of "transcendental education . . . allowed Louisa's active mind to expand along its own lines and accustomed her to think for herself."[345] A noticeable percentage of early-twentieth-century accounts of the house—unlike the hundreds of discussions of the 1912 play—suggest the possibilities for individuality. Perhaps the separate rooms of middle-class houses simply enable a degree of independence, unlike plays, with one stage across which all the characters troop. When the house first opened, there was at least some awareness of its atypicality and individuality. At a time when *Little Women* had come to represent entrenched domesticity, its tangible monument, despite the domicile's etymological link to the domestic, was a permeable text.

Perhaps the play is the thing that gives least scope for individuality, most firmly making *Little Women* an icon of domesticity, ossifying it. The Three Little Women series ossifies it as well, though these books also attempt to merge entrepreneurialism with domesticity, the difficulty of which is enacted by finally stripping Constance of anything to do. Then again, the final volume was published after the successful Broadway play and perhaps borrows its themes. As for the illustrations of *Little Women*, most foreground the decorative and domestic; the tract society reprint, for example, frames the book as the triumph of a woman overcoming adversity and as the triumph of fashion, without reconciling or even negotiating between the two. Only in the house, in the early decades of the twentieth century, do I see a fruitful multiplicity of meanings, a mutual questioning of individuality and domesticity. Yet what is underscored by all these manifestations of popular interest —whether the house, the play, the spinoffs, the illustrated editions— is that in these decades when Alcott's academic reputation was declining, her reputation among more common people was, in contrast, cresting.

CHAPTER 3

Outwitting Poverty and War, 1930–1960

When Selznick wanted me to do *Little Women*, I hadn't read the book. (Kate Hepburn once accused me of never having finished it, which is a lie.) Of course I'd heard of it all my life, but it was a story that little girls read, like Elsie Dinsmore. When I came to read it, I was startled. It's not sentimental or saccharine, but very strong-minded, full of character, and a wonderful picture of New England family life.

—*George Cukor*

The mid-twentieth century was the heyday of scholarly dismissal of Alcott. Most literary scholars and members of the intellectual elite, not to mention the young George Cukor, did not consider Alcott worthy of notice. As a reviewer of Cukor's 1933 film noted, *Little Women* was "often mentioned by the intelligentsia as a horrible example of sweetness and light in literature."[1] A journalist reviewing Katharine Anthony's biography of Alcott a few years later pontificated that "books of the 'Little Women' school have always given this department a severe head-ache" and went on to wonder how anyone could find in Alcott's books "a general worth beyond their amusement value."[2]

Most intellectuals were not even amused. But among the general population *Little Women* was still very popular, even if it was declining from its peak at the beginning of the century. As for how the novel was interpreted, it and its adaptations allowed some attention to women's independence by the 1930s, an attention that declined after World War II. The most visible manifestations of interest and interpretation were the 1933 and 1949 film versions, but there was also a surge in dramatizations, illustrations, and biographies of Alcott, not to mention adaptations screened on television.

ᴄ⁓

With respect to scholarly disinterest, Vernon Louis Parrington's classic *Main Currents in American Thought* (1930) is emblematic: it includes a reference to Louisa M. Alcott in the index, but the textual reference to "the grotesque vaporings of Alcott" is actually to Bronson. In the 1948 three-volume *Literary History of the United States*, edited by Robert Spiller and others, the indexed reference to Alcott in the main text leads one to a tangential mention of her work being available in Sweden—not, in short, to a direct discussion of her writing. Nor does Alcott's name appear in such major works of criticism, what would shortly be considered classic works, as R. W. B. Lewis's *American Adam* (1955) or Richard Chase's *American Novel and Its Tradition* (1957), or in such histories as Robert E. Spiller's *Cycle of American Literature* (1955). In 1952, Edward Wagenknecht ingenuously noted that *Little Women* was beloved and added, "It needs—and is susceptible of—little analysis; critics have, therefore, generally neglected it."[3] Only a maverick outside the academy, the TV and radio personality and critic-at-large Clifton Fadiman, someone condemned by the academy as hopelessly middlebrow, would be willing to declare *Little Women* one of ten works in English most likely to be "universally alive" in five hundred years.[4]

Outside the United States, a British novelist writing in the *Times Literary Supplement* reproved Alexander Cowie for "barely mention[ing]" Alcott in *The Rise of the American Novel* (1948)—but it was only a "small criticism."[5] A commentator writing for a New Zealand newspaper equivocated, "There are some books which are not very big ones but manage to acquire an immortal fate. Such a book is 'Little Women.' It is difficult to place this book as a work of art; yet there are few in successive generations who do not read it with something like enjoyment."[6]

On the few occasions when Alcott was discussed in highbrow venues, she was likely to be misremembered or misquoted. Many critics, for instance, quoted or alluded to a claim that Alcott had said of *Adventures of Huckleberry Finn* (1885), "If Mr. Clemens cannot think of something better to tell our pure-minded lads and lasses, he had best stop writing for them."[7] The earliest version that I've tracked down appears in *The Mauve Decade* (1926), by the literary gossip Thomas Beer. He suggests that his source is a letter to a Frances Hedges Butler. Such a letter does not appear in *The Selected Letters of Louisa May Alcott* or in the calendar of Alcott's letters.[8] Nor does the breezy, gossipy style of Beer's book inspire confidence. Indeed, critics have recently discovered that letters that Beer elsewhere attributes to Stephen Crane are fabricated.[9] It seems likely that the Alcott comment is too. The many earnest repetitions of it simply reflect the desire of many midcentury and subsequent critics to classify Alcott with children and with prim self-righteousness, fencing her off from what they want to consider works of mainstream literature by, for instance, Twain, forgetting that his *Adventures of Huckleberry Finn* and *The Adventures of Tom Sawyer* were also literature for the young.[10]

For Alcott was often dismissed because of her associations with children—at this time when critics disparaged what they considered children's literature but were nonetheless apt to find adolescent quests quintessentially American. For nonacademics, such as the Hollywood gossip columnist Louella Parsons, *Little Women* might be the "typical American novel."[11] But not for the intellectual elite, and for them Alcott herself was childish. "Did she never mature intellectually?" a British reviewer of Madeleine Stern's biography asks. "Was the revolt from Philosophy too complete?"[12] Such an attitude appears with particular clarity in a 1938 review by Odell Shepard, who was, not coincidentally, Bronson's Pulitzer Prize–winning biographer. Shepard claimed that Louisa "never emerged from adolescence," that "she never grew up."[13] In fact,

> living almost always among intellectuals, she preserved to the age of fifty-six that contempt for ideas which is normal among boys and girls of fifteen. . . . She seems to have felt, moreover, that love, marriage, and child-bearing were interruptions of serious business—although she never quite made out what the serious business of life really is, unless it be earning a livelihood. (393)

Earning a livelihood isn't serious business? Certainly it wasn't for the improvident Bronson. Just what is the serious business of life? Perhaps it's war, for Shepard goes on to indict Alcott for referring to the conflict between France and Prussia as a "silly little war": "These words show the bounce and swagger of a mind that has never really faced life's darker mysteries" (393). Such as what it's like to nurse dying men in wartime perhaps? One reason for her popularity, Shepard concludes, is "that the American public is itself immature in thought and mood" (393).

Perhaps the fullest expression of midcentury critical dismay with Alcott appeared in a review in the *Times Literary Supplement* in 1957. The Reverend Robin Alastair Denniston, only minimally concerned with the edition of *Little Men* that is his pretext, describes Jo and Professor Bhaer as "conducting a rare collection of little horrors up the steep paths of virtue."[14] He then temporizes that *Little Women*, "it is fair to say, is beyond the reach of criticism. When a book like this is so loved and cherished—and not merely by the unintelligent—any critic who feels he should discuss Miss Alcott's sentimentality and priggishness will be shown the door." Yet still, "how can [Alcott] go on reporting the conversations and plays of these egregious infants, as if they were so important?" Finally, after particularizing the failings of the March family books, Denniston makes a summary judgment, seemingly more even-handed than the opening sentences, thanks to convenient catchwords of midcentury criticism—*sentimental, classic, universal*—and claims that Alcott's books "are not sentimental rubbish, but they are not classics either, in the sense that they have a relevance outside their time and place, a universal message to communicate." By the standards of midcentury criticism, Alcott's continuing popularity didn't even hint at "universality."

Nor did Alcott fare well with critics who focused on finding quintessentially American works, the pursuit of which seemed to dominate criticism of American literature at this time, as Nina Baym has eloquently demonstrated.[15] Forget that Alcott was not an expatriate, that she did not spend the better part of a decade or more outside the United States, as James and Twain did. Forget that she provided a window on the American middle-class family. A story about a boy and a man rafting down the Mississippi could be quintessentially American, but not one about a family of women guarding the home front during the Civil War. If American works are about the individual in opposition to family and society, the individual testing himself in the wilderness, as midcentury critics were fond of claiming, then *Little Women* does so only in rather subtle ways.

Nevertheless, the 1940s did witness an early stirring of what would eventually blossom into full-blown academic interest in Alcott. In 1943 Leona Rostenberg published her discovery that Alcott had written thrillers under the name A. M. Barnard.[16] Her partner, Madeleine Stern, embarked on a decades-long career of publishing about Alcott, starting with journal articles in the 1940s and including the 1950 publication of what became the standard biography. Stern wrote the best literary appraisal of Alcott at this time, applying the terms and perspectives of midcentury criticism: in an essay published in the scholarly *New England Quarterly* she addressed style and characterization, realism and episodic structure, and Alcott's ability to give a local flavor while nonetheless offering a universal appeal.[17] Stern did not, however, have an academic affiliation.

⁓

The popular response to *Little Women* at midcentury, especially in the 1930s, was very different from the academic disregard and disfavor, as one can gauge by tracking it in the media and material culture.

The novel was frequently the topic of prize-winning essays on a child's favorite book, whether a girl praised it for providing "the best models for girls in this modern world" or asserted that readers "felt as though we were being confided in."[18] In a high-school poll in Milwaukee in 1931, Alcott was outpaced by Zane Grey overall, but *Little Women* was the favorite book among girls.[19] In an *American Girl* magazine contest in 1932, the most popular book was *Little Women*; the most popular character, Jo. One girl wrote that "if Jo March could come alive the world would be a much gayer and cheerier place than it is today."[20]

That same year the Newark Public Library's 150 copies of *Little Women* were "in use all the time."[21] The book was a popular borrowing in the American Merchant Marine Library, and a New York newspaper claimed that it "has a reading in our libraries that exceeds any book in English fiction."[22] In 1941 the writer and editor Leo Lerman hazarded that "'Little Women' probably sells more every year than most best sellers."[23] According to a midwestern library database, five small-town libraries acquired fourteen copies of *Little Women* in the three midcentury decades, about 60 percent of what they had acquired in the previous three decades,[24] so there was some decline overall compared with earlier in the century.

Among adults, a series of Alcott clubs that started in Indiana in 1931, "to inspire high ideals in homemaking," was still going strong in 1977.[25] Speakers at meetings of other women's clubs discussed Alcott, purveying such chestnuts as that Charles Dickens had introduced her to the editor Thomas Niles.[26] (Alcott never actually met Dickens.) Adults were still trying to create clubs for the young, as in the earlier period, now perhaps "'Little Women' clubs for girls below scout age"[27]—which very young age may speak to the age positioning of the novel or of the phrase *little women*. Sometimes, as with the young Jane Addams and other girls in earlier decades, *Little Women* featured in group play or enactments. Girls in upstate New York and subdebutantes in Washington, DC, called themselves Little Women and took on the names of Alcott's characters.[28] More tongue in cheek, a group of Hollywood chorus girls formed "a club called: 'Little Women of Hollywood.' They take names from the Louisa May Alcott classic."[29]

By the 1950s *Little Women* was still popular but less likely than earlier to be a preeminent favorite. In some places and for some individuals it still was; for example, it came in first in polls of the young people's departments of a Chicago branch library and the San Mateo Public Library.[30] Yet overall the novel was less likely to be the foremost favorite of the young. In 1950 and 1956 it was one of many favorites among some schoolchildren in New York.[31] In 1956 *Little Women* was not one of the top choices of New York–area high-school students remembering what they had liked when young; the one tenth grader who is cited as naming it was rather self-conscious, claiming that at one point she had "practically memorized" the book but then "had a violent opposite reaction and would not touch any literature at all about virtuous young ladies."[32] A ninth-grade girl in California was glad that there would be a televised version in 1958, because "the book is so boring I could never get into it. . . . But I want to know the story so this will be an easy way to find out."[33]

Nevertheless, girls who grew up during this midcentury period and went on to have prominence in the arts and in politics—whether as a National Book Award–winning poet or punk rocker or secretary of state—often remembered finding validation in Alcott's work. For Joan Didion the Marches may have been too perfect, but those for whom *Little Women* was significant, sometimes life-changing, include Barbara Bush, Ursula Le Guin, Shirley Temple, Sonia Sanchez, Susan Sontag, Judith Krantz, Gloria Steinem, Jane Yolen, Bobbie Ann Mason, Laura Bush, Connie Chung, Patti Smith, Sara Paretsky, and Hillary Clinton.[34] "I read 'Little Women' a thousand times," claimed Cynthia Ozick. "Ten thousand."[35] Miss Manners (Judith Martin) claimed, in turn, that *Little Women* had been "where I learned that although it's very nice to have two clean gloves, it's even more important to have a little ink on your fingers."[36] The political consultant James Carville listed it as a favorite; the immigrant Juris Jurjevics, who would go on to become a leading editor, loved it.[37] Among adults during this period, *Little Women* came in ninth in a survey of "most interesting books"—not just books for children—conducted by Gallup's American Institute of Public Opinion.[38]

Little Women was popular outside the United States as well. In the 1930s it was reported as "a continuous best seller in England," even if a bookseller in Cheltenham suggested that it was especially popular at "Sunday school prize-givings. Children do not seek it of their own volition."[39] In 1941 it was one of the most frequently borrowed books at a miners' library in Wales, and it featured prominently on a waiting list at a library in Devon.[40] In 1942 it was the choice of the war-torn British children who were polled for "the book they wanted broadcast in dramatized version" on the radio at Christmastime.[41] It was the childhood favorite of the broadcaster Gloria Hunniford, the choreographer Arlene Phillips, and presumably the comedian Marty Feldman (but he was probably joking).[42] Dame Jacqueline Wilson, who went on to become Children's Laureate, "read *Little Women* over and over again."[43] In 1952 in Leeds, a dramatization of the novel was performed in honor of Queen Elizabeth's coronation "because the theme it represents of family love, strength and unity is considered to be exemplified by the British Royal Family."[44]

In France, the expatriate Elliot Paul told an anecdote about the oddly assorted reading of the proprietor of a Parisian goldfish shop, reading that included *Les soeurs Marx* (The Marx sisters). Which is to say, *Little Women*, given that a literal translation of Alcott's title, "Petite femmes," "would have a meaning which would have distressed Louisa May" and given that *March* might sound like *Marx* to the average Frenchman. Those who bought the book were disappointed by the absence of "the zany qualities" of the Marx brothers.[45] Unfortunately, the story is probably apocryphal. A related anecdote has the bookstore owner Sylvia Beach offering Frank Harris, whose writing favored sexual explicitness, a copy of *Little Women*: "He jumped at the title, which to someone with an obsession like his could only have the French meaning of petites femmes."[46]

Elsewhere, according to media reports, the novel was banned in East Germany in 1948 and in Soviet-controlled Hungary in 1950, but in 1958 it was on the shelves of an Israeli reading room and was cited as popular in Thailand; two years later it was mentioned as popular in Italy.[47] By 1949 there had been seven translations of *Little Women* into Chinese.[48] In Japan in 1931, when Alexander Woollcott was giving a speech at a girls' school and was groping for the name of the school that Jo had founded, a Japanese girl "helped me out by supplying 'Plumfield' in a stage whisper."[49] Alcott's works were among the most popular offerings of the U.S. Information Library in occupied Japan after World War II; indeed, one publisher gave its series of translated girls' literature a title that echoed that for *Little Women*.[50] The novel was, furthermore, a favorite of the future empress Michiko, who made a point of visiting Orchard House when in the United States, and of the Finnish Leena Maissen and the Australian cultural critic Peter Craven.[51] The Italian writer and scholar Marisa Bulgheroni found in Jo a model of rebellious femininity, and the Indian writer Neera Kuckreja Sohoni credits *Little Women* with giving her "the romantic dream of marrying a 'Larry'-like male," as she calls him, and raising daughters.[52]

In the United States *Little Women* was still recommended as reading for the young in, for example, Nancy Larrick's influential *Parent's Guide to Children's Reading* (1958) and in many lists published by local librarians across the country throughout this period and beyond. The novel appeared in a 1930 listing of "Forty Books for the Young" recommended by the U.S. Division of Education, as one of five juvenile titles on a 1933 list of one hundred best books by American women, and on the Grolier Club's 1946 list of "100 influential American books."[53] It has appeared repeatedly in editions of *Good Reading*, prepared by the Committee on College Reading of the National Council of Teachers of English.[54] In 1941 Alcott was the representative author in a New York Public Library listing of eleven "Women Who Helped Mold America," although the caption under her picture in the *New York Times Magazine* was defensive: "The progressively trained youth of today may class 'Little Men' and 'Little Women' as A No. 1 sissies, but if it hadn't been for Louisa May Alcott's books there might be no progressive education."[55] *Little Women* was still read frequently in schools; even if a boy preferred boys' books, he could nevertheless "pretend Jo is a boy" and like it pretty well.[56]

The novel continued to figure strongly in the library canon, yet librarians were not as wholehearted about it as they had once been. In 1947 Alice Jordan could not fail to mention *Little Women* in an account of "children's classics," but she noted that the book had endured "in spite of its sentimentality and doubtful English."[57] Sarah Wadsworth has traced a winnowing in the Alcott canon: she notes that the 1893 catalog of the American Library Association included six Alcott titles but that by 1951 the list included just three and in 1961 just two.[58] Interest in Alcott was declining.

Nevertheless, librarians and educators marked the centenary of Alcott's birth in 1932 with displays and celebrations. *Little Women* had always figured importantly during National Book Week—and would continue to do so—but it was especially prominent in 1932. From Binghamton to Berkeley, libraries and bookstores displayed Alcott titles and portraits and dolls dressed as the Little Women.[59] Women's clubs sponsored talks and readings; schools and other groups sponsored dramatizations. The Concord Players, which claimed descent from Alcott's amateur stage productions in Concord, started mounting decennial productions of *Little Women*; in 1932 a production of de Forest's version featured descendants of Alcott's sister Anna.[60] Another group organized a party "with birthday cakes bearing candles to be lighted by children in the costumes of foreign lands in which Alcott books have been published."[61] And NBC Radio featured a production of *Little Women*.[62]

Many newspapers across the United States and abroad featured pieces about Alcott as well. The *Boston Globe*, for instance, published a serialized biography over six days in July. It also reported on the letters that child fans were still sending Alcott, maybe fifty a year, in which they expressed their appreciation of *Little Women* and explained how they and their friends pretended to be the Little Women, or commented on the weather, or inquired whether Alcott had written other books, perhaps offering to send three cents for a copy of one.[63] The *Overland Monthly* honored the centennial in 1933—it wasn't the only journal confused about exactly when the anniversary was—by reprinting a letter in which Alcott described her writing, her reading, and her dislike of being hounded by fans.[64] A New Zealand newspaper reprinted an article from the *Christian Science Monitor*: the piece begins, "It is not often that a nation celebrates the centenary of an author whose major book still holds its own as a 'best seller.'"[65] The *Ladies' Home Journal* reprinted snippets of Alcott's writing, prefacing them by noting that "in these uncertain times, there is a greater need to cherish the joys of family life" and that Alcott "represents the ideals of home and family life which the JOURNAL has ever tried to encourage." Yet the snippets do not just celebrate self-sacrifice and finding meaning in housekeeping but also encourage girls to "see a little of the world" and find independence, underscoring "women's right to any branch of labor for which they prove their fitness."[66]

Indeed, journalists writing in the midst of the Depression were more likely than earlier commentators to acknowledge how the Alcotts coped with poverty, given "these uncertain times." Long associated with nostalgia for a traditional past, *Little Women* now was sometimes seen as carrying hints of women's independence, perhaps of women working to overcome poverty. Writers noted in passing that Alcott "knew the discipline of poverty," that her life showed "the courage that it takes to outwit the handicap of poverty."[67] One for a Delaware newspaper discussed how "the poverty that limited [the Alcotts] and which [was] so fully described in the stories by Louisa Alcott" actually "made them fall back on the life of the mind, and on simple fun; and no one who ever knew anything of that family could help but admire the consequences."[68]

As part of the centennial celebration, the *Elementary English Review* focused its November 1932 issue on Alcott. And Lucile Gulliver (the editor at Little, Brown who responded to children's letters to Alcott) published a book-length bibliography itemizing editions of Alcott's work, including a listing of twelve languages into which the book had been translated, including Czech and Finnish.

Newspapers continued to allude to Alcott frequently throughout this period whether in lists of library purchases or of famous people born on November 29 or in quizzes on children's pages. They also purveyed misinformation. In one of his syndicated "5-Minute Biographies," Dale Carnegie garbled various anecdotes and told how Alcott, bored with writing her "sentimental masterpiece," would "whistle for her dog" and tramp through the woods.[69] (She liked cats. She didn't have a dog.) Novel and author could be so associated with domesticity and mothering that a columnist in the Midwest might misremember "the busy mother that Louisa May Alcott was when she found time to write 'Little Women' while her children pulled at her apron strings."[70] (She never married. And it was more than a decade after Alcott wrote *Little Women* that she took on the care of her dead sister May's child, Lulu.)

One can gauge trends in popular magazines by tracking items indexed in the *Reader's Guide to Periodical Literature*. In the half-century before 1940 there were twice as many items about Alcott as there were in the half-century afterward

Yet the ratio of the number of pieces about Alcott to the number about her father, Bronson, active in the Transcendentalist circle, doubled. About midcentury,
then, popular interest in Alcott declined, even if she outpaced a more scholarly
nineteenth-century figure in general-interest magazines.

As for material culture, in the nineteenth century Alcott may have been one of
thirteen writers represented in the Authors card game, but she became a notable
material presence in the middle of the twentieth century. In 1940 a five-cent
stamp featured a portrait of her head; in 1943 a ship was named after her.[71] And
"cute" quartets of young chimps at the Bronx Zoo were named Meg, Jo, Beth, and
Amy—three times between 1952 and 1960.[72]

This was also the era of *Little Women* dolls, whether they were created by the
couturiers of dolldom or were handcrafted or indeed paper dolls. Madame Alexander inaugurated her annual release (still going strong) of Little Women dolls in
1933, timed to coincide with the RKO film.[73] In 1935 an exhibit in New York City
featured three dolls whose hair was presumably locks from three Alcott sisters; by
the following decade Little Women dolls were a fixture in doll exhibits.[74] Some
enthusiasts demonstrated their flair for the domestic by creating their own dolls.[75]
The novel especially lent itself to twentieth-century dollmaking because, as one
writer claimed, it derived from "a period of quaint charming costume, quite a
point to consider in pleasing doll lovers."[76]

For despite some attention to Alcott's poverty and independence, her name
was still associated with old-fashioned charm. Retro fashions, whatever the era
they were invoking and especially if they were for the young, were likely to be
deemed a Little Women look.[77] Adult fashions were implicated as well: in 1939 a
Bloomingdale's fashion expert reporting on the latest fashions in Paris suggested
that the "well-dressed woman" would "look like one of Louisa Alcott's 'Little
Women' with . . . tiny lace ruffles, fitted jacket coats, wool jersey skirts gathered
on yokes across the hips and evening accessories of pastel violets."[78] Tiny lace
ruffles indeed.

✐

Another index of popularity is the surge in biographies and newly illustrated editions. There were eight new book-length biographies between 1930 and 1960.[79] In
1933 Cornelia Meigs published *Invincible Louisa: The Story of the Author of "Little Women,"* a juvenile biography that would go on to win the Newbery Medal,
awarded annually to the outstanding work of American children's literature. The
literary critic Austin Warren, reviewing the book sympathetically in the premier
scholarly journal for American literature (in what is probably the only review of

a Newbery Medal winner ever to appear in *American Literature*), described Alcott as "a modern woman, eager for independence and a career, but without the modernist's clamor for 'self-expression.'"[80]

Juvenile biographies have continued the tradition of purveying role models more than other biographies have, even when they attempt to probe more of a subject's complexity; the hallmark of Meigs's biography is an emphasis on Alcott's commitment to her family. Meigs concludes, "The whole of what she had wanted from life" was "just to take care of them all."[81] When the Alcott family was in crisis at Fruitlands, Meigs reports, Charles Lane wanted to persuade Bronson "to give up such small things as family love, loyalty and devotion to one's own. He did not know that it is upon such things that the very structure of life is built. It was in those dark and desperate days that Louisa learned to know the truth of what family life should be, learned it and never forgot" (68). Meigs claims that despite the depression that Bronson felt after the failure of Fruitlands, "he was happy to be with [his family], but the fearful struggle had shattered him. He was worn out, he was ill unto death. He had worked so desperately on the Fruitlands farm, trying to draw from those unwilling acres a living for his family, for his companions and his idea! He was tired with this outward struggle; he was still more worn from the battle of doubt within" (70). In short, Meigs has to work hard to bring Bronson back within the circle of his family, to make him "happy" despite all appearances and despite that inward doubt about whether he should have stayed with his wife and daughters or joined Lane—but at least she tackles the difficult issue of his struggle with depression.

Another crux that Meigs has to deal with if she's to maintain her focus on Alcott's commitment to family is Alcott's distaste for Orchard House, the house on which the *Little Women* house is largely modeled. Meigs admits that Alcott "cherished an unreasoned enmity for the house" (120) but is at some pains to explain it. Perhaps it arose because the house was meant to provide a comfortable place for Alcott's dying sister Elizabeth, who died before they could move in. Or perhaps Alcott associated it with her own illness after her stint as a wartime nurse. Yet elsewhere Meigs notes that when May returned from Europe shortly after their mother died, "Louisa gave into her hands, with a sigh of relief, the task of keeping house in Concord. Fame threatened to become an occupation in itself and leave Louisa no time for actual living" (226). Perhaps the culprit was fame or maybe it was cooking and cleaning. Meigs notes that a later summer home in Nonquit (as she spells it) "had one glorious feature in Louisa's eyes: 'it was without the curse of a kitchen'" (243). And the fictional Marches had the fantasy of a devoted family retainer to handle much of the housework. When Alcott was in Concord, housekeeping was what she was expected to do. Maybe a desire to care for her family—"just to take care of them all"—wasn't her sole aim in life.

Later in the decade, Katharine Anthony's *Louisa May Alcott* (1938) billed itself as the first biography of Alcott for adults. It was excerpted in both highbrow and middlebrow venues: in the *North American Review* in 1936, in the *Woman's Home Companion* in 1937–38. This last was accompanied by illustrations by Norman Rockwell, featuring Bronson as much as Louisa. In one image our bird's-eye view of Louisa sitting on a stool before Bronson situates her head above his, though highest of all is that of a sculptured bust, its head aligned almost in parallel with Louisa's—but which resembles Ben Franklin, beardless, more than Bronson's favorite Plato. (A tribute to Louisa's self-making instead of Bronson's ethereal musings?)

Anthony's biography provides a partial corrective to Meigs's, recognizing Alcott's contradictory approach and avoidance with respect to her family: "She lived for them. But she could not live with them."[82] Yet the biography is riddled with errors, as Odell Shepard pointed out in a review.[83] And Anthony is guilty of what I might call an anxiety of immaturity (so is Shepard, for that matter).

Anthony starts by proclaiming that previous biographical works, "whatever their nature and purpose, are classed as children's books" (vii). (Maybe so. Cheney's and Moses's books did tend to drift to the nursery.) But her own book, Anthony insists, "was not written for children," and indeed Alcott's life merits "consideration by adult intelligences" (vii). Later metaphors sustain the efforts to be adult: Anthony belittles the parents, Abba and Bronson, by calling them "unsuspecting infants" when it comes to family responsibility; Louisa's dislike for "the paraphernalia of adult femininity," such as hairpins, means that although "precocious in many ways, she was still childishly below her age in many others" (13, 76–77). A disinterest in hairpins is childish? Any woman's failure to subscribe to normative middle-class femininity is, in fact, one of Anthony's hobbyhorses. She tends to find it a bit perverse when women enter the labor force: she says of Alcott's mother, "Just when her family needed her attention most, she decided to go forth and become a wage-earner" (74). I might counter that just when her family was verging on starvation she decided to find a way to fend it off.

Anthony's focus on the "adult" is further sustained in her discussion of *Little Women*. For she stresses that it is a novel, by which she means to follow the nineteenth-century differentiation of novels from (children's) stories. More specifically it is a love story about Jo and Laurie: "For only a novel could achieve such abounding and enduring popularity. The story of Jo and Laurie is a gay and charming romance, with a touch of autumnal sadness in the ending which allies it with love-stories like Romeo and Juliet's" (171). Apparently, quest stories don't count as novels, nor do family stories.

In any case, Anthony finds heterosexual romance everywhere—and hence, if such love is the marker of adulthood, she justifies her "adult" interest in Alcott. Louisa, Anthony argues, fell in love with the young Pole Ladislas Wisniewski, whom she met in Europe and who would become a partial model for Laurie. Possibly so. Anthony would not be the only biographer to revel in such a view. But other romances that she posits are more idiosyncratic. She cites one of Alcott's relatives as claiming, with respect to the editor Thomas Niles, "There was some talk of a marriage between Mr. Niles and Aunt Louisa . . . but I don't think there was ever anything in it" (224). Anthony concludes, "If there was ever a romance it was a brief one" (227). (Anthony has a penchant for hinting at something a little outrageous, then partly denying it, but leaving open what she must hope is an inviting possibility.) She is even less judicious with respect to Alcott's mother, Abba with whom Anthony finds frequent fault. Most commentators portray Abba as the key force wanting to extricate Bronson from Charles Lane and the communitarian Fruitlands experiment. Anthony doesn't exactly deny that, but she notes tha Abba was the one who later wrote to invite Lane to visit and subsequently implies given that he stayed an extended time, some of it while Bronson was away, tha Abba had a love affair with the visitor. (Anthony might as well have argued tha Abba had an affair with Bronson's brother, who stayed with the family when Bronson was in England, or with any of a number of other visitors to the house hold.) Alcott's novel *Moods* (1865, rev. 1882), about a woman torn between he husband and another man, must therefore be about Abba, Bronson, and Lane The evidence is flimsy at best.

The most scholarly biography, though, and the definitive one, was Madeleine Stern's *Louisa May Alcott* (1950). Stern researched journals and letters, as wel as works that Alcott had published under pseudonyms (the sensation stories) and hard-to-locate early reviews. Her Alcotts are more complex than those of many previous biographers: the parents consider separating; Louisa doesn't want to liv in Concord. And Stern sanely sticks to available information: her Abba Alcot does not conduct a steamy love affair with Charles Lane. Reviewers praised the biography as authoritative, perhaps finding the experience of reading it "pleas antly reminiscent of one's first reading of 'Little Women,'" except that the writ ing is characterized by an "almost total absence of sentimentality," a welcome absence.[84] Even Odell Shepard, in the pages of *American Literature*, praised the

"factual information" in the book, although he would have liked more interpretation, and he continued to belabor what he viewed as Alcott's "failure to grow
up."[85]

As for the biographer Marjorie Worthington, she had "always been in love with
Jo March" and had been consciously or unconsciously gathering materials for
Miss Alcott of Concord (1958) all her life, and once she began writing, she wrote
in what Alcott would call a vortex, completely absorbed, as if inspired.[86] A fellow novelist, Worthington recognizes that Alcott may have kept leaving Orchard
House to find a "room of her own" in which to write: at home "there were too
many distractions even for a woman writer, and heaven knows most of them write
in anything but the ivory tower reserved for male authors" (185). Yet as if to carry
on the "love" theme invoked in her preface, the thrice-married Worthington wor-
ries at the possibilities for heterosexual romance. Alcott must of course have been
in love with Wisniewski (here misspelled *Wisinewsky*). Maybe he even proposed
to her. How remarkable that she never complained of her spinsterhood, especially
since she'd written "one of the immortal love stories of our time, that of Jo and
Laurie" (209). Surely Alcott regretted that she was single. Might there have been
a romance during her months in New York? Might she have sacrificed romantic
love because she was so intent on caring and providing for her mother? or because
she didn't want to burden a potential husband with the Alcott debts? In any case,
Worthington concludes, Alcott proved to be one of the best Americans, even if
not one of the greatest.

The juvenile biographies that followed Meigs's during this period were simultaneously more derivative than hers and more inventive. They hewed closely to
the norm of providing role models and to other contemporary norms for juvenile
biographies: they often focused on the subject's early years, often avoided unpleasant details, and often fictionalized their accounts.[87] These biographers tended to
shy away from exploring family difficulties, such as the possibility that the family
could have broken up at the close of the Fruitlands experiment. And all were
rather inventive with details. All invented dialogue, for instance, and were often
cavalier about historical details. Most drew on Ednah Cheney's 1889 biographical compilation of Alcott materials, but as for more recent sources, they seemed
as likely to consult a film version of the novel as to draw on a recent biography
of Alcott, with Louisa perhaps sliding down a banister, like Katharine Hepburn.

Jean Brown Wagoner becomes inventive in *Louisa Alcott, Girl of Old Boston*
(1943) when she embroiders on Alcott's comment that neighbors' chickens were
dismayed at supplying feathers for dolls' turbans: the sentence is fleshed out into
several scenes, including one in which Louisa is chased as if a chicken thief, and

outraged adults throw sticks at her. In *The Story of Louisa May Alcott* (1955), Joan Howard doesn't just mention that the Alcotts hid an escaped slave but invents a name for him and has him explain to Louisa, "You're always in a hurry to get things done. . . . I'm that way myself. That's why I ran away."[88] Indeed. And Pamela Brown (*Louisa*, 1955), even if unusually willing to address the possibility of the family's breakup, invents a rather implausible speech for Louisa. After Bronson describes the possibility of leaving the family as his "greatest act of self-denial," his daughter scolds him: "I'm tired of self-denial. I don't believe God wants us to deny ourselves things like loving each other. I think He wants us to enjoy each other—otherwise He wouldn't have given you Mother and Anna and me and the babies. And now you've *got* us, you don't want us. That's not self-denial—it's—it's just ingratitude."[89] Louisa sounds rather like a child of the 1950s, reared under the permissive regimen of Dr. Benjamin Spock.

Reissues of *Little Women*, often newly illustrated, were also popular during this period. Five relatively undistinguished editions appeared in the 1930s, but there were at least eighteen newly illustrated English-language editions published between the end of World War II and 1960. These postwar editions include a notable one illustrated by Louis Jambor (1947). His images in many ways hark back to the concerns of the thirties, often foregrounding work: the frontispiece shows the four sisters sewing, later chapter heads show Amy and Meg polishing cups or jars, and the final illustration is not the usual harvest tableau under a tree but an active scene of apple picking.[90] Other illustrators provided less active scenes. Or at least scenes with less productive activity. Hilda van Stockum (1946) was puckish depicting Aunt March's parrot grasping Amy's hair, and her illustration of the act of writing featured not Jo but a couple of her pet rats. This artist was also more likely to feature children, including Professor Bhaer playing bear, Meg's twins Daisy and Demi, and the urchins who scramble for Amy's contraband pickled limes. Van Stockum may simply have delighted in children, with six of her own, but the focus on progenitiveness was also consonant with the baby boom that began that year. The British Dorothy Colles (1954), best known for her child portraits, focused more on flowers and finery, but she also included boisterous children. Barbara Cooney (1955) tended to feature moments of discomfort—the parrot grasping Amy's hair, Jo scorching Meg's hair, Meg trying to get free of a kitten scrambling up her back, Amy's foot caught in plaster. Yet like van Stockum and Colles, she also featured children: her penultimate image does depict apple picking, but dominating the foreground is a young boy perched on a branch precariously reaching for an apple.

Other illustrators in this period focused more on clothing. Albert de Mee Jous

set (1950) delighted in drapery, whether he depicted a young woman coyly peek-
ing from under a parasol, artfully posed to reach a mailbox, preening in front of
a mirror, gracefully draped on a sofa or stile, framed by an arch of greenery at a
flower booth, or pensively leaning on a chair. The British S. Van Abbé (1948) and
the American Jill Elgin (1955) also delighted in drapery, and especially fashion.
Van Abbé seems to have found the 1933 film especially inspiring: his Amy, for
instance, is a dead ringer for Joan Bennett. The cover image for Elgin's book,
as I noted in the introduction, features a recumbent Jo out of the 1940s, but the
interior illustrations are often vigorous: in the image of Jo and Laurie dancing,
Elgin adeptly conveys the wild "swing and spring" of their polka. She had learned
well from her previous experience drawing comic strips for the Girl Commandos
and the Blonde Bomber series.

Reisie Lonette (1950) was also attentive to fashion, with an emphasis on the
quaint and charming. Her girls wear ruffles and ribbons and fashionable hats:
while scribbling in the attic, Jo poses somewhat archly, wearing a quaint mobcap
reminiscent of illustrations by the nineteenth-century Kate Greenaway. Lonette
was nevertheless more likely than other illustrators of this era to depict Jo writing
or Amy drawing. Her early image of family togetherness is looser than others'; a
later image of togetherness includes Father, returned from the war: the six family members face us from behind the piano in two rows, three lined up in back,
three in front. Their regimented lineup may hint at a greater regimentation in the
family now that Father has returned. For Elinore Blaisdell (1946) the image that
most strongly evokes family togetherness is not her early image of the four sisters,
in which Jo is singeing Meg's hair, Meg looking none too pleased, but one of the
family harmoniously clustered around the piano after Father returns. Some books
thus foregrounded the father's return, a fitting emblem at the end of World War
II. But all of these postwar illustrators, with the exception of Jambor, emphasized
traditional feminine associations, whether children or clothes. All of their works
were congruent with the postwar emphasis on domesticity and consumerism.

∽

Then there are the translations onto stage and screen. They signal—the screen
versions especially—the continuing relevance of *Little Women* even as they also
influenced how it was perceived and indeed renewed interest in the novel. The
most telling adaptations of *Little Women* in the 1930s were the 1933 RKO film and
John Ravold's 1931 dramatization for the stage; later significant milestones include
the 1949 MGM film and the 1958 television musical.

No dramatized version was particularly successful on Broadway during this
period. There were brief revivals of the de Forest play in New York in 1931, 1932,

1944, and 1945 and in London in 1941—all in December, for the holidays. There was also some talk of staging musical adaptations in the 1940s and 1950s—one called *My Little Women*, one called *Jo*—but they never made it to Broadway, at least not during these decades.[91] One did make it to London's West End, however, as I will note later.

Versions of *Little Women* continued to be staged frequently by community players in North America, especially early in the period, and perhaps as a senior-class play, especially later. For example—to choose three relatively quiet years, when film releases and other events weren't inciting special interest—in 1930 there were productions in towns or cities in Wisconsin, Illinois, Iowa, Quebec, and Pennsylvania; in 1948, in Wisconsin, Iowa, Alaska, Texas, Massachusetts, Pennsylvania, Ohio, Maryland, Maine, Washington, Utah, and North Carolina; in 1958, in Utah, Michigan, Tennessee, and Colorado.[92]

Dramatic versions were staged frequently in the United Kingdom as well, especially during and soon after World War II, if one can judge by the frequency of notices in the British Newspaper Archive—some as community or repertory productions, some as roadshow offerings from London. Notices make no mention of the Civil War setting of the novel or the home front but do suggest that the performances were popular.[93] It's nevertheless plausible that the focus on a family thriving despite privation during wartime contributed to the popularity. A columnist in Derby commented on the crowds of schoolgirls in the audience and also, "strange as it may seem, quite a number of men in uniform."[94] These men to the contrary, the prevalence of women and the young in the available audience and as available actors—because less likely to be "called to the Colours"[95]—probably contributed to the popularity of productions of *Little Women*.

Even as de Forest's version continued to be performed, a spate of new dramatizations appeared in the first dozen years of this period, including plays by John Ravold (1931), Roger Wheeler (1934), Arthur Jearue (1939), Pauline Phelps (1939), Sara Spencer (1940), and Kristin Laurence (1941); a couple more followed in the next couple of decades. Many of these playwrights, like subsequent ones, foreground romance, sometimes speed-dating through the various couplings, and often diminish Jo's independence and writing. In response to Aunt March's offer of Plumfield at the end of one play, an uncharacteristically submissive Jo demurely responds, "That is for my Professor to decide."[96] This playwright also adds touches that emphasize religion: her Marmee, unlike Alcott's, inscribes Bible verses in New Testaments that she gives the girls for Christmas. Other writers add some modern touches: maybe Amy smuggles lime candy to school instead of pickled limes. The writers also generally try to incorporate as many incidents from the novel as possible, the prefabricated press release for one claiming "more of the beloved elements in the book than any other [motion picture or play] that has ever been offered."[97] The more incidents from the novel that a play crams in, the more it nevertheless seems to evade strong feelings: in one play, there is no burnt manuscript for Jo to forgive; in another, Amy still falls through the ice, but she knew the middle of the river wasn't safe for skating, so Jo is less culpable.

The most intriguing new stage version, frequently performed during the next few years and still sometimes staged, was John Ravold's. He too foregrounds the romances and works in the incidents that readers of Alcott's *Little Women* are most likely to remember. He too de-emphasizes self-sacrifice and the weaknesses that each girl must overcome. Amy still burns Jo's manuscript, but because of romantic jealousy—"Laurie told me he loved you more than me," she tells Jo—this after a scene in which Amy and Laurie stagily fold a blanket together, repeatedly *"fold[ing] it toward the middle and each time they almost kiss."*[98] Jo regrets her intemperate response to the loss of her manuscript within seconds; it's Amy whose contrition isn't expressed till the end of the act. So Jo's anger and pride are not particularly targeted for change; instead Amy's romantic jealousy is key.

As for the relationship between marriage and independence, Ravold, like de Forest, includes Marmee's strictures on not marrying for riches while omitting her advice that it is better to be a happy old maid than an unhappy wife. Indeed, his Marmee has earlier said, "Take Mother's advice and marry some worthy man and make homes for yourselves and get something more than selfishness out of life" (I, 29): Alcott's encouragement of self-sacrifice has devolved into strictures on not remaining a selfish old maid like Aunt March.

Yet Ravold also increases the incoherence of the relationship between marriage and independence by advocating not just marriage but also careers, with dialogue that diverges radically from Alcott's. Aunt March becomes a supporter of careers for women: when she critiques a rehearsal of Jo's Christmas play for its "deplorable state of imperfection," we could dismiss her as simply curmudgeonly, but she may instead be encouraging artistic development, since she later claims credit for Jo's success ("I had to drive her to [succeed] when she was younger") and indeed for Jo's not prematurely marrying "some local yokel, and hav[ing] a baby or two to interfere with her career" (I, 25; III, 71). It's also Aunt March who seems intent on Amy's developing her artistic bent, noting a teacher's report of the girl's "great talent" in drawing and adding, "If you improve, I promise to send you to Europe when you are ready" (I, 29). Minutes later Amy would almost seem to be refuting Aunt March when she says to Laurie, "I think a girl should be a girl, for then she's preparing her life for marriage and motherhood" (I, 30).

In the next act Amy states that she is "to leave for Rome to study painting under the masters"—so perhaps she has indeed been applying herself—but we may well wonder to what end when she adds, "Mr. La[u]rence informed Aunt March he was sending Laurie to Europe next month" (II, 51). Unlike Alcott's Amy, Ravold's has known her true vocation—Laurie—all along. As for Jo, the play ends with Professor Bhaer's proposal and includes no mention of how or whether she might continue her writing.

Particularly memorable are Ravold's anachronistic additions. The stage directions for act 3 indicate that it takes place in 1866. Yet Meg blithely broaches her discussion of marital difficulties by telling Marmee she's "contemplating a divorce" (III, 61)—hardly a common action in the 1860s, and certainly not something Meg would allude to so casually. Later Meg prattles to her husband about reelecting Lincoln president, and Brooke chides her for confusing Andrew Jackson and Andrew Johnson when speaking of a running mate but not—it's 1866, after all—for resurrecting a corpse. And while it's plausible to make a reference to the invention credited to Morse (the March family in Alcott's novel receives a telegram), it's a decade too early to refer to that credited to Bell. Another remarkable addition is the attribution of an extraordinary little jingle to a visiting Ralph Waldo Emerson. It comprises "ten verses of pithy humour" (III, 76), we are told, although Mr. March reads only two couplets:

> There was an old man very rosy and fat
> Who continually wore a high beaver hat.
>
> . . . .
>
> And there was an old maid very thin and prim
> Who was casting amourous glances at him. (III, 77)

It doesn't even scan well. Ravold's version has continued to be produced in recent decades, but in at least one production, at the University of Albuquerque in 1966, actors performed it as high camp.[99]

Ravold's dramatization is unusual for the extent to which it amalgamates modern chic and a jumble of things past. But its heightened artifice simply underscores the nostalgia constructed by all of the dramatic incarnations of *Little Women*. All create a lavender-scented bygone New England. Ravold's play, in particular, perpetuates the conflation of the Marches and the Alcotts and highlights the Concord connection, in this case by bringing Emerson to the household, an Emerson who has authored a frivolous jingle. Both revered and belittled, this Emerson emblematizes the workings of nostalgia, in which the past becomes simple; the natural, artificial; the transcendent, oddly jocular; the authentic, a replica.

In 1940 Ravold's script became the book for an operetta. This version, with lyrics by Frederick Howard and music by Geoffrey O'Hara, has been pared of Ravold's worst solecisms: there's no mention of divorce, no Lincoln as current candidate, no jingle by Emerson. Much of Ravold's earlier dialogue remains (with the addition of a brief scene or two from the RKO film), but instead of highlighting the Concord connections, the operetta foregrounds American ones. At this time when the country was facing the possibility of yet another war, Professor Bhaer's German background is finessed by having him enthuse about having become a citizen and indeed having fought in the Civil War under Grant—whereupon the company sings a patriotic "America, Thou Blessed Land."

As with many musicals, the romances (and their associated duets) are prominent, although Jo's "If I Were Only a Man" provides some counterpoint to the saccharine. So do several numbers featuring Aunt March, whose feminism is here largely omitted; instead she fills the role of the feisty female of midcentury Broadway musicals. She sings, "Highty, Tighty, . . . How could you have joy as a poor fellow's wife?" and "It's All Just a Matter of Opinion . . . I'm a pessimist . . . what ever comes, I'm seldom disappointed."[100] In the penultimate song she celebrates Amy's marrying Laurie: Marmee may have earlier stated that "happiness can be had in a plain home" (II, 77), but the song "You Can Love a Man with Money" is rather more memorable. Its ironic lyrics include

Choose a man above your station
With real cash, not imitation,
Folks have died of slow starvation,
So you're better off with gout. (III, 133)

Frivolousness has given way to irony, simultaneously celebrating and satirizing gold digging.

⸻

The most memorable artifact of the 1930s, the most significant homage to Alcott, was the 1933 RKO film. It was enormously popular when it was released. Exhibitors early on may have been concerned whether it would "appeal to the hey-hey modernes—the 18 to 25 year old gang which seems to be yelling for something snappy, spectacular and jolting in all its entertainment," but in New York the film played to "unheard of audiences at the Music Hall in Radio City, breaking all-time attendance record of this gigantic playhouse"; "on the 16th day an enterprising press agent snapped a picture of a crowd four or five deep and more than five blocks long waiting to get into that enormous theater to see it."[101] It was "a 'sensation' in Dubuque," "played five weeks in Seattle, with nothing but standing room on the last day of its engagement," and broke records in Boston and in Milwaukee, where the newspaper reported that "the squad cars had to be called to get order out of the lines"; indeed, it left a "trail of broken box-office records . . . across the country."[102] It tied for fourth place among the highest-grossing films of 1933.[103] The movie may not have won the Academy Award for best picture, but it did win a public poll for best picture of the year conducted by *Photoplay*.[104] The public loved it.

Like the 1912 Broadway play, the film version "depends upon atmosphere and characterization and not upon action or movement."[105] In 1932 the studio polled the public as to whether the story should be modernized or its original setting and action should be retained: the votes were no to modernization, apparently three to one.[106] So RKO made sure to stress the authenticity of its reproduction of Concord and especially Orchard House—the film promised to be "one of the most authentic productions ever filmed in Hollywood," according to one columnist.[107] The director George Cukor later noted being pleased that the set designer Hobe Irwin "made no chi-chi. . . . We reproduced the Louisa May Alcott house with great taste and detail."[108] The studio publicized its care in re-creating the wall-paper at Orchard House, the furniture, the pictures on the walls, even the uniform of an 1864 messenger boy.[109] The costume designer detailed his careful research through issues of *Godey's Lady's Book*, his staff's sandpapering of cuffs to make them look worn, Jo's relative shabbiness compared with the rest of the sisters, Amy's "pathetic attempt at chic" early on with her odd bits of bric-a-brac.[110] By playing up the idea of authenticity, the studio was able to satisfy the public's interest "in the biographical form of story, in early American life, in antiques and Victorian dress."[111] The film also provided Christmas-card photo-ops of New England in winter: "The glimpses of the snow-covered ground of Concord . . . are depicted so naturally that one is apt to think of them as being real instead of studio-made."[112] In short, *Little Women* was a "nostalgic triumph," one of RKO's "most important" movies, "revitaliz[ing] interest in the 'classics' and in costume pictures."[113]

The screenwriters Sarah Y. Mason and Victor Heerman, who won an Academy Award for their adaptation, inevitably telescoped some elements of the book: the dance that Jo and Meg attend is not at the Gardners' but next door at the Laurences', and it's Aunt March who takes Amy to Europe, not Aunt Carroll, who can therefore be eliminated. The writers also avoided imposing a rising plot on the material: in Cukor's words, "It wasn't slicked up. . . . No plottiness."[114] Cukor's idea of adaptation was that, in the words of a biographer, "the essence of the original should determine the film's style," retaining "a book's weaknesses and strengths."[115] Not tying things together retained "the book's vitality" (76).

Cukor presumably vetoed a version of the script "in which Jo's novel becomes a smash success" because he wanted "to present a less idealized view" (76). He also retained Beth's trajectory of illness–recovery–illness–invalidism–death despite his sense of its awkwardness. When technical difficulties required twenty takes of Katharine Hepburn's Jo weeping at Beth's deathbed, and the actress finally turned aside and vomited out of frustration, Cukor said, "Well, that's what I think of the scene, too" (77). But he retained it. Mason and Heerman also adroitly compressed dialogue: Alcott's Aunt March referring to John Brooke as variously "this Cook," "this Rook," "your Mr. Book" (Alcott 181–82) becomes "this Rook or Hook or Crook." Alcott's references subordinate him with respect to class and cheating; Mason and Heerman reduce the class references by eliminating "Cook" and underscore what Aunt March perceives as Brooke's finagling to get at Meg's potential wealth, by hook or by crook. The film medium, like the stage, readily enabled visual actions to amplify themes and characterization, but it also allowed more scene changes (the screenwriters didn't have to try to stage most of the action in the March family parlor). The cinematic version could underscore Jo's tomboyishness by having her slide down a banister at Aunt March's house.

Overall the screenplay tones down the moral messages, while playing up Jo's tomboyish independence and quirkiness. There may be a sacrifice of a Christmas breakfast, as in the book, but there are no Vanity Fair temptations for Meg to overcome, no burning of Jo's manuscript, and indeed no temper that Jo needs to tame. Professor Bhaer does criticize Jo's writing of popular sensation stories, yet not because they're morally degrading but because they have "such artificial characters, such artificial plots, villains, murderers and—and such women."[116] Well, okay, there is the suggestiveness of "such women." But his primary objection seems to be an aesthetic one: artificiality. Bhaer reassures Jo that she has talent but says that she should focus on "the simple, beautiful things" that she knows (304). And the excuse that later brings him to visit her in Concord is the chance to give her a copy of her book—"such truth, such simple beauty" (318)—just published by a friend of his.

As for tomboyish independence—Hepburn's Jo, unlike Alcott's, dusts Aunt March's banister by sliding down it, neatly leaps a fence, and also fences with Laurie almost as soon as she meets him. These activities would have been improprieties in the 1860s even for Alcott's Jo—never mind later going to the opera with Professor Bhaer without a chaperone, as Hepburn's Jo does—so there are attempts to modernize. Marmee may not deliver a better-to-be-happy-old-maids speech, but Jo's greater physical freedom, at least early in the film, becomes an embodied metaphor for freedom for women. Indeed, after the obligatory outdoor views of New England in winter that begin all the major film versions, the film turns not to Christmas-won't-be-Christmas-without-any-presents but to showing the employment of each March woman: Marmee working at a war-relief center, Meg as a governess, Jo reading to Aunt March, Amy at school, Beth at home. Molly Haskell has noted that in the thirties and forties the screen showed "more working women, from trucking company CEOs to Macy's shopgirls," than in the seventies and eighties.[117] And work is indeed prominent in this film. Even at the end, Jo's prospective husband would seem to approve of her writing, enabling its publication.

To some degree Jo's tomboyishness is contained by her propensity to fall down, especially early on, and especially to show lots of crinoline. The novel and some dramatic versions have her fall while demonstrating to Amy how to faint onstage. The cinematic Jo falls there and elsewhere: she slips on ice while walking (instead of simply being reprimanded by Meg for running); she tumbles while fencing with Laurie.[118] Falling functions complexly, showing Jo's awkwardness and her imperfect attempts at boyishness, while also—those glimpses of crinoline—enabling her to be subjected to a sexualized gaze.

For, of course, like most adaptations of *Little Women*, this one foregrounds romance: Cukor claimed that there was "no love interest until the last quarter of the picture" (59), yet as Jonathan Kuntz later noted of the tamer identities that the girls take on as they mature, "Desire has been channeled into romance and legitimized through marriage."[119] Certainly some advance notices played up romantic expectations. One referred to the novel as "the favorite love story of generations of America."[120] Another called the film "today's favorite romance" and added an exclamation that must have been boilerplate, given the inapplicability to *Little Women*: "A lilac tree, a waterfall and youth aflame!"[121]

Not only was the film popular with the general public, as I've noted, but reviewers were enthusiastic too: *Little Women* was "a perfect picture," "an amazing triumph," "one of the outstanding productions of the year," "one of the most delightful films of these many years," "a masterpiece of Americana," "a swell picture."[122] Even "one of the finest pictures ever made. Hock your watch and take the whole family."[123] In Britain, E. V. Lucas claimed that the film was "one of the most satisfactory pictures I have ever seen."[124]

Reviewers were especially enthusiastic about the authenticity of the setting, the direction of Cukor, and the acting of Hepburn, who "demonstrates her greatness more emphatically in this picture than in anything she has yet done."[125] Sometimes Alcott, Cukor, and Hepburn receive equal credit for the film's success.[126] Sometimes more kudos go to Cukor: this "story about four sisters of a relatively quite sentimental generation could have become a thoroughly wishy-washy picture," but Cukor's "characteristic fine taste and restraint . . . kept all of the proceedings credible and free from mawkishness."[127] Cukor, who later won an Academy Award for directing *My Fair Lady*, thought *Little Women* the picture for which he most deserved an Oscar.[128]

"The best of the many 'depression films,'" one critic wrote, the movie "has a relevance for an American audience today that it would not have had ten or even five years ago," since it can be read as "an allegory of the transcendental virtues triumphant over material emergencies."[129] The sisters "live a life that leaps over all boundaries of poverty and circumstance," another reported.[130] In Britain a writer speculated that the spectacular success of the film in the United States might have been a reaction against modern impersonality, that viewers had turned with relief to a portrayal of poverty that was nevertheless placed in "a world of stable values and sheltered family life, where simple human feelings—joys, sorrows and affections—are all-important."[131] An American situated the book as a response to "the depression of the Civil War."[132] Recent critics suggest that the film simultaneously invokes poverty (not a "biting poverty," though) and offers many of the escapist pleasures of the costume drama.[133] It's a poverty without "bread lines and Hoovervilles" but rather bathed in "the comfortable glow of nostalgia."[134]

Many contemporary commentators, however, reduced the complexity of "the age of *Little Women*" (of its setting? its time of writing?) to nostalgic simplicity. The film was praised for evoking "a much simpler, and strangely happy time," the "simple family life" of "the era which made America great," or both film and novel might be associated with the "simpler days" of childhood.[135] As in responses to the 1912 play, critics found in the production "a true and convincing picture of what we like to believe a typical American home."[136] The characters and "the snug New England town in which they live," another reviewer claimed, are "touched by the sentimental melancholy which surrounds things that happened long ago"; or the film portrays "wholesome, sentimentally warm life in an earlier and simpler America."[137]

Simplicity, typicality, sentimental melancholy—the film is nostalgic. One enthusiastic reviewer called it "unique in its well nigh plush album re-creation of other days."[138] Another urged, "The picture should go into the archives of Americana because it preserves something precious in our tradition that can never come back again."[139] Tallulah Bankhead "sobbed uncontrollably" upon seeing a rough cut of the film; Cukor told her, "You are weeping for your own lost innocence," and explained that the film allowed adults "to relive nostalgically the period of their own youth."[140] Or perhaps the youth of the nation: "It lavishes its sentimentalism not only upon the family tie but also upon country and flag."[141] A critic could be so overcome by nostalgia as to seem to be reviewing an entirely different production, anticipating 1939's *Gone with the Wind*: "Romantic glories of the 'Sixties, days when women were dainty as well as beautiful, and men bowed with the grace of knighthood, are brought back in 'Little Women.'"[142] Another critic, who called the settings and costumes "quaint and authentic," didn't stop to tease out the tensions between the two terms, how quaintness suggests a nostalgia likely to be at odds with historical accuracy.[143] Only four decades later would a critic recognize the complexity of these intertwining themes: "The rich contradictory sense of family—the guilt, rivalry and undying loyalty—is deftly conveyed by George Cukor whose detailed direction blends irony with humor and nostalgia."[144]

As for the dangers of sentimentality, one reviewer found that the book's "sweetness has been preserved but . . . becomes suffocating."[145] Yet most reviewers were more positive regarding the film's evocation of sentiment, even when they were less positive about the novel. The critic for the *Nation* suggested that it has "long been the custom to refer to Louisa M. Alcott's masterpiece as the classic expression of a certain kind of American sentimentalism" but went on to review the film positively.[146] A critic who accused Alcott of "sugared sentimentality" found the film redeemed by "the truly excellent cast . . . set against the perfect background."[147] One proclaimed, "The electric Kate disturbs the Alcott tradition," given that "graceful feminine Jos . . . would have satisfied the preconceived type," but Hepburn "strips the Victorian hoyden of her too syrupy goody-goodiness."[148] In other words, the "saccharine narrative 'Little Women' was Katharine Hepburned into the ten best films of the year."[149] Indeed, Hepburn's Jo "skirts the dangerous edges of sentimentality" or "puts a firm edge on sentiment" or "raises what might have been an over-sentimental cry-fest into art."[150] "This generation has come to think of Louisa M. Alcott as a sentimentalist," another stated, adding, "But there is less sentimentality in the tears shed while watching her 'Little Women' than there is in the laughter induced by Miss West's vulgarities and rhythmical hip movements—if by sentimentality we mean that which emanates from an exaggerated and false emotion. The first is a natural reaction to fundamental sensations and the other a cultivated pose."[151] More recently a commentator has stated that the screenplay "captures the essence of Miss Alcott's novel with fidelity and without mawkishness."[152] Yet some modern viewers disagree. Some find Hepburn's performance mannered or stagy: Janet Maslin calls the film "badly dated."[153] But another recent critic argues that such apparent "'unnaturalness' exactly coincides . . . with the moment at which the contradictions within the ideological project become available": when Hepburn's star presence and independence start to acquiesce to patriarchy, the "'natural' awakening of 'femininity'" is "disturbingly denaturalized."[154]

Contemporary critics sometimes addressed the ways in which book and film did speak to independence for women, certainly more often than critics of the drama had two decades earlier. After all, the film's rising star, Katharine Hepburn, who had trailed her parents to suffrage rallies as a child, was becoming an icon of trousered independence. The film version also created more visual evocations of independence—the fences and fencing—than the play had. One reviewer suggested that Hepburn exaggerated Jo's mannishness.[155] But another exclaimed that "nowhere in all literature can be found a girl quite like Jo!"—"long, gangly, bemused, fiery Jo."[156] More recently, Andrew Britton has traced the complex ways in which Hepburn's Jo channels her opposition to patriarchy and then regulates female desire not just through a final heterosexual coupling but also through the example of Beth. Jo eventually speaks an aside to a heavenly Beth—"Fun, isn't it, Bethy?"—when the family is reunited, "addressing her in preference to the Father, and appears to be set, in the face of divine interdiction, to recreate the previous disposition of the family."[157] Which is to say, a woman-centered one.

As for reception overseas, one report was that the film was only moderately successful in Germany, but the *Washington Post* claimed that it "was shown to capacity houses in every capital of Europe."[158] A report from Britain suggested that "grandmothers and mothers, and the younger generations all flocked to see it."[159] According to a story recounted in a New Zealand newspaper, the film magnate Samuel Goldwyn told an assistant, "'Little Women' is a swell picture. Chase this Louisa Alcott dame; maybe she can write us some more stuff."[160] The writer gets in a dig at Goldwyn but also speaks to the popularity of the film.

Individual exhibitors were still finding creative ways to publicize films, and *Little Women* had "a background worth plenty of dough to exhibitors in the way of tie-ups and community support," according to a trade paper.[161] Theaters sponsored coloring contests for children, invited teachers and community leaders to a preview showing, or offered a special matinee to benefit civic groups.[162] One cosponsored a full-page newspaper ad with local businesses, urging that "little women" need properly fitted shoes or healthy milk products or scientifically produced cosmetics, or maybe the "little woman" can bring her better half to look at proper and comfortable furniture.[163] A number of newspapers published a series of six three- or four-frame comic strips drawn from images in the film.[164]

But there weren't as many merchandising tie-ins for this picture as there would be for subsequent ones. An edition of the novel—or rather a redaction of the film, beginning not with the sisters cozily at home but with Civil War soldiers marching through Concord, as the film does—featured still photographs on alternate pages. Like other novelizations, *Louisa M. Alcott's Little Women* (1934) relies heavily on available stills, repurposing them in unusual parts of the novel; the sequence of images becomes particularly incoherent in the vicinity of Beth's illness, as if to avoid the taint of sentimentality, depicting, say, Jo at Aunt March's (using an image from the beginning of the film) at a point when there's no mention in the text of Jo's going there. (A 1936 French redaction, entitled *Les quatre sœurs Marsch*, was similarly cavalier with the placement of stills.) The film sparked sales of all of Alcott's books, an increase found surprising at the time.[165] The National Council of Teachers of English was quick to capitalize on this popularity and distribute a study guide for the film to, presumably, 17,956 high schools.[166]

The film also sparked other interests: in visiting Orchard House, in re-creating Joan Bennett's hairstyle for young girls, and in embroidery (misremembering that "the heroines of the book embroidered samplers").[167] Madame Alexander, as I've already noted, began creating Little Women dolls in 1933, but she doesn't appear to have been licensed by the producers of the film—and she wouldn't have needed to be, as long as she was basing her dolls on a novel in the public domain. Accounts of fall 1933 fashions may allude to *Little Women* when noting a current vogue for pinafores and for velveteen dresses with striped taffeta bows, or for evening gowns of ribbed crepe, but a reporter would use *Little Women* as a marker for "the days when Louisa Alcott heroines were leading ladylike existences" rather than noting a direct tie-in with the film.[168]

One spinoff of the film was a parodic Jack Benny radio skit called "Miniature Women." Mary Livingstone mimics Hepburn's drawl, and the skit also pokes fun at Jo's writing: she writes poetry in a hencoop and produces flatfooted verse ("Fifteen years, fifteen years we have been together, rain or shine, all the time, in fair or sloppy weather"). The skit deflates Hepburn/Jo and constrains the potential for independent womanhood when Livingstone turns down her millionaire neighbor Tom's proposal, declaiming, "I am a genius," and adds, "The man I marry must be middle aged."[169] Yet since "parody always implicitly reinforces even as it ironically debunks,"[170] the skit is a tribute as well. In order to appreciate the parody, one needs some familiarity with the book or the film, directly or by hearsay; in rewarding the "insider," someone in the know, the skit celebrates knowing *Little Women*.

∽

The postwar period marked a return to domesticity as a nation, or more precisely, a turn to a new kind of domesticity: the home became a "psychological fortress," a buffer against the aftermaths of the Depression and World War II and now the Cold War. The period engendered "the first wholehearted effort to create a home that would fulfill virtually all its members' personal needs."[171] And it witnessed a resurgent emphasis on domesticity among purveyors of and respondents to *Little Women*. The most widely visible responses to *Little Women* at this time were film and televised versions.

The 1949 MGM film drew on the 1933 one, re-using much dialogue (the screenwriters Mason and Heerman were joined in the credits by Andrew Solt) and many stage sets. But this film foregrounded Technicolored fashion, commodities, and shopping, and it was less episodic, the plot more streamlined. (When June Allyson's Jo returns home from New York, for instance, she tells Meg that she and the Professor write to each other and that she is about to send him her book manuscript—thus rationalizing the published book that, in both film versions, he brings her at the end.) In the words of George Cukor, "The later version made the mistake of slicking it up"; and as Carol Gay adds, "'Slicking it up' tends to force the girls' adventures on the pathway to finding husbands."[172]

As for shopping, just as Marmee is producing a letter from Father at the front, Aunt March arrives, bringing gifts of Christmas money. So instead of listening to this longed-for letter, the girls run off to shop at a general store. They browse first for themselves, perhaps coyly trying on a hat, but decide to get gifts for Marmee instead; the camera then lingers on these gifts proudly displayed under a Christmas tree. Consumerism may eventually be corralled in the service of family, in a proud display, but it curiously delays what in other versions of the story becomes an iconic scene of family togetherness.

Like the 1933 film, this one downplays moralizing; it has also become more reticent about what might be deemed potentially erotic. When Beth goes to thank Mr. Laurence for his gift of a piano, she does kiss him on the cheek but, in a medium-close shot, is less clearly sitting on his lap than in the 1933 film. Bhaer no longer excoriates Jo's writing for including portrayals of "such women," that suggestive phrase, but for depicting "fainting women." And in New York Jo and the Professor are not constantly in and out of each other's rooms; indeed, there's no indication that Bhaer is ever in hers.

Allyson's Jo is also less rambunctious than Hepburn's—no sliding down the banister at Aunt March's, no spilling food on her dress at the party, no fencing when she and Laurie meet. Instead she scorches her skirt at this meeting, giving Peter Lawford's Laurie a chance to pat out the sparks, in effect a spanking. In both cases—the fencing and the scorching—Jo falls and her skirt slips up, in Hepburn's case showing the viewer a little too much petticoat and pantalettes; in

Allyson's, showing them to Laurie, who quickly pulls down the skirt and resumes the spanking. The result is a repositioning of a kind of mild violence not as fencing between equals but as rescue and erotic subordination.

Yet Allyson's Jo, like Hepburn's, does clamber down a trellis and does attend the opera with Bhaer unchaperoned. And she leaps over fences, although the first time she tries to do so she falls, giving her watching sisters a chance to titter. Indeed, that's the opening action — not, as in the 1933 film, the scenes of Marmee and her daughters at work. Jo may get up and try again, but still the pratfall frames how we're to view her boyishness: it's not an extension of working or, as in the case of Hepburn's successful slide down the banister in her opening scene, a kind of subversion of authority (refashioning the domestic work of dusting). Nor do scenes of the March women's work feature elsewhere in the 1949 film. Meg and Jo talk of starting work soon, as a governess and a companion, but we do not see them doing such work. (We briefly glimpse Jo's work later as a governess in New York, a scene retained from the earlier film but moved to bedtime, when she tells — or the child tells her — the Goldilocks story. In short, it's not clear who is doing the work here.) In the postwar world of 1949, women's work is deferred. Or maybe Jo can write; she does, after all, finally write a novel, one titled *My Beth*. But the value of writing is at least somewhat diminished. Jo's remuneration for a story, her first, is now $1.00 instead of $1.50, and upon seeing the check Laurie complains about her cooping herself up in the attic to write instead of spending time with him, all for "one measly little dollar." He does not, as in 1933, proclaim her "the celebrated American authoress" (263). The change justifies her later claim that one reason she won't marry him is that "you hate my scribbling." But it also contributes to the film's overall devaluing and containing of women's work.

To judge by the reports in the media, this film was not as popular as the 1933 one; there are no accounts of standing room only or needing to get out squad cars. But it nevertheless tied for tenth place among the top-grossing films in 1949.[173] Reviewers were not especially enthusiastic. The most positive ones stated that the director, Mervyn LeRoy, successfully "bring[s] to life once more the faded sentiments and the tintyped situations" or that, given a plotless story dealing with "the trivial affairs which make up family life," the film "is something approaching a triumph," or at least "leaves you content. And this is its peculiar magic."[174] Bosley Crowther praised the early scenes for portraying "substantially the sort of glee and humor that Miss Alcott originally described," yet later, he noted, the film becomes maudlin.[175] No one proclaimed this *Little Women* the best picture of the year or urged anyone to hock the family jewels to see it.

Negative responses were legion. Reviewers compared the March sisters to "cardboard figures in an old family album" or called them "exquisite puppets that strike high emotional attitudes instead of the lively, wholesome females of a still fresh and winning children's book."[176] Some praised June Allyson, perhaps attributing to her "a refreshing breeziness and bounce"; or maybe she wasn't "the true tomboyish Jo that Hepburn was," but she was still "an interesting and an effervescent character."[177] Others, however, found her "a tissue-brained Jo," "pretty good at working up convulsive sobbing fits," or "a selfish, possessive, conceited and tyrannical little baggage, given to outbursts of tears when she cannot get her own way, but having little warmth."[178] Crowther wasn't alone in thinking that "she can't hold a bayberry candle to the Jo of Katharine Hepburn."[179]

Sentiment and nostalgia were frequently invoked. Sometimes more or less positively, as when a reviewer claimed that scenes evoked "the subdued dignity of Currier and Ives prints" or noted that Allyson successfully "walk[ed] a narrow chalkline between sentiment and sentimentality."[180] But others found the film "sweet and cloying," "a sentimental Technicolored Valentine," the settings "candy-hued," the house "a Technicolored dream house of the Eighteen Sixties American school," the "eyes glisten[ing], Murine-filled, flesh glow[ing] with funeral parlor falsity"; and the costuming made "Marmee March's brave little alpaca-clad brood . . . [look] like very flossy ladies of fashion. (Never mind that the Civil War is raging.)"[181] One who refers to Alcott's novel as a tearjerker describes the final scene of the film, emblematic of the whole, thus: "A pastel, picture-postcard rainbow rises out of the subsiding suds and sentiments to arch the happy ending."[182] If the 1933 film had a critic "sniffling furtively . . . this one left me dry-eyed."[183]

In Japan in 1950, on the other hand, the film was praised as portraying "noble sentimentality." The U.S. Central Motion Picture Exchange promoted it as "literary and artistic" more than a "woman's film"—the latter was stressed in marketing in the United States—though it touted the emphasis on family unity as well. *Little Women* did quite well in the theaters, showing in a Tokyo theater for a full month.[184]

More recent critics generally find the 1949 film the least successful of the three major Hollywood versions, often because of its "primary emphasis on the romance plot"[185] and its foregrounding of consumerism. It's a "syrupy Christmas-card remake," "remembered chiefly because it featured Elizabeth Taylor as Amy, wearing a blond wig," with Christmas an occasion for two shopping sprees, marking out "the national female pastime for the next decade."[186] Carol Gay points to the downplaying of the Civil War context and the Marches' poverty and the turn instead to "hilarity and cuteness," with Concord resembling "an Oz populated by pretty people."[187] The main demurral to such a reading comes from Pat Kirkham and Sarah Warren, who argue that the film should be seen at least in part as belonging to the genre of the Hollywood musical and that it offers a "critique by humour" of fashionable femininity, deeming Taylor's Amy especially parodic.[188] They seem to be picking up on cues offered by Anne Hollander, who suggested that the 1944 musical *Meet Me in St. Louis* set the tone for the performances of several actors who appeared in both films—borrowing "a warm spirit of family harmony sustained by music, not morality." She also noted that, "as usual for a film from this period, every head is forever perfectly coiffed, and the girls' faces are thoroughly made up."[189] Given this context, it may be difficult to read the girls' fashionable perfection as parody. Still, the exaggerated performances of femininity do lend themselves to a camp reading: for a recent French critic, "Le sans-gêne du sous-texte lesbian m'étonnera toujours" (The casual lesbian subtext always astonishes me).[190]

This film was accompanied by extensive cross-merchandising, thus extending the endorsement of consumerism beyond the screen. Newspaper advertisements featured Little Women coats, Little Women dolls, a Little Women scarf featuring scenes from the film, even milk—as enjoyed by Margaret O'Brien (Beth) and Elizabeth Taylor (Amy).[191] One newspaper account noted that the Little Women were selling "soap and breakfast foods"; indeed, "just one tie-up, for example— Hallmark's 'Little Women' greeting-card dolls—gave the film producers access to some 15,000 greeting-card counters and display windows in department stores, gift and greeting card shops."[192]

As for televised redactions, 1958 marked the production of a television musical version of *Little Women* (CBS), most notable for the fact that Beth doesn't die. Previous musical renditions included Eleanor Everest Freer's *Scenes from Little Women* (1934), the 1940 Ravold revision discussed earlier in this chapter, and a 1955 production in London of *A Girl Called Jo*; the first foregrounds courtship scenes and offers music with predictable lyrics ("Oh, Marmee! dear Marmee!/Don't cry, don't cry/'Cause Daddy must not die!"), and reviews of the last were "generally indifferent," including one that called it "neither good Alcott nor good musical."[193] None of these musicals were memorable.

By 1958 there had also been at least seven nonmusical televised versions in English, ranging from a production of Marian de Forest's 1912 play, broadcast by NBC in 1939, to a six-episode BBC production in 1958.[194] The postwar years were a fertile time for broadcasting versions of *Little Women*. In keeping with the postwar turn to the home, the domesticity portrayed in the novel was generally highlighted. Broadcasting a domestic drama, furthermore, might be construed as

Little Women, the scarf—with Margaret, June, Elizabeth, and Janet
Scarf, 1949, from the author's collection.

helping to domesticate television. TV was advertised as a way of bringing the family together, promoting harmony,[195] much as all had clustered around the radio a
decade or two before or, earlier, around the kerosene lamp as a family member
read out loud. Furthermore, as advocates of the new medium of television sought
acceptance, they would not be averse to claiming some of the status of what could
be considered classic texts, much as early film producers had done. An ideal text
would be a classic that fostered domestic values.

The 1958 musical was the TV version that made the biggest splash. Several
months before the broadcast, the composer-lyricist Richard Adler, known for his
Tony Award–winning music for the Broadway successes *The Pajama Game* and
Damn Yankees, casually mentioned in an interview that he hadn't really wanted
to do *Little Women*: "There's no story really except Beth's illness. In the movie she
dies; in the book she doesn't." He added, "I'll probably catch it from the public
for not letting her die but if we're going to get belted we might as well catch it
for sticking to what Louisa May Alcott intended."[196] He had apparently consulted
only part 1 before going into production, and indeed part 1 is all that the program

addresses. And he did catch it. Some shouted, "Kill Dick Adler."[197] Or perhaps it was a telephone respondent for the agency producing the film who claimed, "We're going to let Beth live and kill Dick Adler."[198] The sponsor's advertising agency claimed that 98 percent of Americans "remembered" that Beth died.[199] The sponsor asked Adler to reconsider, given that "an angry public is not a buying public," and he presumably responded, "Beth dies over my dead body." Yet he eventually figured out that it's only in the first volume of the book that Beth survives, and then he claimed that in a single hour "there isn't time to go into the 'Good Wives' part."[200] Columnists had great fun with the interchanges, noting, for instance, the irony that "the ones who wrote letters clamoring for the demise of Beth were those who loved her most."[201]

Aside from the matter of Beth's death, Adler took a number of other liberties. Part of the challenge was choosing which incidents to include in an hour-long program that was, furthermore, a musical: any forward action in the plot would be slowed frequently to accommodate the musical numbers. When Marmee reads a letter from Father, singing "The Letter," that's fine. But then there's the number "Dance, Why Not?" Of course, a musical would have to include the book's early dance scene, a spectacle that had also received attention in the 1933 and 1949 films. Yet it's curious that the number focuses on Mr. Laurence teaching Amy to dance. (Amy didn't go to the ball in Alcott's novel, nor indeed was the ball at the Laurences', although both changes appear in the two midcentury films, which Adler had referred to in an interview; he may have been working from the films as much as from the novel.) Meg is more waspish in Adler's version than in the novel: she, not Amy, is the one who tells Jo that she "detest[s] rude, unladylike girls."[202] Yet perhaps Meg peremptorily orders Jo around to facilitate the introduction of Jo singing, "I'm the man of the family." Jo responds, in the song, by ordering her sisters around and demanding respect ("bring my slippers double quick," and they'd better "scrape and bow" to her). The song—arguably the highlight of the production—could conceivably be seen as parodying traditional masculinity, in keeping with the gender play of the book. And Jeannie Carson performs Jo with a panache reminiscent of an ambiguously gendered Mary Martin crowing, "I want to fly." Carson's performance is consistent with the feisty female role common in midcentury musicals (a role that Aunt March had played in the 1940 operetta). When a commentator criticized her pronunciation by suggesting "she'd been taking lessons in hick dialect from Ado Annie,"[203] the comparison highlighted a similarity to another feisty musical female. This naturalization of Jo in a standard role defuses some of the subversive potential for gender play. Yet if musical numbers can provide a glimpse of utopian possibilities, as Richard Dyer has argued,[204] then here, in this song, even if the lyrics poke fun at Jo's desires, we can glimpse a potential rethinking of gender roles.

There are also hints of the utopian in Jo's opening song, "How Do You Write a Book?," even if she is here seeking advice not on how to publish but, more fundamentally, on how to write.[205] Alcott's Jo may have received some advice on her writing (in part 2 of the novel, the part that Adler was seemingly unfamiliar with), but basically figuring out how to write was not an issue for her in part 1, set in the early 1860s. The 1950s were apparently a different matter. Still, the film opens and closes with Jo writing. This framing might have been to accommodate the production's sponsor: Schaeffer crafted advertisements for its pens that were coordinated with the program, beginning one with, for instance, "In Louisa May Alcott's day people wrote with scratchy points." Yet the framing also serves to mitigate, to some degree, the heightened emphasis on romance in so many dramatic and cinematic adaptations.

Adler later suggested that "the reviews were good," while admitting that *Variety* "correctly" pointed to the trimming necessary for an hour-long program and called the production "a fluffy petit four for dainty palates with not much to sink the choppers into."[206] Actually, the production was panned. This "most disappointing," even "bungled televersion" was "the most boring TV 'special' of the season."[207] Adler's lyrics "were unbelievably trite and his melodies much too contrived."[208] One reviewer quipped, "As far as I'm concerned, Beth died anyway. So did Meg, Jo, Amy, Marmee, Laurie and the old colonel. They died very early in the play and were buried under an avalanche of fudge."[209] Another noted, "Faced with an almost hopeless antique like the Louisa Alcott story, the decision backstage seems to have been to smother its gush in a thick coating of Richard Adler tunes, then turn the cast loose and let them fend for themselves."[210]

‿

The middle decades of the twentieth century were a time when Alcott's "almost hopeless antique" was frequently belittled, unread. If at the beginning of the century it was a byword for the traditional and quaint, it was now also associated with the innocent and naïve—and often lambasted. In 1949, when James Baldwin wanted to decry *Uncle Tom's Cabin* for being sentimental, his yardstick for "self-righteous, virtuous sentimentality" was *Little Women*.[211] Writers also turned the innocence they associated with *Little Women* to humorous effect.

Humorous juxtapositions had appeared as early as the nineteenth century, when a journalist reported seeing, in the cars, a sweet young girl reading a book whose jacket proclaimed it was *Little Women*, but when she was jostled, the book that flew out was a handbook on poker.[212] By the middle of the twentieth century such juxtapositions of the innocent with the less so by way of *Little Women* flourished. There was that anecdote of the French Marx sisters, of course, and whether they were risqué "petites femmes." In 1934 a cartoon in *Life* magazine depicted two leggy and befeathered chorus girls, one saying to the other as she reads a letter, "Ma's coming to New York—and she thinks we're in 'Little Women'!"[213] In the 1950s, a U.S. delegate to the United Nations found a resolution "so meek it wouldn't have scared Louisa May Alcott."[214] More pointedly, a satirist poking fun at those trying to find the real author of Shakespeare's plays wrote an essay attributing *Little Women* to Jack London, precisely because, cozy and innocuous, it was "the antithesis of everything London had known, the epitome of the life he longed for."[215] A joke, in short. Speaking of jokes: "Are you sure that contraption will gather up every single bit of dirt?" a housewife asks the vacuum-cleaner salesman, formerly a seller of books. "Lady . . . I ran this cleaner over a copy of *Lady Chatterley's Lover*, and when I was finished, it was Louisa Alcott's *Little Women*."[216] Julie Wilhelm has written tellingly of the functions of humor in destabilizing gender and class within *Little Women*;[217] I'd argue that the humorous use of the novel in popular culture destabilizes some of the same norms by attributing them to *Little Women* and thus also destabilizes whatever position *Little Women* has in culture. In destabilizing femininity, writers poke fun at its performance, as Alcott does, but also at the performers.

Not everyone was belittling the novel at this time. Occasionally associations with *Little Women* play out with some complexity. In 1941 the book was a clue in a newspaper murder mystery in the *Baltimore Sun*: our detective realizes that the reason that an old edition of part 1 of *Little Women*, but not a first edition, was found under the body of Willie the Mope in a rare-books library is that thieves have been pilfering first editions and replacing them with similar but less valuable books.[218] Part of the point of the story is the odd juxtaposition of a thug and *Little Women*. But also our bespectacled hero knows that a first edition of part 1, appearing before the publisher knew whether there would be a part 2, wouldn't have "Part 1" on its spine. Yet he's not smart enough to figure out, on his own, the domestic mystery that constitutes a subplot: why his wife has suddenly started asking him to bring home odd foods like dill pickles. Domesticity can be mysterious too. It is, to some extent, revalued, just as *Little Women* is, both within and by the story. And *Little Women* did garner some respect in the media in midcentury. Alcott's book was "important to letters because it painted the American scene so accurately," a film reviewer noted in 1933.[219] A reviewer of an Alcott biography in the *New Yorker* noted in 1958, defending the importance of literature for children, that Alcott "may be the most widely read transcendentalist today."[220]

Overall *Little Women* was looked down upon by the intelligentsia in the mid-twentieth century; the novel had almost reached its nadir of critical avoidance and aversion. It continued to be popular with others, yet as the decades wore on, its general popularity appears to have declined, and it was increasingly belittled in popular contexts. Furthermore, the novel spoke differently to the general public before and after World War II. In popular contexts, heterosexual romance may have been particularly to the fore throughout. Yet some possibilities for women's independence and work were possible in the prewar period, even if often in uneasy, unresolved juxtaposition to romance. In the postwar period, however, romance, domesticity, and now consumerism held almost undisputed sway.

CHAPTER 4

Celebrating Sisterhood and Passion
since 1960

Snow-drops hang like tears.
  Shy, sweet, saintly Beth has died.
  One down, three to go.

—*David M. Bader*

But there can be no doubt that echo enriches, that it is more than
shadow and inert simulacrum.

—*George Steiner*

Humorists have continued to have fun with *Little Women*, still associating it
with innocent simplicity. In 1970 Gerald Nachman imagined it reworked as "an
outspoken film about militant feminism," since the "Women's Liberation Front"
was "an inevitable outgrowth of the activities of the girls in the novel"; Beth would
die tragically in "a tastefully done abortion scene. . . . 'Little Women '70' is the
story [Alcott] meant to write all along."[1] Which is truer than he realized—the
politics part. As for Beth's death, it's a popular target. The satirist P. J. O'Rourke
responded to the cheeriness of the novel—less pungently than Oscar Wilde responded to the death of Dickens's Little Nell—with, "Didn't everyone sigh with
relief when Louisa May Alcott finally killed off Beth in 'Little Women'?"[2] David
Bader's humorous haiku that is the first epigraph to this chapter, though, is a
richer text. In the final line he too is dismissive of Beth's death. But if we adopt a
perspective closer to Jo's—and indeed the colloquialism of the line is in keeping
with her penchant for slang—we might remember the loss of sisters as happen-
ing through marriage as well as death. The chronology isn't exact—Meg is lost

to marriage before Beth dies—but for many latter-day readers Jo too is eventually lost through marriage. A terse wryness similar to Bader's is captured in a graphic rendition by Lisa Brown, one of her "three panel reviews," expanded, in this case, to four panels. Jo, Meg, Amy, and Beth are each assigned a panel and an adjective: *smart, sweet, spoiled*—and *dead*.[3]

This final chapter on the afterlife of *Little Women* tracks more than fifty years, with the 1960s marking a turning point in Alcott reception. Although the novel is still a favorite with many, direct popular interest has continued to decline, even as academic interest has greatly increased, and a more diffuse popular interest, manifested in adaptations broadly defined, has accelerated. The echo of *Little Women* continues.

                                                                       *

By 1960 *Little Women* was no longer assigned much in schools, at least not in the regular public-school curriculum; it appeared with some frequency, though, on summer reading lists, especially, it seems, for schools with religious affiliations. If in the nineteenth century Alcott's novel was criticized for not being sufficiently doctrinal, it's now often seen as a repository of traditional values, including by evangelicals and home schoolers.[4] *Little Women* is also revered by groups that make unusual bedfellows for evangelicals: followers of the Goddess, those seeking the Best Gay Novels of All Time, and proponents of drug experimentation.[5]

For the text is permeable, inviting a multitude of approaches. Not all readers like or identify with Jo; some favor Amy, Beth, or Meg.[6] Some, like the scholar Roberta Seelinger Trites, recognize an internal split: "Amy was my reality, but Jo was my goal."[7] Some readers see *Little Women* as celebrating domesticity; others, independence. A recent rumor circulating in the blogosphere is that Alcott's book has been subject to banning, the reasons variously being for creating female characters that are too independent or for creating ones that are not independent enough. The Office for Intellectual Freedom of the American Library Association, however, has received no reports of challenges.[8] *Little Women* simply generates enough partisanship, still, that people want to believe that it has been attacked.

Nevertheless, in recent decades the novel's popularity has declined in polls, although it did place fourth on "A Children's All-Time Bestseller List," based on the responses of three hundred bookstores in 1977, and second in a 1987 poll of adults leading Reading Is Fundamental programs across the country.[9] In 1969 *Little Women* was "still one of the most circulated books in the New York Public Library."[10] In 2014 the Rhode Island public library system has at least 127 hard copies, not counting scores of audio books, condensed versions, and story spinoffs.

(Yet just last month when I went to check out yet another juvenile biography featuring Alcott's image on the cover, the middle-aged woman behind the counter needed to ask, "Who is this Alcott?") The novel is currently rated an average of 4.5 (out of 5) among twelve hundred amazon.com readers; most of those who rate it lowest are unhappy not with the original novel but with a particular edition, whether for being incomplete, abridged, or poorly illustrated. Readers on goodreads.com, more than eight hundred thousand of them, rate *Little Women* 3.98; the most negative reviewers find the novel boring and saccharine. In informal annual surveys of childhood favorites in my Children's Literature course, *Little Women* has slipped from second or third place in the early 1980s to generally ninth or tenth place in the 1990s to rarely making it into the top ten—maybe not even being mentioned by the fifty or so students present—during the past decade.[11] Holly Blackford suggests that for the girl readers she interviewed a decade ago, the coming-of-age novel is less relevant than it once was, given all the sources of information about growing up available in various media; she cites one reader who found Jo attractive and similar in some ways to herself yet "sort of but not really" important.[12]

As for esteem, *Little Women* was named to the White House Library in 1963, and it figured on the Library of Congress 2011 list of "Books That Shaped America."[13] It has remained prominent on other lists as well: on the Children's Literature Association's list of best children's books, memorialized in three volumes entitled *Touchstones: Reflections on the Best in Children's Literature* (1985–89), on E. D. Hirsch's list of "what every American needs to know" in his 1987 *Cultural Literacy*, on a 2005 listing called *A Bookshelf of Our Own: Works That Changed Women's Lives*, and on National Public Radio's 2013 "100 Must-Reads for Kids 9–14." Alcott herself appears on a 1986 list of the twenty-five most important American women and was one of ten women elected to the National Women's Hall of Fame in 1996.[14] In 1999 on the National Education Association's list of the top one hundred books, *Little Women* ranked forty-seventh among teachers' favorites, sixty-second among children's. The difference may hint at some decline in interest among the young. By 2012, in any case, the novel was not one of the fourteen Massachusetts books on the NEA's "50 State Booklist."[15]

Librarians and educators still frequently recommend the book, especially during Children's Book Week or as a Christmas gift. The centennial of *Little Women*, in 1968–69, was celebrated across the country, with displays of dolls and books and perhaps a cake decorated with hand-painted figures.[16] The publisher announced that fan mail was still rolling in, with young girls perhaps describing how they played at being the four sisters.[17] The sesquicentennial of Alcott's birth, in 1982 was less widely commemorated, but there were local festivities. In Fayetteville, New York, for instance—where *Little Women* was "still one of the most popular children's books in the Fayetteville library"—the event was marked by a short film, a reading, and doll and period-costume displays.[18]

In other contexts, discussion of *Little Women* appears routinely in children's-literature textbooks for college students, from May Hill Arbuthnot's pioneering *Children and Books* (1947), where *Little Women* receives praise for marking an epoch, to Carrie Hintz and Eric Tribunella's *Reading Children's Literature* (2013), where the novel is a key exemplar of domestic fiction and the authors praise "the psychological complexity of [Alcott's] characters."[19] John Walsh, the host of Fox's *America's Most Wanted*, recommends *Little Women* as one of four "great reads for children," glossing it thus: "Inexplicably evergreen, trend and taste-defying 1868 classic."[20] The British littérateur John Sutherland recommends it in the pages of the *Guardian*, calling it "sentimental, but irresistible; the novel shows Alcott to be one of the great storytellers of fiction, and not just for girls growing up."[21] Yet even as the Canadian feminist Michele Landsberg included *Little Women* on a 1987 list of recommended reading, she regretted Jo's eventual "taming" by the "antifeminist Alcott."[22]

The novel has continued to be a childhood favorite of many who grew up during the last half-century—many teachers and librarians, along with such notables as the actresses Julianne Moore, Winona Ryder, and Tram-Anh Tran and the writers Barbara Kingsolver, Mary Jo Salter, Sarah Schulman, John Green, and Perri Klass, who named her daughter after Jo.[23] And perhaps Madonna—although when she announced that she had "mended her ways and was now rereading *Little Women*" she may simply have wanted to be provocative.[24] For the writer Anna Quindlen, however, "*Little Women* changed my life."[25] The young bell hooks, later an activist critic, found "remnants of myself in Jo, the serious sister, the one who is punished," making her "a little less alone in the world."[26] The Puerto Rican writer Luis Negrón tells of being spellbound by a library copy of the Illustrated Classics edition, but then his father called him a fag for reading it and his mother tore up the book.[27] A Pennsylvania seventh grader claimed in a prize-winning essay, "Many of our modern heroines from astronauts to Supreme Court Justices, owe some of their success to having met and been inspired by Jo March when they were young girls!"[28] A nine-year-old stated, "It's real . . . it has a little bit of everything. It's got love and drama and death and a little bit of mystery . . . the kind that really happens to people."[29] Another act of homage is Gretchen Anderson's *Louisa May Alcott Cookbook* (1985), a book of nineteenth-century recipes for foods mentioned in *Little Women*—created when Anderson was nine, published when she was twelve. The roster of notables for whom the novel was a favorite is shorter in this chapter than in the previous one, which may reflect, in part, the fact that many young women have yet to make their mark but also probably some decline in the novel's impact. Other anecdotal evidence suggests indifference on the part of many young girls, including those visiting Orchard House.[30]

In England, *Little Women* was the favorite book among ten- to fourteen-year-olds in 1971 but was no longer in the top twenty in a similar survey in 1999.[31] In recent polls of adults, the novel has continued to fare well: in a BBC poll in 2003 *Little Women* was one of twenty-one favorite novels; in 2007 in an online poll of most precious novels it came in eleventh.[32] In 1991 more than twenty editions were listed in *British Books in Print*, and in 1993 Alcott came in twentieth among authors whose books were most borrowed, just after Shakespeare.[33] Anecdotal accounts are mixed: in 1995 a reviewer found few girls who had read Alcott's text; in 2000 a journalist reported that "our daughters love this book."[34] In 1994, before the release of Gillian Armstrong's film version, another journalist noted both that *Little Women* was "Puffin Classics' second-best seller" and that "no girl of my acquaintance has read to the end of it."[35] Indeed, the Booker Prize–winning novelist Hilary Mantel reports hating Jo March "like poison."[36] Charles Spencer, brother of Princess Diana, "was unable to get beyond the horribly twee first page."[37] The novel was nevertheless a childhood favorite of a number of notable women, including Diane Abbott, MP, the Welsh novelist Carole Cadwalladr—and J. K. Rowling.[38]

Around the world, the book has been translated into more than fifty languages.[39] And many nations have had multiple editions and retranslations: between 1946 and 1995 there were at least fourteen new Dutch editions.[40] UNESCO's online Index Translationum lists more than three hundred editions of translated versions, whether of part 1 or part 2 or both together, whether abridged or otherwise, between 1977 and 2009.[41] The translations are in thirty-seven languages published in forty-two countries, including most European nations, several Latin American ones, and Japan, China, South Korea, India, Sri Lanka, Indonesia, Israel, Egypt, and Iran. Seven countries produced more than a dozen editions: Spain, Italy, Japan, Chile, China, Greece, and France.

More anecdotally, one commentator suggests that *Little Women* is not all that popular in Germany,[42] a claim tentatively supported by the Index Translationum, which lists only three new editions in Germany between 1978 and 2009, fewer than for most European countries and far fewer than for Spain, Italy, Greece, and France. There are sporadic reports of some popularity in Africa, specifically in South Africa and Sierra Leone, and the novel was part of a Battle of the Books between middle schools in Hong Kong.[43] Among individuals, *Little Women* has been a favorite with Princess Caroline of Monaco and with Lara Dutta, the East Indian who became Miss Universe in 2000.[44] A Philippine journalist remembers thinking, as a child, "Hey, this book is all about me and my sisters."[45] Four Malaysian sisters, all actresses, identify themselves as Meg, Jo, Beth, and Amy.[46] For the Greek Cypriot Eleni Meleagrou, who "read Little Women over and over," the loss of the book in a house that "became part of the occupied Turkish zone . . . became symbolic of the violation and destruction of the land of my childhood."[47]

As for other forms of homage, the Chilean writer Marcela Serrano has written a modernized spinoff, *Hasta siempre, mujercitas* (Farewell, little women, 2004): the critic Alma B. Kuhlemann Cárdenez describes it as combining overt references to *Little Women* with the Gothicism of Alcott's sensation stories, the Jo figure's false accusations of rape contributing to the downfall of the family.[48] The Korean Park Kyung-ni's *Daughters of Pharmacist Kim* (1962), about four daughters, appears to draw on Alcott's novel; so too do several Italian works, Lidia Ravera's thriller *Bagna i fiori e aspettami* (Water the flowers and wait for me, 1986) and the sequel, *Se lo dico perdo l'America* (If I say I miss America, 2012), and also Letizia Muratori's metafictional *Letterature da guardarobiera* (Literature from the cloakroom, 2012).[49]

Other tributes have appeared in South Korea and Italy as well. A Korean manga version, written in English, retains most of the action of part 1 of *Little Women* and much of Alcott's dialogue. It also retains references to *Pilgrim's Progress*, which are often omitted in modern adaptations, and even adds references to God and to praying: unlike in Alcott's book, the family ends Christmas Day, and the second chapter, by "praying for Father on the battlefield."[50] The publisher may be catering to the relatively large numbers of Christians in South Korea while also targeting an international audience) or may simply be exaggerating the association of anything from the United State with Christianity.

In Italy, the choreographer Caterina Sagna's *Sorelline* (Little sisters, 2001) was inspired by *Little Women*. Elisabetta Chicco Vitzizzai's *Piccole donne in cucina: Scene di vita familiare nel capolavoro di Louisa M. Alcott* (Little Women in the kitchen: Scenes of family life in the masterpiece of Louisa M. Alcott, 2012) apparently provides a gastronomical tour of the novel and of Alcott's New England, including a recipe for the turnovers that Meg and Jo carry in their muffs. And the March sisters have been translated into mice, in *Piccole donne* (2007) and *Piccole donne crescono* (2010), retellings in the wildly popular Geronimo Stilton series, an Italian children's publishing phenomenon (more than 60 million books sold worldwide). This abridgment, part of a series of retellings of children's classics in which the characters are visually depicted as mice, retains the main events of the novel, although the story begins not with Christmas and coziness and a letter from Father but with an invitation to the Gardiners' New Year's party. Presumably more inviting to modern young readers?

Little Women is particularly popular in Japan. Aiko Moro-oka has reported that eleven of Alcott's books have been translated into Japanese.[51] Another Japanese professor points to a 1980 survey by a news company in which *Little Women* was second in popularity among books for girls; she offers as a reason the centrality of motherhood in the novel and in Japanese culture.[52] Yet another professor assigned students a project based on *Little Women* because she could assume their familiarity with the story—even if what some were familiar with was an anime redaction.[53] *Little Women* features in at least five Japanese manga and four anime, whether as a single episode or in a series of forty-eight. A number of books about Alcott have appeared in Japan as well. William T. Anderson's photo-biography *The World of Louisa May Alcott: Little Women*, for instance, was first published in Japan in 1992; only in 1995 was it reprinted in English as *The World of Louisa May Alcott*. When the crown prince and princess visited the United States in 1987, they made a point of visiting the home of this author whose work "is very popular among Japanese schoolchildren."[54] Even before then, Japanese visitors to Orchard House far outnumbered those from any country other than the United States.[55]

The house has continued to be a popular tourist mecca. Only rarely in the past century has a different one been singled out for attention as an Alcott home. One of the few instances occurred in the 1940s when the radio personality Ted Malone, on a pilgrimage to a series of authors' homes, broadcast the Louisa May Alcott episode from Wayside (what the Alcotts had called Hillside). It's emblematic that this Alcott broadcast ran into technical glitches and wasn't actually aired.[56] Orchard House had prevailed once again. In 1983 it was the historic home in Concord "most frequently visited."[57] In 2014 readers rate it first among the eighteen Concord tourist attractions on tripadvisor.com. Accounts of travel to New England, and especially Concord, continue to include a stop at "the place where we all grew up."[58]

Overall in the popular imagination, *Little Women* is still associated with innocent simplicities, especially in contrast with things modern. An article on women in roller derbies in *Esquire* in May 1969 (by Candice Bergen) makes no reference to the novel in its body but is titled "Little Women"; the subtitle reads, "What has forty wheels, seven tits, and fights?" A humorist imagines a publisher agreeing to publish the novel nowadays only because "Twentieth Century Fox is offering $500,000 for the title, only."[59] In 1981 a sportswriter describing the professional golfer Amy Alcott opined—obviously without having read *Little Women*—that she "would dismay Louisa May. This Miss Alcott does not appear in public in her sweet little Alice blue gown."[60] Less humorously, a 1996 legal argument for increasing restrictions on the Internet proffered the evidence that a computer search for *little* plus *women*, as if for a book report, led one to a "site featuring 'Hot Pictures of Naked Women.' "[61] (A recent Google search failed to elicit such a site.)

Little Women has also continued to feature prominently in material culture. The U.S. Post Office issued a twenty-nine-cent stamp featuring *Little Women* in 1993. Madame Alexander's perennial dolls have been joined by Ashton-Drake, Effanbee, and Robin Woods, among others, and at least four different versions of paper dolls. A porcelain collector's doll depicts an elegant Jo, "a very refined and proper young lady"; a collector's plate features the more appropriately elegant Amy or perhaps a reproduction of a Jessie Willcox Smith image; and there are Tasha Tudor figurines of the sisters too.[62] On etsy.com one can find a book safe fashioned from a copy of the novel, "shabby chic" Alcott books for adding "a spot of color" to a room, a Tea with the Little Women necklace, and a paper bridal bouquet fashioned out of a copy of *Little Women*. The women in the rock group 3LW named themselves after the novel; a current jazz/rock group, all men, calls itself Little Women. Alcott's novel has continued to be an occasional touchstone for fashion, invoked especially when a designer harks back to the nineteenth century, though when a commentator refers to "19th Century fashions reminiscent of Louisa May Alcott's 'Little Women' and 'Little Lord Fauntleroy' trouser suits for dining at home," one may wonder if he or she is guilty of a grammatical lapse or simply associates *Little Women* with Katharine Hepburn.[63]

❦

The final decades of the twentieth century witnessed a galvanic shift in Alcott's critical reputation. Leona Rostenberg had published her discovery that Alcott had written thrillers under the name A. M. Barnard in 1943, as I noted in chapter 3, but it wasn't until 1975 that her partner, Madeleine Stern, started publishing reprints of Alcott's pseudonymous and anonymous thrillers, beginning with the collection *Behind a Mask*. Publication of these stories of seduction and intrigue, of ghosts and vengeful women, created some stir in the popular media but also excited scholars. The tales suggested new ways of looking at Alcott's *oeuvre*, focusing on the passions raging beneath the apparent calm and decorum, the "civil war" and the "Civil War" behind the scenes of *Little Women*.

The wave of the feminist movement that emerged in the 1960s had a significant impact on Alcott's reputation and reception as well. It invited attention to previously devalued works by women and created new ways of appreciating them. Feminists' early emphasis on equal rights, what is sometimes called liberal feminism, would hardly have been anathema to Alcott, who was vocal in her support of working women and women's suffrage. Yet liberal-feminist themes are not particularly salient in *Little Women*, at least not to a modern reader. As someone who whistles, runs, talks slang, and carelessly spills coffee on her best dress, Jo is the sister who least conforms to prevailing norms for femininity. She also earns money through her writing. But her eventual marriage to Professor Bhaer and her willingness to give up her published writing (at least until the last book in the series) can seem to be capitulations to prevailing norms, especially if one feels that an individual literary work must have a unified effect, that whatever happens early is subordinate to the ending. Such capitulations may seem even less forgivable since Alcott herself did not indulge in them. Certainly not all feminists have forgiven her. In the 1970s prominent feminist critics were often dismissive of Alcott's little women. Sandra M. Gilbert and Susan Gubar, for instance, lamented Jo's "learning to write moral homilies for children instead of ambitious gothic thrillers"—which would have been "assuredly major," they suggest, unlike literature for children.[64] (Scholarly prejudice against Alcott is often linked with an age prejudice.)

Nevertheless, a feminist approach that emerged in the late 1970s, focusing on women's traditions and their connections with other women, is particularly hospitable to study of Alcott. In discussing "communities of women," for instance Nina Auerbach gives *Little Women* equal billing with Jane Austen's *Pride and Prejudice* (1813), a work that had retained at least a foothold in the U.S. academy during the middle decades of the twentieth century.[65] In some respects *Little Women* comes off even better in Auerbach's analysis, since Alcott's women are more truly supportive of one another than are Austen's.

Feminist approaches have also spurred interest by scholars in other countries British intellectuals have not shown great interest in *Little Women*: in 1995 leading feminists interviewed for the London *Observer*, responding to Alcott's "critical renaissance" in the United States, were ambivalent or even hostile, the novelist Linda Grant calling *Little Women* "a sickening book" and the BBC executive Liz Forgan calling it "profoundly unfeminist, truly dangerous stuff for little girls."[66] But a scholarly collection whose title translates as *Louisa May Alcott: The Road to "Little Women,"* edited by Aiko Moro-oka, appeared in Japan in 1995, and at least seventeen other scholarly essays on Alcott were published there in the 1980s and 1990s. In Italy, scholars such as Sabrina Vellucci have explored Alcott's work.[67] In

Louisa May Alcott: Petites filles modèles et femmes fatales, published in France in 2001, Pascale Voilley takes issue with some feminist arguments, but her claims that *Little Women* is a classic and also an American myth owe much to feminist scholarship.

And feminists have revalued sentiment and sentimentality. In a front-page essay in the *New York Times Book Review* in 1965, reprinted from the London *Times,* Brigid Brophy tackled the charge of sentimentality: "The dreadful books are masterpieces," she admitted, drying her eyes, but she made that admission "with some bad temper and hundreds of reservations."[68] Two decades later, in *Sensational Designs* (1985), Jane Tompkins moved beyond ambivalence to find value in what had been dismissed as sentimental novels by examining the cultural work that such books undertake. More recently, Hildegard Hoeller points to the ways that sentiment is "the central counter-term to individualism" in American culture.[69]

By the 1980s feminist engagement with poststructuralism led to a willingness to value not just some presumed unified effect of a work of literature, with special emphasis on its ending, but also its contradictions. A work becomes powerful if it captures key cultural conflicts and does not fully resolve them: a disjunction between overt and covert messages can be valued as a source of power. *Little Women* purveys mixed messages regarding the position of women: whom should the sisters marry? Or should they marry? In chapter 1 I cited an 1869 letter in which Alcott complained of the pressure to marry Jo off, though "out of perversity" she "made a funny match for her."[70] Laurie, the charming boy next door, has always been the most popular romantic choice with the reading public. Scholars too have devoted considerable energy to the issue, whether they condemn Professor Bhaer, Jo's eventual choice, as too much a father figure or praise him for his feminine or cosmopolitan qualities, whether they condemn Laurie's wealth, which would have made Jo's life too easy, or praise him for having supported Jo's writing.[71] Whichever arguments one finds persuasive, the impassioned attention that Jo's choice receives is a testament to the power of *Little Women.* And perhaps, through its divergence from the happily-ever-after ending with the handsome young prince, the choice of Professor Bhaer even leaves unresolved the question whether a woman has to marry. By providing a "perverse" choice, Alcott leaves cultural conundrums—what makes a good spouse? what is suitable work for a woman? should a woman, in fact, marry?—invitingly open.

Which is also a way of saying that responses to Alcott often enact, even now, a central feminist tension between an ideal of autonomy and an ideal of connectedness. Does Jo provide a model of independence, even if she then capitulates to marriage and stops writing? Or does she embody a sense of connectedness with a community of women? And does she then nullify that community or expand it when she undertakes the education of boys but also some girls in *Little Men?* Does Jo submit to prevailing cultural norms or contest them? Or perhaps negotiate among competing norms or deconstruct them? Does the intensity with which the competing ideals are evoked illuminate key cultural conflicts in the ensuing centuries—and therefore account for the book's impact on popular and scholarly imaginations?

Other relevant developments in feminist criticism include an increasing emphasis on recognizing differences among women, starting with those associated with race, class, and sexual orientation and going on to include age. Girls are females too. And children's literature is literature. *Little Women* has been the touchstone for feminist interest in children's literature in essays in such flagship journals as *Signs* and *American Literature*. In *New Literary History* a case study of response to *Little Women* fleshes out Catharine Stimpson's discussion of canons, making room for affective response—a reply, if you will, to the midcentury debate over Alcott as "beloved" or, more negatively, "sentimental."[72]

Not just in feminist criticism but in literary scholarship more generally children's literature has gained increasing attention. The educators and librarians who functioned as the guardians of children's literature early in the twentieth century had been attending to Alcott all along. But in the last few decades, study of children's literature has emerged within literary criticism, and the scholarly journals that cater to this field, such as *Children's Literature* and *The Lion and the Unicorn*, have been receptive to Alcott since their early years in the 1970s. Recently *Little Women* has also provided a touchstone in criticism informed by queer, materialist, and masculinity studies. And outside literary criticism, it and its sequels figure in scholarly discussions of spirituality, ethics, and educational theory. Dismissiveness, condescension, and marginalization of Alcott and other authors of children's literature are now less common than they were during most of the twentieth century.

Significant scholarship has also appeared in conjunction with new editions of Alcott's work. Not only is there the work of establishing a text (the original 1868 text of *Little Women* or the expurgated 1880 one?) but the accompanying introductions or afterwords are often significant contributions to scholarship. Such scholars as Ann Douglas, Elaine Showalter, Madelon Bedell, and Valerie Alderson have written commentaries that go well beyond the standard brief appreciation and salient biographical facts. Showalter has also edited an edition of the March family trilogy for the Library of America (2005); Anne Phillips and Gregory Eiselein have edited a Norton Critical Edition of *Little Women* (2004)

Daniel Shealy has edited an annotated *Little Women* (2013). Such suturing of popular culture and serious scholarship, as scholars reach out to a broader public, is an emblem of how *Little Women* exists at the interface of the two. Scholars are attending to Alcott because she has been so popular—often because she was so important to them in their own childhoods.

Thus, thanks to the current women's movement and the publication of her lost thrillers, Alcott's work is receiving serious attention in the academy, especially in the United States but also elsewhere. Her work is increasingly available to college students, whether in stand-alone editions or in such anthologies as the *Heath Anthology of American Literature* and the *Norton Anthology of American Literature*. The MLA's online bibliography indexes 393 items of Alcott scholarship since 1960, as of this writing. Scholarly attention to all figures has exploded in recent decades, so comparing scholarly attention to Louisa with that to her father, Bronson, gives a better sense of how recent interest in Louisa has taken off: before 1960 Bronson had a slight edge in the MLA's bibliography (27 items addressing Bronson, 20 addressing Louisa); since then there have been more than four times as many items devoted to Louisa; since 2000, more than fourteen times as many.

Still, I can't help wondering if scholarly attention to Alcott might be a sign of her decline in general popularity. As I've already noted, some evidence suggests that she does not have the same riveting appeal for young women now in their teens and twenties that she had for their predecessors. The increasing efforts to institutionalize Alcott, to hail the importance of her work as literature, may be an attempt to compensate for some erosion of her power to speak to a general public. If she is starting to disappear from popular memory, scholars may need to work all the harder to memorialize her.

‿

Yet *Little Women* still has much appeal. Adaptations and other re-visionings— dramatizations, spinoffs, illustrated editions—have burgeoned. Some treat the novel as a classic, memorializing Alcott's own words. Some attempt modernization, speaking both to the continuing relevance of the novel and to its lack of relevance, its need for updating.

Stock-company and local-theater performances of *Little Women* have continued apace in the United States, especially around the Christmas holidays. Since 1960 at least fifty-eight new English-language scripts have been published or performed, including musical versions and parodies.[73] Some are one-act plays; others are full length, usually in two acts. Most full-length productions focus on a few key scenes, for instance, the nearly-Christmas opening. Some stick closely to the novel, reproducing long stretches of Alcott's dialogue; others attempt to modernize the language and the cultural setting. Some have been significantly influenced by one or more film versions. Writers generally try to balance three conflicting urges: reproducing the most remembered scenes (such as the opening Christmas-won't-be-Christmas); foregrounding those that lend themselves to visual performance or spectacle (such as the melodramatic play within a play, the dance, and the revelation of Jo's cut hair); and perhaps creating a plot with a rising action and a climax (usually by foregrounding the possibilities for romance). Writers also try to address modern sensibilities, perhaps playing down the sentimental: bedside scenes with the dying Beth are now fairly rare. Playwrights vary in the extent to which they foreground Jo's writing. Those that do often end with Jo starting to write the opening scenes of the play or the novel, or else the Professor's excuse for turning up is to deliver Jo's published manuscript. Rare is the play that, like Sandra Fenichel Asher's *Little Women* (2001), makes writing and creating fiction central: not only does she incorporate extensive sections of Alcott's story "The Banner of Beaumanoir" in addition to Jo's play within the play, but Asher also includes the almost never included scenes of the girls reading their "Pickwick Portfolio" contributions, the Camp Laurence picnickers playing the story-game Rigmarole, and the sisters' letters to Marmee and Father.

Several playwrights underscore parallels with Alcott's life by interweaving scenes featuring the author, whether she narrates or else enacts scenes from her childhood, or both. (These versions generally work in references to Emerson and Thoreau as well, thus both celebrating a national literary heritage and elevating Alcott's work through its association with leading figures of the American Renaissance.) Some, starting in the 1990s, begin with an older Jo in her attic, perhaps looking at each sister's chest and remembering their girlhoods.

Occasionally a writer changes the plot: maybe Amy claims to have burned Jo's book but, she later reveals, hasn't really, and in this version Jo is eager to marry ("And our lives would be complete, girls / If someone would sweep us off our feet, girls," she warbles with Meg), and so, at the end, after being spanked by her lord and master, she agrees to marry Laurie after all.[74] Anger and the urge for independence are here reduced to foreplay. Some playwrights publish introductions in which they claim to have hewed closely to Alcott's own words or perhaps her intentions (she didn't really want to write part 2 and marry Jo off, so they'll stick to the story in part 1). And then they proceed to make numerous changes: perhaps the blood-and-thunder tale that Jo reveals she has written is changed to one of Alcott's fairy stories.[75] (So as not to shock any children in the audience?) A modernized version, a spinoff in which Beth loves playing Monopoly and the girls lament that after giving food to a Vietnamese family all that will remain is leftover quiche, apparently features a date rape.[76]

A symptomatic recent dramatization is David Longest's *Little Women of Orchard House* (1998, perf. 1996); his amalgamation of Alcotts and Marches reveals much about contemporary conflations and confusions about the novel, Alcott's life, and the lives of her neighbors. Longest's intent is to bring together "the world of reality and the fictional world of one of America's greatest women writers of all time."[77] He's one of those who weave in scenes with an authorial Louisa. He claims to have taken "the greatest care . . . to use the exact words" of *Little Women* and also Alcott's journals ([6]). Yet he takes great liberties with plot and incident. Early on, for instance, Bronson is leading his young family through a woods to find the new house he has located for them, near an orchard, but he is going in circles, whereupon they encounter Thoreau for the first time. Henry, who has been living near Walden Pond, directs them to Orchard House. "Just like a storybook house!" (I, 19), the young Louisa exclaims upon sighting it. Most of the factual details are wrong here: that's not how the family first glimpsed the dilapidated house that Bronson was to name Orchard House, and Thoreau's sojourn near Walden Pond occurred a decade earlier. Metaphorically, though, the plot captures some of Bronson's cluelessness with respect to practical matters and also, more significantly, the impact of the house upon subsequent fans, once the physical house was repaired and the fictional one created—becoming both a metaphoric and literal storybook house. When Longest has the adult Louisa claim that Orchard House is "where we lived our lives" and "also where I set my story" (I, 13), he captures the mythology about the house—that the Alcotts had lived there when the sisters were young—but not its reality.

Overall, Longest foreshortens the final episodes, modernizes some details, sometimes a bit incoherently, and heightens the cattiness of interactions among females. With respect to the foreshortening, in the second and final act, after little indication of any special attraction, Laurie seems to propose to Amy just because she's the only March sister available; she's insulted when he playfully suggests as much, but when we see them in the next scene, they're married. As for modernized details, Jo's job, for instance, is to read to Aunt March (she's never described as a companion), and when Jo objects to the choice of novels (no Belsham's essays here) as too boring, her aunt oddly rewards her by doubling her salary and allowing her to select more gripping reading. Mr. Laurence gets to complain both that Laurie doesn't practice piano enough—a modern plaint—and that the boy has been too fond of the piano—the nineteenth-century one. Regarding the cattiness,

Meg's premature departure from a dance is very different from its equivalent in the novel. In the play, the Moffat and Gardiner girls are all rather snooty at Annie Moffat's coming-out party, Annie insisting that Meg follow behind her, so that the latter's charms don't overshadow her own. When Meg states that her friends call her Meg, Belle Gardiner retorts, "Well that's all very fine dear child, but you aren't my friend yet, now are you, Margaret?" (I, 81). So Laurie, who has overheard "the vultures," as they're called in the stage directions, whisks Meg away, announcing that the ladies can call him Theodore instead of Laurie: "Because you're not my friends. I don't recall anyone blowing the horn to signal the start of hunting season!" (I, 82). Hardly the talk of an admirable nineteenth-century gentleman. Longest creates a *Little Women* that capitalizes on the classic Concord connections, conflating fact and fiction, while stripping the play of its historical details and manners and also diluting the feminist aspects, especially the sense of community among women, newly resonant with scholars. This jumble of old and new speaks to the multivalent and contradictory positioning of the novel for modern readers.

Dramatic versions of one sort or another have also been performed in England, Scotland, Australia, and Ireland (in which last Laurie apparently endows a Christian fundamentalist college). In 1989 a British theater critic expected that a staging of such an old novel wouldn't "be much of a draw," but the Manchester Opera House "was packed to the roof."[78] In 2004 the comedy team Lip Service produced a parody called *Very Little Women*. Three actors played eleven roles, with a butch Marmee, Amy played by a wooden puppet—at least until Beth dies and frees an actress—and John Brooke played throughout by a mannequin. According to a reviewer, the audience saw Laurie only from the waist up ("I wish we could see more of you!" Jo says), the rabbit puppet that Beth plays with continues to move after she dies (as a visible soul hurtles across the stage to heaven), and there are "transvestism, false bosoms and more kittens than you can shake Amy's detachable wooden head at"—all mocking but still showing "obvious affection for the text."[79]

As for musical versions, besides the four noted in the previous chapter, I have found traces of at least twelve more, not counting an opera based on Alcott's life and a musical version of one of her sensation stories. In addition, many locally created dramatizations of *Little Women* include some music, even if it's not always clear from newspaper reports whether the music extends beyond Beth's and perhaps Laurie's playing a little piano, as indeed they do in the novel. In general, musical versions favor romantic duets, ensemble singing about family togetherness, and of course the early dance scene where Jo meets Laurie, whether it takes place at the Gardiners', as in the novel, or at the Laurences', as in the films.

A musical called *Jo* played off Broadway for a couple of months in 1964. Like other recent redactions, it omits most of the sisters' trials but not their romances. Unlike most stage adaptations, this one omits the opportunities for spectacle in the sisters' play rehearsal, but Jo's later scene with a New York editor does allow for a duet about stories about flaring passions, haunted hallways, epileptic fits, incestuous feelings, a rabid hound, and a grocer's boy who turns out to be the Prince of Wales (not all of these figure in Alcott's corpus). Professor Bhaer easily persuades Jo to forgo such stories, and the play ends with the two under the inevitable umbrella. One reviewer found the musical "melodious and warmly appealing"; another said, "It's not just nice and unpretentious, it's really quite good."[80] Yet another lambasted it as "pretty sticky kid stuff": "Even if you love Tinker-Bell, you may find Jo hard to take."[81] A nine-year-old reported that "it was a very sad show because Jo's sister, Beth, died." (What did she die of? "Spring fever.")[82]

Thomas Hischak, himself the author of a dramatization, found *Jo* fairly predictable but better than the 2004 *Little Women: The Musical*, which was not especially successful on Broadway but is now "a favorite with schools and community theatres."[83] In 1998 the composer Kim Oler and the lyricist Alison Hubbard had won a Richard Rodgers Award to subsidize production of a musical, but they were dismissed in 2000 and replaced with Jason Howland and Mindi Dickstein.[84]

The Howland-Dickstein version reached Broadway in 2004. Maureen McGovern's performance as Marmee was particularly notable: she was nominated for a Drama Desk Award, and reviews of her performances both in New York and on the road were enthusiastic. Yet response to the production overall was lukewarm. While *Time* magazine described it as "the most adult new musical of the Broadway season," *Variety* called it "pleasant but staid."[85] One reviewer found the lyrics "snappy," yet they "often outpace and outdo [the] music"; other critics found the songs "too bland, both musically and lyrically," with melodies that "have that McMusical familiarity that's neither offensive nor memorable" and lyrics that "are largely so generic they could slide right into a variety of different musicals."[86] More acerbic critics complained that the "depiction of Jo as a frenzied, belting demon seems hopelessly out of place in this story" or referred to the "crashing banality" of the show, with its "interchangeable tunes" and a book that "criminally shorthands (and shortchanges) the evergreen Louisa May Alcott novel."[87]

The production ran for 137 performances, at a time when a successful run would have been at least twice as long.[88] The audience was positive but not thrilled. In a Zagat survey to determine whether audience members would recommend the production, 74 percent said they would, a rating that ranked *Little Women* thirty-eighth out of forty-eight major productions on and off Broadway in late January 2005.[89] A twelve-year-old familiar with the book was "dazzled by the sets and by the enactments of Jo's swashbuckling tales" but "felt cheated not to view a deathbed scene onstage."[90] Journalists enjoyed highlighting human-interest stories about who was in the audience at various road-show stops. In Boston, Meg, Jo, Beth, and Amy were not only onstage but in the audience as well—four adult sisters, along with their Alcott-fan mother—and the Patriots linebacker Tedy Bruschi also attended.[91] In Columbus, a similar quartet appeared, this foursome without their mother, who had died of cancer three weeks earlier.[92] Participants in the show were fond of reporting on the men in the audience—the father in the front row who cried, the young men who came to the stage door to request an autograph from the production's Jo, not to mention Bruschi. But it's as if to naturalize such unusual men.

In any case, after its thirty-city tour this musical version has continued to be produced with some frequency by school, community, and repertory groups across the continent, including in French in Quebec.[93] In one week in May 2013, according to broadwayworld.com, the show was being performed in seven cities. Reviewers of community productions are more likely to be enthusiastic than the Broadway reviewers, perhaps calling the show "inspiring and exhilarating."[94] Still, one in California complained of the story's "series of events that dash ahead like dramatized Cliffs Notes and often discard moments of substance."[95] An Australian production in 2008 received lukewarm reviews: this "heart-warming musical" had a "cloying story" and "familiar Broadway feel," with most songs "either anonymous or overwrought."[96] In the Philippines, a production offered "a warm, winsome energy and a richly suggested inner life."[97] In Germany, a school production was described as "wirklich gelungen" (truly successful), although the praise was directed more to the participants than to the play.[98] Overall, the logo, with its simple line drawings of four overlapping sisters in profile—the ad agency consciously avoided the iconic "mother sitting in a chair surrounded by her four daughters"—seems more memorable than the show's music.[99]

For the lyrics are indeed bland. The most interesting are perhaps those for "Off to Massachusetts," which is charmingly inconsequential, rhyming *Massachusetts* with *two sets* (dishes), *suzettes* (crepe), and *glue sets* (model boats). The power ballad "Astonishing"—"I only know I'm meant for something more / I've got to know if I can be Astonishing"[100]—has had a significant afterlife beyond the musical production. But its lyrics and those of the musical's other songs lack the verve of those in long-forgotten musical versions from the forties and fifties, like Aunt March's ditty, quoted in chapter 3, about choosing "a man above your station," thus avoiding "slow starvation"—or "you're better off with gout." In 2004, adjectives do the heavy lifting: everything is astonishing and amazing.

Allan Knee's book, echoing the structure of Mark Adamo's 1998 opera, starts in New York and then covers most of the plot in a flashback. He incorporates the best-remembered incidents, including Jo's cut hair, Beth's dying (offstage), Jo and the Professor reconnoitering under an umbrella. But to show Jo's impulsiveness, Knee adds an incident in which she rushes outside to cut down one of the Laurences' trees for a Christmas tree. So an angry Mr. Laurence comes to the March household: that's how the Marches meet the Laurences. Jo's vandalism and theft are not judged particularly reprehensible; she just has to do some chores for the Laurences and agree to send the tree to the impecunious Hummels. Which she does—asking the newly introduced Laurie to do the delivery, not caring enough about the act of contrition and benevolence to do it herself.

Knee's Jo also writes: the musical foregrounds her blood-and-thunder stories. The story we hear in act 2, which Jo has enacted for an editor and reenacts for Professor Bhaer, seems to be an amalgam of Alcott's "operatic tragedy" with "Snow White," "The Three Billy Goats Gruff," and Angela Carter's "The Bloody Chamber": there's a hag and also a troll guarding a bridge, and the heroine adroitly fends off the villain until her sword is knocked from her hand, whereupon the hero appears to deliver the final blow—and then reveals himself as her sister. Jo later starts writing a story that is rather like *Little Women*, echoing the opening of the novel (and not the first scene in the play). As in film versions, Bhaer gets the book accepted by a publisher, though here it's the same one who printed Jo's blood-and-thunder story. "Sometimes when you dream/Your dreams come true/In extraordinary ways," she croons after she and Bhaer kiss and she announces that they will start a school together.[101]

Still, as seems inevitable in adaptations for popular audiences, there's an emphasis on romance. Meg is of course courted by Brooke, and Laurie proposes to Jo onstage. As for Professor Bhaer, the play starts in New York: "If we meet him early on," the director noted, "we have a relationship to root for."[102] Yet although we're told that he and Jo spend time together, she seems, onstage, to have relatively little interest in him as a person. If the goal of showing him early is to motivate their eventual romantic union, it's no more convincing than the hurried coupling of Amy and Laurie. Hardly Astonishing.

During these decades there continued to be numerous television adaptations.

I've noted that before 1960 there had been at least seven *Little Women* English-language specials, episodes, or miniseries; since then there have been at least twelve television films, miniseries, series, ballets, an opera, and anime, produced in the United States and also in Britain, Germany, Japan, Italy, and Turkey—not counting "Little Women" episodes in such series as *Little House on the Prairie* and *The Wonder Years*. Film critics often consider *Jane Eyre* the novel most frequently adapted to film and television since the 1930s, with almost two adaptations every decade;[103] but given all its television adaptations, *Little Women* would seem to have an edge, with at least twenty-three adaptations in various languages.

These include two made-for-television movies, both in two parts. One was a rather tedious 1970 production by the BBC, which an Australian has described as reminding him "of everything ghastly and poisonous and false in the book."[104] The production features a Jo with a 1960s bouffant hairstyle and a Hannah who is visually coded white yet speaks with a marked southern drawl reminiscent of stereotypical screen mammies. (A number of international visualizations of Hannah make her black; the producers of this version seem to offer an odd compromise.) Jo drawls some too, a bit like a British actress who hasn't quite mastered an American accent, perhaps an attempted echo of Katharine Hepburn. The acting is not particularly strong: in the first half, for instance, Amy and Laurie oscillate between bland and petulant, with little in between. In the understated words of a *Times* reviewer, "The performances were altogether too robust."[105] The three-hour-plus framework, here and in the 1978 television movie, allows attention to aspects of the novel that other adaptations routinely omit, such as the married Meg's efforts at housekeeping and the relationship between Laurie and his grandfather, which receives even more attention than it does in the novel.

Some changes in this adaptation seem due to its budget; others, to the British context. The budget was apparently low enough that the producers needed to rely on obviously painted outdoor backdrops and couldn't afford the cornflakes or cornstarch that have simulated snow in other productions: Amy's fall through the ice while skating becomes a summertime fall off a dock. The British context seems to have led to such changes as omission of Laurie's British visitors, whom Alcott had not portrayed altogether positively (one cheated at croquet), and to some fiddling of class issues (Jo can be a governess in New York without losing too much caste but no longer jostles elbows with the hoi polloi by staying in a boarding house). Perhaps because the book is to represent Americanness more than women's independence, but also because the recent women's movement was still very young, there is some diminishment of Jo's achievement and independence. We do see her writing, and there's a reference to her writing a book, but it's Professor Bhaer who has achieved a publication that Mr. March admires. It's not through Jo's inheritance that she and Bhaer will be able to start a school for boys but through his being offered a position—and thus it's to be his school, not theirs. He may joke at the end that it's the duty of a good German wife to be obedient to her husband, but the laugh doesn't entirely erase Jo's willingness to be subordinate.

More notable was a 1978 NBC production. One reviewer dismissed it as "irrelevant, palid [sic] and as substantial as spun sugar."[106] But others were positive about Susan Dey's performance as Jo, perhaps finding the film as a whole "tolerably sweet and wholesome," certainly better than most TV versions of "cherished novels."[107] A reviewer in Australia called the production "workmanlike, if sugary."[108] One for the *Los Angeles Times* found the cast solid but the "ambience more reminiscent of Knott's Berry Farm than 19th-century Concord, Mass."[109] This claim about the ambience is apt, even if the production did win an Emmy for outstanding art direction for a series. As for the acting, Dey conveys Jo's variety of emotions and her tomboyish exuberance (even if she does lose a race to Laurie—not a footrace but on horseback). Dorothy McGuire's Marmee is more troubled by doubts and uncertainties than in other versions, with the result that she seems rather weak-willed. Meredith Baxter Birney is adequate as Meg, and she gets more screen time than most Megs do, with some attention to her married life. And considerable play is given to cross-purposes between Laurie and his grandfather. Robert Young's Mr. Laurence even strikes Laurie, thus diverging from his star persona, not exactly an unflappable grandfather-knows-best; indeed, Jo is the one who usually knows best for the two men. William Shatner is a plausible Professor Bhaer, even if his German accent slips at times—though it's not till the sequel that Bhaer, played by a different actor, gets to be where no man has been before, as I note below.

In part this film echoes previous ones—we see Jo climb out an upper-floor window and, here, down a tree before she sets off to the offices of the *Spread Eagle* with her story manuscript (also, for some reason, when she goes horseback riding with Laurie). It anticipates the 1994 film by providing a voiceover by Jo, this time often to provide details of the Civil War context. Suzanne Clauser's script sticks more closely to the novel than many film versions do. Yet the changes include prolonging Beth's near death, in the first half, to the point of having her sisters and even Marmee assume, for a few moments, that she is dead (to jerk tears?), even while having her discreetly die offstage later on; calling Jo home from New York not because of Beth's dying but, a bit implausibly, because of Meg's pregnancy (perhaps to give more play to Jo's drawn-out denial of Beth's impending mortality?); and keeping feisty Aunt March alive at the end (as if anticipating the possibility of a sequel?). And Bhaer puts his foot down when Jo says she doesn't want to put off their wedding for a year: "The decision is mine. I will take care of you as I see fit." "Yes, Friedrich," she replies meekly.[110] Capturing 37 percent of the TV audience, the movie was popular enough that the producer created a short-lived TV series that aired the following spring. The series covers the time between the end of *Little Women* and the beginning of *Little Men*, showing, for instance, an unmarried Jo caring for an ailing Bhaer and spending the night, apparently becoming sexually aroused.[111]

As for other television versions, in 1976 NBC presented an hour-long ballet adaptation of *Little Women* in its *Special Treat* series of programs for children.[112] Joanne Woodward narrates, as a reminiscing Marmee, in a production made up of vignettes from the novel, strung together in a plot that foregrounds Meg trying to attract John Brooke (played by New York City Ballet's Edward Villella, who also receives credit for choreography). Beth doesn't die here, but viewers don't seem to have been particularly upset: there was no media uproar as there had been for the 1958 TV musical. Maybe it doesn't matter so much with ballet, which may be seen as more commonly taking liberties with a preexisting text.

For the production foregrounded not the best-remembered scenes from the novel but dance scenes and scenes that could lend themselves to physical movement. Amy still burns Jo's manuscript—so that they can perform a dance that mimes fighting. But unlike in the novel, Amy's schoolteacher, Mr. Davis, teaches a physical-culture class, and Meg as governess teaches four young girls to curtsey and later reads them Brer Rabbit tales so that they can hop like bunnies. Several pas de deux feature Meg and Brooke, concluding with their wedding. The reviewer Judith Martin criticizes the production for being neither play nor ballet: as a play it fails because TV close-ups reveal "the same lipsticked smiles, stretched over bony faces, . . . on all the girls" and "only the jolly, danceable scenes are chosen"; as a ballet, because the dancing is so "constantly interrupted."[113]

Indeed, the target audience for the production is puzzling. Martin suggests that the short dance scenes might appeal to an audience with short attention spans. Yet the novel has rarely been seen as targeting the very young. And there is relatively little of the physical liveliness and humor in this production that might appeal to seven-year-olds and can be found in productions of *The Nutcracker*. So it's quite odd to watch the production with its original advertising, the graceful ballet interrupted by hyperactive ads for Alpha-Bits cereal, Nestlé's Quik, and Kenner action toys.

As for the big-screen version, the 1994 Hollywood film, the Columbia Pictures executive Amy Pascal (Amy Beth Pascal, actually—her mother was an Alcott fan) had wanted to film *Little Women* for years; only once she was a powerful executive was she able to do so.[114] Studios favored action films, and "the very title summons up preconceptions of treacly do-gooders in a smarmy children's story," as Roger Ebert opened his review. But then he remembered that he had found the novel "really GOOD" when he was young, and it "seems to have grown up in the meantime," or maybe director Gillian Armstrong simply focused on the serious themes. He gave the film three and a half stars out of four, praising the ensemble acting for "creating the warmth and familiarity of a real family."[115]

All three major Hollywood versions open with a snowy village scene (an American version of a heritage film—not a stately manor but snowy New England), yet what ensues in each is significantly different: whereas the Depression-era film showed the women at work and the postwar film showed a pratfall, undermining June Allyson's boyish attempt to leap a fence, this one offers Marmee's return from work at a settlement house and the reading of a letter from Father. It thus opens with an early adumbration of family togetherness, echoing many illustrators' clustered fivesome. This scene was a late addition to the film. Only later do we encounter the scene that came first in an early draft of Robin Swicord's screenplay when we watch Laurie gazing toward Orchard House and then cut to the sisters conducting a meeting of what is here called the Pickwick Society.[116] Dressed in drag, they read what they have written. Thus the scene captures Laurie's longing, the sisters' accomplishments, especially Jo's writing, and some visual gender bending. Opening with the warmly glowing image of the matriarchal family, one of the few additions to the early draft, may simply be a way of starting with the received iconography. Maybe the gender bending of the Pickwick scene was still too progressive to open a Hollywood movie. Or maybe there simply is less gender bending overall in this version, Winona Ryder's Jo less of a physical tomboy than Hepburn's or Allyson's.

In any case, the film is in dialogue with Alcott's text, Alcott's other writings, other film adaptations, and the audience; it's a work in its own right, not just an imitation attempting to replicate an originary text. Like previous films, this one omits the moral preaching of Alcott's narrator, but it adds feminist preaching, usually by Marmee, on issues ranging from women's votes to corsets. As the writer Robin Swicord noted in an interview, she and her coworkers "wanted to say what was not being said, particularly to young women and about young women" and to purge this version of the clichés added to previous adaptations, especially the bitchiness that "trivialized what happens between sisters."[117] In adding feminist material from Alcott's other writings, Swicord aligns the film with Alcott's life, an alignment further reinforced by Ryder's retrospective voiceover, positioning her as narrator/writer. Ryder's Jo may not fence or leap fences, but she does eventually let her hair down. As in most visual adaptations, the hair styles are anachronistic, and loose hair here seems to signal the possibility of romance, as does the loose gauzy dress that Jo wears when receiving Laurie's marriage proposal. Yet even as it endorses romance, this version incorporates such Alcott scenes omitted from previous Hollywood versions as Amy's burning of Jo's manuscript: there's no longer a need to shield us from the dangers of anger. Indeed, "I rather crave violence," Jo admits to Beth (not something she says in the novel), talking partly of her writing but also of a general willingness to engage with strong sensations. The publication of Alcott's sensation stories has colored perceptions of the novel.

The film also includes scenes that appeared only in previous film versions, not in the novel, such as Professor Bhaer taking Jo to the opera (even if they watch discreetly from the backstage wings, thereby finessing the improbability of Jo's possessing an opera dress). The music of opera is apparently too useful a filmic device for signifying romance, and indeed, after Bhaer translates some of the love lyrics, he and Jo kiss. We glimpse some of the opera here, a production not of *Faust* as in the early draft of the screenplay—which would have drawn on the Professor's German background, though the theme of selling one's soul to the devil might have been disconcerting—but of Bizet's *Les pêcheurs de perles*. It's an anachronistic performance for the 1860s,[118] but the theme of two men competing for a woman's love might seem more appropriate. In this film version too Bhaer condemns Jo's early writing of sensation stories, yet for writing not of "such women" but of "lunatics and vampires." "You should be writing from life, from the depths of your soul," he later tells her. And, again as in the other film versions but not in the novel, he is instrumental in getting Jo's novel about her family published.

Nevertheless, Armstrong's film incorporates many more overt gestures toward women's independence than both earlier films and the novel do—and also more scenes of Jo writing than the earlier films do. It still ends, though, as do the other major film versions, not with the novel's family gathering in an orchard but with Jo and Bhaer agreeing to marry. Ryder claims in the "Making of *Little Women*" featurette, included on the CD, that the movie is "not just about this girl who wants to be a writer. It's about falling in love and getting your heart broken and breaking people's hearts, and it kind of touches on just about everything." Writing would seem not to be one of Ryder's priorities. And at least one reviewer found that "her telling lack of backbone inevitably encourages interest in her romantic endeavors far more than any career moves."[119] Yet as Deborah Cartmell and Judy Simons point out, the film elides the novel's tensions between writing and romance by merging them, implicitly linking Jo's true writing, writing that is true to her self, with her awakening sexuality.[120]

Reviews were quite positive, more positive than those for the 1949 film version but less wildly so than those for the 1933 one. An occasional reviewer found the film a bit smug or sugary, but others found it "magical," "entrancing," with "a touching naturalness"; "charming, intelligent and beautiful"; "gently feminist, historically genuine, and emotionally satisfying"; "surprisingly sharp and intelligent"; "a beautiful, touching gem of a film"; "a must-see for everyone"—in short, "a perfect holiday gift for the entire family."[121] Even "one of the most impassioned and heartfelt family sagas ever made in this country."[122]

Little Women was not a blockbuster, but it was successful, "the surprise hit of the Christmas season," grossing $27.5 million in three weeks, "attracting multigenerational female moviegoers in unparalleled numbers."[123] It eventually grossed more than $50 million domestically, although it ranked only twenty-seventh among top-grossing films in 1994.[124] Still, the novel has been one of the "few literary properties that prove to be box-office successes no matter how many times they are remade."[125] Anecdotal reports of moviegoers vary. One commentator stated that most girls on a *USA Today* teen panel were lukewarm about the movie (most hadn't read the book).[126] In other reports, a twelve-year-old said, "It *was* good. . . . Even though not all that much happened," and an eleven-year-old boy claimed, "It's great—and it's not just for girls!"[127]

Enthusiasm elsewhere in the world tended to be tempered, although British reviewers were positive. For them the film was "immensely well done," more engaging than a Merchant-Ivory production and giving "back to the book some of its original pioneer feel," and "an unexpected triumph. Even the 1933 version must look to its laurels."[128] Australians, perhaps especially appreciative of the film's Australian director, were positive too, finding the film "a gentle gem," "unashamedly sentimental yet its strength is never wallowing in mush."[129] French reviewers praised Armstrong's lively humanism and the exceptional execution, "à mi-chemin entre l'esthéthism suranné de certaines cartes de Nöel victoriennes et celui plus austere de certains film scandinaves" (midway between the outdated estheticism of certain Victorian Christmas cards and the more austere one of certain Scandinavian films).[130] Yet Italian reviewers variously found the subtlety of the book flattened, the film "inutile e noiosa" (pointless and tedious), leaving a "retrogusto amaro" (bitter aftertaste).[131] A German reviewer called the film "einen durchaus irritierenden Kostuemfilm" (a thoroughly irritating costume drama).[132] A Jamaican found the movie good but thought it "sadly might put most movie-goers to sleep."[133]

Tie-ins included dolls, jewelry, scented products, and lace-trimmed night-gowns.[134] There were at least six book tie-ins, including novelizations by Laurie Lawlor.[135] One, sized to fit on mass-market paperback racks, included a section with black-and-white stills from the film; another, larger but with fewer pages, in-terspersed more numerous color stills—which were as inadequately coordinated with the adjacent text as is common in such productions.[136] The film pushed an edition onto bestseller lists for several weeks in 1995.[137] And its success helped to boost tourism in Concord and encouraged publishers to reissue Alcott biogra-phies, letters, and collected fiction and to issue new items, paying an "incredible advance" for "a lost Alcott novel," A *Long Fatal Love Chase*.[138] It also generated enough interest in Alcott that, as happened after the 1933 film, a different com-pany produced a version of *Little Men* shortly afterwards, but with little critical or financial success.

Despite the many strengths of the 1994 film version, though, arguably the most striking adaptation in recent years is Mark Adamo's opera of *Little Women*, which premiered in Houston in 1998 and was broadcast on PBS in 2001. A "phenomenal success,"[139] it has achieved a remarkable seventy productions, across the United States and also in Canada, Mexico, Australia, Belgium, Israel, and Japan. Its great popular appeal is due in part to its relationship to a well-known text but also to its incorporation of lyricism in addition to atonality and of features of musical theater indebted to Sondheim and Bernstein. Adamo tempered the inevitable nostalgia with astringency; indeed, the small company that originally commissioned the opera rejected it for not having "the nostalgic, homespun quality that Adamo had worked so hard to avoid."[140] As one critic noted, "The balance of sentiment and irony is close to ideal."[141] Furthermore, this chamber opera requires only a small orchestra, and the vocal demands are not too strenuous, making it suitable for young voices and thus conservatory productions. Staying largely in the middle of singers' ranges also makes it easier for the audience to understand the dialogue, a characteristic especially important for a "demotic subject," without the raging passions of traditional opera.[142] Finally, in the words of the director who initially commissioned the music, the opera is "a soprano's paradise . . . and anyone who has ever done opera casting knows that the sopranos far outnumber the other voices."[143]

Far more than any other musical version of *Little Women*, this one has received high praise, sometimes invoking the term *masterpiece*, even if only "some sort of masterpiece."[144] More than one reviewer thought it likely to become an American classic—to "earn a chance at the title of 'greatest American opera.'"[145] Critics found it "engaging," "brilliant," "masterly and often poetic."[146] They occasionally faulted the opera for its focus on "everyday occurrences—hardly the sort of behavior that engenders heroic action or consequence, which are needed if the audience is to forge an emotional bond with [the heroine]."[147] The criticism here sounds a little like dismissals of women's writing as quotidian, as not addressing what's truly important, or dismissals of children's literature. Indeed, a reviewer of an Australian production, while noting Adamo's "verve and freshness," faults the attempt "to explore existential themes of change," since "a simple children's story such as this is not the vehicle with which to do it."[148] Others critiqued the composer for doing "nothing to upset [the] comfort" of the story's familiarity, creating "benignly listenable tunes that occasionally sound like capable music theater writing" or else "the kind of approachable, easily digested score that's becoming increasingly common in contemporary opera."[149] Yet as a critic for the *New York Times* noted, "The piece has taken some critical knocks for its lyricism and the facile appeal of its subject. But it does everything an opera should do. Not least, it leaves an audience moved."[150]

One of the few critics who discussed the libretto praised it: the use of rhyme "may make the words seem slightly old fashioned," but it also enables "both the possibility of humor and wit as well as a rapid shift to operatic poetry in the aria sections."[151] For another critic, however, it wasn't the libretto that counted. The greatest ones look ridiculous on the page, he argued in his brief against adapting a novel such as *Little Women* to opera: "Opera is anti-poetical, anti-novelistic, anti-intellectual."[152]

The reviewer of an American production for the London-based *Opera* referred to "Adamo's sub-Sondheim idiom—with a few wrong-note passages thrown in to give his score contemporary street cred" and doubted "if it's for export."[153] But *Little Women* has nevertheless done well outside the United States. According to excerpts on Adamo's website, a London reviewer claimed that this opera "appeals with soft-spoken conviction to head as well as heart"; an Israeli reviewer found it "compelling"; a Mexican reviewer, "destined to be a classic of American opera"; and in Australia it was "magically transporting," "an opera for our time," "an absolute gem."[154]

This opera is a conscious reinterpretation of the novel. Adamo seems to have resisted one of the temptations experienced by other adapters of *Little Women* to stage or screen, namely, that of playing to the audience or to the audience's memory. Early in the twentieth century, adapters made sure to include scenes that members of the audience were likely to remember from the novel: the playwright Marion de Forest started drafting her 1912 Broadway play by writing from memory, thus including what she remembered best; the director Harley Knoles claimed that his 1919 film version encompassed all the best-remembered scenes.[155] It's harder to find similar direct evidence for subsequent adaptations, but certainly the Hollywood film industry, wanting to recoup the cost of mounting a film and to secure the audience that would be lured by the film's title, would be attentive to such an urge (remember that 1932 poll of whether RKO should modernize the story or retain the nineteenth-century setting). Another motive can be to foreground scenes that particularly lend themselves to the medium into which one is translating a work; such seems to have been the dominant principle for the ballet adaptation shown on NBC in 1976. One advantage, of course, is that a production guided by one of these motives can be true to the dailiness, the relative plotlessness, of the book. Alternatively, and indeed commonly, if an adapter seeks more emplotment, especially one that resonates with what is perceived as a broad audience, he or she may foreground the romance narratives.

What Adamo did, in contrast, was seek to construct a classically plotted narrative that wasn't based on heterosexual romance. Romance is certainly present, but it doesn't drive the story: it seems to function more as a marker of a broader theme of change. Much as Beth leaves Jo through dying, Meg leaves through marriage. (We do get to see Meg's wedding—I suppose that weddings offer too much of an opportunity for spectacle and music for an opera composer to resist.) Laurie and Amy leave Jo through marriage too. Then, at the very end, Professor Bhaer appears at the entrance to Jo's attic, and she extends her hand to him and invites him in. Yet there's no direct proposal and acceptance, no culminating cozy image of the two under an umbrella.

Mary Forsell posits that this ending, in which Jo doesn't explicitly accept a marriage proposal, leaves us with "a lingering question mark," but Elizabeth Keyser argues that Adamo ultimately valorizes marital love by making the loves between Meg and John, Laurie and Amy, and Mr. and Mrs. March prominent and by "giving Bhaer almost the last word."[156] Adamo himself has called the opera "a love story among four girls"—not the love stories of four girls—yet he also admits that he didn't view the novel as "about a woman struggling to become an artist."[157] I'd argue that heterosexual romance is less central here than in other Alcott adaptations: Adamo focused instead on Jo's battle with time, her attempts to make time stand still, the struggle between the "Perfect as we are" that she voices in opposition to Meg's (and Laurie's and Beth's) "Things change, Jo."

Adamo omitted scenes deemed peripheral to this struggle. There's no Amy burning Jo's manuscript, no rescue of Amy from the icy river, no Meg being tempted by Vanity Fair, no Beth being given a piano by Mr. Laurence, indeed no Mr. Laurence, and no hair cutting by Jo to provide money for Marmee's trip to an ailing Father. Indeed, Adamo omits the Civil War. A title shown at the beginning of the PBS broadcast sets the story in "New England after the Civil War," but there's no other reference to the war in the production; the war is simply a verbal marker of the nineteenth century. Or, one could argue, it has been translated metaphorically into a different kind of conflict, Jo's battle with time.

It's not necessary for an adaptation of *Little Women* to have a traditional plot; it's possible to stage one that retains the relative plotlessness of Alcott's novel. But I do think that Adamo's plotting succeeds as an interpretation of the novel—and as a work of art in its own right. Thomas May argues that "the emotional directness and clarification which opera uniquely provides can enrich a story we had thought was already told."[158] We can also appreciate Adamo's opera as an independent work that is simultaneously intertextual with a previous work or works: we don't have to insist on fidelity, even if exact fidelity were possible.

The music, of course, is an important facet of Adamo's medium. He himself brilliantly explicates the interweaving of musical themes in his notes for an online course.[159] Opera aficionados have been somewhat mixed in their judgment of the music. Adamo combines atonal recitative, forwarding the action, with lyrical arias. For some reviewers he achieved the right balance; for others, not.[160] Still, the interweaving of motives and words is noteworthy. As Richard Dyer notes, the "characters echo one another's words but think their own thoughts."[161]

Besides having many aspects of poetry, of recurring and modulating themes, the medium enables contrapuntal effects between words and music: at the end of the prologue, the orchestral "things change" leitmotif plays against Jo's vocal insistence that she can "rewind the spool" of time.[162] The medium also allows for another kind of simultaneity. Sometimes the characters sing together, and indeed critics praise the ensembles—the trios, the quartets, even an octet.[163] And sometimes characters sing or speak over one another, in a way that is difficult to represent on the page. In the family parlor in act 1, scene 2, for instance, Jo is teasing Meg about John Brooke, Mr. and Mrs. March are discussing the family finances, and Beth is composing an accompaniment to John Bunyan's hymn "He that is down need fear no fall"—as indeed she does in the novel. Onstage all happens simultaneously, although Beth is largely drowned out until her father asks to hear her music. She obliges, modestly noting that she hasn't finished the piece yet; her composition won't be completed until act 2, after she dies, when the orchestra completes the music.

As for this discussion of finances, Mr. March says that he does not want to let Niles republish a work of his, since "the Niles publish entertainment./They do not publish thought" (I.ii, 44). He thus inaugurates what Adamo calls the art/entertainment motive ("Course" 42+). A version of this issue is, of course, central to the writing efforts of Alcott's Jo. Should she write sensation stories, to make money, or should she write what she knows? In Alcott's version the issue is largely a moral one; certainly her Professor Bhaer condemns the writing of sensation stories as "put[ting] poison in the sugar-plum": "There is a demand for whiskey, but I think you and I do not care to sell it."[164] In the opera, Bhaer's "You can do better than this, Jo" (II.ii, 66), is ambiguous. Since it immediately follows his saying, "There's a market for opium, too," a phrasing that parallels Alcott's, substituting a substance more condemned now, he seems to imply that she could do better morally. Jo, however, chooses to define *better* in aesthetic terms when she asks, "Well, if the opera isn't,/and my stories aren't,/what's 'proper' art?" (II.ii, 66). She thus seems to be making Bhaer less a patriarchal authority trying to police his little woman's morality and more an aesthetic supporter of his companion's artistic quest. Bhaer's response is to sing Goethe's "Mignon's Song" (something that Alcott's Jo had heard him hum and that she later sings with him), thus answering that Goethe sets a standard to aspire to or perhaps, since the aria ends with an address to "mein Geliebter," "my beloved" (II.ii, 66, 67), that love should supersede art for her. (And it hints at the question whether Adamo's own translation, of novel to opera, aspires to art or to sentiment.)

With respect to Jo's question about the standing of opera, in Alcott's novel opera has high status, whether Meg goes to one when she visits the Gardiners or else a gathering at the Chesters' house discusses it. Jo's subtitling of her melodramatic play "An Operatic Tragedy"—an opus neither particularly operatic nor tragic—invokes the grandeur of both modes, whether she is hoping to shed some on her own work or is being ironic. When in part 2 Laurie goes off to Vienna to compose, he even attempts an opera, but because of her decidedly prosaic and unsentimental "oddities, faults, and freaks . . . Jo wouldn't be put into the Opera at any price" (329). In Alcott's *Little Women* opera is associated with high class and high culture—and indeed those are my primary associations with the art form.

Yet Adamo situates opera somewhat differently with respect to class, or at least nationality, within his opus, and not just because he chooses to focus on faulty, freakish Jo. As in the Hollywood movie versions, Jo and Bhaer go to the opera—something that would have been unthinkable for them to do, unchaperoned, in the novel or in Victorian society. But as I've already suggested, there's something about the visual and aural spectacle of opera, together with a music that often bespeaks passion, that lends itself to a romantic turn in the visual and aural medium of film (or maybe Hepburn simply wanted an excuse to wear her grandmother's opera gown). We don't see Adamo's Jo and Bhaer at the opera, just in the midst of a conversation as they return. "But that's why I loved it!" she exclaims. "So lurid and preposterous./Though I *would* have liked to understand the words" (II. ii, 62). Bhaer responds—"grandly," according to the liner notes—that "Italians make opera./They do not make art" (II.ii, 62). What? Opera is not art? Then I think of my working-class Italian grandmother, who loved opera. Opera didn't know class distinctions in early-twentieth-century Italy. (As Adamo states in an interview, referencing his Italian American background, "Opera is Italian naturalism.")[165] And, apparently, nineteenth-century Germans, despite the presence of Wagner, tended to consider opera inferior to concert music: Beethoven, after all, composed only one opera.[166] So Adamo is having a bit of a joke at his own expense, perhaps also undermining Bhaer. Adamo plays it out a bit more when Jo goes on to say, "Couldn't they print the words on a banner,/unspool it in front of the stage,/so you could read what they were saying as they sing it—" (II.ii, 63). Bhaer replies, "It never would work, Miss March" (II.ii, 63). The popularity of surtitles in modern opera productions undermines Bhaer's artistic judgment even more. The exchange also resonates with the rest of the libretto: it suggests some questioning of traditional boundaries between high and low art, thus creating some space for a demotic opera like Adamo's and for a potential revaluing of Jo's potboilers, and maybe of Alcott's *Little Women*, though the suggestion is not further pursued.

A related theme pertains to the functions of art. The prologue opens on a scene that comes late in Alcott's novel: Laurie has returned from Europe and meets Jo in her attic, their first meeting after he and Amy marry. When he leaves, Jo conjures up the memory of the way things were some years before, the majority of the opera thus situated as a flashback. Or one could say that she composes the story of the opera: she mimes an orchestra conductor as she conducts Laurie back through the trap door and proclaims, "No one's leaving,/no one's dying—" (prologue, 29). The story is thus an effort to stop time and also a palliative for loss, much as Alcott herself performed alchemy on her own family in creating her novel. Yet the function of art in relation to reality is troubled in the opera. The club of sisters shown in the following scene is not the Pickwick Club but the Barristers Club, not a confabulation of writers penning a portfolio but teasing inquisitors demanding truthful answers to questions, as they sort laundry. The game allows for some economical characterization and revelation of plot detail (for example, the loss of Meg's glove, which we'll later learn Brooke has), but it also privileges "truth" over storytelling, thus undermining the value of (Jo's) artistic creation.

Another scene in the novel that would lend itself to a thematics of the role of art, and often to visual performance in adaptations, is the rehearsal of Jo's play. What Adamo offers instead of a play rehearsal is Jo composing—rehearsing fragments of—a story. Compared with the novel, the opera focuses more on her creativity than on performing gender, even if she does mime the role of the male villain with some gusto. Intriguingly, the composing bits are in temporal counterpoint with Jo's protestations to the later Laurie (not physically present) that "we're perfect as we are" (I.i, 38); that is, she switches back and forth between an imagined conversation with Laurie and the action of the melodramatic story she is composing. Or in the words of Adamo's program notes, "her long-lined F-major *cantilena*" is disrupted by "careening dodecaphonic comedy."[167] When Jo's composing reaches a point when she is at a loss for a word—when, for instance, she falters, "The count in a perfect . . . perfect . . ." (I.i, 38, ellipses in original)—she shifts to her imaginary address to Laurie. Then after six or seven lines she shifts back, pivoting on a single word. In this instance she tells Laurie, "How often are your sisters, your nearest sisters/Your dearest fren . . ." (I.i, 38, ellipsis in original). And she comes up with *Frenzy*, a word that undermines some of the sentimentality of the sororal image she has been weaving even as it completes the thought in the earlier melodramatic section and returns her to composing mode: the count is in a perfect frenzy. The link hints at the underside of the sororal story and its connection to Jo's potboilers, implying a link between composing and "reality." At the same time, the presumably "real" segments are addressed to an imaginary Laurie, and the sisters Jo describes are imagined at a distance—"See the way we blend?" (I.i, 38), she observes—and are thus not, in the "real" time of the production, "real."

The multiple meanings in such a scene suggest a richness in the functions of art, a richness reinforced in the final scene when the sisters together refer to "a half-enchanted family/We'll never be again" (II.iv, 77). *Half-enchanted* suggests both the fantasy elements of the entire story and the sorcery of Jo's re-creation of it. So it's a little puzzling to have heard Jo sing, just moments earlier, "No games now./No fairy stories, no 'let's pretend,'" since "Things end." She needs to let go of her sisters: "It's not in my control" (II.iv, 76). Is that dismissal of stories a disavowal of Jo's creativity? Or is it just leading up to a recognition not that things end but that things change? When at the very end she welcomes her Professor with the words "Now is all there is" (II.iv, 78), she has moved into a recognition that things change. Musically, Adamo notes, these words are sung to "a melody of almost the same shape as . . . 'Perfect as we are,' . . . but with its last pitch breaking free of the old theme's enclosed seventh, reaching even higher for change and possibility" ("Course" 82). But if Jo is indeed reconciled to things changing, there seems to be little room for creativity, the inspired attempt to stop change. Love has superseded art.

Yet maybe this self-contradiction is what makes the opera memorable, what makes it live. Adamo's adaptation is a rich reinterpretation that stands on its own even as the audience plays its unfolding against the memory of Alcott's novel. Thomas May posits that the "all-too-human dilemma" of Things Change vs. Perfect As It Was can be "a metaphor for a more specific sense of crisis in the world of opera today."[168] It also functions as a metaphor for the positioning of *Little Women*, the tug of war between Alcott's "perfect as it was" text and the inevitable changes in how readers now read it, whether they re-vision it in private readings or in public fora.

∼

Few re-visionings open up and expand on Alcott's text as Adamo's does. The numerous condensed versions, which have been especially popular since the middle of the twentieth century, rarely do, whether they retain the original language or dumb that down as well—whether to attract a less patient modern reader or perhaps a very young one. Paratextual materials in editions for early readers may stress that after a child has thus been introduced to a story's main themes, "the desire to tackle the original, unabridged version of the story will naturally emerge."[169] Perhaps. Or maybe, like the ten-minute condensed version published in newspapers a century ago, an abridgment simply gives cheap access to cultural capital without its having to be earned the hard way.

Most abridgments begin with Jo's usual "Christmas won't be Christmas without any presents." Sometimes, though, the adapter mangles it: I can only guess that the desire to avoid two-syllable words except when absolutely necessary must have inspired the following: "Christmas will not be fun if we don't get new things."[170] Other versions begin not *in medias res*—it's too confusing to young readers to begin with dialogue?—but with a paragraph that sets the scene: "While the snow fell quietly outside their New England home, the four March sisters stayed warm by the fire in their cozy living room."[171] An afterword tells us that Dr. Arthur Pober, EdD, who is not credited with the abridgment but who did provide some discussion questions and perhaps oversaw the project as a whole, "is a recognized authority in the areas of media and child protection" (153). Protection indeed. Another version, a British abridgment in the Oxford Bookworms Library, is keyed to a website where one can calculate the number of words in a given book—this

Little Women has 14,920—and one's teacher can register the word count in a reading diary to qualify one for a certificate. Whereas the questions at the end of Dr. Pober's edition focus on what-would-you-have-done and how-would-you-feel, those at the end of this one focus on decoding, including identifying statements as true or false and pairing "the right character," one of the March sisters or Laurie, with a "thing," such as "love letters" or "warning about thin ice," and writing about it.[172] Reading *Little Women* becomes, for the very young, a matter of one arbitrary right answer, a way to close off options.

Most abridged editions omit Alcott's incorporated texts—the sisters' letters to their parents in Washington, the "Pickwick Portfolio," to which each contributes, the story-game Rigmarole. (Occasionally a brief text oddly adds an incident, such as a cat accidentally tipping ink onto Meg's hat.) They also generally delete some of the overt moralizing, often omitting as well the temptations and trials of one or more of the sisters. Yet even as the redactors attempt to modernize, and even if their paratextual paraphernalia tend to emphasize Alcott's interest in reform regarding women's issues, they may streamline some of her subtle commentaries out of the text. The afterword to the 1989 Reader's Digest condensed version notes, "The social conscience engendered by her parents drew her to use this attention [brought by fame] in active support of women's suffrage and prison reform. She was also a spokesperson for the view that women should receive the same pay as men for the same work."[173] In the text of this edition, Amy asks Meg whether three years seem like a long engagement:

> "I've got so much to learn, it seems a short time to me," answered Meg, with sweet gravity.
> "You have only to wait. *I* am to do the work," said John. (87)

A clear putdown of women's work: from a man's perspective, acquiring cooking and other housekeeping skills doesn't count. In the original version the second paragraph begins thus: " 'You have only to wait. *I* am to do the work,' said John, beginning his labors by picking up Meg's napkin, with an expression which caused Jo to shake her head" (184). What the redaction loses, in part, is the reversion to Jo's bracing perspective, to her shaking her head, not endorsing a romance that will break up the March family and also, coincidentally, make Meg more dependent on a man than she had been, given Father's absence in most of the book. The condensing also loses the irony that undercuts John's claim to doing all the work, given that the narrator reduces his work to picking up a napkin.

Translations of *Little Women* too are often abridged, in addition to being redacted in other ways, sometimes considerably. Claire Le Brun notes that even French translations done in the past three decades significantly attenuate the feminism of the book, soften Jo's appearance, and minimize her anger and literary ambitions. Emblematic is the change to Jo's desire to be a horse, to be able to run for miles: a more feminine gazelle may be offered instead, or the reference to an animal is omitted entirely. And in one recent French translation, as in the foundational 1880 one, Jo ends *Les quatre filles du docteur March* by marrying Laurie.[174] Still, whether in spite of the mistranslation or because of it, *Little Women* has been a significant presence in France, if one judges by the frequency of translation and also the presence of scholarly work, as I've noted earlier in this chapter.

In a study of recent translations into Dutch, Mieke Desmet closely examines three very different ones: they range from a 1983 version that stays close to the source text, albeit abridging it, to a 1993 mass-market one that aims for a younger audience and has not only minimized the moralizing but "reduced the creativity theme considerably and . . . neutralized the gender ambiguity instead creating a fairy-tale like romantic story."[175] Indeed, in this latter version—possibly a re-translation from the French, given that its title is not the usual *Onder moeders vleugels* (Under mother's wings) of most Dutch editions but *De vier dochters van Dr March*—Jo agrees to marry Laurie only if he becomes a farmer. Which he has apparently been planning to do anyway. So they marry.

☙

Yet another way in which the autobiographical *Little Women* has been re-visioned is through retelling Alcott's life. Authorial biography has a complex relationship to literary texts and to scholarly criticism. In the eighteenth and nineteenth centuries an author's biography was often considered central to a reader's understanding of and relationship to a text, yet with the mid-twentieth-century rise of the New Criticism, scholars have condemned having recourse to the author as resorting to the Intentional Fallacy. If one is studying a work of literature, one should trust the words of the text, not what an author says he or she meant or is inferred as having meant. For Catherine Belsey, critical biography has unfortunately become "not an aid to reading but a substitute for it," yet "outside of academic publishing, very few other varieties of criticism are offered to the general public."[176] One way in which many readers, old and young, pay homage to a text and try to enrich their understanding of it is by turning to the author's biography.

Biography is also of interest for its own sake, not just as an adjunct to a text. The biographer Nigel Hamilton traces two primary impulses for writing and reading biographies: commemorating the past and gaining insight into human character.[177] The former leads to idealizations of character; the latter, to examination of vices as well as virtues. The former was the prevalent approach in the Victorian era; the latter has come to the fore in the twentieth and twenty-first centuries.

And of course biography is of special interest to readers of Alcott's fiction because of the long association of many elements of the work with her life. According to a reviewer of a recent biography, "Louisa May Alcott has become a popular heroine nearly as beloved as her most famous creations, the March sisters," thanks to her pioneering accomplishments as a writer and a Civil War nurse and also her devotion to service and duty.[178] Pascale Voilley has stated that Alcott's life, like those of Emerson and Thoreau, "constitue un texte qui prend place parmi ses œuvres" (is a text that takes its place among her works).[179]

Similar impulses inform juvenile biographies. Authors are people too—so goes a saying popular in some elementary classrooms. Teachers like young students to connect to reading and hope to enable such connection by humanizing the author; they also like students to connect to writing, to think of themselves as authors. Many encourage the student to learn something about the author, an enterprise that has supported a proliferation of juvenile biographies. Biographical study has long been considered important for the young, to provide such connections and indeed to provide role modeling, whether the role to be emulated is one of writing or of living an exemplary life. Before about 1960 such role modeling was largely of the latter sort: in most juvenile biographies authors were idealized. Since then there has been greater attention to providing insights into human character, allowing a child reader "to know that others shared the doubts and fears he or she feels and yet were able to work out a productive and fulfilled life."[180] In the words of an introduction to one juvenile biography, "Biography can inspire not only by adulation but also by realism."[181] The biographical impulse is complicated in Alcott's case because her best-known fiction is so autobiographical. "We really lived most of it," she claimed of *Little Women.*[182] So homage to Alcott is especially likely to take a biographical turn, even as some biographers rely too much on the novel as a source.

Since 1960 there have been eight or more book-length biographies for adults and more than two dozen juvenile biographies. Many of the biographies for adults are composites, whether in terms of genre (biography–cum–social history) or subject (family or dual biographies). And the biographers are still finding new information and interpretations, for instance, that the ailment that Alcott suffered from in her final decades was probably lupus. Or maybe Alcott finally knuckled down to writing *Little Women*, the girls' book she'd promised Thomas Niles, only because producing such a book was a condition for Niles's publishing a work by her father, Bronson. Some biographers also continue to proliferate possible romances—maybe Bronson had romantic interests in younger women, maybe Abba had an affair with Charles Lane. Among biographies targeting adults, John Matteson's Pulitzer Prize–winning *Eden's Outcasts: The Story of Louisa May Alcott and her Father* (2008) is particularly notable for its grace and insight. Matteson treats both father and daughter sensitively, acknowledging the difficulties of living with an improvident father or with a daughter's mood swings (hypothesizing that she was what would now be called bipolar).

The earlier Alcott biographies targeting the young—those written before 1960 but also those in the 1960s and 1970s—were particularly likely to focus on providing a worthy role model in Alcott, to immerse us in the story by fictionalizing parts of it, and to convey "an impressive unity of character and purpose."[183] Martha Vicinus has noted that juvenile biographies of Florence Nightingale published shortly after World War II tended to emphasize romance, or rather failed romance, thus undermining the presumed focus of such a biography on memorializing a successful public figure.[184] The Alcott biographies published in the 1950s and also since then have often continued to focus on Alcott's personal qualities more than her public value, her celebrity more than her fame.

Among the juvenile biographies published since 1960, some are short picture books; most are longer, often with occasional illustrations. Most were first published in the United States, although some first appeared in England, Australia, France, Spain, or Brazil. Some focus on Alcott's early years, or maybe just the months at Fruitlands or her Civil War experiences. Some biographers quote frequently from Alcott's journals and other writings; indeed, some focus almost entirely on her girlhood diaries. Some still invent dialogue. Some are inventive with other details, maybe inventing characters, such as a fellow Civil War nurse in Washington, a redhead called Pinky, whose creation serves little purpose other than to provide local color, as it were. Various biographers erroneously suggest that the vegetarian Alcotts fixed a goose for a Christmas dinner (even if they ended up giving it to poor neighbors) or that Charles Dickens introduced one of Alcott's manuscripts to an editor. According to one book, Louisa rode on the wagon transporting the family's belongings to Fruitlands, while her sister Anna dutifully trudged alongside (selfish Louisa); according to another, it was Anna who rode, while Louisa happily sloshed through the mud (messy Louisa). A few, surprisingly few, draw on Stern's standard 1950 biography (Matteson's is too recent for most). Even after the publication of Alcott's journals and selected letters in the 1980s, many have drawn primarily on Cheney's 1889 much-edited and much-excised compilation of Alcott's journals, now conveniently in the public domain.

Many recycle—and embellish—the same stories about a young Alcott being rescued from the Frog Pond on Boston Common by a black boy; getting lost and being found, lying against a Newfoundland dog, by the town crier; putting on plays
in a Concord barn; bursting in awkwardly with her sisters upon the Transcendentalist Margaret Fuller, who had come to view the model children.[185] And writers
also draw on one another, almost incestuously. "Bronson Alcott believed that
all children, boys *and* girls, deserved to be educated. He believed that children
should be treated with as much respect as grownups. He believed their opinions
were important," says one in 1986.[186] "Unlike many people of his day, Bronson
believed that girls as well as boys should be allowed to go to school. . . . He asked
their opinions and treated them with respect at a time when most other adults
thought children 'should be seen and not heard,'" says another two years later.[187]

Until the last couple of decades, many juvenile biographers have been at pains
to explain why Alcott never married—why, in effect, she's an undesirable role
model. They speculate, variously, that Alcott liked to be free, never found the
right person, worried that she might tire of a mate, or felt it would be hard to find
someone willing to be financially responsible for her family. And what a shame
that Ladislas Wisniewski—the young Pole whom she encountered briefly in Europe and who served as a partial model for Laurie—was so much younger than
she, "for they were boon companions and might very easily have married, had
they been more of an age."[188] Surely she couldn't have considered marriage "as
unpleasant as she sometimes said."[189]

The more recent juvenile biographies, especially those targeting young adults,
are more likely than earlier ones to mention Alcott's personal and family difficulties, perhaps to make her seem like a modern adolescent. Still, many fail to mention Alcott's dislike for Concord or the possibility of the family breaking up at the
end of the communal Fruitlands experiment, not to mention Alcott's thoughts
of suicide. Only a few, like Amy Ruth (1999), acknowledge the conflicting pulls
of family and independence; only a few play out some of the conflicts that the
Alcott family experienced and hint that Alcott may have cherished the family so
much precisely because it was under threat. Similarly, only since the 1990s, Hilary Crew suggests, do juvenile biographers address the full contents of Alcott's
sensation stories.[190]

Of the juvenile biographies published in the 1960s and 1970s, the most carefully researched is Aileen Fisher and Olive Rabe's *We Alcotts* (1968), written from
the perspective of Alcott's mother. The authors don't shy away from the more difficult topics, but perhaps in part because of the perspective they've chosen—"we
Alcotts"—they do stress the importance of family togetherness. Their Abba Alcott

says of her life with her husband, "Our greatest success all along was our family, our being together."[191]

Notable among the many juvenile biographies published in more recent decades is Norma Johnston's (Nicole St. John's) *Louisa May: The World and Works of Louisa May Alcott* (1991). Informed by the scholarship to date, it's eminently readable, indeed witty. Johnston observes, for instance, that in *Little Women* the magazine *Olive Branch*, to which Alcott had contributed an early story, has been "renamed, wickedly, the *Spread Eagle*."[192] This biography has the depth and specificity of a biography for adults; indeed, its target audience is not immediately apparent.[193] Johnston is willing to grapple with the difficulties that Bronson and Abba Alcott experienced in their marriage, and her Louisa is a figure of some complexity. In the words of the *Kirkus* reviewer, "Johnston, bless her, succeeds in reconciling the loving family in Little Women with the facts of Alcott's rich but extraordinarily demanding life."[194]

Homage to Alcott and to *Little Women* can also take the form of re-visioning Alcott's life, at times intermingling it with Jo's in *Little Women* or with that of the biographer. Among works targeting an adult audience, Susan Cheever's *Louisa May Alcott* (2010), not classed as fiction, interweaves comments on this novelist's own relationship with her novelist father, echoing Alcott's with Bronson. Kit Bakke's *Miss Alcott's E-mail: Yours for Reforms of All Kinds* (2006), labeled a bio-memoir on its title page, is categorized by librarians as fiction. Yet beyond the device of imagining an e-mail exchange with Alcott, resulting in several messages presumably from Alcott, most of the text consists of biographical and contextual discussions of Alcott and musings by Bakke on connections with her own life. Particularly interested in Alcott as worker and reformer, roles that Bakke connects to her own work as a nurse and as a participant in the militant Weather Underground in the 1960s and 1970s, Bakke is rather dismissive of *Little Women*. There's homage here to Alcott, if not to *Little Women*, with the novel functioning as a foil to the life.

Most reworkings of Alcott's life are more overtly fictional; many belong to "the new subgenre that imagines the love life of spinster authoresses," to quote from a *Kirkus* review.[195] One author claimed that she wanted "to explore, in fiction, the character of Laurie and what experience might have led [Louisa] to write *Little Women* and end it the way that she did, without Jo and Laurie ending up together."[196] For Patricia O'Brien in *The Glory Cloak* (2004), the failed romance is with the Virginia blacksmith John Sulie (as O'Brien calls him), who, in this version, survives the wounds that brought him to the Civil War hospital where Alcott was a nurse. O'Brien's Louisa, however, isn't bold enough to return to him when an invented sidekick of a cousin, working now with Clara Barton, finds him, so Louisa's cousin has a one-night stand with him instead—and pregnancy ensues, along with the cousin's eventual reconciliation with Alcott. In Kelly O'Connor McNees's *The Lost Summer of Louisa May Alcott* (2010) the suitor is entirely invented, a shopkeeper, whom Alcott meets while summering with her family in New Hampshire in 1855. She leaves him waiting at a train station, ready to elope, when she has second thoughts about how she'd fit in writing with housekeeping and looking after his spoiled little sister. And of course, in the spirit of modern sexual mores, they have made love, though in this case no pregnancy results. In R. R. Smythe's time-slipping *Heart Murmurs* (2013), the central romance does not involve the Alcott sisters but a modern young author, an Alcott fan, who falls in love with Bronson's illegitimate son, who turns out to be a creature of the young author's invention.

Dramas that rework Alcott's life also often focus on the erotic but are less likely to be heteronormative. Although *Little Women* has invited queer readings by scholars, and more than a century ago Marion Ames Taggart portrayed what was at least a schoolgirl crush on an older girl in *The Little Women Club*, modern reworkings of the novel or the biography have rarely given play to the nonhetero-sexual erotic—except in these plays. In his two-act *Romance Language* (1985), Peter Parnell rethinks the sexuality of a number of nineteenth-century figures, and his Alcott is at least a bit queer: with a Tahitian prince in tow, she yearns for Thoreau and ends up having a bit of rough sex with George Armstrong Custer. The Split Britches production of *Little Women: The Tragedy* (perf. 1988) is a meditation on pornography in which Louisa, who is also at times Jo, is torn between the prudent and the lurid, between heaven and hell: a reviewer for a London performance characterized the production as "combin[ing] soft-core lesbian burlesque with acute self-mocking cabaret" and called it an "irreverent coup."[197] In Carolyn Gage's one-act *Little Women Incest* (perf. 1990), Jo and Louisa argue: Jo doesn't want to be married off to that "seedy, self-righteous bigot," Professor Bhaer;[198] she wants Louisa to burn those drafted pages, to admit to having been raped by her demanding father, and to admit her love for the lesbian Jo. Louisa refuses.

～

Another kind of adaptation or re-visioning—another kind of homage—is the spin-offs of the novel. During the first-wave women's movement, in the first two decades of the twentieth century, a number of authors wrote juvenile spinoffs, as I've noted in chapter 2. Perhaps because it too marks a time of uncertainty and it's important to graft new circumstances to old traditions, the second wave has also led to spinoffs—what the critic Julie Sanders might describe (borrowing from Gerard Genette) in terms of grafting, "the rootstock . . . conjoined to a new textual form."[199] In recent years such grafting has appeared especially in novels targeting adults. The writer Lynne Sharon Schwartz, not herself the author of a published spinoff, suggests at least a partial rationale: *Little Women* was a book that she felt passionately about when she was eight, a book that she "wanted to possess even more intimately than by reading. . . . Only later did I understand that I wanted to have written *Little Women*, conceived and gestated it and felt its words delivered from my own pen." More precisely, "I wanted to write my version of *Little Women*, what Louisa May Alcott would write were she in my place, or if I were she, yet living my life."[200] The spinoffs also function as interpretations, sometimes exploring aspects of the novel that have not been explored in other contexts. *Little Women* may not match *Pride and Prejudice* and *Alice's Adventures in Wonderland*, which are reported as having inspired more than 70 and 150 spinoffs, respectively,[201] but my own tally for Alcott's novel—excluding dramatic renderings, fiction that makes brief allusions to her work, fiction that primarily focuses on her life, and short fiction—currently numbers fifty-seven.

Recent spinoffs for juveniles include prequels and paraquels. Fifteen prequels appear in Susan Beth Pfeffer's Portraits of Little Women series (1997–98) and four in Charlotte Emerson's Little Women Journals series (1998), the latter being tie-ins with Madame Alexander dolls. In the former series, little Jo may befriend a blind girl or little Beth may meet Abraham Lincoln. Emerson has also written what might be called paraquels, or parallel novels, stories that happen about the time of *Little Women*, between the scenes: in *Jo's Troubled Heart* (1998) the title refers not to a romantic interest but to Jo's slightly troubled relationship with her sisters (were they deceiving and teasing her when she temporarily swapped jobs with Beth, shortly before Christmas?).

Not till the last three decades do there seem to have been more reworkings of the sort popular a century ago—rethinkings of the novel, usually translating it to a modern era. John Stephens and Robyn McCallum rightly suggest that "retold stories" are more common in literature for children than in that for adults,[202] and that was certainly true of retellings of *Little Women* a century ago. Recent retellings of *Little Women*, however, commonly target a more adult audience.

First, though, there have been some juvenile reworkings. A couple involve time travel. Just before 1960, in Edward Eager's *The Time Garden* (1958), a quartet of modern children accompany Jo, Meg, and Laurie to help a needy family and narrowly escape being kidnapped. In Jane Langton's *The Diamond in the Window* (1962), a girl dreams herself into a scene as one of Beth's dolls; a journalist has described the novel as "a sort of Mary Poppins meets the Transcendentalists."[203] Other reworkings are modernizations. The British Hilary McKay's *The Exiles* (1992) offers the summer misadventures of a constellation of characters similar to that in Alcott's novel: four sisters, staying with an older woman (their grandmother), and a helpful neighboring boy named Graham. "When I grow up," the second youngest announces, "I bags Graham to marry."[204] She's the one who inadvertently starts the fire that burns not her sister's manuscript but their grandmother's books. A similar constellation of characters appears in Jeanne Birdsall's *The Penderwicks* (2005): four sisters, this time living with their father, and a neighboring boy who wants to pursue music. One character has, in fact, read *Little Women*.[205] In Jacqueline Shannon's *Big Guy, Little Women* (1985), the Marsh family move next door to Lori, who notes their eerie similarities to the March family; she tries to save Bethanny's life (getting her fired from working in the school nurse's office) and temporarily loses her own tutor/boyfriend B.G. (the *B* stands for *Brook*, of course) to the airhead eldest, Megan. In Heather Vogel Frederick's *The Mother-Daughter Book Club* (2007), four middle-school girls and (most of) their mothers spend the better part of a year working their way through Alcott's novel; by the start of seventh grade the ex-supermodel mom has allowed her daughter to play ice hockey, the mother of the shy girl has returned to her family, and the two other girls are launched on careers in writing and fashion design. In Megan McDonald's *Rule of Three* (2009), part of The Sisters Club series, two of the three young sisters read *Little Women*; the one called Joey decides to grow her hair to cut it off for a worthy purpose, in her case to make wigs for children with cancer.

A significant reworking that targets a young audience is Lauren Baratz-Logsted's *Little Women and Me* (2011). The first-year high-school student Emily March is literally sucked into *Little Women* when she starts to reread it for a class assignment: she becomes the middle sister of five. Having identified with Jo—"Every girl who has grown up in the last hundred years or so wanting to be a writer, including me, has Jo March to blame"[206]—Emily adores Beth and finds Amy annoying. Yet since she can't now be Jo but has her as a sister, she finds Jo rather bossy. Emily's presence changes the story somewhat: now she's the one who rescues Amy from drowning; she's the one who wins a prize for a story. She also finds Laurie hot and initiates a French kiss with him, much to his consternation. Yet eventually Emily urges Jo to do whatever it takes to be the niece who goes to Europe—and thus end up marrying Laurie. (It turns out that Amy is a time-traveling interloper too. She ended up with Laurie only after she entered the novel in 1881; before then, Jo married him.) When Emily returns to the present day, she discovers that the story retains her changes: Jo ends up with Laurie. Emily acknowledges "how I changed the story even as it changed me" (307). In short, Baratz-Logsted provides a commentary on reading Alcott's work, offering a somewhat offbeat perspective on Jo, on how a reader might view her if not primarily identifying with her, and a slight exaggeration—or interpretation—of Alcott's view of Amy, as a rather greedy interloper who must be from another world. Finally, of course, Baratz-Logsted's book enacts the wish-fulfilling fantasy of many readers when Emily changes Alcott's novel permanently (or at least until the next time traveler), so that Jo marries Laurie. In short, not only may readers be affected by a story (perhaps inspired to write, like Jo) but their reading changes the story (perhaps returning it to what the narrator construes as the original author's original intention—but changing the received story nonetheless).

Another suggestive reworking is a 1977 episode of the long-running family television series *Little House on the Prairie*. The petted and spoiled Nellie Olesen, daughter of the town's shopkeeper, is especially enthusiastic about acting in a dramatized version of *Little Women*. Her mother writes a script that foregrounds Nellie as Meg. The rewriting could thus function as a way to rethink Meg, except that her dialogue and actions are bland (she does little more than enthuse about sewing as she sits sewing) and the never-to-be-admired Nellie has taken on the role. Nellie is, furthermore, upstaged. Not by the central character of the series, Laura Ingalls, who, as Beth, simply serves tea to Marmee and Meg. But by another schoolmate named Ginny Clark, who, as Jo, arrives onstage and takes off her bonnet to reveal that she really has cut her hair. The show is then stopped in favor of the "real" drama of the series, as Ginny explains that she has cut her hair to buy her widowed mother a dress to wear to the performance—and thus somehow enables Mrs. Clark finally to accept the courting of the widower who has accompanied her. This heterosexual ending parallels the ending of Alcott's novel, even if *Little Women* here becomes, for the two men credited with the screenplay, a marker of effete domesticity well worth replacing with the "reality" of *Little House on the Prairie*. As Laura's older sister, Mary, concludes, playacting may be all right, but "real life's a whole lot better."[207]

Then there are the mashups, often targeting a young adult audience. In Lynn Messina's *Little Vampire Women* (2010), the Marches are vampires, but they're "humanitarians" and thus conscientiously avoid feasting on humans (that pet rat in Jo's attic is not a single rat but a series of them, in other words, snacks). The Laurences, however, are humans. Thus Messina gets to rethink the role of, say, Beth, who not only adroitly deflects a stake aimed at Jo but expresses gratitude to Mr. Laurence by biting him and turning him into a vampire. In Porter

Grand's *Little Women and Werewolves* (2010), the Marches are the humans and the Laurences are the werewolves. So the Marches get to be benevolent to the poor misunderstood werewolves, who are decent most of the time (a stance rather belied by the bone-chilling descriptions of some full-moon depredations). And Beth again acts counter to type: she falls madly in love with the elderly Mr. Laurence. Another mashup (target audience unclear) is Jane Nardin's *Little Women in India* (2012), which transplants the Alcottian/Austenian May family to India at the time of what the British called the Mutiny. Catherine (a writer), Jane (too keen on being fashionable, early on), Elizabeth (a rather self-centered artist), and Fanny (annoyingly self-sacrificing) are separated from their parents and hide in a village, where they learn how much the Raj oppresses Indians. Jane takes to farming, though, so when she turns down Lieutenant Palliser, marries the tutor James Keats, and goes to England she'll take up—no, not gardening, but farming.[208] (Maybe there's a hint of Beatrix Potter there too.)

Mashups and other rewritings also appear on fanfiction sites. Fanfiction.net alone offers several hundred *Little Women*–related stories, beginning in 2005, ranging in length from a couple hundred words to more than 150,000. Most of the fiction is in English, although a dozen or so pieces are in Spanish, and there's an occasional item in French, German, or Portuguese. Most fans, especially in the earlier years, try to reimagine the novel with a Jo/Laurie pairing, an acknowledgment of mutual love if not marriage. Maybe Amy dies, or she and Laurie divorce, or Laurie gets Jo pregnant and so she has to marry him, or they're united in the afterlife, or maybe Jo simply accepts him when he first proposes. One fan comments that Alcott "makes me so mad, if she had just written it right in the first place we wouldn't have to go and kill off and divorce her characters!"[209] Another notes, as if in response, "But then again, we might not have such beautiful fanfic as we have on here then, I suppose. That's one consolation."[210] Fans are not just "textual poachers" but members of an "interactive audience," responding to and critiquing one another.[211] Fanfiction provides a window on readers reading.

Some of these engaged and committed readers experiment with other romantic pairings, perhaps Laurie and his tutor John Brooke, perhaps Beth and the British visitor Frank, perhaps Jo and a woman she'd met in New York. Some flesh out the perspectives of characters other than Jo on events in the novel, perhaps Laurie's or Amy's or even Mrs. Hummel's. Some undertake collaborative efforts whether they take turns drafting chapters or create a fiction that responds to an idea in a previous fiction. A few create mashups, perhaps with *Dr. Who* or *Batman* or *Pride and Prejudice*. Several are vampire versions published the year before Messina's book. But most stay within the fictional universe of Alcott's novel. Only a few modernize their stories—unlike many writers of commercially published spinoffs, who transpose a version of the March family to modern times. Indeed almost as telling as the stories themselves are community members' responses to the various fictions, and even though members often praise new approaches, there's a strong norm in the community to stay close to "canon," to Alcott's mores and characterizations. So few try, say, to punish Amy with a rape or to rethink Beth by making her more powerful, as some commercially published spinoffs do (although one futuristic version does transfer Beth's intelligence to a computer). All of the fanfictions speak to the enduring appeal of the novel, maybe especially when the writers undertake wish-fulfilling revisions of the plot, but such revisions still need to stay true to what the fans consider canonical about Alcott's writing. The authors tend to want to enter the world of the novel rather than to re-create it in the present.

Among adult reworkings, one appeared, arguably, as early as 1932, when El-len Glasgow published *The Sheltered Life*.[212] The novel opens with nine-year-old Jenny Blair Archbold being paid a penny a page by her southern grandfather to read *Little Women*, which she never completes. Thereafter Glasgow's novel does not seem to be a reworking, although Allison Speicher argues that the older generation of women living with the girl constitutes the three older sisters and that Jenny Blair represents Amy. But Jenny Blair later fails to overcome an infatuation with a married man, and the novel ends in tragedy. She never finished *Little Women*, never learned its lessons. Glasgow's novel thus constitutes an indictment of the values of southern society, "a society dominated by beauty and appearances; a society which is hollow beneath its elegant veneer."[213]

Other early reworkings include Dorothy West's *The Living Is Easy* (1948) and Lucille Fletcher's *The Daughters of Jasper Clay* (1958). West's forceful Cleo reads *Little Women* to the elderly woman for whom she is a companion. Then, as she makes her way into genteel African American circles in Boston, she dupes her three sisters and their children into joining her, without their husbands. Cleo gains the reunion she has dreamed of, but the harmony of this Plumfield equivalent is temporary: all the marriages founder, including her own, as her husband's wholesale business falls apart, thanks to the exigencies of World War I and a changing corporate economy. For West, a participant in the Harlem Renaissance, Alcott's novel portrays a goal of harmony and gentility that an African American, at least, can't achieve.[214]

Alcott's novel is also re-visioned in a gritty urban twentieth century in Fletcher's book.[215] The four white sisters live not with Marmee but with a fiercely protective and strict father. Instead of providing emotional support, he provides obstacles—

to college, to husbands. The youngest sister, golden-haired Ann, is spoiled and petted and gets to travel, like Alcott's Amy, although across the country instead of across the ocean, and not, finally, through the good offices of her forbidding Aunt Miriam but on her own. Chasing a vision across the country (like Bronson?), Ann lies and steals to follow her dream. The human embodiment of this dream, golden haired like herself, would be, unlike Alcott's Laurie, a poor romantic match for her, since he's gay—even if they hadn't fatally crashed. (Then again, Alcott's Laurie lends himself to a queer reading.) This modern reworking is more punishingly patriarchal than the nineteenth-century novel: Alcott's idealism can't overcome patriarchy, or perhaps can't survive in the twentieth century.

Among reworkings published since 1960, some include incidental references to reading *Little Women*, or to dressing up as the Little Women, or to a Little Women's Book Club.[216] Among those in which Alcott's novel functions largely as a prop is Perri Klass's *Other Women's Children* (1990), but she assimilates her predecessor's novel more fully than many do: *Little Women* becomes a talisman, something to which the pediatrician Amelia turns for guidance and solace as she struggles with her own family (she becomes estranged from her husband) and with the death of a patient from AIDS.

Many books that focus on four or five sisters or women friends also seem to draw on Alcott's novel. Those with the closest echoes include the *New York Times* bestseller *Sisters* (2007), in which Danielle Steel narrates the lives of four adult sisters who live together for a year. The youngest, the Amy equivalent, is a super-model with an eating disorder (and is improbably drugged, kidnapped, raped—so much for little sisters whose lives seem too easy). The next youngest doesn't die, like Beth, but is blinded in an accident, effectively killing her career as a painter—but her loss brings the sisters together. The year ends with all happily in heterosexual relationships. In Lorna Landvik's *Angry Housewives Eating Bon Bons* (2003), five close friends are like sisters—like the sisters in *Little Women*, they note in passing. The friend that the others designate Amy is the one who likes to wear revealing clothes and to talk about sex, although she eventually becomes a minister; the one they designate Beth is not the one who would appear to be dying at the end, but she has been sufficiently self-abnegating to be subjected to domestic abuse. The Laurie figure, whom the friends vote to admit to their book club, is a gay neighbor.

A more concerted reworking is Gabrielle Donnelly's *The Little Women Letters* (2010). In this postfeminist sequel to Alcott's novel the three London Atwater daughters are direct descendants of Jo March Bhaer. They are Emma, the eldest, sensible one, who marries at the end of the novel; Lulu, the main focalizing character, dreamy and a bit adrift; and Sophie, the rising young actress. Only three sisters? Maybe so that one won't have to die—although Sophie does manage to become deathly ill as a result of an allergic reaction. She survives. Lulu discovers old family letters in the attic and loves learning about "Grandma Jo," about whom there's a family tradition that she'd published something, now forgotten. Lulu particularly needs to hear, in the letters, that Grandma Jo was much loved by her family. So maybe there's hope for Lulu, who always feels the odd one out. Her parents keep urging her to make something of her degree in biochemistry, and she does want to find a career, but she also wants to find a man. She ends the novel with plans to go to cooking school and with a promising man. What seems to matter most to the daughters, as Emma finally says, is being "part of a long line of women in the family who fell in love and got married. . . . Mom's always saying that times have changed for women, but this is something that's stayed the same, this falling in love and promising to be together forever."[217] Family was certainly important in Alcott's novel, and the three surviving March sisters did indeed marry, but this postfeminist celebration of traditional marriage, this apparent scaling down of women's careers, seems regressive. Still, Donnelly offers a viable reading of the novel, one whose main contours have appealed to many during the last century and a half.

More strikingly, the last three decades have witnessed a spate of novels that more complexly re-vision Alcott's work. Some authors ponder the impact of semi-autobiographical writing on the rest of one's family, as in Judith Rossner's *His Little Women* (1990) and Katherine Weber's *The Little Women* (2003). Others rethink Mr. March's role, rather negatively in Joyce Carol Oates's *A Bloodsmoor Romance* (1982) and Barbara Kingsolver's *The Poisonwood Bible* (1998), more positively in Geraldine Brooks's *March* (2005).

The thesis novels, the ones that try to make an argument about the relationship between autobiography and fiction, tend to be the least successful even if they raise intriguing questions. In an interview in 1914, when the first authorized dramatization of *Little Women* was touring the country to great acclaim, John Alcott said he had "no doubt that many of [his aunt's] friends could read between the lines and find themselves or bits of themselves in her stories." One of the reasons why the Alcott family had delayed granting permission for a dramatization, he stated, was that "to us 'Little Women' was the story of our home and our family, a theme too intimate for the publicity to which the stage might subject it."[218] The interviewer does not pause to consider the mutual implications of the two statements. And indeed, critics have rarely pondered the impact of Alcott's semiautobiographical novels on her family's dynamics, and the possible blowback on her writing, beyond noting, perhaps, that her father seemed happy enough to bill himself as the father of the Little Women when he went on lecture tours, or perhaps her sister May referred to "that horrid stupid Amy as something like me even to putting a cloths [sic] pin on her nose."[219] Two recent novelists, however, have explored the issue.

In Rossner's *His Little Women*, Sam Pearlstein has four daughters by three wives. The youngest, the Amy equivalent, is vapidly beautiful; the next youngest, the stand-in for Beth, commits suicide. The older two share Jo's qualities: the second oldest is the focalizing character, and the oldest is a novelist named Louisa, who has written a partly autobiographical novel called *Joe Stalbin's Daughters*. Rossner plays out the implications of undertaking such an enterprise by having a distant family member sue Louisa for libel. As the narrating sister states, "My father said once that when Louisa discussed some familiar incident or argument he could recognize the words or deeds, but they'd become part of a story that was foreign to him." Then again, as a lawyer at the trial says, the court should not make a decision that would ground "authors' flights of fancy because we want to soar with them out of everyday life and into realms the imagination makes interesting."[220] As one reviewer noted, this thesis portion of the novel seems "vaguely mechanical and perfunctory," the implications not fully worked through.[221]

They are somewhat more worked through in Weber's *The Little Women*. Joanna and Amy, dismayed over their mother's affair with a graduate student, move from their home on the Upper West Side to stay with their older sister Meg, a student at Yale, and a young man named Teddy, as Alcott's Laurie was sometimes called (Beth was a turtle that died, or maybe the equivalent of Beth's death is the death of their "imaginary family perfection").[222] In this postmodern rendition, Meg and Amy get to write back to their sister, as she writes a book about them. "I hate this feeling I have of being an unwelcome guest at my own party with every critical remark I make, but the way you depict Amy seems condescending to me," notes Amy (111). Meg adds that her own namesake "seems like a generic character, a grim and humorless older sister who carries the weight of the world on her shoulders" (111). The author Joanna later notes that she omitted, from the story proper, that Amy had deleted Joanna's journal from her hard drive, since "I had a concern that it could make readers unsympathetic to Amy" (232). But of course even as she offers implicit criticism of Alcott's inclusion of the comparable incident and thus of the biased depiction of Amy, she includes it nonetheless. The book is ultimately not a novel after all, Meg asserts, but "a manifesto of the way you wish everything had been or the way you insist on thinking everything was" (235). Indeed, the novel functions less well as a novel with fully realized characters than as a meditation on Alcott's work and on its implications for the relationship between "real" life and fiction.

Among the novels that rethink the role of Mr. March, *The Poisonwood Bible* offers Nathan Price, who goes to the Congo in 1959 as a missionary with his wife and four daughters. Kingsolver plays out the oldest sister's materialism and the seismic implications of another sister's death—to choose a couple of Alcott-inflected themes—against a backdrop of decades of turmoil in the region, the national fight for independence paralleling the familial one.[223] The most telling portrait is of the father, a commentary not so much on Mr. March as on Bronson Alcott, whose passion for grand ideas at the expense of his family's financial security had a profound impact on his daughters. Price is rigidly committed to his beliefs, to his view of Christianity, which he wants to impose on the village where they live. He does not realize how little real effect he has on the local population; he never learns enough of the culture or the language to realize that he keeps saying, as he garbles the language, that Jesus is poisonwood, which is to say, poison to the touch. By the end, Nathan is crazed and alone.

In *A Bloodsmoor Romance*, Oates rewrites *Little Women* as a sensation story with a fastidious Victorian narrator.[224] Her nineteenth-century sisters become, variously, an actress, a medium, a man, and the inventor of the disposable diaper. The compliant one, who doesn't escape, nevertheless so fully accedes to the instructions of her husband, who is fond of sexual asphyxia, that she kills him. As for the father, he's a pedagogue and also a high-minded but improvident inventor: he aspires to creating a perpetual-motion machine. He devolves, however, to accepting money to invent what turns out to be the electric chair and then turns his attention to a weapon of mass destruction.

Not all the re-visioned family patriarchs are so crazed. In the Pulitzer Prize–winning *March*, Brooks, who apparently loved *Little Women* as a child but has also referred to it somewhat dismissively as "a wonderful but limited morality tale for young people,"[225] creates what is sometimes called a parallel novel, using the setting or world of a previous one, not translating it to a different time or place. Brooks fills in what happens to Mr. March during the Civil War, while he is off where the fighting is. She also draws on Alcott family background. Like the fictional Mr. March, March serves as a chaplain during the Civil War; like Bronson Alcott, March has been a peddler. Yet he is less improvident, less driven by ideas, than Bronson. It's his wife who has ardent beliefs: she is such an ardent abolitionist that he wants to please her by donating more money than he can afford. March is a complex character, sympathetically portrayed as someone at the mercy of a wife who has trouble controlling her emotions, also someone whose ideals are tested by war. We see the atrocities of war and the guilt of a survivor. And as in recent novels based loosely on Alcott's life, there is an additional love interest—this time not for Louisa but for March, an affair, an understanding at least, with a cultured and intelligent former slave whom he met when a peddler and whom he encounters again during the war. One reviewer faults the characters' "prolonged moral exhibitionism," but others find the book "a moving and inspirational tour de force," "an ingenious counterpoint" to *Little Women*, a work that "enhances rather than appropriates its sister work" such that "Louisa May Alcott would be well pleased."[226]

⌒

A final kind of re-visioning of *Little Women* has been the issuing of re-illustrations. Newly illustrated English-language editions have appeared, on average, more than once a year since 1960, almost seventy of them (for a total of more than a hundred since 1868)—and these don't include editions whose only illustrations are on the cover (sometimes these re-use earlier images, perhaps by Jessie Willcox Smith or Frank Merrill or even a non-Alcott-related photograph of four sisters by Lewis Carroll). There have been at least twenty-six newly illustrated editions of French translations; the number of illustrators worldwide who have tackled *Little Women* is probably more than two hundred. Most of the editions would be called illustrated books: they offer occasional images that focus on key textual moments (Amy's skating accident, perhaps, or Jo's cut hair or Beth's sickbed). Like images produced earlier in the century, recent ones are frequently bathed in nostalgia, with quaint old-fashioned yet anachronistic dresses, ditto hairstyles. Watercolors with muted or pastel tones are popular, if color is included, although in most books line drawings predominate. Illusionistic or realistic styles are common, though occasionally the style draws more on comic books, and indeed some books *are* comic books, manga, or graphic novels.

There are also picture books and easy readers, with images on every page turn, accompanied by a radically condensed text. These books are more likely than other editions to use bright colors and to draw on nonillusionistic styles, such as that of Claymation animated films. One picture book, called *Christmas with Little Women* (1986), based on the first chapter of Alcott's novel, depicts a brightly colored, rather raucous crew, especially a madcap, mobcapped, red-and-white-stockinged Jo, a Pippi Longstocking without pigtails.

Most of the images, whether in illustrated or picture books, are workmanlike but not particularly distinguished. Some illustrators imitate previous images, particularly those by Merrill and also stills from film versions, especially when they choose iconic scenes, such as Jo and Professor Bhaer under the umbrella. Some of the echoes may be unconscious, the originals perhaps absorbed in childhood. Others are more overt copies, whether they function as plagiarism or homage. Some illustrators labor to find ways to distinguish among the four sisters. If the images include color, the artist may simply give them different-colored dresses. In a 1989 edition whose illustrations are credited to the Pablo Marcos Studio, the sisters have different hairstyles: Jo has a bouffant pouf on top of her head, a style almost possible in the 1860s but more reminiscent of the 1960s, especially with her escaped curling tendrils, anticipating *Jersey Shore*'s Snooki.

As in earlier periods, many artists illustrate the scene in which Jo and Laurie go skating and Amy follows but falls through the ice. Illustrators who are inclined to stress the decorative and domestic aspects of the novel may forgo this scene, preferring to show Jo's tearful repentance afterwards, or if they do depict it they have tended, like May Alcott in 1868, to produce fashion plates. Others, more interested in action, may show the rescue, beginning with Merrill in 1880. Still, the fact that he shows Laurie already having reached Amy, plus the near-horizontal lines of the image and of many similar to his, conveying a certain stability, mitigates some of the danger of the accident. Only in the last few decades—only since critics have started excavating the novel's subtexts of anger, aggression, and ambition, in the wake of the publication of Alcott's sensation stories—have illustrators tended to focus directly on Amy's fall. She has burned Jo's manuscript, the work of several years, and Jo fails to warn Amy of thin ice and is temporarily immobilized when her sister calls for help. The accident thus acknowledges Jo's anger and also points to the dangers of female independence, as well as threats to the iconic foursome—Amy could die, and Jo's ambition and anger have clouded her judgment and attentiveness. Even recent illustrators who depict the fall often have difficulty capturing the emotions, resorting perhaps to an echo of Edvard Munch's *The Scream* to show Jo's horror, while a startled Amy looks almost as if she's floating or else a vertical Amy seems to be blossoming from the ice.[227]

In general, as artists have increasingly depicted disruption, they have decreasingly shown the sentimental, even as they continue to foreground fashion and romance and the decorative. Among those favoring the decorative are many commissioned to illustrate limited or collector's editions. The existence of such editions—published by, for instance, the Franklin Mint or the Folio Society—is testament to a kind of classic status for the novel, in the minds of the common reader if not academics. I suppose the collectors of these editions are assumed to be indulging in nostalgia—and thus interested in the moments when couples dance or picnic or are wedded or meet under an umbrella, with Jo at Beth's sickbed thrown in for good measure. Certainly these are favored scenes in such editions. The illustrators tend not to feature Jo writing, although Amy may be depicted sketching—or writing.

Other artists foreground romance and the decorative as well—and happily illustrate the "Castles in the Air" scene in which Laurie follows the sisters when they take their sewing and sketching outside: to him and to the narrator, "It *was* rather a pretty little picture" (115). The British Alexa Rutherford's illustrations (1978), for instance, show the girls relaxing in graceful poses. And the traditionally feminine Amy appears somewhat more frequently than tomboy Jo does in this edition. An image of Amy and Laurie at Valrosa is the frontispiece for part 2 (here called *Good Wives*); there's no illustration of Jo under the umbrella with Professor Bhaer, and at most one in which Marmee appears, in the background. Amy appears to embody the favored subtext of the illustrator, who makes graceful decorativeness more important than ambition or even than Marmee-centered togetherness.

Other illustrators, even before the most recent wave of the women's movement, have foregrounded Jo's writing or, at times, Amy's drawing, thus stressing independent creativity. Lauren Rizzuto has commented on the coordinated frontispiece and title page of a 1962 edition illustrated by Betty Fraser: Marmee and three daughters cluster over a book, but Amy, the artist, is independently to the right, drawing a book of their portraits.[228] Fraser subtly reframes the novel to feature the artist more than the writer. In short, an illustrator can choose to foreground Amy to emphasize the decorative, as Rutherford did, or to underscore female creativity. (Fraser actually does both.) More often, to highlight creativity, illustrators such as Tasha Tudor, Derek James, and the French pair Rozier-Gaudriault feature Jo writing.

Tudor (1960), who has won Caldecott Honors for her illustrations for other books, created pencil and watercolor images that suggest a tension between the pulls of independence and romance, between creativity and nostalgia. On the one hand, she provides a number of illustrations of Jo writing or Amy drawing, including a cover image that depicts the latter. On the other hand, half of the eight color plates feature the potential romantic partners Jo and Laurie. The frontispiece, however, depicts a different romance: that of Laurie and Amy, thus foreshadowing a final pairing. Both figures look to the left, arresting our gaze, possibly even hinting at an impediment to forward movement—in countries that read left to right we generally read pictures left to right—but in any case not immediately inviting us to the title page and the rest of the book. Amy is at the piano, thus potentially creative, but Laurie towers over her, visually surrounding her, one arm outstretched as if to turn a page, compositionally hinting at an embrace, but the

"Play something, Amy."

Tasha Tudor plays on the text
Illustration by Tasha Tudor for *Little Women* (New York:
World, 1969). Reproduced by permission of Tasha Tudor
and Family Inc.

pose also confines her. Neither smiles. And what she is doing is not her preferred
creative outlet. Music is instead an elegant feminine accomplishment: Laurie has
given up his musical ambitions, and Amy here becomes his extension, enacting
his desires. The caption reads, "Play something, Amy." He's in command. Yet in
the novel she declines his request, politely asserting herself. The image thus illus-
trates a nonexistent hypothetical. In the novel Laurie proposes to Amy not by going down on one knee nor by employing the courtly language of subservience but
in rather egalitarian fashion: when they are rowing together, he asks if they "might

always pull in the same boat" (336). Yet Tudor reinstates the patriarchal by adding a scene of domination to the novel, emphasizing the dominance compositionally, and positioning the image prominently (she or her editors) as the frontispiece.

Some editions published in the last two decades feature a number of small illustrations in the margins, using the images as annotations—what Margaret Mackey calls "primitive quasi-hypertext."[229] A 1996 Viking edition includes illustrations from a 1988 edition by Gallimard, a leading French publisher. Every page spread has an illustrated sidebar, or inset, usually with an explanation or caption. Most of the illustrations are "found" images—of Alcott and her family, Dickens, fashion plates, the immigrant Irish, nineteenth-century advertising, even of Winslow Homer paintings. The other images are attributed to the French artist Jame's Prunier and vary in style and quality. The best are generally watercolor or pen and ink. Some make striking use of light and shadow. Some position small figures to gaze with the viewer at vast landscapes, inviting us to muse beyond the figures to an elsewhere, whether to a Celestial City visible beyond the clouds or to storm clouds that signal civil war ("I gave my best to the country I love, and kept my tears till he was gone," the caption reads).[230] The cover features a version of the sororal and maternal fivesome reading Father's letter, in warm earth colors, against a backdrop of a gray and white and raw umber army camp; the cannon in the foreground is a bit threatening (is the family, not directly in its line of sight, nevertheless under threat?), but the lines of the cannon and a line of soldiers draw us to the horizon and the upper right, beyond the frame.

Most of the editions I've been discussing are illustrated books, books with occasional images, images that don't usually forward the narrative. In a well-designed picture book, in contrast, words and images are synergistic: they need each other in order to make meaning or to forward the narrative. (Graphic novels too create a synergy between words and images.) The images in illustrated books are undertheorized; I want to discuss the functions of the images in such books before I go on to examine the work of a couple of intriguing artists.

Many commentators during the last two centuries simply treat the illustrations in illustrated books as handmaidens, as "primarily decorative," to quote a 2009 critic.[231] But a few critics of Victorian novels have begun some theorizing. For most critics, the images may enrich the text, maybe play out themes and symbols and parallels, maybe even ironize the text. But the images are subordinate. It's true that the words are usually created first, and the relatively small number of pictures may mean that they are less likely to play an equal role in forwarding the narrative. Yet the illustrations can do much more than echo the words or provide decorative tailpieces.

Michael Steig captures three possible stances when he says, with respect to Dickens's novels, that "the illustrator is at once collaborator, attempting to express the author's intention visually; interpreter, offering his own comments on the meaning of the work; and perhaps even an *artist*, sometimes creating independently valuable works of art."[232] I'm not sure I'd use the term *collaborator* to characterize the first mode, nor would I insist on authorial intention. But this mode does suggest the subservience of the images to the words, and of the artist to the author—the common assumption. The second mode, that of interpretation, gives the illustrator an opportunity to bring something new—to augment the text, to critique or ironize it, to hint at subtexts or at future developments. In the words of another critic, an illustration "may suppose, support, subvert, explain, interpret, and critique its verbal partner, entering into a complexly reciprocal, interactive, and often compellingly persuasive dialogue."[233] More impressionistically, to quote one of Alcott's illustrators, Shirley Hughes, an illustrator should give author and reader "not what they want exactly, but what they never dreamed they could have."[234]

Recent theorizing about adaptations, which I've discussed in chapter 2, can be helpful here too. No longer is the goal simply to be faithful to an "original" work. The relationship between versions of a text can be dialogic, the "adaptation" creative rather than simply imitative. Illustrations too can be in dialogue with a given text; they may be creative works in their own right, not just imitations of an originary text.

And that brings us to Steig's third mode, the possibility of "creating independently valuable works of art." Such a characterization could apply to what are sometimes called artist's illustrated books (*livres de peintre* or, later, *livres d'artiste*). I'm not here referring to recent artists' books, or book art, a kind of conceptual art that plays off the idea of bookishness. Instead I'm referring to a phenomenon from earlier in the twentieth century: limited editions, usually handmade, with prints by Picasso, Matisse, or another artist. Such artists "favored full-page, non-integrative illustrations or separate suites of individual prints. This underscored their character as autonomous images which, rather than illustrating a text, merely alluded to its content or accompanied it."[235] The images are not altogether independent of the words that they accompany or are enmeshed with. They parallel the text, maybe even provoke or transform it. A couple of illustrated versions of *Little Women* verge on this aesthetic.

One is illustrated by Robert Heindel, for a 1982 limited edition published by the Franklin Library. His six black-and-white images, all half-length portraits in semi-silhouette, are striking. Yet their relationship to the text is not clear. There are no captions nor other indications of which characters they depict. They could accompany any novel set a century or so ago; indeed, the clothing and hairstyles of the women are reminiscent of turn-of-the-century Gibson girls and evoke Edith Wharton more than Alcott. In keeping with the tenets of artist's illustrated books, the images are independent of the text, but they do not parallel it. I have trouble finding a conceptual relationship between images and text.

In contrast, Mark English's stunning images for a Reader's Digest condensed version (1967, 1989) are indeed parallel; they are like paintings inspired by *Little Women*. Each is self-contained, as if in a gallery, not impelling us forward with implied movement to the right. The eight color plates focus on the decorative; in his case the images combine illusionistic faces (when they're depicted) with flattened but textured and often floral surfaces. English also favors abstraction, playing with form and light even as he includes recognizably human figures. These illustrations, in which he tried "to come up with something unique and different,"[236] apparently marked a turning point in his career, opening many doors.

I won't go into detail about the different states of the illustrations in the 1967 and 1989 editions. Suffice it to say that in the earlier edition the images are printed on stock paper and dispersed through the text, without captions; the later one has glossy plates gathered in a gallery, with captions.[237] Thus in the 1989 edition we're likely to look at the images all at once, in the context of one another more than in that of the novel, hence reinforcing their independence from the novel.

As for the images themselves, one shows anachronistic bicycles, boaters, and mutton-chop sleeves, from the 1890s rather than the 1860s. Together with the text, it creates what David Skilton would call a "chronological mermaid . . . , half in one time and half in another."[238] The combination evokes an imprecise earlier era, rather romantic, visually beautiful, through images that often counterpoint their captions and the rest of the text. Heindel has characterized English as "a romantic, sensitive to the female, soft, and warm—as much as he's a tough guy, he's a warm fuzzy person. . . . Whenever he did an illustration, there was always such great feeling for humanity."[239] The critic Jill Bossert notes that English "felt his illustrations of fictional characters should prod a reader's imagination—not be exact depiction. This asked more participation by, hence greater reward for, the viewer."[240] If, as Susan Gannon suggests, most illustrators of *Little Women* "accent the formulaic and conventional at the expense of effects readers might find surprising or discomfiting,"[241] English offers some surprises, even if he doesn't altogether escape the conventional.

Consider his choice of scenes: not for him the family foursome, the skating accident, the cut hair, Jo writing, the umbrella, or other commonly illustrated scenes. English mostly chooses offbeat moments, before or after or outside dramatic scenes, generally moments that do not directly forward the narrative. He shows the exterior of the family house; Beth turned aside from the piano; the breaking up of Laurie's picnic with the visiting Vaughns; Marmee leaving for Washington to tend to Father; Christmas dinner upon Father's return; Jo crying after Amy leaves for Europe; Jo's departure from Professor Bhaer in New York; and Amy with Laurie at Valrosa in France. The images offer what Skilton calls a "diegetic arrest," which in *Bleak House* allows "for the expectancy necessary for suspense."[242] Their arresting function is different in Alcott's less linear novel, which is focused not on solving a mystery of origins but on the dailiness of family life. English invites us to observe and linger in the world of the March family, a world that he portrays as old-fashioned, romantically beautiful, and essentially patriarchal.

The scenes all include fresh flowers, sometimes in addition to a floral design—as befits a domestic novel? or a novel about young women? (It's difficult to determine the kinds of flowers, so it's not as if English is playing the nineteenth-century game of deploying flowers as emblems—as when Alcott's Beth works an image of pansies, for thoughts or remembrance, into the slippers she gives Mr. Laurence.) Five of English's eight scenes are situated outdoors, which is unusual for illustrations of this domestic novel. Four images depict modes of transportation: carriages, bicycles, and a train—again, unusual. Perhaps, like Laurie at the outset, English is positioning himself on the outside looking in; perhaps his perspective is attuned to that of Jo, the sister focalized in the novel and the one most eager to be outdoors and about. Also the one most eager to be moving, most eager to run when she should walk, ladylike; the one most eager, perhaps, to be transported—in English's images, she's the one about to board a train, and it's women (unidentified) who hold the bicycles.

The caption for the first image reads, "The four sisters sat knitting away in the twilight, while the December snow fell quietly without, and the fire crackled cheerfully within."[243] Yet no sisters are evident in the image, which shows the dark exterior of a Victorian city house with light gleaming from the windows and snow patterning the whole. Nevertheless, the warm browns and glowing interior suggest coziness, setting the house apart from the carriage and walkers in front, yet it's part of the scene too, since the pattern of falling snow covers all the dark areas of the image, both foreground and background.[244] Elizabeth Keyser suggests, regarding the curtain that has sometimes prevented Laurie from seeing inside the March family house, "Isn't it that very curtain, literally shielding the little women from the masculine gaze, that keeps the world cozy within and alluring from without?"[245] Not showing us the interior makes it all the more alluring. As for the snow pattern, Bossert points to English's "fascination with optical illusion" and adds, "His complete mastery of drawing gives him the freedom to throw down hundreds of what are essentially circles of equal size—as snow or carpets of flowers or fruit on trees. The viewer can easily read the underlying shapes—house, garden, mountain—while enjoying the thrill (there's no other word for it) generated by seeing large areas awash in polka dots."[246]

The partial carriage in the lower right heads to the right; the walkers in the lower left head to the left. The house and its windows emerge from the ambient darkness and the snow screen, the bay window especially bright. This window frames what figure in Alcott's text as chrysanthemums or Christmas roses; the visual pattern of the blooms echoes that of the snow, as if the outside continues inside. It also provides yet another screen hiding the inside scene of the sisters knitting.

The house in the image is not Orchard House or another recognizable Alcott home—it's as if English wanted to evoke the Victorian era more generally. One could perhaps argue that he hints that the standard association of *Little Women* with Orchard House belies the fact that there were so many Alcott homes (the family moved at least twenty times in Alcott's first twenty-eight years). Nor does this image directly convey sisterly togetherness. Instead, we infer coziness from the glowing inside the otherwise dark house: as English would want, our imaginations are prodded by the lack of "exact depiction." Indeed, he evokes the coziness more strongly than direct portrayals of the sisters do, while also hinting that the home is a haven from the public world, even as he contextualizes the story in the public world more than the novel does at this point.

The house looms large in popular thinking about *Little Women*. In part that has to do with the prominence of Orchard House as a memorial and a museum. But the domicile is also key to the domesticity associated with the novel. And the house is something tangible that can be visualized in an illustration. Male illustrators in particular tend to foreground the house, from the outside, as if they, like Laurie, are on the outside gazing in.

English's direct image of family togetherness is coordinated with the end of part 1 of the novel, and this image, along with the house and another scene, was chosen for the Society of Illustrators Annual Exhibition.[247] This juried exhibition includes art from advertising, magazines, and books; unlike the American Library Association's Caldecott Medal, it is awarded to individual images, not entire books, and there's no evidence that the jurors evaluate the relationship between an illustration and any text it accompanies. Like those of a couple of

The four sisters sat knitting away in the twilight, while the December snow fell quietly without, and the fire crackled cheerfully within.

Mark English almost looks in on the Marches
Illustration by Mark English for *Little Women* (Pleasantville, NY: Reader's Digest, 1967). Reproduced from the 1989 reprint edition by permission of The Reader's Digest Association, Inc., White Plains, NY.

Alcott's illustrators from the 1940s and 1950s, English's key image of family togetherness occurs once Father returns from the war and the family gathers around a Christmas dinner.

In some ways this image complements the opening one: it's as if we've come inside to the warm interior glow. (The bright balls reappear, though their colors are varied and suggest a Christmas tree—there's none in Alcott's novel—more than a pot of roses.) Yet this togetherness image reinscribes the patriarchal family. The patriarch is implicit in other artists' images of the women of the family clustered to hear his letter, but he is often an absent visual presence. Here, however, he and Brooke, Laurie, and Mr. Laurence are visually present. "There never *was* such a Christmas dinner as they had that day," the caption reads. Yet it's not the dinner itself but the dinner party that receives visual attention, crowded around a small table. The men are at rest, at the right, some looking left, where there's more action. On the far left, a woman extends an arm to pour a teapot. In the center, one is either rising or sitting down. Two of the women seem to wear aprons (not something they should wear when entertaining). The women are more active than the men, but it's to serve the men. One man, standing back and to the right, surveys and slightly dominates the scene. He seems to correspond to Brooke, Laurie's tutor, eventually Meg's husband—not yet a man with much command in the novel. He seems to be a surrogate for English, surveying and somewhat detached, much as English's illustrations are from the text, but marrying the text nonetheless.

The woman in the center, rising or sitting, is bathed in light—or maybe her chair is—yet her outline blends into her surroundings. One could argue that, in keeping with the strand of feminist theory that celebrates connection and community, she is interdependent with the rest, both pictorially and familially. Or maybe she is relatively indistinguishable from her domestic role as she merges with the table. Or maybe the indeterminacy of her form simply reflects English's overall concern with design, with composition and the ambient play of light, as much as with the characters he depicts. We may not see a sumptuous display of food—"such a Christmas dinner"—but we see a sumptuous display of family, of women's relational work, and of visual effects.

The final image depicts Amy and Laurie near Nice, at Valrosa, where, in Alcott's text, "roses blossomed everywhere" (315). The caption reads, "'Try lower down, and pick those that have no thorns,' said Amy, gathering three of the tiny cream-colored ones that starred the wall behind her." In the image Amy does hold "the tiny cream-colored ones," but there aren't any "starr[ing] the wall behind her," nor do roses feature elsewhere in the image. A profusion of flowers cascades in front of the two figures, but they resemble daisies more than roses. Nor do the flowers seem to be planted and growing but rather an arranged spray, merging with the pattern on Amy's skirt. If for Alcott the roses ground Amy in a natural setting—she's been too willing to be swayed by superficial social norms of attractiveness and luxury—English's flowers make her a hothouse beauty. He seems less entranced by simplicity. (And his image pushes me to see Alcott's own emphasis on grounding Amy.)

Nice has been a favorite setting for illustrators favoring the decorative, such as Alice Barber Stephens and Jessie Willcox Smith a century ago. They tended to glory not just in the natural setting but in the minutiae of dress. English is more interested in the overall texture and design. And his Amy is curiously reclining against the upright Laurie, dependent on him, though he does not dominate her by his height on the page—but neither is he the observer or supplicant of the earlier Nice illustrations. English's Amy dominates the page visually, but Laurie seems to be putting her on display, his head turned to her as if she were a ventriloquist's dummy—or maybe he is poised for a vampiric bite.[248] And nowhere do we see the sketchbook that she should soon be picking up. Indeed, nowhere in English's illustrations, unlike in those of many other artists, do we see women writing or drawing. In the novel, writing and drawing emblematize possibilities for women's independent action. Still, as I've noted, English does provide women with some outlets for movement.

In short, Mark English's images are stunning and evocative, although in at least one of their subtexts, their embrace of the patriarchal, and indeed in their very artistic independence, they may implicitly constrain and belittle Alcott's text. They don't so much replicate the text as work in parallel with it, allude to it, raise questions, perhaps provoke it. Like the images in an artist's illustrated book, they are works of art in their own right. Illustrators of *Little Women* have often emphasized the decorative and romantic and domestic. In recent years they have often nostalgically foregrounded heterosexual romance but also allowed for expression of anger and disruption and independence, including Amy's independence as an artist. English tends to foreground domesticity and interdependence and the traditionally feminine; his Jo even weeps in one image, something she rarely does in modern illustrations, which tend to temper sentimentality. Yet he created his images before the 1970s, when responses to Alcott were allowing for more anger and danger. His women have the potential not so much for emotional or financial but for spatial and technological independence. And in his house image he creates a scene that simultaneously sets the domestic world apart from the outside world and also lures the viewer to it, without stereotyping its domesticity. This is his image that works best for me: it's suggestive yet in keeping with the premises of the novel. When he turns to identifiable figures, it's hard for English to resist Victorian stereotypes, but the house image hints at the possibilities for creating an illustrated book whose images can be independent, fine art, yet still work in tandem with the text of *Little Women*.

In the past half-century, the interest of the young in *Little Women* appears to have abated—certainly in terms of percentages, whether or not in terms of raw numbers—even as recommendations of the novel continue to be robust. But *Little Women* has permeated American culture in other ways, more than it had in earlier periods. In about a third of the time since the novel was first published, more than half of the various re-visionings have appeared. Recent television versions haven't kept pace with their frequency in the 1950s, yet the total number of TV and film versions since 1960 is almost equivalent to the number before then, and the number of illustrated editions and dramatizations in this period is 50 percent greater. The number of biographies and spinoffs produced in the past half-century is more than double that of all the previous years, and the number of musical renditions is triple. Not only do such re-visionings illuminate how the permeable text that is *Little Women* continues to speak to the modern condition but they have also enabled the text to infiltrate modern culture. The accelerating popularity of the musical versions, a more consciously artificial mode than most other dramatizations, perhaps accommodates a sense of how dated, and hence artificial, the manners of the novel now seem—yet how strongly the emotions, conveyed by music, still resonate. Similarly, the accelerating popularity of spinoffs may address some need to translate the novel for a modern audience, in these changing and disorienting times, even as it speaks to how deeply embedded *Little Women* is in the psyche of modern writers. Partly attesting to how similarly embedded it is for modern scholars is that since 1960 scholarship addressing *Little Women* has exploded—by one measure more than a hundredfold.

Looking to the future, I don't see any abatement of scholarship, and I expect to see more spinoffs and other adaptations, including in new media. Sony is planning another feature-length film adaptation of the book, and there have been a number of references to the novel on television: Bart Simpson reads *Little Women*, as has the mayor of *Buffy the Vampire Slayer*, and as do Joey of *Friends* and Alex of *Modern Family* (though she relents when Lily refuses to listen). Two other recent redactions, both modernized spinoffs, neither in book format, provide a glimpse of future possibilities.

One focuses on the house. In *The March Sisters at Christmas*, presented on television by Lifetime in 2011, four very modern sisters try to fix up Orchard House, here a white-columned colonial, so that their parents will not be tempted to sell it. Jo and Teddy are friends—"with absolutely no benefits," he laments to John. Jo ghost-tweets for a living, Amy makes nude photos available through one of the tweets, so Jo loses this job, also the opportunity to ghostwrite an autobiography. But no matter: an editor, Mr. Bhaer, is quite taken with both her and her unpublished novel. At the end, three sisters seem headed for romantic pairings—and Beth is allowed to live. Domesticity lives on.

The other focuses on cars, and hence potential for movement (though the depicted cars are more often parked, lined up outside a school, than moving). *Little Women Big Cars* (2012+) is online programming, or branded entertainment, offered by AOL and sponsored by Allstate Insurance. Currently with two seasons of five-minute episodes, it features four soccer moms, one named Meg, in interrelationships with their children, partners, and one another. And accompanied by advertisements, although your friendly and too-helpful Allstate representative doesn't physically appear in the plot line till the middle of the second season. Meg, the one with a professor husband, is a not-so-stay-at-home Mom, overinvolved in volunteering for Cherry Branch Elementary School—not quite the same as Jo's active direction, with her professor, of Plumfield School. Barbara, the divorced career woman, dates A.J., the sexy soccer coach and Laurie equivalent; the possibilities for romantic triangles are transferred beyond the sisterhood to external rivals when Barbara's and A.J.'s exes hook up. The pink-gloved Rocky, always ready with showy fashion tips, may not sculpt her young daughter in the same way the artistic Amy does but more directly shapes her, seeking tooth veneers and hair extensions, to enhance her success in beauty pageants. Amy's traits are thus exaggerated, as often happens in spinoffs, but not maliciously here or punitively. No one seems to correspond to Beth; only in supernatural spinoffs does it seem possible to empower the saintly sickly Beth. Unless Connie counts: plump but happy with her body in the first season, or at least mostly so, she is effectively killed off in the second, replaced with a different, slimmer actress. The unattainable perfection of Beth continues to haunt us.

Or perhaps her possibilities do. The possibilities for all four sisters, whether domestically ensconced in the house or with kinetic potential in cars, continue to haunt us, hover before us, beckon us, in the twenty-first century.

Notes

Abbreviations

Acadi.	Academic OneFile. go.galegroup.com.
Adamo.	Mark Adamo. www.markadamo.com.
APSO.	American Periodicals Series Online. ProQuest. proquest.com.
BNA.	British Newspaper Archive. www.britishnewspaperarchive.co.uk.
CA.	Chronicling America, Library of Congress. chroniclingamerica.loc.gov.
CDNC.	California Digital Newspaper Collection. cdnc.ucr.edu/cdnc.
CR.	*Louisa May Alcott: The Contemporary Reviews.* Ed. Beverly Lyon Clark. Cambridge: Cambridge Univ. Press, 2004.
CustomN.	Custom Newspapers. InfoTrac. infotrac.galegroup.com.
ebrary.	ProQuest. proquest.com.
EBSCO.	EBSCO Host. web.ebscohost.com.
GBks.	Google Books. books.google.com.
GNA.	Google News Archive. news.google.com/archivesearch. The archive has been undergoing a slow dismantling since I garnered most materials, in 2010–11.
Guard.	*Guardian* (London). guardian.co.uk.
HathiTrust.	HathiTrust Digital Library. www.hathitrust.org.
InfoTrac.	infotrac.galegroup.com.
JSTOR.	www.jstor.org.
Letters.	*The Selected Letters of Louisa May Alcott.* Ed. Joel Myerson and Daniel Shealy. Assoc. ed. Madeleine B. Stern. Boston: Little, 1987.
LexN.	LexisNexis Academic. www.lexisnexis.com.
LION.	Literature Online. lion.chadwyck.com.
MOA.	Making of America (Cornell University). moa.library.cornell.edu.
NA.	Newspaper Archive. newspaperarchive.com.
NYHN.	Old New York State Historical Newspaper Pages. fultonhistory.com /Fulton.html.
PP.	Papers Past, New Zealand newspapers. paperspast.natlib.govt.nz/cgi-bin /paperspast.
ProQ.	ProQuest. proquest.com.

ProjM.   Project Muse. muse.jhu.edu.
Taylor.   Taylor & Francis Online. www.tandfonline.com.
TDA.   Times Digital Archive. InfoTrac. infotrac.galegroup.com.
TLS.   TLS Historical Archive. find.galegroup.com.

Introduction

Epigraph: John Frow, "Afterlife: Texts as Usage," *Reception: Texts, Readers, Audiences, History* 1 (Fall 2008): 15, receptionstudy.org.

1. Carolyn Steedman, *Strange Dislocations: Childhood and the Idea of Human Interiority, 1780–1930* (Cambridge, MA: Harvard Univ. Press, 1995), 12.

2. Barbara Sicherman, *Well-Read Lives: How Books Inspired a Generation of American Women* (Chapel Hill: Univ. of North Carolina Press, 2010), 57.

3. Kathryn R. Kent, *Making Girls into Women: American Women's Writing and the Rise of Lesbian Identity* (Durham, NC: Duke Univ. Press, 2003), 16, 43.

4. Rosalind Coward, *Female Desires: How They Are Sought, Bought and Packaged* (1984; reprint, New York: Grove, 1985), 203.

5. Holly Virginia Blackford, *Out of This World: Why Literature Matters to Girls* (New York: Teachers College Press, 2004), 21, 26.

6. See James L. Machor, *Reading Fiction in Antebellum America: Informed Response and Reception Histories, 1820–1865* (Baltimore: Johns Hopkins Univ. Press, 2011), 38.

CHAPTER 1:   Becoming Everyone's Aunt, 1868–1900

Epigraphs: Review of *Little Men*, *New York Times*, 17 June 1871, 2 (CR 140); H. R. Hudson, "Concord Books," *Harper's Monthly*, June 1875, 27; Frank Preston Stearns, *Sketches from Concord and Appledore* (New York: Putnam's, 1895), 82.

1. Entry dated September 1867, *The Journals of Louisa May Alcott*, ed. Joel Myerson and Daniel Shealy (Boston: Little, 1989), 158, hereafter cited parenthetically as *J*.

2. And she also perhaps, as Barbara Hochman has argued with respect to *Uncle Tom's Cabin* (1852), helped to legitimate reading the novel at a time when novel reading was still suspect (*"Uncle Tom's Cabin" and the Reading Revolution: Race, Literacy, Childhood, and Fiction, 1851–1911* [Amherst: Univ. of Massachusetts Press, 2011], 78–103).

3. Louisa M. Alcott, *Little Women, or Meg, Jo, Beth and Amy: Authoritative Text, Backgrounds and Contexts, Criticism*, ed. Anne K. Phillips and Gregory Eiselein (New York: Norton, 2004), 17, hereafter cited parenthetically.

4. See, e.g., Steven Mailloux, "The Rhetorical Use and Abuse of Fiction: Eating Books in Late Nineteenth-Century America," *boundary 2* 17.1 (Spring 1990): 133–57.

5. For a somewhat different argument that Marmee's message is subverted, see Elizabeth Lennox Keyser, who explores the implications of Jo's quoting Aunt Chloe of *Uncle Tom's Cabin* (*Little Women: A Family Romance* [New York: Twayne, 1999], 45).

6. For a persuasive argument that Marmee's Christmas gift is the New Testament and not *Pilgrim's Progress*, see Anne K. Phillips, "The Prophets and the Martyrs: Pilgrims and Missionaries in *Little Women* and *Jack and Jill*," in *"Little Women" and the Feminist Imagination: Criticism, Controversy, Personal Essays*, ed. Janice M. Alberghene and Beverly Lyon Clark (New York: Garland, 1999), 222–23.

7. Van Wyck Brooks, *New England: Indian Summer, 1865–1915* (New York: Dutton, 1940), 65.

8. Part 2 continues to be known as *Good Wives* in Commonwealth countries, leading to some confusion as to what constitutes the text of *Little Women*: just part 1, or both parts together? A Canadian commentator read it as two books and found it "more successful that way," given the "distinct break in tone and emphasis" (Nora L. Magid, "Clear the Stage for a Repeat Performance," *New York Times*, 9 Nov. 1969, BRA64 [ProQ]). All data in this paragraph are from Joel Myerson and Daniel Shealy, "The Sales of Louisa May Alcott's Books," *Harvard Library Bulletin*, n.s., 1.1 (Spring 1990): 69–73.

9. Frank Luther Mott, *Golden Multitudes: The Story of Best Sellers in the United States* (New York: Macmillan, 1947), 309, 8.

10. Jno. R. G. Hassard, "The New York Mercantile Library," *Scribner's*, Feb. 1871, 363; The Lounger, *Critic*, 6 Feb. 1886, 71 (APSO); Hamilton W. Mabie, "The Most Popular Novels in America," *Forum*, Dec. 1893, 510.

11. See Caroline Maria Hewins, "Reading of the Young" (1896), reprinted in *Library Work with Children*, ed. Alice I. Hazeltine (White Plains, NY: Wilson, 1917), 43. Alcott's works also appear frequently in individual librarians' lists of children's favorite titles in the 1890s — see Kate McDowell, "Understanding Children as Readers: Librarians' Anecdotes and Surveys in the United States from 1890 to 1930," in *International Perspectives, c. 1500–1990*, ed. Shafquat Towheed and W. R. Owens, vol. 1 of *The History of Reading* (Houndmills, UK: Palgrave Macmillan, 2011), 151, 153.

12. "Evangelist Prize Sunday-School Library," *New York Evangelist*, 2 Aug. 1894, 11 (APSO).

13. "Miss Louisa M. Alcott," *Boston Herald*, reprinted in *New York Times*, 28 Apr. 1880, 2 (ProQ).

14. "Top 20 Circulating Authors" and "Top 20 Circulating Books," What Middletown Read, Ball State University Library, www.bsu.edu/libraries/wmr/. My recalibration of the data leads me to include *An Old-Fashioned Girl* and *Little Men* among the top twenty books. Rather different are the data reported by Christine Pawley for the town of Osage, Iowa, in 1890–95: no work by Alcott is on the list of the public library's twenty-one most popular titles, nor is she among the twenty most popular authors; she is, however, the seventeenth most popular among girls (*Reading on the Middle Border: The Culture of Print in Late-Nineteenth-Century Osage, Iowa* [Amherst: Univ. of Massachusetts Press, 2001], 92, 96, 111).

15. Anne Trubek, "What Muncie Read," *New York Times*, 27 Nov. 2011, BR43 (LexN).

16. Yet it's not the case that the percentage of borrowers from white-collar backgrounds was lowest for *Little Women* among Alcott books, although *Under the Lilacs* did seem to appeal especially to borrowers in blue-collar families.

17. In 1888–98 Roberts Brothers printed about 161,000 copies of *Little Women*, 124,000 copies of *Little Men*, 85,000 copies of *An Old-Fashioned Girl*, and 68,000 copies of *Under the Lilacs* (Myerson and Shealy, "Sales," 69, 72, 73, 80).

18. Jonathan Rose, "The History of Education as the History of Reading," *History of Education* 36.4–5 (July–Sept. 2007): 598 (Taylor). Barbara Ryan responds that a fan letter can have multiple functions, including as "a platform for self-advocacy" ("One Reader, Two Votes: Retooling Fan Mail Scholarship," in *Methods, Strategies, Tactics*, ed. Rosalind Crone and Shafquat Towheed, vol. 3 of *The History of Reading* [Houndmills, UK: Palgrave Macmillan, 2011], 73).

19. Alcott to Thomas Niles, 5 Aug. 1871, in *Louisa May Alcott: Her Life, Letters, and*

Journals, ed. Ednah D. Cheney (1889; reprint, Boston: Roberts, 1891), 203; Alcott to John Seely Hart, 13 Sept. [1871], *Letters*, 161; Alcott to Mary Mapes Dodge, 17 Sept. [1874], *Letters*, 237.

20. Alcott to Viola Price, 18 Dec. 1885, *Letters*, 296.

21. Louise Chandler Moulton, "Louisa May Alcott," in *Our Famous Women: An Authorized Record of the Lives and Deeds of Distinguished American Women of Our Times*, by Louise Chandler Moulton et al. (Hartford, CT: Worthington, 1884), 46.

22. Alcott to Edward Marston, 5 Oct. [1873], *Letters*, 179; Alcott to Mrs. H. Koorders-Boeke, 7 Aug. 1875, *Letters*, 193. In 1880 two Dutch admirers wrote that "your pretty books . . . are read by old and young, who enjoy them each in their way; they revive the old hearts and heads, by making them think back at their own youth, and they encourage the young ones, to do as much good as possible" (Betsy van Brakel and C. v.d. Meer v. [Kuffeler?] to Alcott, 9 Aug. 1880 [MS Am 800.23 (25), Houghton Library, Harvard University, hereafter cited as Houghton Library]). An undated letter from "a lovely old Dutch lady" claimed, "There are so many wise and truthful things in this book that I want my children, my grandchildren and my great-grandchildren to enjoy it" (quoted in "Letters to Author of 'Little Women,'" *New York Sun*, 29 Dec. 1912, 3 [NYHN]).

23. "Louisa M. Alcott," *Washington Post*, 8 Mar. 1888, 4 (ProQ).

24. "A Letter to Miss Alcott," *Christian Union*, 21 Aug. 1884, 187 (APSO).

25. Gracie P. Hill to Alcott, Oct. 1886, and Charlie W. Soule to Alcott, 15 Oct. 1886 (MS 800.23 [85] and [195], Houghton Library).

26. Reprinted in Gloria T. Delamar, *Louisa May Alcott and "Little Women": Biography, Critique, Publications, Poems, Songs and Contemporary Relevance* (Jefferson, NC: McFarland, 1990), 146.

27. Reprinted as "Miss Louisa M. Alcott," *New York Times*, 28 Apr. 1880, 2 (ProQ). Moulton quotes a remarkably similar letter (thus suggesting that the letter wasn't entirely fabricated, but also hinting at a common nineteenth-century casualness regarding transcription): the author claims she "cried quarts over Beth's sickness. If you don't have her marry Laurie in the second part, I shall never forgive you, and none of the girls in our school will ever read any more of your books" (Moulton et al., *Our Famous Women*, 43).

28. Dorothy Lundt, "Miss Alcott," *Boston Evening Transcript*, 10 Mar. 1888, 8; Literary Affairs in Boston, *Book Buyer*, May 1888, 135; Frances Crane, "'Little Women' and Little Men," *Chicago Daily Tribune*, 13 Apr. 1888, 9 (ProQ).

29. Satie S., letter, Aunt Patience's Writing Desk, *Christian Union*, 21 Jan. 1880, 66 (APSO).

30. Louise Chandler Moulton, "Louisa May Alcott," *St. Nicholas*, May 1888, 626, quoted in Daniel Shealy, "'Work Well Done': Louisa May Alcott and Mary Mapes Dodge," in *"St. Nicholas" and Mary Mapes Dodge: The Legacy of a Children's Magazine Editor*, ed. Susan R. Gannon, Suzanne Rahn, and Ruth Anne Thompson (Jefferson, NC: McFarland, 2004), 187. Another young fan reportedly "could not sleep nor eat, absolutely refusing to be comforted" after learning of Alcott's death ("The Children and Miss Alcott," [Boston newspaper?, Mar. 1888?] [MS Am 800.23 (284), Houghton Library]).

31. "Thirty-Eight Graduate," *Cedar Rapids (IA) Evening Gazette*, 10 June 1898, 6 (NA).

32. The middle-class Dorothy Richardson, who had read *Little Women* four times

herself, reported telling the plot to two working women who were unfamiliar with the book and being told, "That's no story—that's just everyday happenings. I don't see what's the use putting things like that in books" ([Dorothy B. Richardson], *The Long Day: The Story of a New York Working Girl, as Told by Herself* [1905; reprint, New York: Century, 1911], 86). Alcott was nevertheless one of the most popular authors in a reading room for working-class girls in Hartford in the late 1880s, where the "girls" chose books from among those provided by middle-class benefactors (see Barbara Sicherman, *Well-Read Lives: How Books Inspired a Generation of American Women* [Chapel Hill: Univ. of North Carolina Press, 2010], 30). Melissa R. Klapper suggests that Alcott's works were popular with immigrant Jewish girls in part because librarians encouraged such reading (*Jewish Girls Coming of Age in America, 1860–1920* [New York: New York Univ. Press, 2005], 207 [ebrary]).

33. Sicherman, *Well-Read Lives*, 30, 25. Sicherman also notes appreciation by a number of others.

34. Martha Freeman Esmond to Julia Boyd, 9 Mar. 1888, reprinted in Herma Clark, "When Chicago Was Young: The Elegant Eighties," *Chicago Daily Tribune*, 3 Jan. 1937, F4 (ProQ).

35. Helen Keller, *The Story of My Life* (1902; reprint, Garden City, NY: Doubleday, 1924), 108 (GBks).

36. Quoted in Niles to Alcott, 11 July 1871 (MS Am 1130.8 [3], Houghton Library).

37. Louella Parsons, Hollywood, *Middletown (NY) Times Herald*, 18 May 1948, 12 (NA).

38. Marian de Forest to Jessie Bonstelle, 31 Mar. 1911 (transcription in MS Am 800.23 [205], Houghton Library).

39. Edna Ferber, *A Peculiar Treasure* (New York: Doubleday, 1939), 36; Teasdale, cited in Lee Jolliffe, "The Magazine as Mentor: A Turn-of-the-Century Handwritten Magazine by St. Louis Women Artists," *American Periodicals* 7 (1997): 59 (JSTOR); Carol Miles Peterson, *Bess Streeter Aldrich: The Dreams Are All Real* (Lincoln: Univ. of Nebraska Press, 1995), 10; Lucy C. Lillie, "Louisa May Alcott," *Cosmopolitan*, Apr. 1888, 162. Elaine Showalter would add Gertrude Stein to the list (*Sister's Choice: Tradition and Change in American Women's Writing* [Oxford: Clarendon, 1991], 42).

40. Mary Church Terrell, *A Colored Woman in a White World* (1940; reprint, Salem, NH: Ayer, 1992), 26; Wells noted that she had formed her ideals on Alcott's and others' stories (*Crusade for Justice: The Autobiography of Ida B. Wells*, ed. Alfreda M. Duster [Chicago: Univ. of Chicago Press, 1970], 21). Overall, although *Little Women* has been mentioned as a childhood favorite by some blacks—including Ann Petry, Sonia Sanchez, Diane Abbott, and Donna Britt, cited in later chapters—the novel seems not to have been as popular with nonwhites as with whites.

41. Theodore Roosevelt, *An Autobiography* (New York: Macmillan, 1913), 20.

42. See Alexander Woollcott to Laura E. Richards, 15 Mar. 1932, in *The Letters of Alexander Woollcott*, ed. Beatrice Kaufman and Joseph Hennessey (New York: Viking, 1944), 108; and Samuel Hopkins Adams, *A. Woollcott: His Life and His World* (New York: Reynal, 1945), 30.

43. Charlotte Yonge to unknown addressee, n.d., in *The Letters of Charlotte Mary Yonge (1823–1901)*, ed. Charlotte Mitchell, Ellen Jordan, and Helen Schinske, www .yongeletters.com; Constance Smedley, *Crusaders* (London: Duckworth, 1929), 230;

Terry, quoted in Cornelia Meigs, *Invincible Louisa: The Story of the Author of "Little Women"* (1933; reprint, Boston: Little, 1935), 242.

44. Frank Swinnerton, *Swinnerton: An Autobiography* (Garden City, NY: Doubleday, 1936), 31.

45. Rudyard Kipling, *From Sea to Sea: Letters of Travel*, vol. 2 (New York: Doubleday, 1899), 161; "To Save Orchard House," *New-York Daily Tribune*, 26 Mar. 1911, 4 (NYHN).

46. See Shirley Foster and Judy Simons, *What Katy Read: Feminist Re-Readings of 'Classic' Stories for Girls* (Iowa City: Univ. of Iowa Press, 1995), 13–16.

47. W. J. Niles to Alcott, 18 Mar. 1871 (MS Am 800.23 [127], Houghton Library).

48. The Magazines, *Sun and Central Press* (London), 12 May 1873, 9 (NA). Reviews of *Life*, ed. Cheney, in *Daily News* (London), 18 Oct. 1889, 5; *Saturday Review* (UK), 9 Nov. 1889, 538; and *Guardian* (London), 2 Apr. 1890, 555 (NA).

49. Edward Salmon, *Juvenile Literature as It Is* (London: Drane, 1888), 21, 22 (GBks).

50. See "Miss Alcott Abroad," *Boston Evening Transcript*, 11 Dec. 1873, 7 (CR 86); and "Louisa May Alcott—Deutsche Übersetzungen," www.xanth.de/alcott/buecher.htm. A common early title was *Kleine Frauen*; a common recent one is *Betty und ihre Schwestern* (Betty and her sisters).

51. *Tydspiegel*, translated and transcribed by Mrs. C. Boeke in her letter to Alcott of 19 Jan. 1877 (MS Am 2745 [86], Houghton Library).

52. See Mieke K. T. Desmet, *Babysitting the Reader: Translating English Narrative Fiction for Girls into Dutch (1946–1995)* (Bern: Lang, 2007), 75.

53. *Constitutionnel* and *Union Jurassienne*, 30 Nov. 1872, quoted (in English) in "Miss Alcott Abroad," 7 (CR 87). A later writer suggested that although "the French read but few foreign books . . . Miss Alcott's tales are at once translated" ("Points in the Copyright Discussion," *Scribner's*, Oct. 1878, 898 [MOA]).

54. Literary Notes, *Chicago Daily Tribune*, 19 Jan. 1873, 4 (ProQ).

55. Quoted (in English) in Odds and Oddities, *Burlington (IA) Hawk-Eye*, 4 June 1881, 7 (NA).

56. See *Brandon (MB) Sun*, 30 Jan. 1981, TV5 (NA).

57. See Claire Le Brun, "De *Little Women* de Louisa May Alcott aux *Quatre filles du docteur March*: Les traductions françaises d'un roman de formation au féminin," *Meta* 48.1–2 (2003): 47–67 (EBSCO), hereafter cited parenthetically. My discussion throughout this paragraph is informed by Le Brun's insights. For a brief discussion of why the book was first translated into French in Switzerland, less Catholic than France, see I. Nières, quoted in Emer O'Sullivan, *Comparative Children's Literature*, trans. Anthea Bell (London: Routledge, 2005), 70.

58. "Miss Alcott's Little Men," *Maine Farmer*, 9 Aug. 1873, 4 (APSO).

59. K.T.W., "A Varied Mental Diet Needed," letter to the editor, *New York Times*, 5 Mar. 1898, RBA156 (ProQ).

60. Local Laconics, *Lima (OH) Daily Times*, 6 Feb. 1889, 4 (NA); L. W., letter to the editor, *St. Nicholas*, Mar. 1886, 394–95 (CR 91); Erin Graham, "Books That Girls Have Loved," *Lippincott's*, Sept. 1897, 432.

61. Katherine Davis Chapman Tillman, *Beryl Weston's Ambition: The Story of an Afro-American Girl's Life* (1893), reprinted in *The Works of Katherine Davis Chapman Tillman*, ed. Claudia Tate (New York: Oxford Univ. Press, 1991), 215.

62. See Daniel Shealy, "The Growth of *Little Things*: Louisa May Alcott and the

Lukens Sisters' Family Newspaper," *Resources for American Literary Study* 30 (2005): 160–77.

63. Mary R. Botsford, cited in *Louisa May Alcott*, by Katharine Anthony (New York: Knopf, 1938), 205.

64. Quoted in Mary Wright Plummer, "The Work for Children in Free Libraries," *Library Journal* 22 (Nov. 1897): 684.

65. Annie Adams, letter to the editor, *St. Nicholas*, Feb. 1878, 300 (CR 88).

66. Margaret Huntingdon, "Miss Alcott: A Letter from England to New York," *Monthly Packet*, Sept. 1890, 273.

67. "Letter to Miss Alcott."

68. Survey respondents quoted in Plummer, "Work for Children," 684.

69. Review of *An Old-Fashioned Girl*, *Springfield (MA) Daily Republican*, 4 Apr. 1870, [2] (CR 97).

70. Thomas Niles to Alcott, 25 July 1868 (MS Am 1130.8 [1], Houghton Library).

71. Alcott to Elizabeth Powell, 20 Mar. [1869], *Letters*, 125. In her journal for November 1868 Alcott noted, "Girls write to ask who the little women marry, as if that was the only end and aim of a woman's life. I *won't* marry Jo to Laurie to please any one" (J 167).

72. Alcott to Powell, 20 Mar. [1869], 125.

73. [Thomas Wentworth Higginson], "Childhood's Fancies," *Scribner's*, Jan. 1876, 358 (MOA).

74. [Mrs. Henry Ward Beecher], review of part 2 of *Little Women*, *Mother at Home*, July 1869, 221 (CR 77).

75. Graham, "Books That Girls Have Loved," 431.

76. Huntingdon, "Miss Alcott," 276.

77. Sicherman, *Well-Read Lives*, 21.

78. Personalities, *New York Graphic*, 18 Dec. 1875, 374, quoted in *Letters*, 208n1. In her journal Alcott noted that she "talk[ed] with four hundred girls, wr[o]te in stacks of albums and schoolbooks, and kiss[ed] every one who ask[ed] me" (Feb. 1875, J 196).

79. Bronson Alcott to Louisa Alcott, 4 Feb. 1875, in *The Letters of A. Bronson Alcott*, ed. Richard L. Herrnstadt (Ames: Iowa State Univ. Press, 1969), 646. Her father was frequently public about Louisa's private life on his speaking tours, a synergistic move that enhanced the celebrity of both.

80. Alcott to Mrs. Woods, 20 July [1875], *Letters*, 193.

81. Clara Gowing, *The Alcotts as I Knew Them* (Boston: Clark, 1909), 28 (GBks).

82. Lydia Maria Child to Sarah Shaw, 18 June 1876, in *Lydia Maria Child: Selected Letters, 1817–1880*, ed. Milton Meltzer and Patricia G. Holland (Amherst: Univ. of Massachusetts Press, 1982), 534.

83. L. M. Alcott, "The Lay of a Golden Goose," *Woman's Journal*, 8 May 1886, 151. In an early manuscript the turkeys "gobble facts & fictions" ("The Lay of a Golden Goose," MS Am 1817 [12], Houghton Library). Thomas Niles discouraged Alcott from publishing the verse in 1870, fearing "its effect would be very prejudicial" (Niles to Alcott, 30 Aug. 1870, quoted in *Little Women Abroad: The Alcott Sisters' Letters from Europe, 1870–1871*, ed. Daniel Shealy [Athens: Univ. of Georgia Press, 2008], 178n1).

84. Louisa M. Alcott, *Jo's Boys, and How They Turned Out: A Sequel to "Little Men"* (1886; reprint, Boston: Roberts Brothers, 1891), 45 (GBks), hereafter cited parenthetically.

85. Gamaliel Bradford, "Portrait of Louisa May Alcott," *North American Review* 209 (Mar. 1919): 402 (JSTOR).

86. Obituary, *Piqua (OH) Daily Call*, 9 Mar. 1888, 2 (NA).

87. Katherine Adams, *Owning Up: Privacy, Property, and Belonging in U.S. Women's Life Writing* (New York: Oxford Univ. Press, 2009), 155, hereafter cited parenthetically.

88. See, e.g., Alcott to Thomas Niles, [Fall] 1886, *Letters*, 299. Latter-day readers are not so different: Sherryl A. Englund argues that Alcott-related publications still favor a youthful photograph ("Reading the Author in *Little Women*: A Biography of a Book," *ATQ*, n.s., 12.3 [Sept. 1998]: 216).

89. Graeme Turner, *Understanding Celebrity* (London: Sage, 2004), 8 (ebrary).

90. See Joseph Roach, "The Doubting-Thomas Effect," *PMLA* 126 (Oct. 2011): 1129, www.mlajournals.org.

91. Barbara Hochman, *Getting at the Author: Reimagining Books and Reading in the Age of American Realism* (Amherst: Univ. of Massachusetts Press, 2001), esp. 13, 22–23.

92. "Louisa M. Alcott," *Victoria Magazine*, July 1880, 6.

93. See, e.g., Alcott to Mrs. Graham, 2 Feb. [1877], *Letters*, 220.

94. See Beverly Lyon Clark, introduction to *CR*, xviii.

95. Clippings in Thomas Niles to Alcott, 20 [Jan.?] 1871 (MS Am 2745 [84], Houghton Library); Personal, *Washington Post*, 12 Aug. 1878, 2 (ProQ); *Boston Traveler*, cited in *The Women Folk*, *Hamilton (OH) Daily Democrat*, 21 Apr. 1887, 1 (NA).

96. Christopher P. Wilson, *The Labor of Words: Literary Professionalism in the Progressive Era* (Athens: Univ. of Georgia Press, 1985), 12. As James L. Machor notes, though, "realism and the realistic went from being a trait defining particular elements of a work of fiction . . . to being a mark of a text's defining generic status and of authorial identity, as manifested in one's overall practice as a fiction writer" (*Reading Fiction in Antebellum America: Informed Response and Reception Histories, 1820–1865* [Baltimore: Johns Hopkins Univ. Press, 2011], 313). Readers didn't define Alcott as a realist, nor her domestic children's novels as part of a realistic genre, so they didn't generally classify her works as realistic.

97. See John Matteson, *Eden's Outcasts: The Story of Louisa May Alcott and Her Father* (New York: Norton, 2007), 261.

98. Susan R. Gannon, "Getting Cozy with a Classic: Visualizing *Little Women* (1868–1995)," in Alberghene and Clark, *"Little Women" and the Feminist Imagination*, 105–10.

99. Alcott didn't much care for Billings's illustrations but found Frank Merrill's "capital" (Alcott to Elizabeth B. Greene, 1 Apr. [1869], *Letters*, 126; Alcott to Thomas Niles, 20 July 1880, *Letters*, 249).

100. For a detailed listing of textual changes, see "Textual Variants," in Alcott, *Little Women, or Meg, Jo, Beth and Amy*, 386–408. Daniel Shealy argues that Alcott "had little or no input" regarding the verbal changes ("Note on the Text," in *Little Women: An Annotated Edition*, by Louisa May Alcott, ed. Daniel Shealy [Cambridge, MA: Belknap Press of Harvard Univ. Press, 2013], ix–x).

101. See Gannon, "Getting Cozy with a Classic," 115–19. Merrill's illustrations also play up humor and drama.

102. See May Alcott, "Alcott's Woodland Gate," in *Classic Concord, as Portrayed by*

Emerson, Hawthorne, Thoreau and the Alcotts, ed. Caroline Ticknor (Boston: Houghton, 1926), 218.

103. Amy Kaplan, "Nation, Region, and Empire," in *The Columbia History of the American Novel*, ed. Emory Elliott (New York: Columbia Univ. Press, 1991), 251.

104. Gowing, *Alcotts as I Knew Them*, 73, 93. For a parallel argument that late-nineteenth-century illustrations of British novels foreground local places as a way of helping to define the nation, see Thomas Recchio, *Elizabeth Gaskell's "Cranford": A Publishing History* (Farnham, UK: Ashgate, 2009), 133.

105. Ann Douglas, introduction to *Little Women* (New York: Signet, 1983), xii–xiii. For an astute discussion of *Little Women* as a "narrative of national recovery" in which the war also functions as a metaphor for "individual struggles against gender norms," see Elizabeth Young, "A Wound of One's Own: Louisa May Alcott's Civil War Fiction," *American Quarterly* 48.3 (Sept. 1996): 439–74, esp. 463, 441.

106. Stephanie Coontz, *The Way We Never Were: American Families and the Nostalgia Trap* (New York: Basic, 1992), 100–101, hereafter cited parenthetically.

107. Review of *Eight Cousins, Overland Monthly*, Nov. 1875, 493 (CR 252).

108. See Gannon, "Getting Cozy with a Classic," 119.

109. Harriet Prescott Spofford, "Louisa May Alcott," *Chautauquan*, Dec. 1888, 161, Spofford's spelling.

110. [Sarah J. Hale?], "Books for Home Reading," *Godey's Lady's Book*, Nov. 1870, 472 (CR 117). Englund points out that the first editions of parts 1 and 2 were standard-sized books with dark cloth bindings, "packaged scarcely differently from adult novels" ("Reading the Author," 211).

111. Quoted in Ellery Sedgwick, *The Atlantic Monthly, 1857–1909: Yankee Humanism at High Tide and Ebb* (Amherst: Univ. of Massachusetts Press, 1994), 206, hereafter cited parenthetically.

112. Salmon, *Juvenile Literature*, 125, 130.

113. M.W.P., "Books for Children—$100 Worth," letter to the editor, *New York Times*, 8 Oct. 1898, BR665 (NA); Augusta H. Leypoldt and George Iles, eds., *List of Books for Girls and Women and Their Clubs* (Boston: Library Bureau, 1895), 1–2 (GBks); Thomas Wentworth Higginson, "A Young Girl's Library," *Ladies' Home Journal*, Nov. 1895, 4 (APSO)—despite "some occasional instance of slang or slovenly expression."

114. George E. Hardy, *Five Hundred Books for the Young: A Graded and Annotated List* (New York: Scribner's, 1892), 64 (GBks); J. W. White, "Traveling Libraries in Wisconsin," *Outlook*, 22 Jan. 1898, 219 (APSO); John W. Stone, "One Hundred Best Books for a Village Library," *Bookman*, Feb. 1898, 522 (APSO).

115. *The Best Reading: Hints on the Selection of Books; on the Formation of Libraries, Public and Private; on Courses of Reading, Etc.*, 4th ed. (New York: Putnam's, 1877), 106 (GBks), spelling as in original. Among the "b" authors are Eggleston, Howells, Trollope, Verne, and Warner; Twain is unranked.

116. Chronicle and Comment, *Bookman*, Dec. 1897, 271 (APSO).

117. "Mr. Putnam's List," *New York Times*, 15 Apr. 1899, RBA243 (ProQ); Walter Pulitzer, "Fifty Best American Novels," letter to the editor, *New York Times*, 15 Oct. 1898, 25 (ProQ).

118. Review of *Little Women, Ladies' Repository* (Boston), Dec. 1868, 472 (CR 66);

review of *Little Women, Ladies' Repository* (Cincinnati, OH), Nov. 1868, 472 (*CR* 65). Delamar cites 1868 and 1869 reviews in *Golden Hours* that suggest *Little Women* is "not harmful" but is not to be read on a Sunday (*Louisa May Alcott and "Little Women*," 147). In ensuing debates as to how religious the books in a Sunday school library needed to be, those who encouraged a broad view often listed Alcott's as exemplary additions; see, e.g., Rev. O. A. Kingsbury, "The Sunday School Library," *New Englander*, May 1881, 358 (MOA).

119. See Janet S. Zehr, "The Response of Nineteenth-Century Audiences to Louisa May Alcott's Fiction," *ATQ*, n.s., 1 (Dec. 1987): 333. For other laments about the lack of religious observances in the novel, see "Letters to Author of 'Little Women,'" 3; and Huntingdon, "Miss Alcott," 276.

120. "Books for the Sunday-School Library," *Christian Union*, 1 June 1882, 512–15 (APSO); Inquiring Friends, *Christian Union*, 14 July 1887, 44 (APSO).

121. "Louisa May Alcott," *Christian Advocate*, 15 Mar. 1888, 176 (APSO).

122. For Dickens, see Philip Waller, *Writers, Readers, and Reputations: Literary Life in Britain, 1870–1918* (Oxford: Oxford Univ. Press, 2006), 188–97; for James, see B. Clark, *Kiddie Lit*, 32–35.

123. See, e.g., Augusta J. Chapin, *General Survey of American Literature: Syllabus of a Course of Six Lecture-Studies* (Chicago: Univ. of Chicago Press, 1895), 15 (GBks); and John Nichol, *American Literature: An Historical Sketch, 1620–1880* (Edinburgh: Black, 1882), 369 (GBks). Sicherman finds Alcott's work included in an American literature course in 1878–79 at a female seminary (*Well-Read Lives*, 24).

124. John Habberton, "Author and Woman," *Cosmopolitan*, Dec. 1889, 254.

125. Templeton, review of part 2 of *Little Women*, Hartford (CT) *Daily Courant*, 1 May 1869, [1] (*CR* 73).

126. Review of part 2 of *Little Women*, *Eclectic Magazine*, June 1869, 757 (*CR* 76).

127. George Parsons Lathrop, "Some New England Authors," *Chautauquan*, Mar. 1887, 361 (APSO).

128. "Miss Alcott's New Book for Old and Young Folks," [Chicago newspaper? 1870?] (*CR* 120).

129. Review of *Eight Cousins*, 493–94 (*CR* 252). For an influential modern rebuttal of attacks on the plotting of women's novels, which often reject the dominant narrative logic (without specifically addressing Alcott), see Nancy K. Miller, "Emphasis Added: Plots and Plausibilities in Women's Fiction," *PMLA* 96.1 (Jan. 1981): 36–48 (JSTOR).

130. J.N., review of *An Old-Fashioned Girl*, *Eastern Argus*, n.d., n.p. (*CR* 123).

131. Review of *Little Men*, *Godey's Lady's Book*, Sept. 1871, 279 (*CR* 152); [Hale?] "Books for Home Reading," 472 (*CR* 117).

132. Samuel S. Green, "Class Adaptation in the Selection of Books—The Fiction Question," *Library Journal* 5 (May 1880): 141.

133. Thomas Wentworth Higginson, *Short Studies of American Authors*, enlarged ed. (Boston: Lee, 1888), 66–67.

134. "Two Books for Children," *Scribner's*, Apr. 1876, 897 (*CR* 260).

135. For example, Bernard DeVoto claimed that "the successful use of an American vernacular as the sole prose medium of a masterpiece is a triumph in technique" (*Mark Twain's America* [Boston: Little, 1932], 318).

136. The Lounger, *Critic*, 3 Apr. 1897, 235 (APSO).

137. [Almaric Rumsey?], review of part 2 of *Little Women, Athenaeum,* 25 Sept. 1869, 399 (CR 79).

138. *"Little Women," Graphic* (London), 26 Nov. 1870, 514–15 (CR 84).

139. Huntingdon, "Miss Alcott," 273.

140. Agnes Macdonell, "The American Heroine," *Macmillan's Magazine,* Oct. 1875, reprinted in *Littell's Living Age,* 30 Oct. 1875, 315, 317.

141. Review of *Little Women, British Quarterly Review* (American ed.), Jan. 1871, 157 (CR 85).

142. [Rumsey?], review of part 2 of *Little Women* (CR 79).

143. Macdonell, "American Heroine," 314.

144. Review of *Little Women, British Mail,* 2 May 1881, 381 (NA).

145. For an alternative reading of Dickens's use of the phrase as comparable to Alcott's, see Sarah Elbert, *A Hunger for Home: Louisa May Alcott and "Little Women"* (Philadelphia: Temple Univ. Press, 1984), 151–52.

146. Obituary, *Times* (London), 8 Mar. 1888, 7 (TDA).

147. Quoted in Margaret Adams, "Author of 'Seven Little Australians' Sees Her Country and U.S. Closely Linked," *Christian Science Monitor,* 18 Apr. 1941, 8. See also, e.g., editor's note to reprint edition of *Six Little New Zealanders* (1917; Auckland, New Zealand: Hodder, 1983), 201.

148. "Louisa M. Alcott," *Victoria Magazine,* July 1880, 7; editorial, *Godey's Lady's Book,* Sept. 1871, 279; review quoted in Zehr, "Response of Nineteenth-Century Audiences," 325; review of *Little Women, British Mail.*

149. José Martí, "La originalidad literaria en los Estados Unidos: Louisa May Alcott," in vol. 2 of *Norteamericanos,* vol. 16 of *Obras completas de Martí* (Havana: Trópico, 1939), 66.

150. "Little Men," *Scribner's,* Aug. 1871, 446 (CR 149). Even this reviewer added, though, that Alcott's works thus far "are only simple 'studies,' and of very narrow range."

151. Alice M. Jordan, *From Rollo to Tom Sawyer and Other Papers* (Boston: Horn Book, 1948), 39; editor of *Harper's* quoted in Frank Luther Mott, *A History of American Magazines,* vol. 2, *1850–1865* (Cambridge, MA: Harvard Univ. Press, 1938), 401.

152. *Zion's Herald,* 2 Sept. 1869, 413 (CR 16); *National Anti-Slavery Standard,* 18 Sept. 1869, [3] (CR 18); C. M. Hewins, *Books for the Young: A Guide for Parents and Children* (New York: Leypoldt, 1882); A. Adams, letter to the editor, 300.

153. John Tebbel, *The Expansion of an Industry, 1865–1919,* vol. 2 of *A History of Book Publishing in the United States* (New York: Bowker, 1975), 600–601.

154. Alcott to Thomas Niles, [June?] 1886, *Letters,* 298. Many reviews of *Jo's Boys* suggest that it is for young and old, but most imply that the primary audience is the young.

155. Review of *A Christmas Dream, Saturday Review* (UK), 3 July 1886, 27 (CR 356).

156. Review of *Jack and Jill, New York Times,* 17 Oct. 1880, 4 (CR 334).

157. See, e.g., R. Gordon Kelly, *Mother Was a Lady: Self and Society in Selected American Children's Periodicals, 1865–1890* (Westport, CT: Greenwood, 1974), 66–74.

158. Review of *An Old-Fashioned Girl, Atlantic,* June 1870, 752 (CR 110). On the gender segmenting of children's literature, see, e.g., Anne H. Lundin, "Victorian Horizons: The Reception of Children's Books in England and America, 1880–1900," *Library Quarterly* 64 (Jan. 1994): 43; and Sarah A. Wadsworth, "Louisa May Alcott, William T. Adams, and the Rise of Gender-Specific Series Books," *Lion and the Unicorn* 25 (2001): 17–46.

159. Roosevelt, *Autobiography*, 20.

160. They rarely did for, say, Mark Twain, whose *Adventures of Tom Sawyer* and *Adventures of Huckleberry Finn* were generally classed together as fiction for all ages, perhaps especially for boys of all ages; in the twentieth century, however, the former became essentially children's literature and the latter a novel for adults (see B. Clark, *Kiddie Lit*, 77–101).

161. [H. E. Scudder], review of *Jack and Jill*, *Atlantic*, Jan. 1881, 124 (*CR* 339); review of *Proverb Stories*, *Saturday Review* (UK), 9 Dec. 1882, 774 (*CR* 57). A later report tells of librarians in a New York City branch library deciding not to replace worn copies of *Little Women* because of "too much love-making in it for young people" (quoted in Anna A. Rogers, *Why American Marriages Fail, and Other Papers* [Boston: Houghton, 1909], 127 [GBks]). For a more positive response, see "Louisa M. Alcott, Her Life and Her Works," *Literary News*, Apr. 1888, 101.

162. [Lyman Abbott], review of *Little Men*, *Harper's Monthly*, Aug. 1871, 186 (*CR* 147); [Lyman Abbott], review of part 2 of *Little Women*, *Harper's Monthly*, Aug. 1869, 455–56 (*CR* 78).

163. Review of *An Old-Fashioned Girl*, *Atlantic*, June 1870, 752 (*CR* 110).

164. [Henry James], review of *Eight Cousins*, *Nation*, 14 Oct. 1875, 250–51 (*CR* 246–47).

165. [No title], [Boston newspaper, Oct. 1875?] (*CR* 251).

166. Agnes Repplier, "What Children Read," *Atlantic*, Jan. 1887, 29, 28.

167. Walter Lewin, review of *Books and Men*, by Agnes Repplier, *Academy*, 10 Aug. 1889, 83.

168. Review of *An Old-Fashioned Girl*, *Atlantic*, 752 (*CR* 110); [Scudder], review of *Jack and Jill* (*CR* 339).

169. "Two New England Women," *Atlantic*, Mar. 1890, 420, 421.

170. Richard H. Brodhead, *Cultures of Letters: Scenes of Reading and Writing in Nineteenth Century America* (Chicago: Univ. of Chicago Press, 1993), 69–106. Most of Alcott's publications in story papers appeared under pseudonyms and would not be tracked down—and would not influence her reputation—till the following century.

171. Alcott to Thomas Bailey Aldrich, 23 Oct. 1883, Yale Collection of American Literature, Beinecke Rare Book and Manuscript Library. I am grateful to Betsey Shirley for sharing her transcription with me.

172. Quoted in Thomas Beer, *The Mauve Decade: American Life at the End of the Nineteenth Century* (1926; reprint, New York: Knopf, 1937), 18. This story, like another that I have traced to Beer and discuss in chapter 3, may be apocryphal.

173. "The Best American Books," *Critic*, 3 June 1893, 357.

174. "A Hundred American Authors," *Critic*, 24 July 1886, 0_1 (APSO).

175. "Miss Alcott and her Work," *Boston Post*, 7 Mar. 1888, 4. But see "Louisa May Alcott," *Boston Evening Transcript*, 6 Mar. 1888, 4, which refers to Alcott's "consummate art."

176. "The Alcotts," *Critic*, 10 Mar. 1888, 119.

177. Obituary, *Independent*, 15 Mar. 1888, 12 (APSO).

178. "Louisa M. Alcott, Her Life and Her Works," 101.

179. Lundt, "Miss Alcott."

180. Walter Lewin, "Obituary: Amos Bronson Alcott and Louisa May Alcott," *Acad*

emy, 24 Mar. 1888, 206; M. D. Conway, "The Alcotts," *Athenaeum*, 24 Mar. 1888, 372; Obituary, *Times* (London), 8 Mar. 1888, 7 (TDA). A year and a half later, though, in reviewing Ednah Cheney's biographical compilation, the British tended to be more negative: see, e.g., "Miss Alcott's Life and Letters," *Spectator*, 16 Nov. 1889, 693; and review of *Life*, ed. Cheney, *Athenaeum*, 9 Nov. 1889, 632.

181. The most significant are collected in Daniel Shealy's *Alcott in Her Own Time: A Biographical Chronicle of Her Life, Drawn from Recollections, Interviews, and Memoirs by Family, Friends, and Associates* (Iowa City: Univ. of Iowa Press, 2005).

182. See, e.g., "An Alcott Anecdote," *Eau Claire (WI) Daily Free Press*, 15 Sept. 1888, 2 (NA), citing Sallie Joy White in *Wide Awake* ("An Alcott Anecdote," Sept. 1888, 264 [GBks]).

183. Zehr, "Response of Nineteenth-Century Audiences," 334.

184. See, e.g., Gale Eaton, *Well-Dressed Role Models: The Portrayal of Women in Biographies for Children* (Lanham, MD: Scarecrow, 2006), 2 and passim.

185. Ednah D. Cheney, *Louisa May Alcott, the Children's Friend*, illus. Lizbeth B. Comins (Boston: Prang, 1888), 19, 32.

186. Cheney, *Friend*, 24. In *Life*, Cheney simply mentions the distaste and offers no context.

187. Alcott to Mrs. A. D. Moshier, 6 Apr. [1878], *Letters*, 228. Alcott also found Concord too conservative (see Alcott to Maggie Lukens, 5 Feb. [1884], *Letters*, 278).

188. Cheney's stresses are consonant with what Martha Vicinus finds more generally in nineteenth-century juvenile biographies of women: a foregrounding of family love and acting not for personal gain but for public good ("What Makes a Heroine? Girls' Biographies of Florence Nightingale," in *Florence Nightingale and Her Era: A Collection of New Scholarship*, ed. Vern Bullough, Bonnie Bullough, and Marietta P. Stanton [New York: Garland, 1990], 96, 93).

189. See, e.g., *Life*, ed. Cheney, 389.

190. "Work of Single Women," *Logansport (IN) Daily Journal*, 18 Dec. 1892, 7 (NA).

191. See, e.g., "The Prince Winked," *New York Mail*, reprinted in *Fredericksburg (VA) Free Lance*, 1 Nov. 1910, 2 (CA).

192. Janice A. Radway discusses the ways in which a successor, the fifty-volume Harvard Classics series (which did not include anything by Alcott), is imbricated in efforts to bring a kind of cultural capital to a broad public, commodifying learning and paving the way for a middlebrow phenomenon like the Book-of-the-Month Club (see *A Feeling for Books: The Book-of-the-Month Club, Literary Taste, and Middle-Class Desire* [Chapel Hill: Univ. of North Carolina Press, 1997], 145–47).

193. See, e.g., Theodore F. Wolfe, *Literary Shrines: The Haunts of Some Famous American Authors* (Philadelphia: Lippincott, 1899), esp. 21, 52–58.

CHAPTER 2: Waxing Nostalgic, 1900–1930

Epigraph: Jessie Bonstelle, citing Grace George, in Helen Christine Bennett, "The Star Lady," *McCall's Magazine*, Oct. 1928, 98.

1. C.F.R., "Louisa May Alcott," *Encyclopedia Britannica*, 1911, now at Online Encyclopedia, http://encyclopedia.jrank.org/.

2. William Peterfield Trent et al., eds., preface to vol. 1 of *The Cambridge History of American Literature*, 4 vols. (1917–21; reprint, New York: Macmillan, 1958), iii; hereafter

the *Cambridge History* is cited parenthetically. For a fuller treatment of the arguments in this paragraph and the next two, see Beverly Lyon Clark, *Kiddie Lit: The Cultural Construction of Children's Literature in America* (Baltimore: Johns Hopkins Univ. Press, 2003), esp. 48–76.

3. Clayton Hamilton, *Materials and Methods of Fiction* (New York: Baker, 1908), 76 (GBks). The 1918 edition, retitled *A Manual of the Art of Fiction*, indicated in its subtitle that it was "Prepared for the Use of Schools and Colleges."

4. "Children," *Life*, 6 Nov. 1919, 790 (APSO).

5. Lewis Mumford, *The Golden Day: A Study in American Experience and Culture* (New York: Liveright, 1926), 161–62.

6. "Our 'Little Women,'" *Rochester (NY) Democrat and Chronicle*, 11 Nov. 1902, 6 (NYHN).

7. "Houston Beauty Appears as 'Meg' in 'Little Women,'" *San Antonio Light*, 28 Dec. 1913, 22 (NA).

8. Joel Myerson and Daniel Shealy provide an invaluable account of the numbers of copies printed through 1909 in "The Sales of Louisa May Alcott's Books," *Harvard Library Bulletin*, n.s., 1.1 (Spring 1990): 69–71. All data in this paragraph are from this source; the data for *Little Men* are on p. 73.

9. See, e.g., "'Little Men' and 'Little Women,'" *Boston Daily Globe*, 22 July 1906, SM12 (GNA); advertisement, *Kendallville (IN) Standard*, 25 Oct. 1906, 6 (GNA).

10. See The Book Mart, *Bookman*, Apr. 1909 through Sept. 2013.

11. See Frederic J. Haskin, "Our Public Libraries," *Syracuse Post-Standard*, 28 June 1909, 2 (NYHN).

12. Notes, *Nation*, 23 Oct. 1902, 327 (EBSCO); "List of New Books on Library Shelves," *Southeast Missourian* (Cape Girardeau), 24 June 1919, 8 (GNA).

13. William E. Sage, "Suffragettes Rejoice," *Cleveland (OH) Leader*, 12 Oct. 1912 (MS Am 800.23 [287], Houghton Library, Harvard University, hereafter cited as Houghton Library).

14. Data from Main Street Public Library Database, Ball State University, cardinalscholar.bsu.edu.

15. Books and Reading, *St. Nicholas*, Sept. 1905, 1053 (APSO); J. Breckenridge Ellis, "The Books Children Prefer," *Dial*, 1 Dec. 1901, 429 (APSO).

16. "Books for All," *Minneapolis Journal*, 17 Aug. 1901, suppl. 1 (CA); The St. Nicholas League, *St. Nicholas*, Oct. 1903, 1136 (APSO).

17. "What the Modern Child Reads," *New York Times*, 1 Dec. 1907, SM1 (ProQ). Admitting the fallibility of using such essay submissions as a gauge, especially since girls' submissions greatly outnumbered boys', the librarian nevertheless averred that Alcott's "name would appear at the head of any list."

18. John Farrar, "What Do American Children Read?" *West Virginia School Journal* 52 (1923): 188–89.

19. Lillian Sewell to Santa, *Atlanta Constitution*, 19 Dec. 1905, 9 (NA); Margaret G. Jones to Santa, *Atlanta Constitution*, 11 Dec. 1905, 7 (NA); Joe Hartness to Santa, *Iowa Recorder* (Greene, IA), 7 Dec. 1904, 1 (NA).

20. Literature, *Massachusetts Ploughman*, 26 Apr. 1902, 2 (APSO).

21. Jessie E. Wilcox, "My Favorite Character in Fiction," *St. Nicholas*, Oct. 1903, 1137

(APSO); Agnes Lee Bryant, "My Favorite Book, and Why," *St. Nicholas*, Mar. 1907, 469 (APSO); unnamed child quoted in Sarah de Bekker, "Librarians Find That Children Have Natural Love of Good Books and Are the Best Critics," *Chicago Daily Tribune*, 7 Mar. 1909, F3 (ProQ); Daisy [Beatrice Clephane], "My Favorite Author," *Washington Post*, 25 Aug. 1912, SM4 (ProQ); Lenore Ballangee, quoted in "High School Department," *Pella (IA) Chronicle*, 29 May 1929, 7 (NA).

22. Frank De Witt Talmage, "Talmage Sermon," *Daily Kentucky New Era* (Hopkinsville, KY), 1 June 1903, 3 (GNA); "Thirty-five Years of Library Reading," *Providence (RI) Journal*, 2 Feb. 1913, V2.

23. "Books New and Old: For the Young," *Atlantic*, May 1903, 700; Rupert Hughes, "Viewing with Alarm," *Bookman*, May 1919, 264 (APSO).

24. "Spirit of Miss Alcott's Best Known Story Retained in the Stage Version of 'Little Women,'" *New York Telegram*, 17 Oct. 1912 (MS Am 800.23 [287], Houghton Library).

25. Col. Gaston Gossips, *Gastonia (NC) Gazette*, 27 July 1949, 2 (NA).

26. Leo Lerman, "Little Women: Who's in Love with Miss Louisa May Alcott? I Am," *Mademoiselle*, Dec. 1973, reprinted in *Critical Essays on Louisa May Alcott*, ed. Madeleine B. Stern (Boston: Hall, 1984), 113.

27. Ruapehu, "A Boy and his Books," *Press* (Canterbury, New Zealand), 9 May 1914, 9 (PP).

28. Quoted in Aaron Latham, "The Lardners: A Writing Dynasty," *New York Times*, 22 Aug. 1971, SM10 (ProQ).

29. [Arthur Walkley], "Just Jo," *Times* (London), 11 Nov. 1919, 12 (TDA).

30. Lavinia Russ, "Not to Be Read on Sunday," *Horn Book*, Oct. 1968, reprinted in Stern, *Critical Essays*, 100.

31. Mary Astor, *A Life on Film* (New York: Delacorte, 1971), 195. *Little Women* was also a favorite of the actress Mary Wickes, who played Aunt March in the 1994 film version (Glenna Nowell, "Who Reads What?" 1993, Gardiner, ME, Public Library, gpl.lib .me.us/celebrity); then again, given the timing of her claim, Wickes might have been plugging the movie.

32. Ann Petry to Barbara Sicherman, 23 July 1994, quoted in Sicherman, *Well-Read Lives: How Books Inspired a Generation of American Women* (Chapel Hill: Univ. of North Carolina Press, 2010), 30.

33. M.J.P., The Theatre, *Wall Street Journal*, 21 Nov. 1933, 3 (ProQ). Another claimed more sardonically, "I assume that everyone has read the book. Apparently everyone has, from what I hear" (J.C.M., The Current Cinema, *New Yorker*, 11 Nov. 1933, 61).

34. John Barry, "Letters Still Come to Louisa M. Alcott," *Boston Globe*, 27 Nov. 1932, B2 (ProQ). Not for nothing was *Little Women* offered as a prize for home canning ("McKinley Offers Newer Prizes," *Decatur [IL] Daily Review*, 14 June 1916, 8 [NA]).

35. F.B., "Prominent People Tell Their Favorite Books as Children," *Chicago Daily Tribune*, 19 Nov. 1927, 14 (ProQ).

36. Walter Prichard Eaton, "The Little Women March On," *Berkshire County Eagle* (Pittsfield, MA), 4 Aug. 1948, 17 (NA).

37. "Best Hundred Books for Children," *Daily News* (London), 25 Jan. 1900, 6 (BNA); Children's Books, *Sheffield Independent* (UK), 28 Jan. 1900, 4 (BNA).

38. Florence B. Low, "The Reading of the Modern Girl," *Nineteenth Century*, re-

printed in *Living Age*, 28 Apr. 1906, 197 (APSO); Constance A. Barnicoat, "The Reading of the Colonial Girl," *Nineteenth Century*, reprinted in *Living Age*, 26 Jan. 1907, 222 (APSO).

39. "Girl Favourites in Fiction," *Westminster Budget*, 1 Apr. 1904, 32 (NA); Harold Spender, "What Do the Children Read?" *Pall Mall Magazine*, reprinted in *Living Age*, 26 Aug. 1905, 557 (APSO); "What Children Read," *Co-Partnership*, Apr. 1911, 55.

40. *The Equipment of Workers* (New York: Macmillan, 1919), 173.

41. G. K. Chesterton, "Louisa Alcott," *Nation*, 1907, reprinted in Stern, *Critical Essays*, 213; Chesterton, *What I Saw in America* (1922; reprint, New York: Dodd, Mead, 1923), 83 (GBks). "At learned ladies' colleges," he noted in the earlier essay, the novel was apparently "handed about secretly, like a dangerous drug" (214).

42. Books and Their Publishers, *Courier* (Dundee, UK), 23 July 1910, 7 (BNA).

43. Lilian M. Faithfull, *In the House of My Pilgrimage* (1924; reprint, London: Chatto, 1925), 33.

44. Hiromi Tsuchiya Dollase, "Shōfujin (Little Women): Recreating Jo for the Girls of Meiji Japan," *Japanese Studies* 30.2 (2010): 250, 258, 248 (Taylor). Kazuko Watanabe dates the first translation to 1891 in "Reading *Little Women*, Reading Motherhood in Japan," *Feminist Studies* 25.3 (Fall 1999): 700 (JSTOR).

45. "The Thread of Literature," *Kai Tiaki: The Journal of the Nurses of New Zealand*, Apr. 1910, 77 (GNA).

46. Topics of the Day, *Press* (Canterbury, New Zealand), 17 July 1911, 6 (PP).

47. Simone de Beauvoir, *Memoirs of a Dutiful Daughter*, trans. James Kirkup (1959), quoted in Sicherman, *Well-Read Lives*, 28.

48. "Favourite Books: An Interesting Vote," *Evening Post* (Wellington, New Zealand), 15 Nov. 1924, 17 (PP).

49. "Girls of To-Day," *Sydney Mail*, 8 Dec. 1926, 51 (GNA); *Sydney Morning Herald*, reprinted as "Louisa Was 'Jo,'" *Evening Post* (Wellington, New Zealand), 27 Aug. 1935, 15 (PP).

50. H. R. Knickerbocker, Daily News Letter, *East Chicago (IN) Times*, 21 Aug. 1926, 7 (NA).

51. E. M. Almedingen, "*Little Women* in Russia," *Horn Book*, Dec. 1968, 673–74.

52. "'Little Women' Dramatic Triumph at Opera House," *Providence (RI) News*, 7 Mar. 1922, 11 (GNA).

53. Henry Tetlow, "Best Books for the Young with a Backward Glance to Ten Alluring Volumes," *Washington Post*, 14 Dec. 1924, SO20 (ProQ).

54. "Alcott Window Display," *Boston Daily Globe*, 13 Nov. 1913, 2 (ProQ).

55. Advertisement, *Chicago Daily Tribune*, 11 Oct. 1919, 7 (ProQ). Fanny Butcher reported that little girls and old women stood in line to see the exhibit ("The Chicago Book Fair," *Bookman*, Nov.–Dec. 1919, 337).

56. "Children Here Read Risque Novels! No! Say Librarians," *Appleton (WI) Post-Crescent*, 16 July 1926, 4 (NA).

57. "Seek Deeper Books," *New York Evening Post*, reprinted in *Los Angeles Times*, 25 Apr. 1927, 14 (ProQ).

58. G. W. Willett, "The Reading Interests of High-School Pupils," *English Journal* 8 (Oct. 1919): 484 (JSTOR). In a less systematic survey, in 1927 the top favorite for girls responding to an essay contest sponsored by the *Youth's Companion* was *Little Women*; it

did not figure among the boys' favorites, although *Little Men* came in fifteenth ("What Are Our Favorite Books? Why Do We Like Them?" *Youth's Companion*, 7 Apr. 1927, 250 [APSO]).

59. Thomas J. Lancaster, "A Study of the Voluntary Reading of Pupils in Grades IV–VIII," *Elementary School Journal* 28 (Mar. 1928): 527 (JSTOR).

60. Carleton Washburne and Mabel Vogel, *Winnetka Graded Book List* (Chicago: American Library Association, 1926), 130. The popularity index entailed multiplying the number of children who read and liked a book by the number of cities in which it was liked (51–52). The "typical" child's comment that the authors provide for *Little Women* is, "The author tells the hardships as well as the joys of the family. You seem to live right with the people in the book and you cry over their sorrow and are happy when some great joy comes to them" (130).

61. Lewis M. Terman and Margaret Lima, *Children's Reading: A Guide for Parents and Teachers* (New York: Appleton, 1926), 74, 125. In their survey of one hundred Stanford graduate students, half the women listed *Little Women* as one of "the ten books read in childhood that could be recalled most easily"—a proportion much greater than that for any other book (69).

62. For a discussion of these canons, see Sarah Wadsworth, "Canonicity and the American Public Library: The Case of American Women Writers," *Library Trends* 60.4 (Spring 2012), esp. 711, 724–25 (ProjM).

63. "'Little Women' in Dramatic Form," *New York Sun*, 14 Jan. 1912, 13 (NYHN). Publicity releases for the 1912 dramatization tended to make grand, unsubstantiated claims.

64. J. F. Bobbitt, A. C. Boyce, and M. L. Perkins, "Literature in the Elementary Curriculum," *Elementary School Teacher* 14.4 (Dec. 1913): 160 (JSTOR).

65. C. W. Hunt (Newark librarian), "Books for Girls of Thirteen," *New York Times*, 17 Aug. 1901, BR7 (ProQ); Rosa Markus, "The Value of Good Books," *San Francisco Call*, 11 Dec. 1910, JS1 (CA); Elizabeth Thompson, Heart and Home Problems, *Janesville (WI) Daily Gazette*, 18 Sept. 1914, 6 (NA); "What Shall We Give That Blessed Child for Christmas? Some Bookish Suggestions from the Princeton Parents' Association," *New York Tribune*, 7 Dec. 1919, VIII4; Cheryl Knott Malone, "Books for Black Children: Public Library Collections in Louisville and Nashville, 1915–1925," *Library Quarterly* 70.2 (2000): 184 (JSTOR); Alice Lindsey Webb, Books New and Old, *Pullman (WA) Herald*, 9 June 1922, II6 (CA); "Make List of Books Suitable as Library for the Young Girl," *Billings (MN) Gazette*, 10 Nov. 1925, 5 (NA); "50 Books to Read before One is 15," *Lethbridge (AB) Herald*, 3 Dec. 1926, 7 (NA).

66. Hamilton W. Mabie, "Mr. Mabie on Books for Young People," *Ladies' Home Journal*, Oct. 1907, 24 (APSO); "The List of One Hundred Books," *St. Nicholas*, Mar. 1900, 445 (APSO); Grace Isabel Colbron, "Choosing the Children's Library," *Bookman*, Oct. 1915, 196–200 (APSO); Jessie Fauset, "Some Books for Boys and Girls," *Crisis*, Oct. 1912, 296; "'Zelda' on Books," *Jewish Daily News*, 4 Aug. 1903, cited in Sicherman, *Well-Read Lives*, 13.

67. Jim Walters, "County Library System All Began with 'Little Women,'" *Los Angeles Times*, 31 July 1994, 14 (ProQ).

68. Fact and Comment, *Youth's Companion*, 28 Sept. 1916, 534 (APSO).

69. "A List of Forty Books," *Alton (IL) Evening Telegraph*, 24 Nov. 1925, 4 (NA).

70. "Two-Foot Book Shelf for School Children," *New York Times*, 9 Aug. 1922, 12 (ProQ). Other national lists that featured *Little Women* are reported in "National Reading Circle Books," *Elementary School Journal* 20.6 (Feb. 1920): 408–10 (JSTOR); "Child Reading List Compiled," *Los Angeles Times*, 1 Dec. 1925 (ProQ); and "Bible Tops List of 'Better Home' Books," *Boston Daily Globe*, 16 Apr. 1923, 5 (ProQ).

71. "Old Books Delight Modern Type Girls," *Berkeley (CA) Daily Gazette*, 9 Oct. 1922, 4 (GNA).

72. Bertha E. Bush, "A Miss Alcott Day," *School Journal* 57.2 (Oct. 1909): 48 (GBks).

73. Fanny E. Coe, preface to *The Louisa Alcott Story Book* (1910; reprint, Boston: Little, 1912), iii (GBks), hereafter cited parenthetically. Little, Brown, the successor to Roberts Brothers, had published *The Louisa Alcott Reader* in 1908, subtitling it *A Supplementary Reader for the Fourth Year of School*; the book is a slightly truncated repurposing of volume 1 of Alcott's *Lulu's Library* (1890).

74. Alan H. Feller, "About School #59," *Baltimore Jewish Times*, 31 July 2009, 27 (ProQ).

75. A.L.P., The Colyum, *San Francisco Call*, 17 June 1912, 6 (CDNC); see also " 'Louise [sic] Alcott Day' Observed by Pupils," *San Francisco Call*, 14 June 1912, 13 (CDNC).

76. "The Best Hundred Books for Children," *Living Age*, 14 Apr. 1900, 132 (APSO).

77. "America Aids London Sick," *New York Times*, 27 June 1928, 12 (ProQ).

78. Bookman, A Reader's Notes, *Manitoba Free Press* (Winnipeg), 10 Aug. 1925, 9 (NA).

79. See Leslie McGrath, "Reading with Blitheness: *Anne of Green Gables* in Toronto Public Library's Children's Collections," in *Anne's World: A New Century of "Anne of Green Gables,"* ed. Irene Gammel and Benjamin Lefebvre (Toronto: Univ. of Toronto Press, 2010), 107–8.

80. Shorter works included a thirty-page volume for the young, Bertha E. Bush's *Story of Louisa M. Alcott* (1905).

81. The *New York Times* reviewed it as a girls' book (see "Real Books for Real Girls," 5 Dec. 1909, LS20 [ProQ]).

82. Belle Moses, *Louisa May Alcott, Dreamer and Worker: A Story of Achievement* (New York: Appleton, 1909), 150, hereafter cited parenthetically.

83. *Scouting for Girls: Official Handbook of the Girl Scouts* (New York: Girl Scouts, 1920), 24 (GBks).

84. Gamaliel Bradford, "Portrait of Louisa May Alcott," *North American Review* 209 (Mar. 1919): 394 (JSTOR), hereafter cited parenthetically.

85. Advertisement, *Syracuse Herald*, 8 Sept. 1919, 18 (NA).

86. "Little Women," in *Boys and Girls of Bookland*, by Nora Archibald Smith, illus. Jessie Willcox Smith (1923; reprint, New York: Derrydale, 1988), 10, 11, hereafter cited parenthetically.

87. Edward D. Nudelman, *Jessie Willcox Smith: American Illustrator* (Gretna, LA: Pelican, 1990), 43.

88. I have not been able to verify those by M. V. Wheelhouse (1909), G. Ridout (1914), and Richard Jones (1915), as well as one perhaps by H. G. Gray (1928 or earlier, possibly a misprint for M. E. Gray?).

89. As Susan R. Gannon also indicates in "Getting Cozy with a Classic: Visualizing *Little Women* (1868–1995)," in *"Little Women" and the Feminist Imagination: Criticism,*

Controversy, Personal Essays, ed. Janice M. Alberghene and Beverly Lyon Clark (New York: Garland, 1999), 123.

90. I am indebted to Lauren Rizzuto for noticing this detail, in "Illustrating *Little Women*, or, Louisa, Jo, May and Amy," paper presented at annual meeting of the Children's Literature Association, Boston, 14 June 2012.

91. "Valrosa! The romance of romances in our girlhood's literature," exclaims Anna Steese Richardson, in "'Little Women': At the Theater with 'Meg,' 'Jo,' 'Beth,' and 'Amy,'" *Woman's Home Companion*, June 1912, 49. Its resonance seems to have faded for the producers of the 1994 film as well, for although an early draft of the script places Amy and Laurie at Valrosa, amid cascades of roses, the final version eliminates the roses and situates the two under an overarching maple tree.

92. See Aileen Fyfe, "A Short History of the Religious Tract Society," in *From the Dairyman's Daughter to Worrals of the WAAF: The Religious Tract Society, Lutterworth Press and Children's Literature*, ed. Dennis Butts and Pat Garrett (Cambridge: Lutterworth, 2006), 25, 28.

93. Flora Klickmann, preface to *Little Women*, illus. Harold Copping (London: Religious Tract Society, 1913), 3, 4, hereafter cited parenthetically.

94. E. Honor Ward, "Introduction," The Girl's Own Paper Index, maths.dur.ac.uk/~tpcc68/GOP/guideintro.

95. George Bluestone, *Novels into Film* (1957; reprint, Baltimore: Johns Hopkins Univ. Press, 2003), 5–6, 64.

96. Linda Hutcheon, *A Theory of Adaptation* (New York: Routledge, 2006), 8.

97. Literary Notes, *Friends' Intelligencer*, 22 June 1901, 394 (APSO).

98. Hildegarde Hawthorne's "An Adventure with 'Little Women'" (*Delineator*, June 1915, 8–10) is a much shorter spinoff. Works with more distant echoes of *Little Women* include *Five Little Peppers*, by Margaret Sidney [Harriett Lothrop] (1881); Ethel Turner's *Three Little Maids* (1900); *Aunt Jane's Nieces*, by Edith Van Dyne [L. Frank Baum] (1906); Carolyn Wells's Two Little Women series (1915–17); and Esther Glen's *Six Little New Zealanders* (1917).

99. Ethel Turner, *Seven Little Australians* (1894; reprint, London: Ward, 1954), 28.

100. Clare Bradford, "Ethel Turner," in *Australian Literature, 1788–1914*, ed. Selina Samuels, vol. 230 of *Dictionary of Literary Biography* (Detroit: Gale, 2001), 400, 396.

101. Joel Myerson, "Louisa May Alcott Travels Down Under," paper presented at the annual meeting of the Children's Literature Association, Boston, 14 June 2012.

102. Patricia West, *Domesticating History: The Political Origins of America's House Museums* (Washington, DC: Smithsonian, 1999), 58; Boston Items, *New York Times*, 1 Mar. 1902, BR13 (ProQ). Melissa R. Klapper notes that the Louisa M. Alcott Club, created by Jewish women for Jewish immigrants, fostered learning about literature and art but also training "to qualify the girls to wait at our own tables" (quoted in *Jewish Girls Coming of Age in America, 1860–1920* [New York: New York Univ. Press, 2005], 116 [GBks]). In Chicago, Hull House sponsored an Alcott Club where one member read aloud while other twelve-year-olds sewed (see Sicherman, *Well-Read Lives*, 173–74). All of these clubs, whether sponsored by children or adults, are very unlike the ones associated with Jane Austen, which were marked by their self-selective exclusivity, as "people linked by complacency over their own taste" (Claire Harman, *Jane's Fame: How Jane Austen Conquered the World* [New York: Holt, 2009], 126).

103. May Hollis Barton, *Four Little Women of Roxby, or The Queer Old Lady Who Lost Her Way* (New York: Cupples, 1925), 5, 27.

104. Marian Marvel, The Business Girl's Corner, *Providence (RI) News*, 19 July 1920, 7 (GNA). For a useful discussion of the embodiments and contradictions of the New Woman, see Elizabeth Ammons, "The New Woman as Cultural Symbol and Social Reality: Six Women Writers' Perspectives," in *1915, the Cultural Moment: The New Politics, the New Woman, the New Psychology, the New Art and the New Theatre in America*, ed. Adele Heller and Lois Rudnick (New Brunswick, NJ: Rutgers Univ. Press, 1991), 82–97.

105. *Youth's Companion*, 21 Oct. 1915, 547 (APSO).

106. Gabrielle E. Jackson, *The Dawn of Womanhood* (New York: Revell, 1908), 138 (GBks), hereafter cited parenthetically.

107. Gabrielle E. Jackson, *Three Little Women's Success: A Story for Girls* (1910; reprint, Philadelphia: Winston, 1913), 66 (HathiTrust), hereafter cited parenthetically as *Success*.

108. Gabrielle E. Jackson, *Three Little Women at Work: A Story for Girls* (Philadelphia: Winston, 1909), 263, hereafter cited parenthetically as *Work*.

109. For a discussion of the turn to consumerism in series fiction after 1900, see Emily Hamilton-Honey, "Guardians of Morality: Librarians and American Girls' Series Fiction, 1890–1950," *Library Trends* 60.4 (Spring 2012): 768 (ProjM).

110. Gabrielle E. Jackson, *Three Little Women: A Story for Girls* (1908; reprint, Philadelphia: Winston, 1913), 18, hereafter cited parenthetically as *Three*.

111. Gabrielle E. Jackson, *Three Little Women as Wives: A Story for Girls* (Philadelphia: Winston, 1914), 61, hereafter cited parenthetically as *Wives*.

112. See Nina Silber, *The Romance of Reunion: Northerners and the South, 1865–1900* (Chapel Hill: Univ. of North Carolina Press, 1993), 122.

113. Barrett Wendell, *A Literary History of America* (1900; reprint, New York: Scribner's, 1909), 337.

114. Amy Lowell, quoted in "Books for Children," *Literary Digest*, 29 Nov. 1919, 31; Annie Carroll Moore, "Books for Young People," *Bookman*, Mar. 1920, 87; Edith Wharton, *A Backward Glance* (New York: Appleton-Century, 1939), 51.

115. Katharine Fullerton Gerould, "Miss Alcott's New England," *Atlantic*, Aug. 1911, 181–82.

116. Gerould, "Miss Alcott's New England," 183. Gerould is presumably adducing reasons for an acquaintance's dislike; the editors of the *Dial* opine that the acquaintance might have been a southerner, given "the lack of enthusiasm with which a Virginian or a Marylander or a Georgian may at times hear the names of the New Englander's literary idols, as may also the denizen of Fifth Avenue" (*Dial*, 16 Aug. 1911, 95 [ProQ]).

117. Louisa M. Alcott, *Little Women, or Meg, Jo, Beth and Amy: Authoritative Text, Backgrounds and Contexts, Criticism*, ed. Anne K. Phillips and Gregory Eiselein (New York: Norton, 2004), 31, hereafter cited parenthetically.

118. According to the OED Online, www.oed.com, *boss* was current in the United States in the nineteenth century; it was slower to achieve respectability in Britain, starting as workmen's slang.

119. See June Howard, *Publishing the Family* (Durham, NC: Duke Univ. Press, 2001), 161.

120. Frances Armstrong, "'Here Little, and Hereafter Bliss': *Little Women* and the Deferral of Greatness," *American Literature* 64 (1992): 453–74.

121. Sally Mitchell, *The New Girl: Girls' Culture in England, 1880–1915* (New York: Columbia Univ. Press, 1995), 66, 73.

122. Hutcheon, *Theory of Adaptation*, 9.

123. Susan F. Beegel, "'Bernice Bobs Her Hair': Fitzgerald's Jazz Elegy for *Little Women*," in *New Essays on F. Scott Fitzgerald's Neglected Stories*, ed. Jackson R. Bryer (Columbia: Univ. of Missouri Press, 1996), 64.

124. F. Scott Fitzgerald, "Bernice Bobs Her Hair" (1920), in *The Short Stories of F. Scott Fitzgerald*, ed. Matthew J. Bruccoli (1989; reprint, New York: Scribner, 1995), 33, hereafter cited parenthetically.

125. Floyd Dell, *Homecoming: An Autobiography* (New York: Farrar, 1933), 218.

126. See Louisa May Alcott to Anna Alcott Pratt, 27 July [1870], in *Little Women Abroad: The Alcott Sisters' Letters from Europe, 1870–1871*, ed. Daniel Shealy (Athens: Univ. of Georgia Press, 2008), 158. It's not entirely clear whether the production was a dramatization of *Little Women* or of the play within the novel.

127. W. H. Venable, *The School Stage: A Collection of Juvenile Acting Plays* (Cincinnati, OH: Wilson, 1893) (GBks); "The Philocalian Society," *Chicago Daily Tribune*, 1 Mar. 1874, 13 (ProQ). For Alcott's approval of Venable's undertaking, see Alcott to William Henry Venable, 21 Nov. [1872], *Letters*, 172.

128. For Ladies Only, *Burlington (IA) Daily Hawk-Eye*, 7 Mar. 1875, 2 (NA).

129. The *"Little Women" Play*, adapted by Elizabeth Lincoln Gould, illus. Reginald Birch, *Ladies' Home Journal*, Jan. 1901, 3–4, 36–37 (APSO); *The "Little Men" Play*, adapted by Elizabeth Lincoln Gould, illus. Reginald Birch, *Ladies' Home Journal*, Dec. 1900, 3–4, 40–41 (APSO).

130. Bennett, "Star Lady," 101.

131. "Trials Beset Manager in Producing Drama," *Pittsburgh Leader*, 29 Sept. 1912; Bennett, "Star Lady," 96.

132. Marian de Forest, "Dramatizing a Novel Is a Chastening Experience," *New York Times*, 5 Mar. 1916, X8 (ProQ).

133. See Anna Steese Richardson, "At the Theater with 'Little Women,'" *Woman's Home Companion*, May 1912, 11.

134. May Lamberton Becker, introduction to *Little Women, or Meg, Jo, Beth, and Amy*, by Louisa M. Alcott (Cleveland, OH: World, 1946), 8–9.

135. *Chicago InterOcean*, quoted in "'Little Women' Staged with Popular Success," *Christian Science Monitor*, 17 Feb. 1912, 24.

136. See, e.g., John Alcott to Marian de Forest, 22 June 1911 and 16 July 1911 (MS Am 800.23 [49, 5], Houghton Library).

137. Jessie Bonstelle Stuart to John Alcott, 24 June 1911 (MS Am 800.23 [205], Houghton Library).

138. Bonstelle Stuart to John Alcott, 24 June 1911.

139. See de Forest to John Alcott, 11 Aug. 1911 and 5 Oct. 1911 (MS Am 800.23 [50], Houghton Library).

140. John S. P. Alcott, "The 'Little Women' of Long Ago," *Good Housekeeping*, Feb. 1913, 185.

141. "'Little Women' at Colonial," *Cleveland (OH) Plain Dealer*, 15 Oct. 1912, 12.

142. In a photograph of a scene later in the act they cluster around their mother, overlapping with and attuned to one another, in a version of the iconic scene of March family togetherness.

143. See Catherine Van Dyke, "'Little Women' As a Play," *Harper's Bazar*, Jan. 1912, 22.

144. Marian de Forest, *Little Women: A Comedy in Four Acts* (New York: French, 1921), II.i, 56, hereafter cited parenthetically, with references to act (and scene, if any), followed by the page in this edition.

145. See Alcott to Louisa Caroline Greenwood Bond, 17 Sept. [1860], *Letters*, 60. See also Ednah D. Cheney, *Louisa May Alcott: Her Life, Letters, and Journals* (1889; reprint, Boston: Little, 1919), 55, 112 (GBks). Richardson noted that de Forest said she frequently consulted Cheney's compilation ("At the Theater," 11).

146. Quoted in Richardson, "Little Women," 49.

147. I've located only one critic who seems to hint at the enhanced attention to romance: "The final settling of the love stories . . . is rather conventional in stage form, but it is probable that in no other way could the play be brought to its conclusion more satisfactory to the average spectator" ("'Little Women' Comes to Hartford," *Hartford [CT] Courant*, 18 Feb. 1913, 11). Although she does not mention *Little Women*, Florence Kiper's contemporary feminist critique of popular plays could also apply to de Forest's, as enacting "the pet American dramatic platitude that love makes right all things" ("Some American Plays: From the Feminist Viewpoint," *Forum* 51 [1914]: 928 [APSO]).

148. To be sure, de Forest omits Marmee's "To be loved and chosen by a good man is the best and sweetest thing which can happen to a woman" (84).

149. Even if aficionados such as Richardson might still, remembering the book, find their "heart ached for him in his first sincere, manly passion" ("At the Theater," 12).

150. Bonstelle Stuart to de Forest, quoted in de Forest to John Alcott, 4 Aug. 1911 (MS Am 800.23 [49], Houghton Library).

151. I have not found the phrase predating Alcott, so it was perhaps less trite when she was writing—possibly she even originated it—but by the time of the play it was clichéd.

152. "Characters That Made 'Little Women' Famous to Be Seen on the Stage," *Chicago Daily Tribune*, 11 Feb. 1912, B8 (ProQ). That wholesomeness would become a reason for praise in many reviews.

153. Bonstelle Stuart to John Alcott, 27 Nov. 1911 (MS Am 800.23 [206], Houghton Library).

154. See William A. Brady, *Showman* (New York: Dutton, 1937).

155. See Silber, *Romance of Reunion*, 168.

156. "Dramatizing Novels Successfully," *New York Dramatic Mirror*, 6 Nov. 1912, 1 (NYHN).

157. Brooks Atkinson, *Broadway* (1970; reprint, New York: Macmillan, 1971), 4, 21, 22, 81.

158. Louis Sherwin, "'Little Women' Is Well Acted in Dramatic Version," *New York Globe*, 17 Oct. 191[2] (MS Am 800.23 [287], Houghton Library).

159. Charles Darnton, The New Plays, *New York Evening World*, 17 Oct. 1912, 21 (CA).

160. A[rthur] W[arren], "'Little Women' Delightful Dramatization of Louisa Alcott's Famous Book," *New-York Tribune*, 17 Oct. 1912, 9 (CA).

161. The contrary reports appeared some months after the first performances: Burns Mantle, "'Follies' 1912 Series Returns to Burlesque," *Chicago Daily Tribune*, 27 Oct. 1912, B1 (ProQ); Matthew White Jr., "The Stage: Looking Back on the Season 1912–1913," *Munsey's Magazine*, June 1913, 407.

162. "Brady Stages 'Little Women,'" *New-York Tribune*, 21 Jan. 1912, 9 (CA); "Little Women," *Wilkes-Barre (PA) Times-Leader*, 22 Jan. 1912.

163. "Step Alive out of Book," *Buffalo (NY) Express*, 23 Jan. 1912, 6 (NYHN); "Teck Box Office Certainly Selling Tickets This Week," *Buffalo Express*, [25] Jan. 1912 (NYHN).

164. Percy Hammond, "'Little Women' Acted at the Garrick," *Chicago Daily Tribune*, 15 Feb. 1912, 9 (ProQ); G.P.G., "Garrick Theater—'Little Women,'" *Detroit Free Press*, 6 Feb. 1912, 4. G.P.G. also reported that the Wednesday matinee on the following day was already sold out.

165. Newsy Stage Notes, *New London (CT) Day*, 22 Mar. 1912, 10 (GNA).

166. Jackson D. Haag, "In the Theaters Last Evening," *Pittsburgh Post*, 1 Oct. 1912, 5.

167. "'Little Women' Dramatized—A Triumph of Sentiment," *Current Opinion*, Jan. 1913, 28; "Four Plays Well Worth Seeing," *Outlook*, 14 Dec. 1912, 787 (APSO).

168. Ralph Graves, "'Little Women' the Week's Novelty at the Theaters," *Washington Post*, 4 May 1913, MT2 (ProQ); Burns Mantle and Garrison P. Sherwood, eds., *The Best Plays of 1909–1919; and the Year Book of Drama in America* (New York: Dodd, 1934), 480.

169. See David Sheward, *It's a Hit: The Back Stage Book of Longest-Running Broadway Shows, 1884 to the Present* (New York: Back Stage, 1997), 10–11, 9.

170. "What the Press Agents Say," *Tacoma (WA) Ledger*, 4 Feb. 1914 (MS Am 800.23 [287], Houghton Library).

171. White, "Stage," 407; [Louis V. Defoe], "Louisa Alcott's Classic of Childhood Gives Its Audience at Playhouse a Delightful Evening," *New York World*, 17 Oct. 1912 (MS Am 800.23 [287], Houghton Library); Darnton, New Plays; W[arren], "'Little Women' Delightful," 9; A[rthur] W[arren], The Playgoer, *New-York Tribune*, 20 Oct. 1912, V2 (CA); "Two Remarkable Plays," *Independent*, 7 Nov. 1912, 1095 (APSO).

172. Quotations from Alan Dale, *New York American*; *New York Herald*; Acton Davies, *New York Evening Sun*; and Adolph Klauber, *New York Times*—all on theater card (MS Am 800.23 [287], Houghton Library).

173. "'Little Women' Is Full of Sunshine," *Brooklyn Daily Eagle*, 17 Oct. 1912, 7 (NYHN). A sign of what many critics at the time sought appears in an account comparing road-show productions in nearby towns: one was cast better, in part because "the girls were all better looking," which is to say, less authentic, whereas the stage setting was more so: "the orchard scene was a little more elaborate and looked more like an orchard" ("'Little Women' at the Court Square," *Northampton Herald*, 10 Feb. 1914 [MS Am 800.23 (287), Houghton Library]).

174. Vanderheyden Fyles, "Fat Trusts in Silk Hats and Jewelry in Front Seats," *San Antonio Express*, 27 Oct. 1912 (MS 800.23 [287], Houghton Library).

175. Ol' Props, "Women Dramatists Have Shone in Season's Productions," *Providence (RI) Sunday Journal*, 11 May 1913, IV3.

176. White, "Stage," 407; "Greatest Matinee Play," *Washington Post*, 4 May 1913, MT2 (ProQ). Apparently, the London performances in 1919 were all matinees, since in

the postwar euphoria "everybody was amusement mad" and, Katharine Cornell noted, "We couldn't get a house for evening performances" (Katharine Cornell, as told to Ruth Woodbury Sedgwick, *I Wanted to Be an Actress* [New York: Random House, 1939], 23).

177. See Jackson D. Haag, "Revival of Shakespeare Bodes Well for the Drama," *Pittsburgh Post*, 6 Oct. 1912, II2.

178. A. S. Hatfield, Amusements, *Salt Lake Telegram*, 2 Dec. 1913, 5.

179. See, e.g., "Little Women," *Parsons (KS) Sun*, 28 Jan. 1914 (MS Am 800.23 [287], Houghton Library).

180. See Sherry D. Engle, *New Women Dramatists in America, 1890–1920* (New York: Palgrave Macmillan, 2007), 10–11.

181. "Little Women," *Washington Post*, 24 Dec. 1911, 12 (ProQ).

182. Marah Gubar, "Entertaining Children of All Ages: Nineteenth-Century Popular Theater as Children's Theater," *American Quarterly* 66.1 (Mar. 2014): 1–34 (ProjM).

183. Adolph Klauber, Topics of the Drama—The Week's New Plays, *New York Times*, 20 Oct. 1912, X5 (ProQ).

184. "Little Women," *Atlanta Constitution*, 9 Nov. 1913, B3 (ProQ).

185. Jack Poggi claims that before about 1910 producers wanted to build a reputation in New York and then go on to make most of their money on the road, but after 1910 the road receipts declined, thanks to the rise of the motion picture, of the automobile (enabling trips to large cities), and of radio (*Theater in America: The Impact of Economic Forces, 1870–1967* [Ithaca, NY: Cornell Univ. Press, 1968], 8, 28, 261).

186. R[alph] G[raves], Last Night at the Theaters, *Washington Post*, 6 May 1913, 5 (ProQ).

187. "'Little Women' at the Oliver," *Lincoln (NE) Journal*, 11 Nov. 1913; Adelphi, *Philadelphia Record*, 30 Nov. 1913 (both MS Am 800.23 [287], Houghton Library).

188. John Brooks, "'Little Women' at Majestic Theatre," *Boston Traveler and Evening Herald*, 30 Dec. 1913 (MS Am 800.23 [287], Houghton Library).

189. Haag, "In the Theaters Last Evening," 5.

190. Haag, "Revival," II2.

191. Sherwin, "'Little Women' Is Well Acted."

192. Shubert, *Kansas City (MO) Independent*, 22 Nov. 1913 (MS Am 800.23 [287], Houghton Library).

193. Montrose J. Moses, "Plays for Parents," *Independent*, 6 Feb. 1913, 305 (APSO).

194. "Playhouse—*Little Women*," *Westfield (NJ) Leader*, 16 Oct. 1912 (MS Am 800.23 [287], Houghton Library).

195. Lea Jacobs, *The Decline of Sentiment: American Film in the 1920s* (Berkeley: Univ. of California Press, 2008), 9–12. With respect to Beth's death, Carol Gay argues, "Louisa doesn't sentimentalize it either in style or focus: but we do" ("*Little Women* at the Movies," in *Children's Novels and the Movies*, ed. Douglas Street [New York: Ungar, 1983], 34).

196. Burns Mantle, Theatrical, *Anaconda (MT) Standard*, 10 Nov. 1912, 20 (NA).

197. For a discussion of the complex and shifting meanings of *sentiment* in *Little Women*, see Lauren Elizabeth Rizzuto, "Reading, Writing, and Illustrating Jo March: The Place of Sentiment in the Sentimental Novel" (MA thesis, Simmons College, 2011).

198. See Howard, *Publishing the Family*, 235.

199. J. B. Firth, "Some Aspects of Sentiment: A Comparison," *Westminster Review* 138 (1892): 125 (GBks).

200. "Some Really Truly Christmas Books," *Book News Monthly*, Dec. 1915, 176.

201. Angela Brazil, "'Little Women': An Appreciation," *Bookman* (London), Dec. 1922, 140.

202. Rowland Grey, "America and the Girl's Book," *Englishwoman*, Mar. 1920, 199, 201, 203.

203. Eye Witness, "Eleventh Paper—Louisa May Alcott's 'Little Women,'" *Chicago Daily Tribune*, 19 Feb. 1922, F1.

204. "Louisa May Alcott," *Appletons' Annual Cyclopaedia and Register of Important Events of the Year, 1888* (New York: Appleton, 1889), 12.

205. Review of *Little Women* (play), *Philadelphia Bulletin*, 15 Nov. 1913 (MS Am 800.23 [287], Houghton Library).

206. "Chautauqua Bringing 'Little Women' Here," *San Jose (CA) Evening News*, 23 Apr. 1917, 2 (GNA).

207. "Not a Drunk in the Cast," *Los Angeles Times*, 12 Mar. 1926, A10 (ProQ).

208. David McCord, "H. T. Parker," *Theatre Arts Monthly*, Oct. 1932, 841, 845. For a fuller discussion of the issues raised in this paragraph, see Beverly Lyon Clark, "*Little Women* Acted: Responding to H.T.P.'s Response," *Lion and the Unicorn* 36 (2012): 174–92.

209. "Music: Death of Parker," *Time*, 9 Apr. 1934, www.time.com.

210. H[enry] T[aylor] P[arker], "'Little Women' Acted," *Boston Evening Transcript*, 30 Dec. 1913, 14. Subsequent references to Parker's review are to this page.

211. See, e.g., Clark, "*Little Women* Acted," 184–85.

212. "'Little Women' at the Playhouse," *New York Post*, 17 Oct. 1912 (MS Am 800.23 [287], Houghton Library).

213. William A. Brady, "Old Times and New in the Theater Business," *Saturday Evening Post*, 13 Sept. 1913, 58. The setting was apparently so "authentic" that the Boston audience applauded the opening scene ("'Little Women' Pleases," *Christian Science Monitor*, 30 Dec. 1913, 10).

214. "'Little Women' Is Full of Sunshine," 7.

215. "Real 'Properties,'" *New-York Tribune*, 13 Oct. 1912, V3 (CA).

216. Bonstelle Stuart to Eunice Alcott, 6 Jan. 1912 (MS Am 800.23 [201], Houghton Library). Critics did indeed find the players familiar, whether or not it was due to the costuming: "All of them were like the familiar portraits in your favorite edition," or they "came plausibly near preconceptions of their parts from the printed page" (W[arren], "'Little Women' Delightful," 9; P[arker], "'Little Women' Acted").

217. Maureen Taylor (www.maureentaylor.com), telephone interview by author, 21 Dec. 2011.

218. See Laurajane Smith, *Uses of Heritage* (London: Routledge, 2006), 71 and passim.

219. "Real 'Properties.'" For a different provenance of the rag doll, or at least *a* rag doll, one proffered by a girl in the audience, see "Gossip of the Stage," *Pittsburgh Dispatch*, 29 Sept. 1912, V4.

220. De Forest to John Alcott, 2 Nov. 1911 (MS Am 800.23 [50], Houghton Library).

221. Richardson, "At the Theater," 10; Richardson, "Little Women," 7. The emphasis on the "real" persists in Jessie Bonstelle and Marian de Forest's *Little Women Letters from the House of Alcott* (Boston: Little, 1914), a compilation of Alcott family letters and journals. They open with an anecdote of a well-to-do young theatergoer, dressed in fur, protesting to her father after watching the play, "But, daddy, it isn't real. There never

was such a family" (2). The editors comment, "But it is real; there was such a family, and in letters, journals, and illustration this little book gives the history of the four Little Women, the Alcott girls" (2).

222. "Little Women," *Springfield (MA) Republican*, 10 Feb. 1914, 3. A. S. Byatt has quipped more recently, "The real fantasy in [Alcott's] world is the solid comfortable dailiness of the March sisters' home life" ("The End of Innocence," *Guardian* [London], 6 Sept. 2003 [Guard]).

223. Edward R. Doyle, "Little Women Now a Play," *Buffalo (NY) Express*, [20?] Jan. 1912 (NYHN).

224. [Defoe], "Louisa Alcott's Classic"; Fyles, "Fat Trusts."

225. Sage, "Suffragettes Rejoice." Even de Forest claimed that "the book was a more or less accurate account of the Alcott family happenings and family vicissitudes, with the result that the play fell naturally into natural scenes, because Miss Alcott had not created, but had chronicled what she had lived and had seen lived in her own home" ("Dramatizing a Novel").

226. Sage, "Suffragettes Rejoice." The subheadlines read, "'Tis a Fine Week for the 'Weaker Sex' at the Local Playhouses" and "Man Doesn't Figure at All, Theatrically Speaking. It is 'The Woman' Against 'Little Women,' and, Strange to Say Both Will Win." The headline writer might be invoking suffragists simply because the play foregrounds women.

227. "Remarkable Achievement in Dramatization," *Life*, 31 Oct. 1912, 2096 (APSO).

228. "Louisa May Alcott's 'Little Women' Has Been Dramatized at Last," *Tacoma (WA) Times*, 20 Feb. 1912, 5 (CA).

229. "Louisa M. Alcott's 'Little Women' at Last on the Stage," *New York Sun*, 25 Feb. 1912, 7 (NYHN). The critic is here invoking Alcott's Meg.

230. Richardson, "Little Women," 7.

231. "Informal Comments on Last Week's Programs," *Pittsburgh Dispatch*, 6 Oct. 1912, V5.

232. "'Little Women' at Court Square," *Springfield (MA) Union*, 10 Feb. 1914 (MS Am 800.23 [287], Houghton Library).

233. According to the actress who played her, though she admitted to never having read the novel (quoted in "'Little Women' Made to Live," *New-York Tribune*, 27 Oct. 1912, 4 [CA]).

234. Sidney Ormond, "'Little Women' Scores a Hit," *Atlanta Constitution*, 14 Nov. 1913, 11 (ProQ).

235. Isma Dooly, "'Little Women' Dramatized," *Atlanta Constitution*, 28 Jan. 1912, C6 (ProQ).

236. "Little Women," *Bookman*, Dec. 1912, 380 (APSO); "'Little Women' at the Wieting," *Syracuse Herald*, 15 Nov. 1914, 8 (NA).

237. "A Fine Play," *Concord (NH) Patriot*, 2 Mar. 1914; Clarence Urmy, "'Little Women' Makes Very Pleasing Play," *San Jose (CA) Mercury-Herald*, 15 Jan. 1914 (both MS Am 800.23 [287], Houghton Library).

238. Lillian B. Schmeidler, "The High Cost of Living Locks the Door of Fairyland," *New-York Tribune*, 21 Sept. 1919, VIII3 (CA).

239. See "'Little Women' in London," *Christian Science Monitor*, 24 Dec. 1919, 8; and "'Little Women' Criticised," *Manchester Guardian*, 11 Nov. 1919, 8.

240. [Walkley], "Just Jo."

241. Stage and Screen, *Providence (RI) News*, 3 Mar. 1922, 22 (GNA). The critic was commenting on how warmly the London audience nevertheless responded to the play.

242. Review of *Little Women* (play), *Illustrated London News*, 22 Nov. 1919, 836, gale group.com. One critic for whom the novel once "was my inseparable companion" said of the drama, "Sentiment hangs upon it like an over-ripe mulberry on a stem" (S.R.D., The Drama of the Day, *Englishwoman*, Dec. 1919, 207).

243. *Morning Advertiser*, *Sportsman*, and *Morning Post*, quoted in advertisement, *Times* (London), 14 Nov. 1919, 10 (TDA); subsequent quotations in this paragraph are from this page.

244. Quoted in "'Little Women' in London," *Literary Digest*, 20 Dec. 1919, 31; subsequent quotations in this paragraph are from this page.

245. Theatrical Notes, *New York Times*, 14 Dec. 1916, 13 (ProQ); "Poli's—'Little Women,'" *Washington Post*, 16 Jan. 1917, 8 (ProQ); "Grandma's Favorite Story in Real Life," *Philadelphia Evening Public Ledger*, 13 Feb. 1917, 15 (CA).

246. Michael J. Toscano, "Another 'Little Women' Loses Its Way on Stage," *Washington Post*, 24 Aug. 2006, TO6 (LexN).

247. Advertisement, *Midland Daily Telegraph* (Coventry, UK), 16 Jan. 1918, 1 (BNA); Victoria, *Courier* (Dundee, UK), 18 Dec. 1917, 2 (BNA); The Triangle Hall, *Western Daily Press* (Bristol, UK), 8 Jan. 1918, 3 (BNA). The Bristol showings were accompanied by "Dainty Afternoon Teas."

248. See "*Little Women*," in *Feature Films, 1911–1920*, vol. F1 of *The American Film Institute Catalog of Motion Pictures Produced in the United States*, ed. Patricia King Hanson and Alan Gevinson ([Berkeley]: Univ. of California Press, 1988), 534. According to the Internet Movie Database (imdb.com), it took a year for Brady to reach an agreement with Paramount to distribute the film.

249. Kathryn Helgesen Fuller, "At the Picture Show," in *Exhibition, the Film Reader*, ed. Ina Rae Hark (London: Routledge, 2002), 45 (GBks); promotional materials quoted in Richard Koszarski, *An Evening's Entertainment: The Age of the Silent Feature Picture, 1915–1928*, vol. 3 of *History of the American Cinema*, ed. Charles Harpole (New York: Scribner, 1990), 70.

250. Koszarski, *Evening's Entertainment*, 66.

251. See David L. Kranz and Nancy C. Mellerski, introduction to *In/Fidelity: Essays on Film Adaptation*, ed. Kranz and Mellerski (Newcastle, UK: Cambridge Scholars, 2008), 1.

252. Benjamin B. Hampton claims that no more than 5 percent of films at this time lacked a box-office star (A *History of the Movies* [New York: Covici Friede, 1931], 194). Dorothy Bernard, the film's Jo, would have been the closest to one, having previously appeared in 83 films, many of them short films. By comparison, Mary Pickford had appeared in 226 films by this year, and a lesser star, Bernard's sometime co-star Blanche Sweet, had appeared in 130.

253. See, e.g., By the Way, *Outlook*, 25 Sept. 1918, 152 (APSO). Favorable comments on the setting in reviews and announcements, some of them probably lifted from studio publicity materials (with wording similar to that in *Outlook*), appeared frequently in newspapers.

254. Quoted in H.U., "Here are Little Women," *New York Tribune*, 7 July 1918, IV4 (CA).

255. "'Little Women' Now Classic of Screen," *Southeast Missourian* (Cape Girardeau), 29 Apr. 1919, 2 (GNA).

256. H.U., "Here are Little Women."

257. "Little Women," *Variety*, 15 Nov. 1918, 45.

258. Taylor, telephone interview, 21 Dec. 2011.

259. A least one contemporary was disconcerted by this change (see "'Little Women' Criticised").

260. See "'Little Women' Proves a Delight at Colonial," *Logansport (PA) Pharos-Reporter*, 17 Mar. 1919, 8 (NA).

261. Advertisement, *Fort Wayne (IN) News and Sentinel*, 15 July 1920, 8 (NA).

262. "The Year's Best," *New York Times*, 11 Jan. 1920, 77 (ProQ).

263. See Koszarski, *Evening's Entertainment*, 34-35; and Jacobs, *Decline of Sentiment*, 80.

264. Harold O. Berg, "One Week's Attendance of Children at Motion Picture Entertainments," *Playground* 17 (June 1923): 165.

265. Koszarski, *Evening's Entertainment*, 28-29.

266. Koszarski, *Evening's Entertainment*, 26-27.

267. Hugo Münsterberg, *The Photoplay: A Psychological Study* (1916), reprinted as *The Film: A Psychological Study* (New York: Dover, 1970), 84, 93.

268. See, e.g., Michael Aronson, *Nickelodeon City: Pittsburgh at the Movies, 1905–1929* (Pittsburgh: Univ. of Pittsburgh Press, 2008), 222.

269. *Wichita (KS) Eagle*, quoted in *Cedar Rapids (IA) Evening Gazette*, 8 Nov. 1920, 13 (NA).

270. William A. Brady to Eunice Alcott, 25 May 1915, and Brady to John Alcott, 11 Aug. 1915 (both MS Am 800.23 [23], Houghton Library). Brady may have been considering *A Modern Mephistopheles* as a possible stage production—he used the term *stage* in connection with it—but he tended to use terms for plays and films interchangeably in his letters about Alcott productions and indeed seems to have thought about the two media in very similar ways.

271. Paul S. Moore, *Now Playing: Early Moviegoing and the Regulation of Fun* (Albany: SUNY Press, 2008), 195; Koszarski, *Evening's Entertainment*, 192.

272. See Samantha Barbas, *The First Lady of Hollywood: A Biography of Louella Parsons* (Berkeley: Univ. of California Press, 2005), 61, 65.

273. See, e.g., "Forsyth Presents Two Big Pictures," *Atlanta Constitution*, 9 Mar. 1919, 3 (ProQ).

274. Advertisement, *Chicago Heights Star*, 20 Feb. 1919, 6 (NA).

275. "'Little Women' Filmed," *Philadelphia Evening Public Ledger*, 21 Jan. 1919, 11 (CA).

276. "Little Women at the Englert," *Iowa City Citizen*, 2 June 1919, 5 (NA); advertisement, *Moberly (MO) Evening Democrat*, 25 Apr. 1919, 4 (NA); Pictures and Plays, *Maoriland Worker* (Wellington, New Zealand), 15 Oct. 1919, 2 (PP).

277. Advertisement, *LeMars (IA) Semi-Weekly Sentinel*, 20 Feb. 1920, 8 (NA); advertisement, *Fort Wayne (IN) News and Sentinel*, 22 May 1919, 20 (NA).

278. See advertisements, *Manitoba Free Press* (Winnipeg), 15 Feb. 1919, 23 (NA), and *Logansport (PA) Pharos-Reporter*, 15 Mar. 1919, 4 (NA).

279. Advertisement, *New Castle (PA) News*, 3 Mar. 1919, 8 (NA).

280. See "Little Women," *Moving Picture World*, 18 Jan. 1919, 391; and Theater Lodi, *Lodi (CA) Sentinel*, 1 May 1919, 8 (GNA). But "do not make the mistake of appealing merely to the children, for their elders all know and love the story," the *Moving Picture World* also advised (391). Indeed a commentator in Indiana suggested that "the greater part of the audiences were composed of middle-aged and grey-haired women. The present generation thought it much too tame" ("The Moral Trend," *Fort Wayne (IN) Journal Gazette*, 23 Jan. 1921, 4 [NA]).

281. "For the 'Kiddies,'" *Manitoba Free Press* (Winnipeg), 22 Feb. 1919, 29 (NA).

282. Advertisement, *Suburbanite Economist* (Chicago), 31 Jan. 1919, 6 (NA); Club News, *Berkeley (CA) Daily Gazette*, 4 Mar. 1921, 6 (GNA); "Matinee to Aid Cripples," *New York Times*, 2 Dec. 1921, 24 (GNA); Notice, *Estherville (IA) Democrat*, 26 Mar. 1919, 13 (NA); advertisement, *Grand Rapids (MI) Daily Leader*, 27 Mar. 1919, 5 (NA).

283. Aronson, *Nickelodeon City*, 221.

284. Advertisement, *Fitchburg (MA) Daily Sentinel*, 17 Feb. 1919, 14 (NA).

285. "'Little Women' at the Majestic," *Hartford (CT) Courant*, 19 Jan. 1919, Z7.

286. "Immense Crowd at Community Program," *Appleton (WI) Post-Crescent*, 23 Oct. 1920, 8 (NA).

287. Advertisement, *Harrisonburg (VA) Daily News-Record*, 20 Dec. 1918, 2 (NA).

288. Advertisement, *La Crosse (WI) Tribune and Leader-Press*, 19 Mar. 1919, 4 (NA).

289. Advertisement, *New Castle (PA) News*, 5 Mar. 1919, 11 (NA). In another ad, in the *Manitoba Free Press* (Winnipeg), 15 Feb. 1919, 23 (NA), the same image and caption seem to accompany yet another film, *Impropaganda*. It's possible that the image was wrongly assigned to *Little Women*, but the text accompanying the Pennsylvania ad does draw on the film's dramatis personae.

290. "Drama: This Holiday Week," *Los Angeles Times*, 1 Jan. 1919, I13 (ProQ).

291. Koszarski, *Evening's Entertainment*, 36, 38, 51.

292. Advertisement, *Mohave County Miner and Our Mineral Wealth* (Kingman, AZ), 28 June 1919, 6 (CA).

293. See Hampton, *History of the Movies*, 201–2.

294. Advertisement, *Philadelphia Evening Public Ledger*, 27 Jan. 1919, 11 (CA).

295. See Film Timetable, *Philadelphia Evening Public Ledger*, 8 Feb. 1919, 16 (CA). I am grateful to Josh Stenger for alerting me to the timing of distribution of copies of the film.

296. "Little Women," *Cedar Rapids (IA) Evening Gazette*, 4 July 1919, 7 (NA).

297. Paramount Theatre, *Evening Post* (Wellington, New Zealand), 13 Oct. 1919, 3 (GNA); Empire Theatre, *Otago Daily Times* (New Zealand), 22 Nov. 1919, 6 (PP).

298. "'Little Women' Shown on Screen," *New York Times*, 11 Nov. 1918, 13 (ProQ).

299. Virginia Tracy, "The Search for the Perfect Picture Play," *New York Tribune*, 16 Mar. 1919, IV4 (CA); subsequent quotations in this paragraph are from this page.

300. In *The Girl and Her Trust* (1912), a short film directed by D. W. Griffith, Bernard doesn't strike me as particularly little. As a "telegraphist" girl who succeeds, despite imminent danger, in telegraphing for help, she's feisty, even if she later wilts. To the

extent that the audience remembered an actor's previous roles—and actors did tend to be seen as types—her feistiness might carry over to her role as Jo. Tracy may, of course, be remembering other roles.

301. "Little Women," *Variety*.

302. "Little Women," *Moving Picture World*, 23 Nov. 1918, 856.

303. Frederick James Smith, The Celluloid Critic, *Motion Picture Classic*, Feb. 1919, 51.

304. "Little Women," *Variety*; "Little Women," *Moving Picture World*, 23 Nov. 1918; F. Smith, Celluloid Critic, 51.

305. "Little Women," *Variety*.

306. Hazel Simpson Naylor, "Little Women," *Motion Picture Magazine*, Feb. 1919, 74.

307. "'Little Women' in London," *Literary Digest*, 20 Dec. 1919.

308. *Morning Advertiser*, quoted in advertisement, *Times* (London), 14 Nov. 1919, 10 (InfoTrac).

309. [Walkley], "Just Jo."

310. See Kevin Brownlow, *The Parade's Gone By . . .* (New York: Knopf, 1968), 349.

311. See Ben Brewster and Lea Jacobs, *Theatre to Cinema: Stage Pictorialism and the Early Feature Film* (Oxford: Oxford Univ. Press, 1997), 103.

312. John Douglas Eames, *The Paramount Story* (New York: Crown, 1985), 19.

313. See David Pierce, "The Survival of American Silent Feature Films: 1912–1929," Library of Congress, Sept. 2013, 1, www.loc.gov/film/pdfs/pub158.final_version_sept_2013 .pdf. Pierce notes, "There is seemingly no rhyme or reason why certain films survived, as neither quality nor critical reputation determined their fates" (21).

314. See, e.g., Frank Thompson, *Lost Films: Important Movies That Disappeared* (New York: Citadel, 1996).

315. See Ken Bloom, *The Routledge Guide to Broadway* (New York: Routledge, 2007), 53 (GBks).

316. And except for Bernard, none was appearing more than six years later on Broadway. Even Bernard appeared only four or five times over thirty years.

317. Theodore F. Wolfe, *Literary Shrines: The Haunts of Some Famous American Authors* (Philadelphia: Lippincott, 1899), esp. 21, 52–58.

318. "Louisa Alcott's Home Christmas Shrine for Booklovers," *Tacoma (WA) Ledger*, 13 Dec. 1912 (MS Am 800.23 [287], Houghton Library).

319. See, e.g., "Orchard House," *Boston Evening Transcript*, 11 July 1903, 5 (GNA).

320. See West, *Domesticating History*, 58, 59.

321. See J. Alcott, "'Little Women' of Long Ago," 187; and Eye Witness, "Eleventh Paper." See also Margaret M. Lothrop, *The Wayside: Home of Authors* (New York: American, 1940), 183.

322. Harriett Lothrop, unpublished document, quoted in Adam W. Sweeting, "Preserving the Renaissance: Literature and Public Memory in the Homes of Longfellow, Hawthorne, and Poe," *American Studies* 46.1 (Spring 2005): 35 (JSTOR).

323. Book Notes from Boston, *Chicago Daily Tribune*, 1 Nov. 1902, 18 (ProQ).

324. Stella M. Livsey, "The Home of the Alcotts," *Outlook*, 9 Oct. 1909, 322 (APSO).

325. *Concord (MA) Enterprise*, 1 Feb. 1911, quoted in West, *Domesticating History*, 67.

326. "New England and Other Matters," *Youth's Companion*, 4 Aug. 1910, ii (APSO); Casual Comment, *Dial*, 16 Mar. 1911, 205 (APSO). The latter appeal was seconded the

next issue in a letter to the editor by Charles Welsh of Scranton ("The Alcott Memorial," *Dial*, 1 Apr. 1911, 256 [APSO]).

327. What Women Are Doing, *New York Sun*, 9 Apr. 1911, 7 (NYHN).

328. "Pennies to Buy Alcott Home," *Chicago Daily Tribune*, 19 Feb. 1911, 6 (ProQ).

329. "Alcott Home, Where 'Little Women' Was Written, to Become Museum," *Mt. Vernon (OH) Democratic Banner*, 18 July 1911, 2 (CA); Florence Taft Eaton, "An American Woman's Letter: The Alcott House at Concord," *Landmark*, Dec. 1925, 757. Or maybe the little girl received only one cent a week for her allowance (see J. Alcott, "'Little Women' of Long Ago," 187).

330. "New England and Other Matters," ii; The Spectator, *Outlook*, 6 July 1912, 552 (APSO); F. Eaton, "American Woman's Letter," 755. By 1926, if not earlier, there were international visitors; see "Louisa Alcott and Memories of Concord," *Age* (Melbourne), 11 Sept. 1926, 4 (GNA).

331. Anne Trubek, *A Skeptic's Guide to Writers' Houses* (Philadelphia: Univ. of Pennsylvania Press, 2011), 12, 5.

332. Quoted in Sheryl A. Englund, "Reading the Author in *Little Women*: A Biography of a Book," *ATQ*, n.s., 12.3 (Sept. 1998): 213.

333. People, *National Tribune* (Washington, DC), 14 Apr. 1910, 8 (CA).

334. West, *Domesticating History*, 42.

335. Patricia West, "Gender Politics and the 'Invention of Tradition': The Museumization of Louisa May Alcott's Orchard House," *Gender & History* 6 (Nov. 1994): 456–57.

336. Spectator, 553, 552.

337. It may provide the architectural setting, but not altogether consistently: David H. Watters notes that at times the parlor seems to be on the second floor, at times on the first ("'A power in the house': *Little Women* and the Architecture of Individual Expression," in Alberghene and Clark, *"Little Women" and the Feminist Imagination*, 187).

338. West, "Gender Politics," 461.

339. West, *Domesticating History*, 85, 65.

340. Lydia Maria Child to Sarah Shaw, 18 June 1876, in *Lydia Maria Child: Selected Letters, 1817–1880*, ed. Milton Meltzer and Patricia G. Holland (Amherst: Univ. of Massachusetts Press, 1982), 535.

341. West, "Gender Politics," 465.

342. See West, *Domesticating History*, 85.

343. Spectator, 552; the first quotation is from a docent.

344. See Watters, "A power in the house," 188.

345. "To Preserve the Home of the Author of 'Little Women' as a Memorial," *New York Times*, 25 June 1911, SM15 (ProQ).

CHAPTER 3: Outwitting Poverty and War, 1930–1960

Epigraph: George Cukor, interview, in *On Cukor*, by Gavin Lambert, ed. Robert Trachtenberg (New York: Rizzoli, 2000), 59. Cukor later admitted that he hadn't finished the novel (see Bill Davidson, "George Cukor," *New York Times*, 30 Apr. 1978, D15 [ProQ]).

1. "Little Women," *Ada (OK) Evening News*, 7 Jan. 1934, 6 (NA).

2. John Selby, The Literary Guidepost, *Sandusky (OH) Register*, 6 Feb. 1938, 4 (NA).

3. Edward Wagenknecht, *Cavalcade of the American Novel from the Birth of the Nation to the Middle of the Twentieth Century* (New York: Holt, 1952), 88.

4. Clifton Fadiman, "Books for Children," *Holiday Magazine*, revised and reprinted in his *Party of One* (Cleveland, OH: World, 1955), 385. Dwight MacDonald, for example, associated Fadiman with what he called "midcult" ("Masscult and Midcult," *Partisan Review* [1960], reprinted in MacDonald, *Masscult and Midcult: Essays Against the American Grain* [New York: New York Review, 2011], 50, 35).

5. [Anthony Dymoke Powell], "National and Natural," *TLS*, 8 Jan. 1949, 17–18 (TLS).

6. Charles Pilgrim, "What London Is Reading," *Auckland Star*, 10 June 1939, 10 (PP).

7. Thomas Beer, *The Mauve Decade: American Life at the End of the Nineteenth Century* (New York: Knopf, 1926), 25. Also quoted in, e.g., Frank Luther Mott, *Golden Multitudes: The Story of Best Sellers in the United States* (New York: Macmillan, 1947), 249; and Alexander Cowie, *The Rise of the American Novel* (New York: American, 1948), 645. The claim continues to be recycled frequently, including in a 2009 biography that appears, oddly, to attribute the claim to a volume that I edited (Harriet Reisen, *Louisa May Alcott: The Woman Behind "Little Women"* [New York: Holt, 2009], 187n).

8. See Joel Myerson, Daniel Shealy, and Madeleine B. Stern, "A Calendar of the Letters of Louisa May Alcott," *Studies in the American Renaissance*, 1988, 362–99.

9. See, e.g., Paul Sorrentino, "The Legacy of Thomas Beer in the Study of Stephen Crane and American Literary History," *American Literary Realism* 35 (Spring 2003): 187–211 (JSTOR).

10. For an account of shifting perceptions of children's literature, and of Alcott and Twain, see Beverly Lyon Clark, *Kiddie Lit: The Cultural Construction of Children's Literature in America* (Baltimore: Johns Hopkins Univ. Press, 2003), 77–101.

11. Louella O. Parsons, "All-American Film," *San Antonio Light*, 25 June 1930, 30 (NA).

12. [Mary Crosbie], "Family Breadwinner," *TLS*, 8 Aug. 1952, 518 (TLS).

13. Odell Shepard, "The Mother of *Little Women*," *North American Review* 245 (Summer 1938): 392, hereafter in this paragraph cited parenthetically.

14. [Robin Alastair Dennison], "Sentimental Journal," *TLS*, 31 May 1957, 340 (TLS); subsequent quotations in this paragraph are from this page.

15. Nina Baym, "Melodramas of Beset Manhood: How Theories of American Fiction Exclude Women Authors" (1981), reprinted in *The New Feminist Criticism: Essays on Women, Literature, and Theory*, ed. Elaine Showalter (New York: Pantheon, 1985), 63–80.

16. Leona Rostenberg, "Some Anonymous and Pseudonymous Thrillers of Louisa M. Alcott," *Bibliographical Society of America Papers* 37.2 (1943), reprinted in *Critical Essays on Louisa May Alcott*, ed. Madeleine B. Stern (Boston: Hall, 1984), 43–50.

17. Madeleine B. Stern, "Louisa M. Alcott: An Appraisal," *New England Quarterly* 22 (Dec. 1949): 475–98 (JSTOR).

18. Mary Catherine Fish, "My Favorite Book," *Washington Post*, 26 Aug. 1934, JP3 (ProQ); Rosemary Dermody, "My Favorite Book," *Washington Post*, 21 Oct. 1934, JP2 (ProQ). Both comments appeared shortly after the release of the 1933 RKO film.

19. "Bay View Pupils Place Zane Grey as Most Popular," *Milwaukee Journal*, 26 Nov. 1931, [33] (GNA). For other local polls in which *Little Women* was the favorite of the young, see "E.H.S. Students Like Classics," *Elyria (OH) Chronicle-Telegram*, 22 Nov. 1930, 13 (NA); and "S. L. Library Circulation Shows Decrease," *Salt Lake Tribune*, 8 Jan. 1935, 22 (NA).

20. "Miss 1932 Prefers Heroines of Yore," *Pittsburgh Post-Gazette*, 9 Feb. 1932, 11 (GNA).

21. John Barry, "Letters Still Come to Louisa M. Alcott," *Boston Globe*, 27 Nov. 1932, B2 (ProQ).

22. "Yo, Ho, and a Good Book," *Amsterdam (NY) Evening Recorder and Daily Democrat*, 27 Oct. 1930, 4 (NYHN); "'Little Women' Revived," *New York Evening Post*, 5 Dec. 1931, 8 (NYHN).

23. Leo Lerman, "An Industry Within an Industry," *Saturday Review of Literature*, 8 Nov. 1941, 6, www.unz.org.

24. Main Street Public Library Database, Ball State University, cardinalscholar.bsu .edu. Acquisitions clustered about the time of the release of the RKO film (1932–34) and at the close of World War II (1944–47).

25. "Groups Form Alcott Clubs," *Anderson (IN) Herald*, 25 Sept. 1977, WW21 (NA).

26. See "J. C. Buie Home Is Colorful Setting for Meeting of Twentieth Century Club on Thursday," *Corsicana (TX) Democrat Sun*, 21 Feb. 1948, 4 (NA).

27. "Invite All Women to Convene at Dunseith," *Turtle Mountain (ND) Star*, 14 July 1932, 1 (GNA).

28. "4 Girls Take Name from Favorite Story of Their Mothers and Grandmothers," *Syracuse Herald*, 27 Dec. 1933, 14 (NA); "Four of Bookland's Most Famous Characters Are Found in Capital Society," *Washington Post*, 5 Aug. 1934, S1 (ProQ). See also, e.g., "Organize First Girls Club at Y.M.C.A.," *Emporia (KS) Gazette*, 20 July 1945, 3 (NA).

29. Harrison Carroll, "Behind the Scenes in Hollywood," *Tyrone (PA) Daily Herald*, 3 July 1934, 4 (NA).

30. "'Trapp Family' Favorite Book at Library Here," *South-End Reporter* (Chicago), 31 May 1950, 5 (NA); "'Gone with the Wind' Wins S. M. 'Favorite Book' Poll," *San Mateo (CA) Times*, 18 Apr. 1959, 4 (NA).

31. "Book Choices of Younger Readers," *New York Times*, 11 June 1950, 194 (ProQ); "Young Readers' Choice of Books for Summer," *New York Times*, 3 June 1956, 270 (ProQ).

32. Nancy A., quoted in "These Books We Loved When We Were Still Quite Young," *New York Times*, 18 Nov. 1956, 312 (ProQ).

33. Quoted in "It's Easier to See Than to Read 'Little Women,'" *Pasadena (CA) Independent*, 16 Oct. 1958, A4 (NA).

34. Didion, quoted in Mirabella Amruta Slee, "'Little Women' Meet Gillian Armstrong," *Age* (Melbourne), 25 Jan. 1995, 16 (LexN); Jane Trager, "Elyria School Abuzz over Letter from Barbara Bush," *Elyria (OH) Chronicle-Telegram*, 9 Mar. 1991, B1 (NA); Ursula K. Le Guin, *Dancing at the Edge of the World: Thoughts on Words, Women, Places* (New York: Grove, 1989), 213; Temple, cited in advertisement, *Kingsport (TN) Times*, 12 Feb. 1948, 3 (NA); Sanchez, quoted in Tanya Barrientos, "'Little Women': Big Influence," *Providence (RI) Journal*, 27 Dec. 1994, E2; Sontag and Krantz, quoted in "Uncle Wiggily's Karma and Other Childhood Memories," *New York Times Book Review*, 7 Dec. 1986, 46, 47; Steinem, quoted in April Simpson, Q & A, *Seattle Times*, 9 July 2009, seattletimes .com; Nadine Epstein, "Children's Book Author Interview: Jane Yolen," *Moment* 38.3 (May–June 2013): 63–64 (ProQ); Mason, quoted in Marie Arana-Ward, "Speaking for the Country," *Washington Post*, 20 Dec. 1998, X10 (ProQ); Laura Bush, "Books: Five Best," *Wall Street Journal*, 30 Sept. 2006, 8 (ProQ); Chung, quoted in Glenna Nowell, "Who Reads What?" 1991, Gardiner, ME, Public Library, gpl.lib.me.us/celebrity; Patti Smith,

Just Kids (New York: HarperCollins, 2010), 10–11; Sara Paretsky, *Writing in an Age of Silence* (London: Verso, 2007), 5; Clinton, cited in "The Book That Changed My Life," *Manila Bulletin* (Philippines), 6 Aug. 2010, mb.com.ph. Elaine Showalter would add Adrienne Rich to the list (see *Sister's Choice: Tradition and Change in American Women's Writing* [Oxford: Clarendon, 1991], 42). In "Louisa May Alcott, Patti Smith, and Punk Aesthetics," paper presented at annual meeting of the American Literature Association, Boston, 24 May 2013, Gregory Eiselein tellingly argues for Alcott's influence not just on "wholesome" traditions of literature but on beat, punk, and queer aesthetics.

35. Cynthia Ozick, "Spells, Wishes, Goldfish, Old School Hurts," *New York Times*, 31 Jan. 1982, BR24.

36. Quoted in "Uncle Wiggily's Karma," 47.

37. "*Little Women* Still Has Big Fans," *Syracuse Herald Journal*, 18 Dec. 1994, M17 (NA); Sarah Crichton, "What We Read as Youngsters: Top Editors Recall Their Favorite Childhood Books," *Publishers Weekly*, 26 Feb. 1982, 121.

38. "What We're Reading," *Wisconsin State Journal* (Madison), 17 Jan. 1939, II1 (NA).

39. Book Notes, *New York Times*, 16 July 1935, 17 (ProQ); Ann Lloyd Morgan, "Preparations for Christmas," *Gloucestershire Echo* (Cheltenham, UK), 23 Nov. 1932, 4 (BNA).

40. Jonathan Rose, "Marx, Jane Eyre, Tarzan: Miners' Libraries in South Wales, 1923–1952," *Leipziger Jahrbuch zur Buchgeschichte* 4 (1994): 189; From the Editor's Chair, *No. Devon Journal-Herald* (UK), 24 Apr. 1941, 4 (BNA). *Little Women* wasn't held by the other two miners' libraries that Rose reports on.

41. Malvina Lindsay, "The Gentler Sex," *Washington Post*, 21 Dec. 1942, B2 (ProQ).

42. Hunniford, quoted in John Koski, Bookworm, *Mail* (London), 3 Apr. 2005, 71 (CustomN); Arlene Phillips, "My Six Best Books," *Daily Express* (UK), 1 Apr. 2011, 48, express.co.uk; Feldman, quoted in "Stars Reveal Favorite Books," *Lima (OH) News*, 29 May 1978, 8 (NA). Pop-eyed Feldman claimed to have been "the only teen in England who could read 'Little Men' and 'Little Women,' by Louisa May Alcott, simultaneously."

43. Jacqueline Wilson, *Jacky Daydream* (London: Doubleday, 2007), 232 (GBks).

44. "English Pick Spencer Play for Festival," *Charleston (WV) Gazette*, 8 Feb. 1953, 51 (NA).

45. Elliot Paul, *The Last Time I Saw Paris* (New York: Random House, 1942), 108, 109. For whatever it's worth, I found no record of *Les soeurs Marx* in the Bibliothèque Nationale or on Google (although a Google search for "petites femmes" did lead to a rather extraordinary series of what are apparently board books).

46. "For Wharton a Car, For James a Go-Cart," *New York Times*, 7 June 1981, A7 (ProQ).

47. See "Soviet Books Sold in the Satellites," *Milwaukee Journal*, 24 July 1952, 35 (GNA); Ralph Thompson, In and Out of Books, *New York Times*, 14 Nov. 1948, BR14 (ProQ); "Hungary's Moralists Link Cinderella with Striptease," *Washington Post*, 15 Dec. 1950, 17 (ProQ); Ray Tucker, News Behind the News, *New London (CT) Day*, 11 Mar. 1958, 6 (GNA); John Sibley, "Pony-Cart Library Delights Thai Villagers," *New York Times*, 8 Feb. 1958, 21 (ProQ); and Lavinia R. Davis, "American Ambassadors," *New York Times*, 8 May 1960, BRA20 (ProQ). *Little Women* was a standard export to represent American culture (see, e.g., I. A., Notes on Books and Authors, *New York Times*, 4 Oct. 1942, BR10 [ProQ]; and C. K. Ogden and E. C. Graham, *Basic English: International*

Second Language [New York: Harcourt, 1968], revised edition of Ogden's *Basic English* [1930], 457–63).

48. Shouyi Fan, "Translation of English Fiction and Drama in Modern China: Social Context, Literary Trends, and Impact," *Meta* 44.1 (1999): 171, id.erudit.org.

49. Alexander Woollcott, "How to Go to Japan," in *The Portable Woollcott*, ed. Joseph Hennessey (New York: Viking, 1946), 300.

50. The publisher called its series Wakakusa-bunko, which echoed what had become the standard Japanese title for *Little Women*: *Wakakusa-monogatari* (Green grass story) (see Hiromi Ochi, "What Did She Read? The Cultural Occupation of Post-War Japan and Translated Girls' Literature," *F-GENS* 5 [2006]: 360–61; see also Tsuyoshi Ishihara, *Mark Twain in Japan: The Cultural Reception of an American Icon* [Columbia: Univ. of Missouri Press, 2005], 64 [ebrary]).

51. See Orchard House newsletter, reprinted in Susan, "Little Women Meets the Japanese," *Louisa May Alcott Is My Passion* (blog), 10 Dec. 2012, louisamayalcottismypassion.com; Leena Maissen, "Global Connections: Working with IBBY," *Bookbird*, July 2002, 17 (ProQ); and Peter Craven, "Love and Longing in the Crinoline and Bonnet Set," *Age* (Melbourne), 4 Oct. 2008, AII27 (LexN).

52. Alessandro Beretta, "Libri cambia," *Corriere della Sera* (Milan), 12 May 2010, 15, archiviostorico.corriere.it; Neera Kuckreja Sohoni, Last Word, *India Currents*, Mar. 2003, 72 (ProQ).

53. "Forty Books for the Young," *Washington Post*, 15 June 1930, JP7 (ProQ); "100 Books Listed as Women's Best," *New York Times*, 20 July 1933, 17 (ProQ); David A. Randall, "Books That Influenced America," *New York Times*, 21 Apr. 1946, 127 (ProQ).

54. I have tracked it in the 1935, 1948, 1960, and 1969 editions. In the earlier ones the novel is described as "tender but not saccharine"; in 1969 it is "sentimental, rather dated."

55. Barbara Auchincloss, "Women Who Helped Mold America," *New York Times Magazine*, 20 July 1941, 14.

56. Jerry Rogers, "Boy Says Stories about Girls Are Not Interesting," *Evening Huronite* (Huron, SD), 28 Oct. 1937, 10 (NA). The novel was recommended, for example, by Delphine Sparks as part of "A Reading Unit in American Literature" in *English Journal* 31 (Sept. 1942): 541 (JSTOR).

57. Alice M. Jordan, "Children's Classics," *Horn Book*, Feb. 1947, reprinted in her *Children's Classics*, 5th ed. (Boston: Horn Book, 1976), 88.

58. Sarah Wadsworth, "Canonicity and the American Public Library: The Case of American Women Writers," *Library Trends* 60.4 (Spring 2012): 714 (ProjM). The 1893 catalog actually named seven Alcott titles.

59. See, e.g., "Students Here Pay Tribute to Famed Author," *Binghamton (NY) Press*, 30 Nov. 1932, 8 (NYHN); and Ida C. Hilbers, "Centennial of Louisa Alcott Being Observed," *Berkeley (CA) Daily Gazette*, 7 Nov. 1932, 9 (GNA).

60. "Alcott Play Staged by Concord Players," *Boston Globe*, 3 Apr. 1932, A40 (ProQ).

61. F. M. Clouter, "An Alcott Bibliography," letter to the editor, *Saturday Review of Literature*, 19 Nov. 1932, 260.

62. See, e.g., "Voice of Romance Makes Bow," *Los Angeles Times*, 16 Nov. 1932, 14.

63. Barry, "Letters Still Come."

64. "Letter from Louisa M. Alcott to Viola Price Franklin," *Overland Monthly*, Aug. 1933, 106.

65. "The Bigness of 'Little Women,'" *Auckland Star*, 14 Jan. 1933, 2 (PP).

66. "When Louisa M. Alcott Wrote for the Journal," *Ladies' Home Journal*, Nov. 1932, 96.

67. "Louisa May Alcott," *Rochester (NY) Evening Journal*, 3 Dec. 1932, 16 (GNA); M.O.W., "Lesson in Life of Louisa May Alcott," *Indianapolis News*, reprinted in *Deer Park (WA) Union*, 15 Dec. 1932, 15 (GNA).

68. Virginia Page, "What Shall I Do?" *Delmarva Star* (Wilmington, DE), 13 Nov. 1932, 20 (GNA).

69. Dale Carnegie, "5-Minute Biographies," *Estherville (IA) Vindicator and Republican*, 23 Aug. 1938, 4 (NA).

70. Out on the Farm, *Moulton (IA) Weekly Tribune*, 22 Jan. 1959, 4 (NA).

71. "Finish 1,000th Liberty Vessel," *Milwaukee Journal*, 29 May 1943, 2 (GNA). A residence hall for federal workers was also named for Alcott ("Residence Halls' Names Selected by FWA Unit," *Washington Post*, 14 Mar. 1943, R1 [ProQ]).

72. "Four 'Little Women' Make a Hit in Debut at Bronx Zoo," *New York Times*, 17 June 1953, 29 (ProQ); "4 Chimp Children Take Up City Ways," *New York Times*, 13 Aug. 1959 (ProQ), 29; John C. Devlin, "4 Little Chimps Make Zoo Debut," *New York Times*, 15 Apr. 1960, 25 (ProQ).

73. See "Dollmaker Likes to Work with the Classics," *Elyria (OH) Chronicle Telegram*, 3 Dec. 1934, 10 (NA).

74. "Galaxy of Dolls to Be Seen Friday," *New York Times*, 22 Dec. 1935, N12 (ProQ); see also, e.g., "Mitchell Library Exhibits Historical Doll Collection," *Racine (WI) Journal Times*, 10 June 1949, 7 (NA).

75. See, e.g., "Woman, Mate Fashion Fancy Dolls for Children of Her Native Italy," *Racine (WI) Journal Times*, 27 May 1953, 20 (NA).

76. Clara Hallard Fawcett, "The Creative Artist and the Doll," *Hobbies*, Oct. 1953, 52.

77. See, e.g., "Boo to Balenciaga!" *Council Bluffs (IA) Nonpareil*, 1 Aug. 1956, 5 (NA).

78. Kathleen Cannell, "Whole Ensemble Often Designed Around a Set of Unusual Gems," *New York Times*, 23 Aug. 1939, 20 (ProQ).

79. Brief biographical sketches continued to appear, in addition to occasional pieces on Orchard House. For the British writer E. M. Delafield (Edmée E. M. de la Pasture), visiting the Alcott House ranked "in my own estimation higher than anything else I have done in America" (*The Provincial Lady in America* [New York: Harper, 1934], 163).

80. Austin Warren, review of *Invincible Louisa*, by Cornelia Meigs, *American Literature* 6 (Mar. 1934): 98 (JSTOR).

81. Cornelia Meigs, *Invincible Louisa: The Story of the Author of "Little Women"* (1933; reprint, Boston: Little, 1935), 246, hereafter cited parenthetically.

82. Katharine Anthony, *Louisa May Alcott* (New York: Knopf, 1938), 276, hereafter cited parenthetically.

83. Shepard, "Mother of *Little Women*," 396–97.

84. Joseph Leach, review of *Louisa May Alcott*, by Madeleine Stern, *El Paso (TX) Herald-Post*, 1 July 1950, 4 (NA).

85. Odell Shepard, review of *Louisa May Alcott*, by Madeleine Stern, *American Literature* 24 (Mar. 1952): 100–101 (JSTOR).

86. Marjorie Worthington, preface to *Miss Alcott of Concord: A Biography* (Garden City, NY: Doubleday, 1958), 9, hereafter cited parenthetically.

87. For a discussion of such norms, see, e.g., Charlotte S. Huck, *Children's Literature in the Elementary School*, 3rd ed. (New York: Holt, 1979), 551–52.

88. Joan Howard [Patricia Gordon], *The Story of Louisa May Alcott*, illus. Flora Smith (New York: Grosset, 1955), 75–76.

89. Pamela Brown, *Louisa*, illus. Sax (New York: Crowell, 1955), 45, hereafter cited parenthetically.

90. C. A. Mold's slightly earlier illustrations for a 1933 British edition also focus on action, such as the tower falling during the play rehearsal or Amy's fall through the ice. Susan R. Gannon discusses the vigor of the Marches in Jambor's illustrations in "Getting Cozy with a Classic: Visualizing *Little Women* (1868–1995)," in *"Little Women" and the Feminist Imagination: Criticism, Controversy, Personal Essays*, ed. Janice M. Alberghene and Beverly Lyon Clark (New York: Garland, 1999), 125.

91. See Sam Zolotow, "War Play Bought by Lindsay, Crouse," *New York Times*, 11 Aug. 1944, 12 (ProQ); Zolotow, "Williams to Name Sponsor for Play," *New York Times*, 10 Dec. 1954, 36 (ProQ); Arthur Gelb, "Broadway Role to Inga Swensen," *New York Times*, 23 Jan. 1958, 20 (ProQ).

92. These results derive from scanning NA and GNA. It's tempting to conclude that *Little Women* was especially popular in the immediate wake of World War II, given the focus then on GIs returning home and women leaving the wartime work force to rebuild the family, but the arbitrariness of the sources (including the fact that my scanning of the 1958 GNA occurred some months after the site started to divest itself of listings) makes such a conclusion uncertain.

93. See "Thespians' Busy Week," *Evening Telegraph* (Dundee, UK), 13 Apr. 1940, 4 (BNA).

94. Joan, in Derby and Joan, *Derby Evening Telegraph* (UK), 25 June 1943, 3 (BNA).

95. "Thespians' Busy Week."

96. Pauline Phelps, *Little Women: A Dramatization of Louisa M. Alcott's Book of the Same Name* (Sioux City, IA: Wetmore Declamation Bureau, 1939), III.ii, 118. Sara Spencer foregrounded writing more, and romance generally less, than other playwrights.

97. "Press Copy—'Little Women,'" in *Little Women: A Dramatization of Louisa M. Alcott's Immortal Novel in Three Acts*, by Arthur Jearue (Minneapolis: Northwestern, 1939), [107]. But Kristin Laurence's dramatization would soon vie for those superlatives.

98. John D. Ravold, *Little Women: A Play in Three Acts* (1931; reprint, New York: French, 1935), II, 51; I, 29, hereafter cited parenthetically, with references to act and page.

99. "Satirical 'Little Women' To Be Presented at UA," *Albuquerque Tribune*, 3 Mar. 1966, D2 (NA).

100. *Little Women: An Operetta in Three Acts*, dram. John Ravold, lyrics Frederick Howard, music Geoffrey O'Hara ([1940]; reprint, New York: French, n.d.), 90, 105–6, hereafter cited parenthetically.

101. McCarthy, "Little Women," *Motion Picture Herald*, 11 Nov. 1933, 27; "'Little Women' Here Next Week," *Charleston (SC) News and Courier*, 26 Nov. 1933, 6B (GNA); Ben Prout, For Your Amusement, *Miami (FL) Daily News*, 7 Dec. 1933, 15 (GNA).

102. "'Little Women' Playing to Large Crowds at Orpheum," *Dubuque (IA) Telegraph-Herald*, 3 Dec. 1933, 8 (GNA); "Famous Classic at Fox Theater," *Spokane (WA) Daily Chronicle*, 11 Jan. 1934, 5; The Stage, *Boston Daily Globe*, 28 Nov. 1933, 19; Nancy

Lee, Reviewing the Screen, *Milwaukee Journal*, 10 Dec. 1933, 20 (GNA); Donald Kirkley, Theater Screen and Music, *Baltimore Sun*, 11 Jan. 1934, 8 (ProQ).

103. See "Actual Receipts at the Wickets Now Decide 'Box-Office Champions of 1933,'" *Washington Post*, 6 Feb. 1934, 14 (ProQ).

104. "Little Women," *Photoplay*, Nov. 1934, 32.

105. Harold W. Cohen, The New Films, *Pittsburgh Post-Gazette*, 1 Dec. 1933, 13 (GNA).

106. See George Shaffer, "'Little Women' Will Be Set in Time of Story," *Chicago Tribune*, 15 Oct. 1932, 19 (ProQ). The reported ratio varied widely.

107. Mayme Ober Peak, Reel Life in Hollywood, *Boston Globe*, 9 June 1933, 31 (ProQ).

108. Cukor, interview, 59.

109. "Now 'Little Women,'" *New York Times*, 30 July 1933, 116 (ProQ); "Bringing 'Little Women' to the Screen Tested Hollywood's Art to the Limit," *Edwardsville (IL) Intelligencer*, 20 Feb. 1934, 5 (NA). Most critics praised the settings, perhaps for being "flawlessly authentic," yet some demurred, perhaps finding too much "opulent hand-someness" (William Troy, "Films: 'Little Women,'" *Nation*, 29 Nov. 1933, 631; James Shelley Hamilton, review of *Little Women* [film], *National Board of Review Magazine*, Dec. 1933, reprinted in *From Quasimodo to Scarlett O'Hara: A National Board of Review Anthology, 1920–1940*, ed. Stanley Hochman [New York: Ungar, 1982], 177).

110. Walter Plunkett, "'Little Women' Attired After Careful Research," *Oakland (CA) Tribune*, 10 Dec. 1933, [47] (NA).

111. "Activities on the Hollywood Front," *New York Times*, 21 May 1933, X3 (ProQ).

112. Mordaunt Hall, "Those Evanescent Shadows," *New York Times*, 26 Nov. 1933, X5 (ProQ).

113. Richard B. Jewell, *The RKO Story*, with Vernon Harbin (London: Octopus, 1982), 68. See also "Public Wants Respectable Film Stories," *Los Angeles Times*, 29 Apr. 1934, A1 (ProQ).

114. Cukor, interview, 59.

115. Emanuel Levy, *George Cukor, Master of Elegance: Hollywood's Legendary Director and His Stars* (New York: Morrow, 1994), 82, 76, hereafter cited parenthetically.

116. *Little Women*, "Combined Script and Transcript," in *Four-Star Scripts: Actual Shooting Scripts and How They Are Written*, ed. Lorraine Noble (Garden City, NY: Doubleday, 1936), 302, hereafter cited parenthetically; the passages quoted are the same in the DVD film version. Noble does not credit the screenwriters, Mason and Heerman.

117. Molly Haskell, *From Reverence to Rape: The Treatment of Women in the Movies*, 2nd ed. (Chicago: Univ. of Chicago Press, 1987), viii.

118. In one instance, Amy was supposed to fall from a chest of drawers, but the script was rewritten so that Hepburn could replace the pregnant Joan Bennett (James Robert Parish and Don E. Stanke, "Joan Bennett," in *The Glamour Girls* [New Rochelle, NY: Arlington House, 1975], 50).

119. Jonathan Kuntz, "*Little Women*," in *Magill's Survey of Cinema*, ed. Frank N. Magill (Englewood Cliffs, NJ: Salem, 1980), 2:990.

120. "'Little Women' Next Week Is Hastings Show," *Dobbs Ferry (NY) Register*, 2 Feb. 1934, 6 (NYNH).

121. Advertisement, *Zanesville (OH) Signal*, 23 Dec. 1933, 8 (NA).

122. "'Little Women' Feature at Fox One of Year's Greatest Films," *Atlanta Constitution*, 31 Dec. 1933, 12A (ProQ); J.C.M., The Current Cinema, *New Yorker*, 18 Nov. 1933, 61; "Favorite Novel of Last Generation Brought to Screen," *Los Angeles Times*, 17 Dec. 1933, A2 (ProQ); Richard Dana Skinner, "*Little Women*," *Commonweal*, 22 Dec. 1933, 217; "Screen: 'Little Women' Is a Masterpiece of Americana," *Newsweek*, 25 Nov. 1933, 32; Eleanor Barnes, "Little Women," *Los Angeles Illustrated Daily News*, 25 Dec. 1933, reprinted in "Katharine Hepburn in Mag's," katethegreatnet.proboards.com.

123. Movies, *Life*, Jan. 1934, 44 (APSO).

124. Quoted in John Walker, *Halliwell's Film, Video and DVD 2006 Guide*, 21st ed. (London: HarperCollins, 2005), 658.

125. Ralph T. Jones, "'Little Women' Four Stars at Fox While Grand Plays Dinner at Eight," *Atlanta Constitution*, 30 Dec. 1933, 8 (ProQ).

126. See, e.g., "'Little Women' Makes Magic Screen Play," *Albany (NY) Evening News*, 9 Dec. 1933, 8 (NYHN).

127. George L. David, Viewed from This Angle, *Rochester (NY) Democrat and Chronicle*, 21 Jan. 1934 (NYHN).

128. Davidson, "George Cukor," D15 (ProQ).

129. Troy, "Films," 630, 631. See also "Little Women," *Photoplay*, Nov. 1934, 32.

130. Skinner, "*Little Women*," 217.

131. The Cinema, *Spectator*, 2 Feb. 1934, 159.

132. "Four Lovely New England Girls and Their Destinies Shown in Romantic Classic," *Pampa (TX) Daily News*, 21 Jan. 1934, 8 (NA).

133. Pat Kirkham and Sarah Warren, "Four *Little Women*: Three Films and a Novel," in *Adaptations: From Text to Screen, Screen to Text*, ed. Deborah Cartmell and Imelda Whelehan (London: Routledge, 1999), 84.

134. Anne Hollander, "Portraying 'Little Women' Through the Ages," *New York Times*, 15 Jan. 1995, B11, reprinted in Alberghene and Clark, "*Little Women*" *and the Feminist Imagination*, 98.

135. Edwin Schallert, "'Little Women' Enchants," *Los Angeles Times*, 25 Dec. 1933, A11 (ProQ); advertisement, *Jefferson City (MO) News and Tribune*, 14 Jan. 1934, 18A (NA); Mae Tinée, "If You Enjoyed 'Little Women' You will Enjoy Film Version," *Chicago Tribune*, 1 Dec. 1933, 17 (ProQ).

136. Nelson B. Bell, "'Little Women' Renews Appeal as Screen Gem," *Washington Post*, 26 Nov. 1933, 12 (ProQ). A promotional comic-strip version of the movie refers to "this ideal American home" (reproduced in Glen Cravath, "Little Women," *The Ephemerist* [blog], www.sparehed.com).

137. The New Pictures (Cinema), *Time*, 27 Nov. 1933, 34 (Acad1); Walter Prichard Eaton, "Romance Comes Back," *Oakland (CA) Tribune*, 11 Jan. 1934, 17 (NA).

138. Schallert, "'Little Women' Enchants."

139. Hamilton, review of *Little Women* (film), 178–79.

140. See Gene D. Phillips, *George Cukor* (Boston: Twayne, 1982), 66.

141. "'Little Women' Film Vogue," editorial, *Greeley (CO) Tribune-Republican*, 18 Jan. 1934, 10 (NA).

142. "Tower Presenting Famed 'Little Women,'" *Salt Lake Telegram*, 19 May 1934, 5.

143. Tinée, "If You Enjoyed 'Little Women.'"

144. Linda Gross, "'Little Women' at the Vagabond," *Los Angeles Times*, 3 June 1976, G16 (ProQ).

145. Iris Barry, Film Comments, *Bulletin of the Museum of Modern Art*, Jan. 1934, 4 (JSTOR).

146. Troy, "Films," 630.

147. Mollie Merrick, "Executive Sees Clean Pictures," *Los Angeles Times*, 16 Feb. 1934, 10 (ProQ).

148. Rush., review of *Little Women* (film), *Variety*, 21 Nov. 1933, 14.

149. Picking the Pictures, *Xenia (OH) Evening Gazette*, 8 Jan. 1935, 2 (NA).

150. Cohen, New Films, 13; New Films in London, *Times* (London), 29 Jan. 1934, 10 (TDA); Rob Wagner, The Movies, *Rob Wagner's Script*, 23 Dec. 1933, 10.

151. Mrs. Walter Ferguson, "Making History," *Pittsburgh Press*, 9 Dec. 1933, 4 (GNA).

152. Gross, "'Little Women' at the Vagabond."

153. Janet Maslin, "The Gold Standard for Girlhood across America," *New York Times*, 21 Dec. 1994, C13 (ProQ).

154. Andrew Britton, *Katharine Hepburn: Star as Feminist* (1985; reprint, New York: Columbia Univ. Press, 2003), 62, 68.

155. Bell, "'Little Women' Renews Appeal."

156. Florence Fisher Parry, On with the Show, *Pittsburgh Press*, 3 Dec. 1933, 27 (GNA).

157. Britton, *Katharine Hepburn*, 116.

158. Claire Trask, "The Screen in Berlin," *New York Times*, 28 Apr. 1935, X4 (ProQ); "Louise [*sic*] Alcott's Ageless Classic Here on Jan. 30," *Washington Post*, 24 Jan. 1937, TR1 (ProQ).

159. "Revolt Against Sex Novels," *Daily Mail* (Hull, UK), 11 Apr. 1935, 5 (BNA).

160. Percy Flage, Postscripts, *Evening Post* (Wellington, New Zealand), 10 May 1935, 6 (PP).

161. "Katharine Hepburn in 'Little Women,'" *Film Daily*, 16 Nov. 1933, 6.

162. See "'Little Women' Children's Party," *Rochester (NY) Democrat and Chronicle*, 26 Nov. 1933, 16C (NYHN); "'Little Women' Offers Chance for Prizes," *La Crosse (WI) Tribune and Leader-Press*, 3 Jan. 1934, 4 (NA); "Little Women Shown in a Preview Here," *Albert Lea (MN) Evening Tribune*, 19 Dec. 1933, 5 (NA); and "Giving Special Showing," *Edwardsville (IL) Intelligencer*, 18 Dec. 1933, 3 (NA).

163. Advertisement, *San Mateo (CA) Times and Daily News Leader*, 30 Dec. 1933, 5 (NA).

164. See, e.g., "Little Women," *Lowell (MA) Sun*, 27 Nov. 1933, 11; 28 Nov. 1933, 13; 29 Nov. 1933, 12; 2 Dec. 1933, 6; and 4 Dec. 1933, 9 (NA).

165. "Story Success 'Unexpected,'" *Los Angeles Times*, 7 Apr. 1934, 7 (ProQ).

166. "Further Testimony of a Great Picture's Hold on the Public," *Washington Post*, 24 Dec. 1933, B2 (ProQ).

167. See "Louisa Alcott House," *Fitchburg (MA) Sentinel*, 9 Oct. 1934, 6 (NA); Kathleen McLaughlin, "Now the Younger Set Has Beauty Clinic of its Own," *Chicago Tribune*, 14 Jan. 1934, G8 (ProQ); advertisement, *Montreal Gazette*, 22 Dec. 1933, 9 (GNA).

168. "Pinafores Return, a Bit Sophisticated," *Washington Post*, 26 Nov. 1933, S7 (ProQ). See also "'Little Women' Styles Copied by Smart Set," *Washington Post*, 30

Dec. 1933, 13 (ProQ); and Germaine, "Paris in the Mirror," *Evening Post* (Wellington, New Zealand), 11 May 1935, 19 (PP).

169. Jack Benny and Mary Livingstone, "Miniature Women," episode 113 of *The Jack Benny Show*, CBS Radio, 11 Feb. 1934, www.myoldradio.com.

170. Linda Hutcheon, *A Theory of Parody: The Teachings of Twentieth-Century Art Forms* (1985; reprint, Urbana: Univ. of Illinois Press, 2000), xii (GBks).

171. Elaine Tyler May, *Homeward Bound: American Families in the Cold War Era* (New York: Basic, 1988), 11.

172. Cukor, interview, 59; Carol Gay, "*Little Women* at the Movies," in *Children's Novels at the Movies*, ed. Douglas Street (New York: Ungar, 1983), 35. Mary Astor, the film's Marmee, similarly knew that "Mervyn LeRoy would make it a very slick show" (Astor, *A Life on Film* [New York: Delacorte, 1971], 196). She added that Elizabeth Taylor delayed production by constantly talking on the phone, "June Allyson chewed gum constantly and irritatingly and Maggie O'Brien looked at me as though she were planning something very unpleasant" (198).

173. See "1949 in Film," Wikipedia, en.wikipedia.org. Margaret O'Brien reported that she was still receiving fan mail for her role as Beth almost half a century later ("Actresses Have Happy Memories of '49 Film," *USA Today*, 20 Dec. 1994, 4D [LexN]).

174. The New Pictures (Cinema), *Time*, 14 Mar. 1949, 104 (Acad1); Marjorie Turner, "'Crushed Velvet' a Sissy Style: First Day Crowd Charmed by 'Little Women,'" *Syracuse Herald*, 22 Apr. 1949, 45 (NA); Philip K. Scheuer, "'Little Women' Revives Era of Gracious Living," *Los Angeles Times*, 18 Apr. 1949, B7 (ProQ).

175. Bosley Crowther, "Metro Fails to Spare Pathos in 'Little Women' Remake Seen at Music Hall," *New York Times*, 11 Mar. 1949, 33 (ProQ).

176. Jane Lockhart, Looking at Movies, *Rotarian*, July 1949, 50 (GBks); Bosley Crowther, "Into the Rainbow," *New York Times*, 20 Mar. 1949, X1 (ProQ).

177. New Pictures, *Time*, 104; Nadine Subotnik, "Alcott Story Pulls Tears Still Again," *Cedar Rapids (IA) Gazette*, 13 May 1949, 20 (NA).

178. "Little Women—'49 Edition," *Wall Street Journal*, 14 Mar. 1949, 8 (ProQ); Wood Soanes, "Old Alcott Story Wins New Praise," *Oakland (CA) Tribune*, 18 Apr. 1949, 13 (NA).

179. Crowther, "Metro."

180. Scheuer, "'Little Women' Revives Era"; "'Little Women' Retains Its Classic Charm," *Pittsburgh Press*, 15 Apr. 1949, 63 (GNA).

181. "'Little Women' Retains"; "Little Women in Color," *Newsweek*, 28 Mar. 1949, 84; Lockhart, Looking at Movies, 50; Crowther, "Metro"; Richard L. Coe, "'Little Women' Lacks a Hepburn," *Washington Post*, 15 Apr. 1949, C13 (ProQ); Frankie McKee Robins, review of *Little Women* (film), *McCall's*, May 1949, 7.

182. New Pictures, *Time*, 104.

183. John McCarten, The Current Cinema, *New Yorker*, 19 Mar. 1949, 82.

184. Hiroshi Kitamura, *Screening Enlightenment: Hollywood and the Cultural Reconstruction of Defeated Japan* (Ithaca, NY: Cornell Univ. Press, 2010), 100–103 (ebrary).

185. Robyn McCallum, "The Present Reshaping the Past Reshaping the Present: Film Versions of *Little Women*," *Lion and the Unicorn* 24.1 (2000): 83 (ProjM).

186. Walker, *Halliwell's*, 658; "Revered in Film and Feminism," *Time*, 19 Dec. 1994, 74; Hollander, "Portraying 'Little Women,'" 99.

187. Gay, "*Little Women* at the Movies," 34, 37. LeRoy had directed *The Wizard of Oz* (1939).

188. Kirkham and Warren, "Four *Little Women*," 89.

189. Hollander, "Portraying 'Little Women,'" 99, 98. Jeanine Basinger also speaks to the prominence of fashion in the films of the 1930s, 1940s, even 1950s, the audiences lured in part by vicarious luxury: "Even a movie about a poor little shop girl had her standing behind the counter in a simple dress trimmed in about two thousand dollars' worth of handmade lace" (A *Woman's View: How Hollywood Spoke to Women, 1930–1960* [New York: Knopf, 1993], 115).

190. Johanne Larue, review of *Little Women* (film), *Séquences*, Jan.–Feb. 1995, 42.

191. See advertisements in, e.g., *Charleston (WV) Gazette*, 4 Mar. 1949, 2 (NA); and *Sheboygan (WI) Press*, 11 June 1949, 5 (NA).

192. Reynolds Knight, "Behind the Scenes in American Business," *Cullman (AL) Banner*, 12 May 1949, 4 (NA). And not explicit tie-ins, but subsequent illustrated editions drew on images from this film version at least as frequently as they did on images from the 1933 one, depicting perhaps a jauntily perched hat or Jo as a June Allyson with bangs.

193. Eleanor Everest Freer, *Scenes from "Little Women"* (Chicago: Music Library, [1934]), 31; "A Girl Called Jo," *Encyclopedia of Popular Music*, 4th ed. (New York: Oxford Univ. Press, 2006), available online at www.oxfordmusiconline.com; *The Stage*, quoted in Ken Mandelbaum, "Little Women of the '50s," Broadway Buzz, www.broadway.com /buzz. But see Elise K. Kirk, who argues that Freer generally deserves more credit for creating fresh and novel chamber operas than she has received (*American Opera* [Urbana: Univ. of Illinois Press, 2001], 242–44). Charles Ives offered not an adaptation but a musical tribute in his *Concord Sonata* (1919, rev. 1947), devoting one movement to "The Alcotts," both Bronson and Louisa.

194. The fullest listing appears in the Internet Movie Database, imdb.com (see esp Louisa May Alcott as writer). Also listed are a 1955 Italian miniseries, *Piccole donne* (RAI, and a 1959 Brazilian version called *Mulherzinhas* (TV Tupi).

195. See, e.g., Ellen Seiter, *Sold Separately: Children and Parents in Consumer Culture* (New Brunswick, NJ: Rutgers Univ. Press, 1993), 26.

196. Quoted in John Crosby, "Musicals for TV," *Sarasota Herald-Tribune*, 23 July 1958, 29 (GNA).

197. See Marie Torre, TV-Radio Today, *Washington (PA) Observer*, 29 Aug. 1958, 1. (GNA).

198. Quoted in John Crosby, "One Word Is Worth a Thousand Pictures," *Hartford (CT) Courant*, 25 July 1958, 20.

199. Milton Esterow, "TV Put in a Dither by 'Little Women,'" *New York Times*, 3 Aug. 1958, 44. Margaret O'Brien, reprising her role in the 1949 film, also wanted Beth to die, though not so much out of loyalty to Alcott as because "she had wanted to do a death scene" ("Little Women Script Revised," *Oxnard [CA] Press-Courier*, 2 Oct. 1958, 13 [GNA]).

200. Quoted in Torre, TV-Radio Today.

201. Donald Kirkley, Look and Listen, *Baltimore Sun*, 16 Oct. 1958, 18 (ProQ).

202. *Little Women*, dir. William Corrigan, *Schaeffer Showcase*, 16 Oct. 1958, CBS TV.

203. Dorothy Kilgallen, The Voice of Broadway, *New Castle (PA) News*, 13 Oct. 1958, 4 (NA).

204. Richard Dyer, "Entertainment and Utopia," in *Hollywood Musicals: The Film Reader*, ed. Steven Cohan (London: Routledge, 2002), 19–30.

205. An odder addition to the production is the song "I Don't Want to Be a Fly," in which Jo tries to persuade Amy to play at being a fly so Jo can play spider (Amy retorts that she'd rather be a dragon), even if it is one way of capturing the antagonism between the two. Then again, this song appears only on the 2009 CD, not in the production as aired.

206. Richard Adler, *"You Gotta Have Heart,"* with Lee Davis (New York: Fine, 1990), 190.

207. Lawrence Laurent, "'Gift of the Magi' Is New 'Special' Tailored, Adler Says, for Television," *Washington Post*, 9 Dec. 1958, B11 (ProQ); Donald Kirkley, Look and Listen, *Baltimore Sun*, 11 Dec. 1958, 16; "Big Boy Critic Blasts 'Little Women' of Screen," *Iola (KS) Register*, 17 Oct. 1958, 8 (NA).

208. Jack Gould, "TV: The March Sisters," *New York Times*, 17 Oct. 1958, 59 (ProQ).

209. Harriet Van Horne, "'Little Women' Treated Poorly," *Albuquerque Tribune*, 17 Oct. 1958, 11 (NA).

210. William Ewald, "'Little Women' Production Was—Well—Simply Awful," *Oxnard (CA) Press-Courier*, 17 Oct. 1958, 11 (NA).

211. James Baldwin, "Everybody's Protest Novel" (1949), in *Notes of a Native Son* (Boston: Beacon, 1990), 14.

212. Woman about Town, *Washington Post*, 23 Dec. 1894, 71 (ProQ).

213. Cartoon, *Life*, Oct. 1934, 18 (APSO).

214. "Scaring Louisa May Alcott," *Time*, 21 Dec. 1959, 19 (Acad1).

215. Don Todd, "Jack London and 'Little Women,'" *Los Angeles Times*, 5 June 1956, A5 (ProQ).

216. Bennett Cerf, *Good for a Laugh: A New Collection of Humorous Tidbits and Anecdotes from Aardvark to Zythum* (1952; reprint, Garden City, NY: Hanover House, 1958), 102.

217. Julie Wilhelm, "'Don't laugh! Act as if it was all right!' And Other Comical Interruptions in *Little Women*," *Studies in American Humor*, 3rd ser., 19 (2009): 63–82 (EBSCO).

218. Pat Frank, "Step by Step," *Baltimore Sun*, 9 Nov. 1941, WM8+ (ProQ).

219. Wood Soanes, "'Little Women' Blush again at Paramount," *Oakland (CA) Tribune*, 2 Dec. 1933, 4 (NA).

220. Review of *Miss Alcott of Concord*, by Marjorie Worthington, *New Yorker*, 18 Oct. 1958, 194.

CHAPTER 4: Celebrating Sisterhood and Passion since 1960

Epigraphs: David M. Bader, *Haiku U.: From Aristotle to Zola, 100 Great Books in 7 Syllables* (New York: Gotham Books, 2006), 26; George Steiner, "The Hermeneutic Motion" (1975), in *The Translation Studies Reader*, ed. Lawrence Venuti, 2nd ed. (New York: Routledge, 2004), 196.

1. Gerald Nachman, "After 'Wuthering,' What?" *New York Times*, 4 Oct. 1970, 109 (ProQ).

2. P. J. O'Rourke, Bookshelf, *Wall Street Journal*, 30 July 1987, 1 (ProQ).

3. Lisa Brown, "Little Women," in *The Graphic Canon*, vol. 2 (New York: Seven Stories, 2012), xi.

4. See, e.g., Helen Reagan Smith's "Louisa Alcott's Despair Turned into Real Success," *Big Spring (TX) Daily Herald*, 29 Jan. 1960, 3 (NA); and Carrie, review of *Little Women*, *Reading to Know* (blog), 3 Dec. 2007, www.readingtoknow.com. But see Mary Van Nattan, who excoriates Alcott—*Little Women* "is not a helpful book for girls and young ladies to prepare them to be content as home makers"—and concludes that "this woman's books ought not be used in a Christian home" ("Louisa May Alcott," *The Home Maker's Corner* [blog], n.d., www.homemakerscorner.com).

5. See Lunaea Weatherstone, "Heart and Home: Everyday Enchantments; Making Friends with Aphrodite and Louisa," *SageWoman* 29 (31 Mar. 1995), 54 (ProQ); S. Hillel Halle, "Group Casts Wide Net in Fishing for Best Gay Novels," *Colorado Springs Gazette*, 1 Aug. 1999, T&B7 (NA); and "The 100 Best Lesbian and Gay Novels," Publishing Triangle, www.publishingtriangle.org. An interviewer stated that Winona Ryder's parents claimed that "Alcott wrote 'Little Women' while stoned on opium"; they actually claimed that she used opium and morphine to ease chronic pain (Aljean Harmetz, "On and Off Screen, Winona Ryder Comes of Age," *New York Times*, 9 Dec. 1990, H24 [ProQ]; Cynthia Palmer and Michael Horowitz, eds., *Sisters of the Extreme: Women Writing on the Drug Experience* [1982; Rochester, VT: Park Street, 2000], 44).

6. See, e.g., Caryn James, "Amy Had Golden Curls; Jo Had a Rat. Who Would You Rather Be?" *New York Times Book Review*, 25 Dec. 1994, 3, 17; Deirdre F. Baker, "When Good Books Go Bad," *Horn Book*, Mar.–June 2006, 281 (EBSCO); and "*Little Women* Question: Which character can you most compare yourself to? Why?" Goodreads, 15 May 2012+, goodreads.com.

7. Roberta Seelinger Trites, "Academic Grief: Journeys with *Little Women*," in *A Narrative Compass: Stories That Guide Women's Lives*, ed. Betsy Hearne and Roberta Seelinger Trites (Urbana: Univ. of Illinois Press, 2009), 11.

8. Shumeka Pickett, Office for Intellectual Freedom, American Library Association, e-mail message to author, 5 Dec. 2012.

9. "A Children's All-Time Bestseller List," *Gastonia (NC) Gazette*, 12 Nov. 1977, [24] (NA); Pamela Davis Diaz, "Louisa May Alcott," *St. Petersburg (FL) Times*, 6 Mar. 1992, 3B (LexN).

10. Geraldine E. LaRocque, Book Marks, *English Journal* 58.2 (Feb. 1969): 288 (JSTOR).

11. Except in 2003–5, when it came in sixth or seventh; most of these students would have been about ten when the 1994 film was released. Barbara Sicherman suggests that women born in the 1960s and 1970s seem less likely to have felt passionate about the book than those born in the 1940s and 1950s (*Well-Read Lives: How Books Inspired a Generation of American Women* [Chapel Hill: Univ. of North Carolina Press, 2010], 29).

12. Holly Virginia Blackford, *Out of This World: Why Literature Matters to Girls* (New York: Teachers College Press, 2004), 12, 87. The thirty-three girl readers seemed more interested in seeking alterity, stories that "actually had little to do with their own experiences" (6).

13. "Libraries: For Well-Read Presidents," *Time*, 23 Aug. 1963, www.time.com; Library of Congress, "Books That Shaped America," 2011 National Book Festival, www.loc.gov.

14. *Ladies' Home Journal*, cited in "Martha Washington Tops Best Women List," *Elyria (OH) Chronicle-Telegram*, 3 June 1986, A2 (NA); "Women Honored for Contributions," *Annapolis (MD) Capital*, 6 Oct. 1996, A3 (NA).

15. "Teachers' Top 50 Books" and "Kids['] Top 100 Books," *Farmington (NM) Daily Times*, 24 Feb. 2002, 21 (NA); "50 State Booklist," National Education Association, www.nea.org.

16. See, e.g., the photograph in the *Charleston (WV) Daily Mail*, 17 Dec. 1968, 7 (NA).

17. Gay Pauley, "Louisa M. Alcott Classic Century Birthday Comes," *El Paso (TX) Herald-Post*, 25 Sept. 1968, B6 (NA).

18. "Celebrate Author's Birthdate," *Fayetteville (NY) Eagle-Bulletin*, 24 Nov. 1982, 8 (NYHN).

19. May Hill Arbuthnot, *Children and Books* (Chicago: Scott, 1947), 24; Carrie Hintz and Eric L. Tribunella, *Reading Children's Literature: A Critical Introduction* (Boston: Bedford, 2013), 203.

20. Quoted in Suzy Belton, "20 Great Reads for Children," *Irish Independent*, 4 Apr. 2011, www.independent.ie.

21. "1000 Novels Everyone Must Read," *Guardian* (London), 20 Jan. 2009, S1 (LexN).

22. Michele Landsberg, *Reading for the Love of It: Best Books for Young Readers* (1986; reprint, New York: Prentice Hall, 1987), 300.

23. Wieland Freund, "'Ich mag keine Sommersprossen': Der Hollywood-Star Julianne Moore hat ihr erstes Kinderbilderbuch geschrieben," *Die Welt*, 7 Feb. 2009, LW6 (LexN); Ryder, cited in "*Little Women* Still Has Big Fans," *Syracuse Herald Journal*, 18 Dec. 1994, M17 (NA); Gerard Lim, "'Ghostwriter's' Tina," *Asianweek*, 29 Jan. 1983, 1 (ProQ); Barbara Kingsolver, *High Tide in Tucson: Essays from Now or Never* (New York: HarperCollins, 1995), 44; Mary Jo Salter, "American Girls," *New York Times*, 15 May 2009, G10 (ProQ); Schulman, quoted in Karen Cook, "The Lavender List," *Village Voice*, 29 June 1999, 155 (ProQ); Marc McEvoy, "Interview: John Green," *Age* (Melbourne), 21 Jan. 2012, theage.com.au; Perri Klass, "Where 'Little Women' Grew Up," *New York Times*, 25 Apr. 1999, 176 (ProQ). Robin Uncapher's informal survey of romance writers and readers suggests that they generally did not feel passionately about the book—because it lacks sexual passion ("Thoughts on *Little Women*," *All About Romance* [blog], 14 Aug. 2006, www.likesbooks.com/234).

24. Quoted in "*Little Women* Still Has Big Fans."

25. Anna Quindlen, introduction to *Little Women* (Boston: Little, 1994), [vi].

26. bell hooks [Gloria Jean Watkins], *Bone Black: Memories of Girlhood* (New York: Holt, 1996), 77.

27. Luis Negrón, "The Pain of Reading," trans. Suzanne Jill Levine, *New York Times*, 7 Oct. 2012, SR10 (ProQ).

28. Katie Pellegrino, quoted in Lea Czar, "Students Reflect on Courage, Confidence and Character," *Gettysburg (PA) Times*, 7 Mar. 2008, B5 (NA).

29. Quoted in Naomi Knickmeyer, Among Other Things, *Ada (OK) Evening News*, 29 Sept. 1968, 7 (NA).

30. See Alice Furland, "Great Minds Live Alike," *New York Times*, 4 May 1997, XX13 (ProQ).

31. "Junior Choice," *Guardian* (London), 9 Nov. 1999 (Guard).

32. David Smith, "The Nation's Love Affair with Stories of Childhood," *Guardian*

(London), 19 Oct. 2003; John Ezard, "Pride and Prejudice the Most Precious as Modern Readers Turn Over an Old Leaf," *Guardian* (London), 28 Feb. 2007; "Books You Can't Live Without: The Top 100," *Guardian* (London), 1 Mar. 2007 (all at Guard).

33. Peter Keating, "Louisa May Alcott's Happy End," *TLS*, 7 June 1991, 11 (TLS); John Ezard, "Hardy a Perennial Favourite but the Bard Trails in 19th," *Guardian* (London), 7 Jan. 1993, 5 (CustomN).

34. Brian Alderson, "Nursery Classics Enjoy Second Childhoods," *Times* (London), 16 Mar. 1995, 33 (Acad1); E. Jane Dickson, "There's Something I'd Really Like You to Read," *Times* (London), 30 Sept. 2000, 8 (Acad1).

35. Jenny Gilbert, "Books for Children Stuck on the Shelf," *Independent* (London), 20 Nov. 1994, 51 (LexN).

36. Hilary Mantel, "Author, Author," *Guardian* (London), 30 Jan. 2009 (Guard).

37. And thus he didn't read it before going to see a stage production, which of course he panned (Charles Spencer, "Terrifying Orgy of Niceness," *Daily Telegraph* [UK], 15 Oct. 2004, 22 [LexN]).

38. Paul Donovan, Pick of the Day, *Times* (London), 11 Aug. 2002, 77 (CustomN); "To Boldly Go Where No Other Book Has Gone Before," *Western Mail* (Cardiff, Wales), 4 Mar. 2006, 4 (LexN); "J. K. Rowling: By the Book," *New York Times*, 14 Oct. 2012, BR8 (LexN). See also Hermione Lee and Sophia Chauchard-Stuart, "Marmee's Girls," *Independent* (London), 4 Mar. 1995, 34 (LexN), for responses from a number of prominent women who were young in the current and previous periods.

39. Denise Lavoie, "Orchard House Brings 'Little Women' to Life," *Manchester (CT) Journal Inquirer*, 6 Jan. 2005, A5 (NA).

40. Mieke K. T. Desmet, *Babysitting the Reader: Translating English Narrative Fiction for Girls into Dutch (1946–1995)* (Bern: Lang, 2007), 191.

41. A comparison with books catalogued in the French Bibliothèque Nationale during these decades suggests that the Index Translationum (www.unesco.org/new/en/culture) may list about half of the published French translations. But it does suggest a lower limit for the numbers of translations.

42. Michael Unverzagt, "Louisa May Alcott: Movies, Animations & Alcott in Germany," www.xanth.de/alcott.

43. See Idette Noomé, "Shaping the Self: A *Bildungsroman* for Girls?" *Liberator* 25.3 (Nov. 2004): 131n8 (EBSCO); Emer O'Sullivan, *Comparative Children's Literature*, trans. Anthea Bell (London: Routledge, 2005), 56; and Jessie Hui, "Word Power Provides the Motivation," *South China Morning Post*, 25 May 2004, www.scmp.com.

44. "Even Royalty Likes to Read," *Idaho Falls Post-Register*, 23 June 1968, 8 (NA); "Miss Universe 2000," *India Abroad*, 19 May 2000, 22 (ProQ).

45. Pennie Azarcon-dela Cruz, "Books that Changed Our Life," blog, *Philippine Daily Inquirer*, Mar. 2008, blogs.inquirer.net.

46. Shuib Taib, "Sisters Are 'Little Women' Personified," *New Straits Times* (Malaysia), 10 July 2006, L15 (ProQ).

47. Eleni Meleagrou, "A Child's Reading in Cyprus," *Washington Post*, 10 May 1992, X13 (ProQ).

48. Alma B. Kuhlemann Cárdenez, "On the Darker Side of 'Paradise': Reading Gender Roles in Marcela Serrano's *Hasta siempre, mujercitas* through the Lenses of Domestic and Gothic Fiction," *Chasqui* 40.1 (May 2011): 141–58 (LION).

49. See Lee Hyo-won, "Park Kyung-ni[']s Works Translated Onscreen," *Korea Times*, 5 May 2008, koreatimes.co.kr; Giovanna Pezzuoli, "Ravera," *Corriere della Sera* (Milan), 5 Feb. 2012, 19, archiviostorico.corriere.it; and Ida Bozzi, "Piccole donne dietro lo specchio," *Corriere della Sera* (Milan), 19 June 2012, 41, archiviostorico.corriere.it.

50. *Little Women*, Manga Literary Classics ([Seoul]: Y.kids, 2007), 23; "Adaptation & Art" are credited to Special Academic Manga.

51. Aiko Moro-oka, "Alcott in Japan: A Selected Bibliography," in *"Little Women" and the Feminist Imagination: Criticism, Controversy, Personal Essays*, ed. Janice M. Alberghene and Beverly Lyon Clark (New York: Garland, 1999), 377–79.

52. Kazuko Watanabe, "Reading *Little Women*, Reading Motherhood in Japan," *Feminist Studies* 25.3 (Fall 1999): 699–700 (JSTOR).

53. Mariko Yoshida, "Playbuilding in a Japanese College EFL Classroom: Its Advantages and Disadvantages," *Caribbean Quarterly* 53.1–2 (Mar.–June 2007): 231–32 (JSTOR).

54. "Japanese Royalty Begin Visit with Look at American History," *Santa Fe New Mexican*, 4 Oct. 1987, A2 (NA).

55. William A. Davis, "Sayonara Tourism as Japan Mourns, Visits to US Drop Off," *Boston Globe*, 12 Jan. 1989, 69 (ProQ).

56. See Ted Malone [Frank Alden Russell], *Should Old Acquaintance* (Haddonfield, NJ: Bookmark, 1943), xi–xiii.

57. "The Orchard House," *Colonial Homes*, July–Aug. 1983, 78.

58. Lori Miller, "Pilgrimage to House of 'Little Women,'" *Cedar Rapids (IA) Gazette*, 1 Jan. 1995, 9C (NA).

59. John Keasler, "Obligatory Sex Pays Off," *Thomasville (GA) Times Enterprise*, 12 Feb. 1976 (NA).

60. Jim Murray, "Little Miss Alcott Comes Out Swinging," *Los Angeles Times*, 2 Apr. 1981, OC_B1 (ProQ).

61. "Judges Examines [*sic*] Issues Regarding Cyberspace Porn," *Texas City Sun*, 23 Mar. 1996, 2 (NA).

62. See advertisements, *Lumberton (NC) Robesonian*, 9 Mar. 1986, W2 (NA), and *Santa Fe New Mexican*, 17 Mar. 1991, W19 (NA).

63. "Paris Fashions a Period Piece," *Washington Post*, 27 Aug. 1966, C1 (ProQ).

64. Sandra M. Gilbert and Susan Gubar, *The Madwoman in the Attic: The Woman Writer and the Nineteenth-Century Literary Imagination* (New Haven, CT: Yale Univ. Press, 1979), 64.

65. Nina Auerbach, "Austen and Alcott on Matriarchy: New Women or New Wives?" *Novel* 10 (Fall 1976): 6–26.

66. Lisa O'Kelly, "Renaissance or No, Alcott Characters Not Real Feminists," *Orange (TX) Leader*, 26 Feb. 1995, 1C, 2C (NA).

67. See, e.g., Sabrina Vellucci, *New Girls: Adolescenti nella cultura statunitense (1865–1890)* (Naples: Loffredo, 2008).

68. Brigid Brophy, "Sentimentality and Louisa M. Alcott," *Times* (London), Dec. 1964, reprinted as "A Masterpiece, and Dreadful," *New York Times*, 17 Jan. 1965, BR1 (ProQ).

69. Hildegard Hoeller, "From Agony to Ecstasy: The New Studies of American Sentimentality," *ESQ* 52 (2006): 343.

70. Alcott to Elizabeth Powell, 20 Mar. [1869], *Letters*, 125.

71. For an illuminating discussion of the arguments, see Michelle A. Massé, "Songs to Aging Children: Louisa May Alcott's March Trilogy," in Alberghene and Clark, *"Little Women" and the Feminist Imagination*, esp. 336–39.

72. Catharine R. Stimpson, "Reading for Love: Canons, Paracanons, and Whistling Jo March," *New Literary History* 21 (Autumn 1990): 957–76.

73. Many additional hard-to-trace community productions have been scripted by the director or a local teen or through the collaboration of the performers. Nor does my count include pastiches, in which, say, Eliza escapes *Uncle Tom's Cabin* to join the March sisters (see Pamela Sommers, "Off the Ice," *Washington Post*, 26 Feb. 1996, B7 [ProQ]).

74. Sheila Corbett, *Little Women* (Birmingham, UK: Cambridge, 1967), I.ii, 32, hereafter cited parenthetically, with references to act and scene, followed by the page in this edition.

75. See Beth Lynch and Scott Lynch-Giddings, *Louisa's Little Women* (Venice, FL: Eldridge, 1997), II.iii, 51.

76. See Steve Groark, "New Look at 'Little Women' Enlightens," *Wisconsin State Journal* (Madison), 21 Jan. 1989, 5C (NA); Gay Strandemo, "'Little Women' Given Careful Thought," letter to the editor, *Wisconsin State Journal* (Madison), 18 Aug. 1989, 15A (NA).

77. David Longest, *Little Women of Orchard House* (Woodstock, IL: Dramatic Publishing, 1998), [5], hereafter cited parenthetically.

78. Jeffrey Wainwright, "Girls in Unmarried Bliss," *Independent* (London), 29 June 1989, Arts14 (LexN).

79. J. D. Atkinson, review of *Very Little Women*, performed by Lip Service / Chester Gateway, 2004, British Theatre Guide, www.britishtheatreguide.info.

80. Jack Gaver, "'Little Women' Provides Story for Warm New Musical: 'Jo,'" *Oakland (CA) Tribune*, 13 Feb. 1964, 14E (NA); Richard P. Cooke, "Tuneful Tomboy," *Wall Street Journal*, 14 Feb. 1964, 10 (ProQ).

81. "Little Women 'Pretty Sticky Kid Stuff,'" *Reno Evening Gazette*, 13 Feb. 1964, 23 (NA).

82. Dream Street, *Uniontown (PA) Morning Herald*, 23 Mar. 1964, 18 (NA).

83. Thomas S. Hischak, *Off-Broadway Musicals since 1919: From "Greenwich Village Follies" to "The Toxic Avenger"* (Lanham, MD: Scarecrow, 2011), 89 (ebrary).

84. See Jesse McKinley, "Big Women, 'Little Women,'" *New York Times*, 2 June 2000, E2 (ProQ). A production of the earlier version in Syracuse in 2009 was positively received as "highly sophisticated classic Broadway," with "memorable tunes driven by full-blooded emotion" (James MacKillop, "Girl Power," *Syracuse New Times*, 2 Dec. 2009, 14+ [ProQ]).

85. Richard Zoglin, "Louisa May on Broadway," *Time*, 7 Feb. 2005, 74 (Acad1); David Rooney, "'Women' Marches a Little out of Step," *Variety*, 31 Jan. 2005, 58 (Acad1). A sixteen-year-old reviewer claimed, "The show deftly transforms the story into a musical" (Caroline Duffy, "'Women': Little Room for Improvement," *Washington Times*, 22 July 2006 [LexN]).

86. Jules Becker, "Earnest 'Women,'" *Jewish Advocate*, 20 Jan. 2006, 34 (ProQ); Louise Kennedy, "Music Yields to Strong Memories in 'Little Women,'" *Boston Globe*, 12 Jan. 2006, H1 (ProQ); Mark E. Leib, "A Little Inspiration," *Creative Loafing* (Tampa,

FL), 10 Feb. 2010, 37 (ProQ); Ben Brantley, "A Tomboy with Gumption (and Her Sisters)," *New York Times*, 24 Jan. 2005, E1 (ProQ).

87. Michael Feingold, "Forced Marches," *Village Voice*, 2–8 Feb. 2005, C67 (ProQ); Trey Graham, "3B or Not 3B," *Washington (DC) City Paper*, 7 July 2006, 38–39 (ProQ).

88. In a September 2005 exchange on The Straight Dope (boards.straightdope.com), participants variously proffer 300 or 400–500 performances as the break-even point for Broadway shows.

89. Zagat Theater Survey, *Wall Street Journal*, 28 Jan. 2005, W7 (ProQ).

90. Quoted in Salter, "American Girls."

91. Carol Beggy and Mark Shanahan, "'Little Women,' Big Fans," *Boston Globe*, 14 Jan. 2006, E2 (ProQ).

92. Mary K. Feeney, "For Real 'Little Women,' Story Strikes a Chord," *Washington Post*, 7 July 2006, WW42 (ProQ).

93. See Alison Mayes, "Sisters' Story Has Universal Appeal," *Winnipeg (MB) Free Press*, 19 Sept. 2012, D4, eureka.cc; Kathryne LaMontagne, "Les quatre filles du Dr March," *Journal de Québec*, 1 Dec. 2012, W18, eureka.çc.

94. "Adventures and Rivalries Weave a Wonderful Tale in 'Little Women—The Broadway Musical,'" *Between the Lines* (Livonia, MI), 10 Sept. 2009, 31 (ProQ).

95. Joel Hirschhorn, "Little Women—The Musical," *Variety*, 9 Sept. 2005, 32 (LexN).

96. Troy Lennon, "Marmee's Refrain," *Daily Telegraph* (Australia), 14 Nov. 2008, F69 (LexN); Jo Litson, "These Charming Women," *Sunday Telegraph* (Australia), 16 Nov. 2008, F99 (LexN); John Shand, "Alcott's Charm Shows, But Could Have Shone," *Sydney Morning Herald*, 14 Nov. 2008, E9 (LexN).

97. Gibbs Cadiz, "In 'Magsimula ka!' and 3 Other Musicals—An Illustrative Moment," *Philippine Daily Inquirer*, 16 Dec. 2010, services.inqrr.nat.

98. Ariane Fries, "Hochprofessionelle Premiere," *General-Anzeiger* (Bonn), 5 May 2012, 26 (LexN).

99. At this time when 63 percent of the Broadway audience was women (2003–4), the head of the production's advertising agency noted the advantage of having "an unbelievably well-known and recognized brand" and chose a logo that was not the typical image but had "a younger-looking spin" (quoted in Michael Kuchwara, "Broadway Taps in to Girl Power," *Elyria [OH] Chronicle Telegram*, 20 Feb. 2005, B6, B7 [NA]). The story is placed under a photograph of a scene in which Marmee sits surrounded by her four daughters.

100. Mindi Dickstein, "Astonishing," in *Little Women: The Broadway Musical*, book by Allan Knee (New York: Music Theatre International, n.d.), 67.

101. Mindi Dickstein, "Volcano—Reprise," in *Little Women: The Broadway Musical*, 115.

102. Quoted in Nelson Pressley, "'Little Women' as Girl-illa Theater," *Washington Post*, 29 June 2006, C5 (ProQ).

103. Critics cited in Kate Cronin, "Eliot Adapted" (honors thesis, Wheaton College, 2011), 9. Among shorter works, *A Christmas Carol* might win the laurels, with forty-seven film and TV adaptations, according to Bob Leddy, "The Greatest 'Carol,'" *Providence (RI) Journal*, 19 Dec. 2013, A16.

104. Peter Craven, "Love and Longing in the Crinoline and Bonnet Set," *Age* (Melbourne), 4 Oct. 2008, AII27 (LexN).

105. Leonard Buckley, "Little Women BBC/1," *Times* (London), 26 Oct. 1970, 11 (TDA).

106. Marilyn Beck, Telly, *Blytheville (AR) Courier News*, 10 Oct. 1978, 12 (NA).

107. Tom Shales, "Sweet 'Little Women,'" *Washington Post*, 2 Oct. 1978, B9 (ProQ).

108. M. MacDonald, "Kate Is a Hard Act to Follow," *Courier Mail* (Australia), 29 Sept. 1985 (LexN).

109. MaryLouise Oates, "'Little Women' in a Slick, Shiny Glow," *Los Angeles Times*, 2 Oct. 1978, E14 (ProQ).

110. *Little Women* (film), dir. David Lowell Rich, NBC, 1978, DVD 2007.

111. See Betty Utterback, "Never Underestimate the Power of Big Nielsen," *Santa Fe New Mexican*, 25 Feb. 1979, TV9 (NA). I have been unable to view these episodes.

112. *Special Treat: Little Women*, 14 Dec. 1976, NBC. An earlier version of the ballet, with the same music but probably different choreography, was screened by NBC in 1969, this time with child dancers and narrated by Geraldine Page. A review service wryly noted that one should forget that this ballet was supposed to be based on *Little Women* and be prepared to watch "sweet and charming traditional ballet steps in pastel frocks of becoming hues" (TV Key, *Lima [OH] News*, 25 May 1969, F12 [NA]). The earliest ballet version may have been one performed in New Zealand in 1944 (see "They Speak English," *Auckland Star*, 6 Dec. 1944, 3 [PP]).

113. Judith Martin, "A Truncated 'Little Women,'" *Washington Post*, 14 Dec. 1976, B10 (ProQ).

114. Gillian Armstrong, interview by Margaret Smith, in "Gillian Armstrong," *Cinema Papers*, Mar. 1995, 6.

115. Roger Ebert, "Sisters Sweetly," *Colorado Springs Gazette Telegraph*, 23 Dec. 1994, AA5, AA6 (NA).

116. [Robin Swicord], *Little Women*, first draft revised (Studio City, CA: Hollywood Scripts, [1993]), 1–3. Swicord has discussed the Pickwick scene as of some significance to her, adumbrating "themes of ambition and transformation" ("Under the Skin: Adapting Novels for the Screen," in *In/Fidelity: Essays on Film Adaptation*, ed. David L. Kranz and Nancy C. Mellerski [Newcastle, UK: Cambridge Scholars, 2008], 19).

117. Quoted in Manohla Dargis, "Reworking *Women*," *Village Voice*, 3 Jan. 1995, 71 (ProQ).

118. See marysueeasteregg, comment, Aug. 2012, "Little Women (Opera Scene – Les pêcheurs de perles)," YouTube, www.youtube.com.

119. David Noh, review of *Little Women* (film), *Film Journal*, Jan.–Feb. 1995, 44.

120. Deborah Cartmell and Judy Simons, "Screening Authorship: *Little Women* on Screen, 1933–1994," in *Nineteenth-Century American Fiction on Screen*, ed. R. Barton Palmer (Cambridge: Cambridge Univ. Press, 2007), 89. For the argument that the film sanitizes economic realities and eradicates tension and ambiguity, see Linda Grasso, "Louisa May Alcott's 'Magic Inkstand': Little Women, Feminism, and the Myth of Regeneration," *Frontiers* 19.1 (1998): 177–92.

121. Barbara Shulgasser, "'Little Women': Politically Correct, Smug," *Hutchinson (KS) News*, 23 Dec. 1994, 3A (NA); Amy Gamerman, "Four Saintly Sisters," *Wall Street Journal*, 29 Dec. 1994, A8 (ProQ); Janet Maslin, "The Gold Standard for Girlhood across America," *New York Times*, 21 Dec. 1994, C13; Richard Schickel, "Transcendental Meditation," *Time*, 19 Dec. 1994, 74; Yardena Arar, "'Little Women': A Christmas Treat," *In-*

diana (PA) Gazette, 22 Dec. 1994, 8 (NA); Jonathan Richards, "Watching a Good Book," *Santa Fe (NM) Reporter,* 28 Dec. 1994, 29 (NA); Movies, *Capital Times* (Madison, WI), 1 Apr. 1995, 3D (NA); Emiliana Sandoval, "'Little Women' Is a Gem of a Film; a Must See," *Santa Fe New Mexican,* 6 Jan. 1995, 26 (NA); "Deja View," *Paris (TX) News,* 12 Feb. 1995, E3 (NA); Bob Thomas, "*Little Women* a Beautiful Holiday Gift," *Brownsville (TX) Herald,* 20 Dec. 1994, 15 (NA).

122. Steve Vineberg, "Alcott & Armstrong," *Threepenny Review* 62 (Summer 1995): 27 (JSTOR).

123. Ruth Reichl, "A Lucky Director's Daring Career," *New York Times,* 8 Mar. 1995, C1 (ProQ); John Horn, "'Little Women,' Big Box Office," *Lawrence (KS) Journal-World,* 13 Jan. 1995, 1D (NA).

124. See *Little Women* (1994), Box Office Mojo, boxofficemojo.com.

125. Doug Nye, "Other Versions of 'Little Women' on Video," *Syracuse Herald-Journal,* 25 Jan. 1995, B6 (NA).

126. Karen S. Peterson, "'Little Women' Lost on Teens of the '90s," *USA Today,* 3 Jan. 1995, 6D (LexN).

127. Quoted in Donna Britt, "The Last No-Action Heroes?" *Washington Post,* 27 Dec. 1994, D5 (ProQ), and in Evan Levine, "Armstrong's 'Little Women' Replays Timeless Charm of March Girls," *Indiana (PA) Gazette,* 8 Oct. 1995, E6 (NA).

128. Kevin Jackson, "Laugh? I Nearly Took out a Subscription to Mensa," *Independent* (London), 16 Mar. 1995, 25 (LexN); Lindsay Duguid, "Falling into Walden Pond," *TLS,* 24 Mar. 1995, 18 (TLS); Geoff Brown, "Respect for Women's Rites," *Times* (London), 16 Mar. 1995, 29 (Acad1).

129. J. Sanderson, "Alcott's Sisters Still Captivate," *Sunday Mail* (Queensland, Australia), 2 Apr. 1995, G141 (LexN); G. Dibble, "Sob Story that Raises a Cheer," *Herald Sun* (Melbourne), 30 Mar. 1995 (LexN). But see Peter Crayford, "Heavy Burden for Little Women," *Australian Financial Review,* 31 Mar. 1995, 19 (LexN).

130. C[atherine] A[xelrad], review of *Les quatre filles du docteur March* (film), *Positif,* June 1995, 51 (International Index to Performing Arts); Johanne Larue, review of *Little Women* (film), *Séquences,* Jan.–Feb. 1995, 42.

131. Emanuela Martini, review of *Piccole donne* (film), *Cineforum,* Mar. 1995, 82; Tullio Kezich, "Riecco le donnine di zucchero," *Corriere della Sera* (Milan), 9 Mar. 1995, 31, archiviostorico.corriere.it; Carlo Avondola, review of *Piccole donne* (film), *Segnocinema* 73 (1995): 59–60.

132. Daumenkino, *Die Tageszeitung* (Berlin), 18 May 1995, 17 (LexN).

133. Howard McGowan, "'Little Women'—A Good Movie, But Oh So Slow," *Gleaner* (Kingsport, Jamaica), 3 May 1995, 13A (NA).

134. See "Revered in Film and Feminism," *Time,* 19 Dec. 1994, 74; "*Little Women* Still Has Big Fans."

135. See Elizabeth Sanger, "'Little Women' Books Hit Stores as Movie Opens," *Cedar Rapids (IA) Gazette,* 25 Dec. 1994, 2C (NA).

136. The simplified language of this rendition generated debate over the dumbing down of U.S. education (see Sally Streff Buzbee, "Simplified 'Little Women' Brings Big Debate," *Capital Times* [Madison, WI], 23 Feb. 1995, 3F [NA]).

137. See, e.g., Paperback Best Sellers, *New York Times,* 12 Feb. 1995, BR36 (ProQ).

138. Connie Lauerman, "Austen's Work Kept Alive by TV, Films," *Fort Walton Beach (FL) Daily News*, 21 Dec. 1995, 10D (NA). Roger Riley, Dwayne Baker, and Carlton S. Van Doren suggest that the film seemed to have an unusually large impact on attendance at Orchard House, compared with the impact of other contemporary films associated with recognizable locations, in "Movie Induced Tourism," *Annals of Tourism Research* 25.4 (1998), esp. 928.

139. George Loomis, "Do We Really Need Another Opera?" *Opera*, Mar. 2005, 298.

140. Kyle MacMillan, "'Little Women' Opera Brought Adamo's Big Break," *Denver Post*, 28 June 2001, E03 (ProQ).

141. Mark Mandel, in *Opera News*, Feb. 2011, quoted in Adamo, "*Little Women*— Critical Acclaim" (Adamo).

142. Bill Rankin, "Adamo: Little Women," *American Record Guide*, May–June 2010, 36 (Acad1).

143. Elaine Walter, quoted in Joseph McLellan, "'Little Women' Marches to a New Beat," *Washington Post*, 21 Sept. 1997, G10 (ProQ).

144. John Rockwell, "Alcott's Sisters Grow from Page to Stage," *New York Times*, 26 Mar. 2003, E5 (ProQ). See also Feldman, "Adamo: Little Women," *American Record Guide*, May–June 2011, 245 (Acad1); T. L. Ponick, "'Little Women,' Big Opera," *Washington Times*, 18 June 2007, B5 (LexN).

145. Jason Serinus, "Thank Heaven for Little Women," *Advocate*, 28 Aug. 2001, 63 (ProQ).

146. Jason Serinus, "Little Victories," *Colorado Springs Independent*, 29 Aug. 2001, 29 (ProQ); Daniel Ginsberg, "A 'Little Women' That's a Little Too Familiar," *Washington Post*, 18 June 2007, C5 (ProQ); Allan Kozinn, "Glimmerglass Distills Power of Acceptance and Faith," *New York Times*, 30 July 2002, E3 (ProQ).

147. Jim Lillie, "Sister Act," *Westword* (Denver, CO), 12 July 2001, 38 (ProQ).

148. Graham Strahle, "Musical Celebration of Sisterhood," *Australian*, 22 May 2007, F10 (LexN).

149. Heidi Waleson, Opera, *Wall Street Journal*, 7 Aug. 2002, D14 (ProQ); David Weininger, "'Little Women' Is Laudable," *Boston Globe*, 13 Dec. 2005, C11 (ProQ).

150. Kozinn, "Glimmerglass," E3.

151. Kenneth DeLong, "Little Women," *Opera Canada*, Summer 2010, 37 (Acad1).

152. Alex Ross, "Sisterhood," *New Yorker*, 22 July 2002 (Acad1).

153. Hugh Canning, Cooperstown, *Opera*, Nov. 2002, 1369.

154. Martin Bernheimer, Financial Times; Ona Binur, *Maa'riv* (Tel Aviv), July 2008; Benjamin Echenique Juarez, *La Reforma* (Mexico City); Strahle, "Musical Celebration of Sisterhood"; Ewart Shaw, *Advertiser* (Australia), May 2007; Barry Lenny, *Rip It Up* (Australia), May 2007—all quoted in Adamo, "*Little Women*—Critical Acclaim."

155. Marian de Forest, "Dramatizing a Novel Is a Chastening Experience," *New York Times*, 5 Mar. 1916, X8 (ProQ); Knoles, quoted in H.U., "Here are Little Women," *New York Tribune*, 7 July 1918, 32 (CA).

156. Mary Forsell, "Making Little Women Sing," *Victoria*, Mar. 2003, 100 (Acad1); Elizabeth Lennox Keyser, "'Things Change, Jo': Reflections on Twenty Years in Children's Literature (The 2003 Francelia Butler Lecture)," *Children's Literature* 34 (2006): 201.

157. Quoted in Janet L. Martineau, "PBS to Air 'Little Women' Opera," *Syracuse*

Herald American, 26 Aug. 2001, SM7 (NA); and Barrymore Laurence Scherer, "Opera: The Man Behind 'Little Women,'" *Wall Street Journal*, 29 Aug. 2001, A12 (ProQ).

158. Thomas May, "Perfect As It Was? No: Things Change," for andante.com, May 2002 (Adamo).

159. See Mark Adamo, "*Little Women*, A Course for Opera America's Distance Learning Program," 22–83 (Adamo), hereafter cited parenthetically as "Course."

160. For the former, see Feldman, "Adamo: Little Women," 245, and Rockwell, "Alcott's Sisters Grow"; for the latter, Stephen Francis Vasta, "Adamo: Little Women," *Opera News*, Dec. 2001, 70 (Acadı).

161. Richard Dyer, "'Little Women' Opera Is a Grand Success," *Boston Globe*, 1 Sept. 2001, C5 (ProQ).

162. Prologue, p. 29 of liner notes to *Little Women* (opera), by Mark Adamo, performed by Houston Grand Opera, recorded 17–18 Mar. 2000, Ondine, ODE988-2D, 2001, compact disc, hereafter cited parenthetically with reference to the act and scene in the opera and the page in the liner notes.

163. See Anthony Tommasini, "Lyricism but Few Modern Bits for the March Sisters," *New York Times*, 29 Aug. 2001, E5 (ProQ).

164. Louisa M. Alcott, *Little Women, or Meg, Jo, Beth and Amy: Authoritative Text, Backgrounds and Contexts, Criticism*, ed. Anne K. Phillips and Gregory Eiselein (New York: Norton, 2004), 280, hereafter cited parenthetically.

165. Quoted in William V. Madison, "The March of Adamo," *Opera News*, Mar. 2003, 46 (Acadı).

166. Edward J. Dent, *The Rise of Romantic Opera*, ed. Winton Dean (Cambridge: Cambridge Univ. Press, 1976), 2–3.

167. Mark Adamo, "Putting Away Childish Things," playbill, Houston Grand Opera, Mar. 1998 (Adamo).

168. May, "Perfect as It Was?"

169. Afterword to *Little Women*, retold by Deanna McFadden, illus. Lucy Corvino (New York: Sterling, 2005), 152, hereafter cited parenthetically.

170. Jacqueline Nightingale, adapter, *Little Women* (Oakdale, NY: Edcon, 1997), sec. A–21. For insights into abridgments of *Little Women*, including various first sentences, see Margaret Mackey, "*Little Women* Go to Market: Shifting Texts and Changing Readers," *Children's Literature in Education* 29.3 (1998), esp. 155–58.

171. Deanna McFadden, adapter, *Little Women* (New York: Sterling, 2005), hereafter cited parenthetically.

172. "Activities: After Reading," in *Little Women*, retold by John Escott, illus. Martin Cottam, 2nd ed. (Oxford: Oxford Univ. Press, 2000), 83.

173. "Louisa May Alcott (1832–1888)," in *Little Women*, condensed ed., illus. Mark English, Reader's Digest Best Loved Books for Young Readers (1967; reprint, New York: Choice, 1989), [163], hereafter cited parenthetically.

174. Claire Le Brun, "De *Little Women* de Louisa May Alcott aux *Quatre filles du docteur March*: Les traductions françaises d'un roman de formation au féminin," *Meta* 48.1–2 (2003): 47–67, esp. 56–57 (EBSCO).

175. Desmet, *Babysitting the Reader*, 227.

176. Catherine Belsey, *A Future for Criticism* (Chichester, UK: Wiley-Blackwell, 2011), 53, 37.

254   NOTES TO PAGES 172–175

177. Nigel Hamilton, *Biography: A Brief History* (Cambridge, MA: Harvard Univ. Press, 2007), 8–10. For a nuanced account of the functions of biography in the nineteenth century, especially belief in its power to shape character, see Scott E. Casper, *Constructing American Lives: Biography and Culture in Nineteenth-Century America* (Chapel Hill: Univ. of North Carolina Press, 1999), 2 and passim.

178. Ruth Graham, "Biography," *Wall Street Journal*, 29 Oct. 2010 (ProQ).

179. Pascale Voilley, *Louisa May Alcott: Petites filles modèles et femmes fatales* (Paris: Belin, 2001), 119.

180. Elizabeth Segel, "In Biography for Young Readers, Nothing Is Impossible," *Lion and the Unicorn* 4.1 (Summer 1980): 8.

181. Matina S. Horner, "Remember the Ladies," in *Louisa May Alcott*, by Kathleen Burke, American Women of Achievement (New York: Chelsea House, 1988), 9.

182. Louisa May Alcott, 26 Aug. 1868, in *The Journals of Louisa May Alcott*, ed. Joel Myerson and Daniel Shealy (Boston: Little, 1989), 166.

183. Gale Eaton notes these general trends for midcentury juvenile biographies in *Well-Dressed Role Models: The Portrayal of Women in Biographies for Children* (Lanham, MD: Scarecrow, 2006), 4.

184. Martha Vicinus, "What Makes a Heroine? Girls' Biographies of Florence Nightingale," in *Florence Nightingale and Her Era: A Collection of New Scholarship*, ed. Vern Bullough, Bonnie Bullough, and Marietta P. Stanton (New York: Garland, 1990), 103.

185. As Hilary S. Crew also notes, in "Louisa May Alcott: The Author as Presented in Biographies for Children," *Children & Libraries* 10 (Winter 2012): 29, 34.

186. Laurence Santrey, *Louisa May Alcott: Young Writer*, illus. Sandra Speidel (n.p.: Troll, [1986]), 8.

187. Marci Ridlon McGill, *The Story of Louisa May Alcott, Determined Writer*, illus. Darcy May (New York: Dell, 1988), 3.

188. Martha Robinson, *The Young Louisa M. Alcott*, illus. William Randell (New York: Roy, 1963), 134.

189. Carol Greene, *Louisa May Alcott: Author, Nurse, Suffragette* (Chicago: Childrens, 1984), 72.

190. Crew, "Louisa May Alcott," 32.

191. Aileen Fisher and Olive Rabe, *We Alcotts: The Story of Louisa M. Alcott's Family as Seen through the Eyes of "Marmee," Mother of "Little Women,"* illus. Ellen Raskin (New York: Atheneum, 1968), 269.

192. Norma Johnston [Nicole St. John], *Louisa May: The World and Works of Louisa May Alcott* (New York: Four Winds, 1991), 174.

193. The eight copies in my state's public library system are shelved in juvenile collections. Johnston's biography of Harriet Beecher Stowe, published by the same press, appears in both adult and juvenile sections; it would seem to matter whether the subject is (currently) associated with children's literature.

194. Review of *Louisa May*, by Norma Johnston, *Kirkus Reviews*, 15 Oct. 1991, Kirkus Reviews, www.kirkusreviews.com.

195. Review of *The Lost Summer of Louisa May Alcott*, by Kelly O'Connor McNees, *Kirkus Reviews*, 1 Mar. 2010, Kirkus Reviews, www.kirkusreviews.com. There's also the rather loosely plotted Louisa May Alcott Mystery series, by Anna Maclean [Jeanne

Mackin], with such titles as *Louisa and the Country Bachelor* (2005)—the country bachelor being not a love interest but a murder victim. Juvenile reworkings include Norma Johnston [Nicole St. John], *Lotta's Progress* (1997), which tells a story of a German immigrant girl whose family was presumably helped by the Alcotts, much as the Hummels were helped by the Marches in *Little Women*; Sheila Solomon Klass's *Little Women Next Door* (2000), which tells of the family's stay at Fruitlands through the eyes of a neighboring girl; and Jeannine Atkins's *Becoming Little Women* (2001), likewise focused on Fruitlands, essentially a biography with invented dialogue and added incidents.

196. Kelly O'Connor McNees, quoted in Alli Marshall, "Summer Fling," *Asheville (NC) Mountain Xpress*, 8 June 2011, 54, brackets Marshall's (ProQ).

197. Christopher James, "Little Women: The Tragedy," *Independent* (London), 13 Sept. 1989, L28 (LexN).

198. Carolyn Gage, *Louisa May Incest* (1990), in *The Second Coming of Joan of Arc, and Other Plays* (Santa Cruz, CA: HerBooks, 1994), 80.

199. Julie Sanders, *Adaptation and Appropriation* (London: Routledge, 2006), 55.

200. Lynne Sharon Schwartz, "True Confessions of a Reader," *Salmagundi*, nos. 88–89 (Fall 1990–Winter 1991): 206 (JSTOR).

201. Ronald Frame, "Destroyed Expectations," *Guardian* (London), 8 Dec. 2012, R12 (LexN); Carolyn Sigler, "Selected Bibliography of *Alice* Imitations and *Alice*-Inspired Works," in *Alternative Alices: Visions and Revisions of Lewis Carroll's Alice Books* (Lexington: Univ. Press of Kentucky, 1997), 387–91; Jan Susina, *The Place of Lewis Carroll in Children's Literature* (New York: Routledge, 2010), 75.

202. John Stephens and Robyn McCallum, *Retelling Stories, Framing Culture: Traditional Story and Metanarratives in Children's Literature* (New York: Garland, 1998), 3.

203. Glenn Rifkin, "A Town That Has a Way with Words," *New York Times*, 18 May 2007, F3 (LexN).

204. Hilary McKay, *The Exiles* (1991; reprint, New York: McElderry, 1992), 162.

205. Anne K. Phillips discusses the intertextuality in "'Certainly Reminiscent of Alcott's Little Women': The Marches, the Penderwicks, and 'the Family Story as Genre,'" paper presented at the annual meeting of the American Literature Association, Boston, 24 May 2013.

206. Lauren Baratz-Logsted, *Little Women and Me* (New York: Bloomsbury, 2011), 36, hereafter cited parenthetically.

207. Dale Eunson and B. W. Sandefur, "Little Women," *Little House on the Prairie*, season 3, episode 14, 24 Jan. 1977, YouTube, www.youtube.com.

208. Nardin "jokes that she has no idea how to plot a story, which is why her first novel follows the structure of a classic tale" (Akshita Nanda, "Late Start, Early Fame," *Straits Times* [Singapore], 18 Dec. 2012 [LexN]).

209. Mere24, review of "Two Roads Diverged," 22 Jan. 2009, www.fanfiction.net.

210. the doctor's next dance, review of "To Look at You and Never Speak," 6 Sept. 2007, www.fanficton.net.

211. See, e.g., Henry Jenkins, *Fans, Bloggers, and Gamers: Exploring Participatory Culture* (New York: New York Univ. Press, 2006), 135 (ebrary). Lauren Rizzuto has discussed the interpretive communities of fanfiction based on *Little Women* in "'Jo March Is Pregnant and Laurie's the Father': Alcott in the Fanfiction Community," paper presented at the annual meeting of the American Literature Association, Boston, 24 May

2013. For a discussion of the way fanfiction enables us to "listen to the stories young people tell themselves," see Catherine Tosenberger, "Mature Poets Steal: Children's Literature and the Unpublishability of Fanfiction," *Children's Literature Association Quarterly* 39.1 (Spring 2014): 22.

212. Earlier potential candidates include Floyd Dell's *Janet March: A Novel* (1923) and Anzia Yezierska's *The Bread Givers* (1925); although each portrays a woman with some strength and resilience, the echoes of *Little Women* are muted. But see Ruth Bienstock Anolik's "'All Words, Words, about Words': Linguistic Journey and Transformation in Anzia Yezierska's *The Bread Givers*," *Studies in American Jewish Literature* 21 (2002): 12–23, esp. 18–19 (JSTOR).

213. Allison Speicher, "When It All Goes South: Re-Imagining Alcott's Little Women in *The Sheltered Life*," *Ellen Glasgow Newsletter* 57 (Fall 2006): 8.

214. For a perceptive reading of West's novel in light of *Little Women*, see Janice M. Alberghene, "Autobiography and the Boundaries of Interpretation: On Reading *Little Women* and *The Living Is Easy*," in Alberghene and Clark, *"Little Women" and the Feminist Imagination*, 347–76.

215. For a brief commentary on the echoes of *Little Women* in Fletcher's *Daughters of Jasper Clay*, see Joanne Bourne, "Brooklyn Enclave," *New York Times*, 16 Mar. 1958, BR41 (ProQ).

216. Works that invoke or somehow echo *Little Women* include the British Kate Saunders's *The Prodigal Father* (1986), Jamaica Kincaid's *Lucy* (1990), Patricia Dienstfrey's *The Woman without Experiences* (1995), Jane Smiley's *Moo* (1995), the British Fay Weldon's *Big Women* (1997, published in the United States as *Big Girls Don't Cry*), Laura Kalpakian's "Little Women" (in *The Delinquent Virgin*, 1999), Chris Bohjalian's *Trans-sister Radio* (2000), Rick Hautala's "Little Women in Black" (in *Required Reading: Remixed*, 2011); and, for the young, Kathleen V. Kudlinski's *Shannon* (1996), Jennifer Donnelly's *A Northern Light* (2003), and Lenore Look's *Alvin Ho: Allergic to Birthday Parties, Science Projects, and Other Man-Made Catastrophes* (2010).

217. Gabrielle Donnelly, *The Little Women Letters* (New York: Simon, 2010), 349.

218. Quoted in A. J. Philpott, "Who Was the Real Laurie?" *Boston Daily Globe*, 4 Jan. 1914, 37.

219. May Alcott to Alfred Whitman, 5 Jan. 1869, quoted in *Little Women: An Annotated Edition*, by Louisa May Alcott, ed. Daniel Shealy (Cambridge, MA: Belknap Press of Harvard Univ. Press, 2013), 178n6. Shealy also notes the ambiguous implications of a sentence in a recently discovered letter in which Alcott indicates that May preferred to have only the line "illustrated by May Alcott" in the book and not "be identified as one of the little women." He adds that it is not clear whether she thought it might be "more professional to be listed as the illustrator" or didn't "want to be identified as Amy" ("Contributor Daniel Shealy reports on a Recent Auction of a Letter from Alcott to her Publisher Regarding *Little Women*," *Portfolio*, Spring 2013, 1).

220. Judith Rossner, *His Little Women* (New York: Summit, 1990), 237, 281. Marilyn French's *Our Father* (1994) similarly plays out the relationships among four daughters of a powerful man by different mothers, but to different effect: she explores the possibilities of creating sisterhood upon the death of the patriarch.

221. Michiko Kakutani, "Sisters in Hollywood and Art Too Much Like Life," *New York Times*, 13 Apr. 1990, C28 (ProQ).

222. Katharine Weber, *The Little Women* (New York: Farrar, 2003), 165, hereafter cited parenthetically; the comments by the sisters are in italics in the original.

223. For a reading of *The Poisonwood Bible* as a "recycling" of the domesticity of *Little Women*, see Kristin J. Jacobson, "The Neodomestic American Novel: The Politics of Home in Barbara Kingsolver's *The Poisonwood Bible*," *Tulsa Studies in Women's Literature* 24.1 (Spring 2005): 105–27 (JSTOR). Jacobson quotes Kingsolver as noting that she certainly "considered that other famous family of 'little women'. . . . But the parallels don't go too far. Louisa May Alcott didn't put any snakes in her book" (124n11). For additional readings of the Alcottian echoes in Kingsolver's, Rossner's, and Brooks's novels, see Betina Entzminger, *Contemporary Reconfigurations of American Literary Classics: The Origin and Evolution of American Stories* (New York: Routledge, 2013), 83–103.

224. For discussion of the correspondences with *Little Women*, see Elizabeth Lennox Keyser, "*A Bloodsmoor Romance*: Joyce Carol Oates's Little Women," *Women's Studies* 14 (1988): 211–23.

225. Susan Wyndham, "Spoils from the Battlefield," *Sydney Morning Herald*, 19 Apr. 2006, N13 (LexN); Ray Chesterton, "Pulitzer Prize Winner's Story Better than Fiction," *Daily Telegraph* (Australia), 19 Apr. 2006, F29 (LexN).

226. Thomas Mallon, "Pictures from a Peculiar Institution," *New York Times*, 27 Mar. 2005, G11 (ProQ); *Los Angeles Times*, *New Yorker*, and *Economist* quoted in Amanda Hodge and David Nason, "Aussie Interloper Joins American Literary Elite," *Australian*, 19 Apr. 2006, L3 (LexN).

227. See also Susan R. Gannon, "Getting Cozy with a Classic: Visualizing *Little Women* (1868–1995)," in Alberghene and Clark, *"Little Women" and the Feminist Imagination*, 134.

228. Lauren Rizzuto, "Illustrating *Little Women*, or Louisa, Jo, May and Amy," paper presented at the annual meeting of the Children's Literature Association, Boston, 14 June 2012.

229. Mackey, "*Little Women* Go to Market," 166.

230. Louisa May Alcott, *Little Women*, illus. Jame's Prunier (New York: Viking, 1997), 105.

231. Sharon Goodman, introduction to "Words and Pictures," in *Children's Literature: Approaches and Territories*, ed. Janet Maybin and Nicola J. Watson (Milton Keynes, UK: Palgrave Macmillan–Open University, 2009), 296.

232. Michael Steig, *Dickens and Phiz* (Bloomington: Indiana Univ. Press, 1978), 3.

233. Robert L. Patten, "Serial Illustration and Storytelling in *David Copperfield*," in *The Victorian Illustrated Book*, ed. Richard Maxwell (Charlottesville: Univ. Press of Virginia, 2002), 92.

234. Shirley Hughes, "Word and Image," in *"Only the Best Is Good Enough": The Woodfield Lectures on Children's Literature, 1978–1985*, ed. Margaret Fearn (London: Rossendale, 1985), 75.

235. Michael Semff, "'L'ordonnance d'un labyrinthe': Sculptors' Contributions to the Illustrated Artist's Book," trans. John William Gabriel, in *Splendid Pages: The Molly and Walter Bareiss Collection of Modern Illustrated Books*, ed. Julie Mellby (New York: Hudson Hills–Toledo Museum of Art, 2003), 51, 53. See also Johanna Drucker, *The Century of Artists' Books* (New York: Granary, 1995).

236. "SI Hall of Fame: Mark English, 1983 Hall of Fame Inductee," interview by Anna Lee Fuchs, Society of Illustrators, www.societyillustrators.org.

237. In the 1967 Reader's Digest four-pack, the images are slightly browner and less sharp than those in the 1989 single-novel reprint. Often glossy printings more closely replicate the artwork, so one might be tempted to give preference to the later renditions; then again, skilled illustrators create artwork specifically for a given production process so that the intended appearance is what is on the printed page.

238. David Skilton, "The Relation between Illustration and Text in the Victorian Novel: A New Perspective," in *Word and Visual Imagination: Studies in the Interaction of English Literature and the Visual Arts*, ed. Karl Josef Höltgen, Peter M. Daly, and Wolfgang Lottes (Erlangen, Germany: Universitätsbund Erlangen-Nürnberg, 1988), 309.

239. Quoted in Jill Bossert, *Mark English* (New York: Madison Square, 2002), 24.

240. Bossert, *Mark English*, 19.

241. Gannon, "Getting Cozy with a Classic," 134. Gannon does not mention English's illustrations.

242. Skilton, "Relation between Illustration and Text," 310.

243. *Little Women*, illus. Mark English, opp. 74. Captions appear only in the 1989 edition.

244. Lori Kenschaft has pointed to the image's echo of the Five of Pentacles in a Tarot deck, featuring two figures in the snow in front of a warmly lit window; the card signifies hardship, such as financial hardship, yet perhaps also the support of loyal partners (personal communication, 3 Oct. 2012).

245. Elizabeth Lennox Keyser, *Little Women: A Family Romance* (New York: Twayne, 1999), 44.

246. Bossert, *Mark English*, 145.

247. The three illustrations are reproduced in *Illustrators 10*, ed. Howard Koslow (New York: Hastings House, 1969), items 207, 227, 367. English was later elected to the Illustrators Hall of Fame.

248. I am indebted to Roger Clark and Kim Miller for the ventriloquism and vampire insights.

Index

Abbott, Diane, 142
Abbott, Jacob, 36
Abbott, Lyman, 36
Academy Award, 87
Adamo, Mark, 155, 162–69
Adams, Katherine, 20–21
Addams, Jane, 14, 106
Adler, Richard, 133–35
Adventures of Huckleberry Finn (Twain),
103–4, 105, 212n160
Adventures of Tom Sawyer, The (Twain),
37, 104, 212n160
"Adventure with 'Little Women,' An"
(Hawthorne), 291n98
Alcott, Abba (Abigail May Alcott), 9, 72,
112–16, 173–75
Alcott, Amy, 145
Alcott, Anna, 9, 21, 40, 50, 82, 116, 173
Alcott, Bronson (Amos Bronson Alcott), 18,
24, 26, 38, 97–100, 242n193; in biogra-
phies, 40, 104, 112–14, 116, 173–75, 184;
compared to Louisa, 44–45, 49, 83, 103,
111, 149; fictionalized, 151, 176, 182, 185;
on tour, 18, 26, 207n79
Alcott, Elizabeth, 73, 97, 112
Alcott, Eunice, 91
Alcott, John Sewell Pratt, 19, 71, 91, 183
Alcott, Junius, 114
Alcott, Louisa May: *Aunt Jo's Scrap-Bag*,
21; "The Banner of Beaumanoir," 150; as
A. M. Barnard, 105, 145; *Behind a Mask*,
145; biographies of, 7, 20, 39, 51–54, 103,
109–16, 171–76, 198 (*see also* Cheney,
Ednah D.); celebrity of, 10, 21, 39, 87,
173, 207n79; *Comic Tragedies*, 50; *Eight
Cousins*, 34, 36; fan letters and, 5, 11,
13–14, 17–18, 20, 109–10, 140, 204n27;
Hospital Sketches, 8, 34–35, 38; *Jack and
Jill*, 36, 37; *Jo's Boys*, 4, 11, 19–20, 34, 48,
211n154; "The Lay of a Golden Goose,"
19; *Little Women* (see *Little Women*);
Little Men (see *Little Men*); *A Long
Fatal Love Chase*, 162; *Lulu's Library*,
50, 218n73; *A Modern Mephistopheles*,
40, 91, 228n270; *Moods*, 34, 39, 114; *An
Old-Fashioned Girl*, 11–12, 31, 35, 36–37,
50, 91, 203n14, 203n17; *Proverb Stories*,
36; *Rose in Bloom*, 37–38; sensation
stories, 7, 105, 114, 143, 152, 174, 187;
sensation stories and modern critics, 145,
149, 160; *Under the Lilacs*, 12, 203n16,
203n17; women's suffrage and, 22, 39, 83,
95, 98–100, 146, 159, 170; *Work*, 35
Alcott, May (Abigail May Alcott Nieriker),
9, 19, 21, 110, 112, 184; as illustrator,
22–24, 187, 256n219
Alderson, Valerie, 148
Aldrich, Bess Streeter, 15
Aldrich, Thomas Bailey: *The Story of a
Bad Boy*, 37
Alice's Adventures in Wonderland (Carroll),
177

Allstate Corporation, 199
Allyson, June, 129–31, 133, 159, 241n172, 242n192
Almedingen, E. M., 49
Alvin Ho (Look), 256n216
American Adam, The (Lewis), 103
American Library Association (ALA) catalog, 34–35, 109
American Literature, 112
American Merchant Marine Library, 106
American Novel and Its Tradition, The (Chase), 103
Anderson, Gretchen, *The Louisa May Alcott Cookbook*, 141
Anderson, William T., *The World of Louisa May Alcott*, 144
Angry Housewives Eating Bon Bons (Landvik), 182
Anthony, Katharine, *Louisa May Alcott*, 102, 113–14
Arbuthnot, May Hill, *Children and Books*, 141
Arcadia, The, 94
Armstrong, Frances, 67
Armstrong, Gillian, 142, 159, 161
Asher, Sandra Fenichel: *Little Women*, 150
Astor, Mary, 47, 241n172
Atkins, Jeannine: *Becoming Little Women*, 255n195
Atlantic Monthly, 28, 31, 35–37
Auerbach, Nina, 146
Aunt Jane's Nieces (Baum), 219n98
Aunt Jo's Scrap-Bag (Alcott), 21
Austen, Jane, 85, 180, 219n102; *Pride and Prejudice*, 146, 177

Bader, David, M., 138
Bagna i fiori e aspettami (Ravera), 143
Baker, S. Josephine, 14
Bakke, Kit: *Miss Alcott's E-mail*, 175
Baldwin, James, 135
Bankhead, Tallulah, 125
"Banner of Beaumanoir, The" (Alcott), 150
Baratz-Logsted, Lauren: *Little Women and Me*, 178–79
Bartelme, Mary, 48
Barton, May Hollis: *Four Little Women of Roxby*, 60, 61–62

Basinger, Jeanine, 242n189
Baum, Frank L. (pseud. Edith Van Dyne): *Aunt Jane's Nieces*, 219n98
Baxter Birney, Meredith, 157
Baym, Nina, 105
Beach, Sylvia, 108
Beauvoir, Simone de, 49
Becker, May Lamberton, 71
Becoming Little Women (Atkins), 255n195
Bedell, Madelon, 148
Beecher, Mrs. Henry Ward, 18
Beegel, Susan, 69
Beer, Thomas, *The Mauve Decade*, 103
Behind a Mask (Alcott), 145
Being a Boy (Warner), 37
Belsey, Catherine, 171
Bennett, Joan, 117, 128, 238n118
Benny, Jack, 128
Bergen, Candice, 144
Bernard, Dorothy, 95, 96, 97, 227n252, 229n300, 230n316
"Bernice Bobs Her Hair" (Fitzgerald), 69
Betty und ihre Schwestern (translation), 206n50
Bibliothèque Nationale, 234n45, 246n41
Big Girls Don't Cry (Weldon), 256n216
Big Guy, Little Women (Shannon), 178
Big Women (Weldon), 256n216
Billings, Hammatt, 24, 208n99
Birdsall, Jeanne: *The Penderwicks*, 178
Bizet, Georges: *Les pêcheurs de perles*, 160
Blackford, Holly, 5, 140
Blaisdell, Elinore, 117
Bleak House (Dickens), 33, 193
Bloodsmoor Romance, A (Oates), 183, 185
"Bloody Chamber, The" (Carter), 155
Bluestone, George: *Novels into Film*, 58
Bohjalian, Chris: *Trans-sister Radio*, 256n216
Bonstelle, Jessie (Jessie Bonstelle Stuart), 6, 49, 70–71, 74–75, 81–82, 226n225
Books for Boys and Girls (Toronto Public Library), 52
Bookshelf of Our Own, A (Felder), 140
Bossert, Jill, 192
Boys and Girls of Bookland (Smith), 56
Bradford, Clare, 60

Bradford, Gamaliel: *Portraits of American Women*, 53
Brady, Alice, 42, 97
Brady, William, Jr., 42
Brady, William A., 6, 42, 75, 81–82; and films, 86–89, 91, 96, 227n248, 228n270
Brazil, Angela, 79
Bread Givers, The (Yezierska), 256n212
Britton, Andrew, 127
Brock, H. M., 55
Brodhead, Richard H., 37
Brontë, Charlotte: *Jane Eyre*, 156
Brooks, Geraldine: *March*, 183, 185–86
Brooks, Van Wyck, 11
Brophy, Brigid, 147
Brown, Lisa, 139
Brown, Mamie, 14
Brown, Pamela: *Louisa*, 116
Brundage, Frances, 55
Buffy the Vampire Slayer (TV series), 198
Bulgheroni, Marisa, 108
Bunyan, John, 165; *Pilgrim's Progress*, 10, 16, 57, 61, 74, 143, 202n2
Burd, Clara, 55
Bush, Barbara, 107
Bush, Bertha E.: *Story of Louisa M. Alcott*, 218n80
Bush, Laura, 107
Byatt, A. S., 226n222

Cadwalladr, Carole, 142
Cambridge History of American Literature, The, 43–44
Carnegie, Dale: "5-Minute Biographies," 110
Caroline, Princess of Hanover, 143
Carroll, Lewis, 186; *Alice's Adventures in Wonderland*, 177
Carson, Jeannie, 134
Carter, Angela: "The Bloody Chamber," 155
Cartmell, Deborah, 161
Carville, James, 107
Case of Peter Pan, The (Rose), 3
Chase, Richard: *The American Novel and Its Tradition*, 103
Cheever, Susan: *Louisa May Alcott*, 175
Cheney, Ednah D.: *Louisa May Alcott,*

the *Children's Friend*, 28–29, 39–40; *Louisa May Alcott: Her Life, Letters, and Journals*, 33, 37, 39–40, 113, 213n180; as source for later biographies, 52–53, 115, 173
Chesterton, G. K., 48
Child, Lydia Maria, 19, 100
Children and Books (Arbuthnot), 141
Christmas Carol, A (Dickens), 249n103
Christmas with Little Women, 186
Chung, Connie, 107
Clauser, Suzanne, 157
Clinton, Hillary Rodham, 107
Coe, Fanny: *The Louisa Alcott Story Book*, 51
Colles, Dorothy, 116
Comic Tragedies (Alcott), 50
Comins, Lizbeth B., 29
Concord, MA, 11, 19, 26, 123, 213n187; Alcotts' home in, 24, 39–40, 70, 97, 100, 109, 112–14, 144, 174; and films, 87, 96, 122, 123, 128, 131, 162; and plays, 81, 120–21, 152
Concord Sonata (Ives), 242n193
Concord Woman's Club, 15, 98–100
Coolidge, Susan (Sarah Chauncey Woolsey), 11
Cooney, Barbara, 116
Coontz, Stephanie, 26
Copping, Harold, 55, 57–59
Cornell, Katharine, 85, 96, 97, 224n176
Cowie, Alexander: *The Rise of the American Novel*, 103
Crane, Stephen, 103
Craven, Peter, 108
Crew, Hilary, 174
Critic, 38
Crowther, Bosley, 130–31
Cukor, George, 102, 122–26, 129
Cultural Literacy (Hirsch), 140
Custer, George Armstrong, 176
Cycle of American Literature, The (Spiller), 103

Daughters of Jasper Clay, The (Fletcher), 181–82
Daughters of Pharmacist Kim, The (Park), 143

Dawn of Womanhood, The (Jackson), 62
de Forest, Marian, 14, 226n225; *Little Women* (play), 70–75, 80, 82, 88–89, 119, 164; revivals of play, 49, 85–86, 96, 109, 117–18, 132, 223n176
de Horne Vaizey, Mrs. George: *Sisters Three*, 60–61
Delafield, E. M., 236n79
Delamar, Gloria T., 210n118
Dell, Floyd, 70; *Janet March*, 256n212
Denniston, Robin Alastair, 104–5
Desmet, Mieke K. T., 171
De vier dochters van Dr March (translation), 171
DeVoto, Bernard, 210n135
Dey, Susan, 16, 157
Diamond in the Window, The (Langton), 177
Dickens, Charles, 12, 30, 46, 106, 173, 189; *Bleak House*, 33, 193; *A Christmas Carol*, 249n103
Dickstein, Mindi, 153
Didion, Joan, 107
Dienstfrey, Patricia: *The Woman without Experiences*, 256n216
Donnelly, Gabrielle: *The Little Women Letters*, 182–83
Donnelly, Jennifer: *A Northern Light*, 256n216
Douglas, Ann, 148
Doyle, Edward, 83
Dutta, Lara, 143
Dyer, Richard, 134, 165

Eager, Edward: *The Time Garden*, 177
Eaton, Walter Prichard, 48
Ebert, Roger, 159
Eden's Outcasts (Matteson), 173
Edgeworth, Maria, 14, 33, 36
Edward, Prince of Wales, 40
Eight Cousins (Alcott), 34, 36
Eiselein, Gregory, 148, 234n34
Elementary English Review, 110
Elgin, Jill, 2, 3, 117
Emerson, Charlotte: *Jo's Troubled Heart*, 177; Little Women Journals series, 177
Emerson, Ralph Waldo, 97, 120–21; home of, 87, 93

English, Mark, 192–98, 258n247
Englund, Sherryl A., 208n88, 209n110
Esmond, Martha Freeman, 14
Exiles, The (McKay), 178

Fadiman, Clifton, 103
Faithfull, Lilian M., 49, 52
Faust (opera), 160
Felder, Deborah G.: *A Bookshelf of Our Own*, 140
Feldman, Marty, 107, 234n42
Ferber, Edna, 15
Fisher, Aileen: *We Alcotts*, 174
Fitzgerald, F. Scott: "Bernice Bobs Her Hair," 69
Five Little Peppers, The (Lothrop), 98, 219n98
"5-Minute Biographies" (Carnegie), 110
Fletcher, Lucille: *The Daughters of Jasper Clay*, 181–82
Forgan, Liz, 146
Forsell, Mary, 164
Four Little Women of Roxby (Barton), 60, 61–62
Frank Leslie's Illustrated Newspaper, 37
Fraser, Betty, 188
Frederick, Heather Vogel: *The Mother-Daughter Book Club*, 178
Freer, Eleanor Everest, 242n193; *Scenes from Little Women*, 131
French, Marilyn: *Our Father*, 256n220
Friends (NBC), 198
Fruitlands, 112, 114–15, 173–74
Fuller, Margaret, 174

Gage, Carolyn: *Little Women Incest*, 176
Gannon, Susan R., 22, 192, 237n90
Garrett, Edmund H., 24–25
Gaskell, Elizabeth, 80
Gaston, Colonel, 47
Gay, Carol, 129, 131
Genette, Gerard, 177
Gerould, Katharine Fullerton, 65–66
Gilbert, Sandra M., 146
Girl and Her Trust, The (film), 229n300
Girl Called Jo, A (musical), 132
Girl Scouts: *Scouting for Girls*, 53
Girl's Own Paper, 57, 58

Glasgow, Ellen: *The Sheltered Life*, 181
Glen, Esther: *Six Little New Zealanders*, 219n98
Glory Cloak, The (O'Brien), 175
Godey's Lady's Book, 122
Goethe, Johann Wolfgang von: "Mignon's Song," 166
Goldwyn, Samuel, 127
Gone with the Wind (film), 126
Good Reading (National Council of Teachers of English), 108
Good Wives (Alcott). See *Little Women* (Alcott): part 2 of
Gowing, Clara, 19, 26
Grand, Porter: *Little Women and Werewolves*, 179–80
Grant, Linda, 146
Grauman, Sid: Grauman's Theater, 93
Gray, M. E., 55
Green, John, 141
Green, Samuel, 31
Grey, Zane, 105
Griffith, D. W., 96, 229n300
Gubar, Marah, 77
Gubar, Susan, 146
Gulliver, Lucile, 110

Haag, Jackson, 78
Hallmark Cards, 132
Hamilton, Clayton, 44
Hamilton, Nigel, 171
Hampton, Benjamin B., 227n252
Harris, Frank, 108
Hart, John S.: *A Manual of American Literature*, 30; *A Short Course in Literature*, 30
Haskell, Molly, 124
Hasta siempre, mujercitas (Serrano), 143
Hautala, Rick: "Little Women in Black," 256n216
Hawthorne, Hildegarde: "An Adventure with 'Little Women,'" 291n98
Heart Murmurs (Smythe), 176
Heerman, Victor, 122–23, 129
Heindel, Robert, 191–92
Hemingway, Ernest, 47
Hepburn, Katharine, 97, 115, 123–24, 126–27, 128, 145, 167, 238n118; subsequent portrayals of Jo compared to, 129–31, 156, 159
Hetzel, Pierre-Jules (pseud. P.-J. Stahl), 16
Hewins, Caroline, 34
Higginson, Thomas Wentworth, 28, 70; *Short Studies of American Authors*, 31–32
Hintz, Carrie: *Reading Children's Literature*, 141
Hirsch, E. D.: *Cultural Literacy*, 140
Hischak, Thomas, 153
His Little Women (Rossner), 183–84
Hochman, Barbara, 21, 202n2
Hoeller, Hildegard, 147
Hollander, Anne, 132
hooks, bell, 141
Hospital Sketches (Alcott), 8, 34–35, 38
Howard, Frederick, 121
Howard, Joan: *The Story of Louisa May Alcott*, 116
Howells, William Dean, 37
Howland, Jason, 153
Hubbard, Alison, 153
Hughes, Shirley, 191
Hull, Henry, 97
Hunniford, Gloria, 107
Hutcheon, Linda, 58

Index Translationum (UNESCO), 142, 246n41
Indianapolis Public Library, 34
Invincible Louisa (Meigs), 111–13, 115
Irwin, Hobe, 122
Ives, Charles: *Concord Sonata* (Piano Sonata No. 2, *Concord, Mass.*, 1840–60), 242n193

Jack and Jill (Alcott), 36, 37
Jackson, Gabrielle E.: *The Dawn of Womanhood*, 62; *Three Little Women*, 62–67; *Three Little Women as Wives*, 65, 68–69; *Three Little Women at Work*, 63, 65, 68; *Three Little Women* series, 60, 62–69, 101; *Three Little Women's Success*, 63–64, 66–68
Jacobs, Lea, 79
Jacobson, Kristin J., 257n223
Jambor, Louis, 116, 237n90
James, Derek, 188

James, Henry, 30, 36
Jane Eyre (Brontë), 156
Janet March (Dell), 256n212
Jearue, Arthur, 118
Jersey Shore (TV series), 187
Jo (musical), 118, 153
Johnston, Norma (Nicole St. John): Lotta's Progress, 255n195; Louisa May, 175
Jones, Richard, 55
Jordan, Alice, 109
Jordan Marsh, 50
Jo's Boys (Alcott), 4, 11, 19–20, 34, 48, 211n154
Jo's Troubled Heart (C. Emerson), 177
Jousset, Albert de Mee, 116–17
Jurjevics, Juris, 107

Kalpakian, Laura: "Little Women," 256n216
Kaplan, Amy, 24
Keller, Helen, 14
Kenschaft, Lori, 258n244
Kent, Kathryn R., 4
Keyser, Elizabeth Lennox, 164, 193
Kincaid, Jamaica: Lucy, 256n216
Kingsolver, Barbara, 141; The Poisonwood Bible, 183, 185, 257n223
Kiper, Florence, 222n147
Kipling, Rudyard, 15
Kirk, Elise K., 242n193
Kirkham, Pat, 132
Klapper, Melissa R., 205n32, 219n102
Klass, Perri, 141; Other Women's Children, 182
Klass, Sheila Solomon: Little Women Next Door, 255n195
Klauber, Adolph, 77
Kleine Frauen (translation), 206n50
Klickmann, Flora, 57, 58
Knee, Allan, 155
Knoles, Harley, 87, 96, 164
Koszarski, Richard, 86–87
Krantz, Judith, 107
Krips, Valerie: The Presence of the Past, 4
Kudlinski, Kathleen V.: Shannon, 256n216
Kuhlemann Cárdenez, Alma B., 143
Kuntz, Jonathan, 124

Ladies' Home Journal, 109–10
La Ganke, Florence, 48
Landsberg, Michele, 141
Landvik, Lorna: Angry Housewives Eating Bon Bons, 182
Lane, Charles, 112, 114, 173
Langton, Jane: The Diamond in the Window, 177
Langworthy, Mrs. B. F., 48
Lardner, Ring, 47
Lardner, Ring, Jr., 47
Larrick, Nancy: A Parent's Guide to Children's Reading, 108
Laurence, Kristin, 118, 237n197
Lawford, Peter, 129
Lawlor, Laurie, 162
"Lay of a Golden Goose, The" (Alcott), 19
Le Brun, Claire, 171
Le Guin, Ursula K., 107
Leigh, Janet, 133
Lerman, Leo, 47, 106
LeRoy, Mervyn, 130, 241n172, 242n187
Les pêcheurs de perles (Bizet), 160
Les quatre filles du docteur March (translation), 16, 171
Les quatre filles du docteur Marsch (translation), 16
Les quatre filles du pasteur March (translation), 16
Les quatre sœurs Marsch (novelization), 128
Letterature da guardarobiera (Muratori), 143
Lewin, Walter, 37
Lewis, R. W. B.: The American Adam, 103
Library of the World's Best Literature (Warner), 41
Lillie, Lucy, 15
Lima, Margaret, 51
Lip Service: Very Little Women, 152
Literary History of the United States (Spiller), 103
Little, Norman, 55
Little House on the Prairie (TV), 156, 179
Little Men (Alcott), 3, 4, 12, 13, 35, 36, 104, 234n42; adaptations of, 51–52, 70, 91, 158, 162; and education, 17, 108, 148; library circulation of, 12, 203n14; prominence of, in early twentieth century, 42, 45, 48, 50–52, 70, 217n58; sales of, 11, 45, 203n17

Little Theatre movement, 81, 86

Little Vampire Women (Messina), 179

Little Women (Alcott): abridged editions of, in English, 1, 54, 139, 140, 169–70, 186, 192, 253n170; abridged translations of, 16, 142, 144, 170–71; anime adaptations of, 7, 144, 156; annotated edition of, 149; awards presented to adaptations of, 122, 125, 153, 185, 194; ballet adaptations of, 156, 158, 164, 250n112; clubs based on, 7, 17, 61, 106, 182, 219n102; comics and graphic adaptations of, 127, 139, 141, 143, 144, 186, 189; critical esteem and, 7, 10, 28–39, 43–44, 103–5, 137; dolls based on, 50, 109, 111, 132, 140–41, 145, 162 (*see also* Madame Alexander Doll Co.); fanfiction about, 180–81, 255n211; film adaptations of, 2, 16, 150, 156, 198 (see also *Little Women* [films]); feminist themes and, 138, 141, 145–48, 152, 171; illustrations and, 7; illustrations and, after 1930, 103, 111, 116–17, 149, 159, 186–98, 237n90, 242n192, 258n237; illustrations and, before 1930, 11, 22–26, 45, 54–59, 82, 101, 208n99, 208n101, 256n219; language in, 24, 31–32, 65–66, 209n113; library circulation of, 6, 11–13, 45–47, 49, 50, 139–42, 203n11, 203n14, 205n32; Library of America edition of, 148; musical adaptations of, 117–18, 121, 132–35, 152–55, 158, 198, 242n193, 248n84, 249n99 (see also *Little Women* [opera]); Norton Critical Edition of, 148; part 1 of, 4, 7, 9–10, 11, 18, 30, 133–35, 136; part 2 of, 9, 11, 18, 24, 30, 36, 134–35, 188, 203n8; Player's Edition of, 55; polls and, after 1930, 105–7, 122, 139–40, 142, 164, 232n19, 245n23; polls and, before 1930, 12, 16, 38, 45, 46, 48–51, 216n58, 217n61; radio adaptations of, 107, 109, 128; Reader's Digest edition of, 170, 192; recommendations of, 28–30, 34–35, 39, 51–52, 108, 140–41, 198, 218n70, 235n56; reviews of, 6–7, 16, 28–38, 46, 114, 140, 210n118; sales of, 6, 10–12, 28, 42, 45, 49, 128; sentiment and, 78–81, 85, 95–96, 104–5, 126, 135, 148, 224n195; spinoffs (fictional) of, after 1930, 143, 149, 150, 176–86, 198–99, 256n212, 256n216; spinoffs (fictional) of, before 1930, 45, 58–70, 101, 219n98; stage adaptation of, on Broadway in 1912, 6, 42–43, 58, 70–89, 95–96, 97, 101, 183 (*see also* de Forest, Marian); stage adaptations of, other, 7, 103, 117–21, 149–55, 198, 248n73; Sunday schools and, 12, 29–30, 31, 56, 107, 210n118; television adaptations of, 103, 106, 117, 129, 132–35, 179, 198–99, 242n194 (see also *Little Women* [TV films]); translations of, into French, 16–17, 170–71, 186, 206n57, 246n41; translations of, into other languages, 7, 16, 49, 107–8, 110, 142–44, 171, 216n44

Little Women (Asher), 150

Little Women (de Forest), 70–75, 80, 82, 88, 119, 164; revivals of, 85–86, 109, 117–18, 132

Little Women (film, 1917), 86

Little Women (film, 1919), 86–97, 164

Little Women (film, 1933), 7, 86, 97, 102, 111, 121–28, 131, 161, 164; influence of, 115, 117, 129–30, 134, 153, 155, 159–60, 162, 166–67

Little Women (film, 1949), 7, 48, 102, 117, 129–33, 161, 242n199; influence of, 134, 153, 155, 159–60, 166–67, 242n192

Little Women (film, 1994), 6, 157, 158–62, 219n91

"Little Women" (Kalpakian), 256n216

Little Women (music group), 145

Little Women (opera), 7, 155, 156, 162–69

Little Women (TV films), 16, 156–58

Little Women, The (Weber), 183–85

Little Women, The Musical, 153–55

Little Women, The Tragedy (Split Britches), 176

Little Women and Me (Baratz-Logsted), 178–79

Little Women and Werewolves (Grand), 179–80

Little Women Big Cars (online series), 199

Little Women Club, The (Taggart), 60, 61, 176

"Little Women in Black" (Hautala), 256n216

Little Women Incest (Gage), 176

Little Women in India (Nardin), 180, 255n208
Little Women Journals series (C. Emerson), 177
Little Women Letters, The (Donnelly), 182–83
Little Women Next Door (Klass), 255n195
Little Women of Orchard House (Longest), 151–52
Little Women Wedded (Alcott). See *Little Women* (Alcott): part 2 of
Living Is Easy, The (West), 181
Livingstone, Mary, 128
Lonette, Reisie, 117
Longest, David: *Little Women of Orchard House*, 151–52
Long Fatal Love Chase, A (Alcott), 162
Look, Lenore, *Alvin Ho*, 256n216
Los Angeles County Library, 51
Lost Summer of Louisa May Alcott, The (McNees), 176
Lothrop, Harriett (pseud. Margaret Sidney), 98; *The Five Little Peppers*, 98, 219n98
Lotta's Progress (Johnston), 255n195
Louisa (Brown), 116
Louisa Alcott (Wagoner), 115
Louisa Alcott Reader, The, 218n73
Louisa Alcott Story Book, The (Coe), 51
Louisa and the Country Bachelor (Maclean), 255n195
Louisa M. Alcott's Little Women (novelization), 128
Louisa May (Johnston), 175
Louisa May Alcott (Anthony), 102, 113–14
Louisa May Alcott (Cheever), 175
Louisa May Alcott (Moro-oka), 146
Louisa May Alcott (Moses), 52–53, 113
Louisa May Alcott (Stern), 104, 105, 114, 173
Louisa May Alcott (Voilley), 147
Louisa May Alcott, the Children's Friend (Cheney), 28–29, 39–40
Louisa May Alcott, Her Life, Letters, and Journals (Cheney), 33, 37, 39–40, 113, 213n180; as source for later biographies, 52–53, 115, 173
Louisa May Alcott Cookbook, The (Anderson), 141

Louisa May Alcott Mystery series (Maclean), 254n195
Lowell, Amy, 65
Lucas, E. V., 124
Lucy (Kincaid), 256n216
Lukens sisters, 17
Lulu's Library (Alcott), 50, 218n73

MacDonald, Dwight, 232n4
Machor, James L., 208n96
Mackey, Margaret, 189
Maclean, Anna: *Louisa and the Country Bachelor*, 255n195; Louisa May Alcott Mystery series, 254n195
Madame Alexander Doll Co., 111, 128, 145, 177
Madonna (Madonna Louise Ciccone), 141
Main Currents in American Thought (Parrington), 103
Maissen, Leena, 108
Malone, Ted, 144
Manchester Opera House, 152
Manners, Miss. See Martin, Judith
Mantel, Hilary, 142
Mantle, Burns, 79
Manual of American Literature, A (Hart), 30
Manual of American Literature, A (other), 43
March (Brooks), 183, 185–86
March Sisters at Christmas, The (TV film), 198–99
Marshall Field's, 50
Martí, José, 33
Martin, Judith (pseud. Miss Manners), 107, 113
Martin, Mary, 134
Maslin, Janet, 126
Mason, Bobbie Ann, 107
Mason, Sarah Y., 122–23, 129
Matteson, John: *Eden's Outcasts*, 173
Mauve Decade, The (Beer), 103
Maxwell, Anne, 88
May, Thomas, 165, 169
McCallum, Robyn, 177
McDonald, Megan: *Rule of Three*, 178
McDowell, Mary, 48
McGovern, Maureen, 153

McGuire, Dorothy, 157
McKay, Hilary: *The Exiles*, 178
McNees, Kelly O'Connor: *The Lost Summer of Louisa May Alcott*, 176
Meet Me in St. Louis (film), 132
Meigs, Cornelia: *Invincible Louisa*, 111–12, 115
Meleagrou, Eleni, 143
Merrill, Frank, 24, 26, 186, 187, 208n99, 208n101
Messina, Lynn: *Little Vampire Women*, 179
Michiko, Empress, 108, 144
"Mignon's Song" (Goethe), 166
"Miniature Women" (radio skit), 128
Miss Alcott of Concord (Worthington), 115
Miss Alcott's E-mail (Bakke), 175
Mitchell, Jessie T., 55, 57
Mitchell, Sally, 69
Modern Family (TV series), 198
Modern Mephistopheles, A (Alcott), 40, 91, 228n270
Mold, C. A., 237n90
Montgomery, L. M., 11
Moo (Smiley), 256n216
Moods (Alcott), 34, 39, 114
Moore, Anne Carroll, 65
Moore, Julianne, 141
Moro-oka, Aiko, 144; *Louisa May Alcott*, 146
Moses, Belle: *Louisa May Alcott*, 52–53, 113
Mother-Daughter Book Club, The (Frederick), 178
Mott, Frank Luther, 11
Moulton, Louise Chandler, 204n27
Moving Picture World, 92, 95, 229n280
Mulherzinhas (TV film), 242n194
Mumford, Lewis, 44
Muratori, Letizia: *Letterature da guardarobiera*, 143
Myerson, Joel, 60, 214n8; *The Selected Letters of Louisa May Alcott*, 103
My Little Women (musical), 118

Nachmann, Gerald, 138
Nagel, Conrad, 97
Nardin, Jane: *Little Women in India*, 180, 255n208
National Council of Teachers of English,

128; Committee on College Reading, *Good Reading*, 108
National Women's Hall of Fame, 140
Negrón, Luis, 141
Nelly, 13
Newark Public Library, 106
Newbery Medal, 111–12
New York Mercantile Library, 11
New York Public Library, 45–46, 50, 139
Nieriker, Louisa May (Lulu), 110
Nieriker, May Alcott. *See* Alcott, May
Nightingale, Florence, 173
Niles, Thomas, 14, 29, 106, 114, 166, 207n83; encouragement of Alcott's writing, 8–9, 11, 18, 172
Nodelman, Perry: *Touchstones*, 140
Northern Light, A (Donnelly), 256n216
Novels into Film (Bluestone), 58
Nudelman, Edward, 54

Oates, Joyce Carol: *A Bloodsmoor Romance*, 183, 185
O'Brien, Margaret, 132, 133, 241n172, 241n173, 242n199
O'Brien, Patricia: *The Glory Cloak*, 175
O'Hara, Geoffrey, 121
Old-Fashioned Girl, An (Alcott), 11–12, 31, 35, 36–37, 50, 91, 203n14, 203n17
Oler, Kim, 153
Olive Branch, 175
Onder moeders vleugels (translation), 16, 171
Orchard House, 24–25, 39–40, 112, 115, 194, 236n79; adaptations of *Little Women* and, 81, 87, 93, 122, 128, 151, 159, 199, 252n138; as museum, 7, 15, 43, 58, 61, 70, 97–101, 194; visitors to, 15, 41, 97, 108, 142, 144
O'Rourke, P. J., 138
Other Women's Children (Klass), 182
Our Father (French), 256n220
Ozick, Cynthia, 107

Pablo Marcos Studio, 187
Page, Geraldine, 250n112
Paramount Pictures, 86, 90, 227n248
Parent's Guide to Children's Reading, A (Larrick), 108
Paretsky, Sara, 107

Park, Kyung-ni: *The Daughters of Pharmacist Kim*, 143
Parker, Henry Taylor, 80–81
Parnell, Peter: *Romance Language*, 176
Parrington, Vernon Louis: *Main Currents in American Thought*, 103
Parsons, Louella, 14, 104
Pascal, Amy, 6, 159
Paul, Elliot, 107
Pawley, Christina, 203n14
Peg o' My Heart (play), 76
Penderwicks, The (Birdsall), 178
Perkins, Frederic Beecher, 28
Petites femmes (translation), 16
Petry, Ann, 48
Pfeffer, Susan Beth: Portraits of Little Women series, 177
Phelps, Pauline, 118
Phillips, Anne K., 148
Phillips, Arlene, 107
Piccole donne (translation), 143
Piccole donne (TV series), 242n194
Piccole donne crescono (translation), 143
Piccole donne in cucina (Vitzizzai), 143
Pickford, Mary, 227n252
Pilgrim's Progress (Bunyan), 10, 16, 57, 61, 74, 143, 202n6
Pober, Arthur, 169
Poggi, Jack, 224n185
Poisonwood Bible, The (Kingsolver), 183, 185, 257n223
Portraits of American Women (Bradford), 53
Portraits of Little Women series (Pfeffer), 177
Pratt, Anna Alcott. *See* Alcott, Anna
Pratt Institute, 28
Pride and Prejudice (Austen), 146, 177
Presence of the Past, The (Krips), 4
Prodigal Father, The (Saunders), 256n216
Proverb Stories (Alcott), 36
Prunier, Jame's, 189
Pulitzer, Walter, 29

Quindlen, Anna, 141

Rabe, Olive: *We Alcotts*, 174
Radio City Music Hall, 121
Radway, Janice A., 213n192

Ravera, Lidia: *Bagna i fiori e aspettami*, 143; *Se lo dico perdo l'America*, 143
Ravold, John D., 117, 118, 119–21, 132
Reading Children's Literature (Hintz and Tribunella), 141
Religious Tract Society, 57
Repplier, Agnes, 36
Rich, Adrienne, 234n34
Richardson, Anna Steese, 219n91, 222n149
Richardson, Dorothy B., 204n32
Ridout, Gladys, 55
Rise of the American Novel, The (Cowie), 103
Rizzuto, Lauren, 188, 255n211
RKO Pictures, 121–22
Roach, Joseph, 21
Roberts Brothers, 11, 21, 24, 45
Rockwell, Norman, 113
Romance Language (Parnell), 176
Roosevelt, Theodore, 15, 35, 69
Rose, Jacqueline: *The Case of Peter Pan*, 3
Rose, Jonathan, 13
Rose in Bloom (Alcott), 37–38
Rossner, Judith: *His Little Women*, 183–84
Rostenberg, Leona, 105, 145
Rowling, J. K., 142
Royal Free Hospital: Little Women bed, 52
Rozier-Gaudriault (Jacques Rozier and Monique Gaudriault), 188
Rule of Three (McDonald), 178
Russ, Lavinia, 47
Ruth, Amy, 174
Rutherford, Alexa, 188
Ryan, Barbara, 203n18
Ryder, Winona, 141, 159–60, 244n5

S., Satie, 14
Sage, William, 83
Sagna, Caterina: *Sorelline*, 143
Salmon, Edward, 28
Salter, Mary Jo, 141
Sanchez, Sonia, 107
Sanders, Julie, 177
San Mateo Public Library, 106
Saunders, Kate: *The Prodigal Father*, 256n216
Scenes from Little Women (Freer), 131
"Scenes from 'Little Women'" (play), 70

Schaeffer Pen Corporation, 134–35
School Stage, The (Venable), 70
Schulman, Sarah, 141
Schwartz, Lynne Sharon, 177
Scouting for Girls (Girl Scouts), 53
Scudder, Horace, 28, 35, 37
Selected Letters of Louisa May Alcott, The
    (Myerson and Shealy), 103
Se lo dico perdo l'America (Ravera), 143
Sensational Designs (Tompkins), 147
sensation stories (Alcott), 7, 105, 114, 143,
    152, 174, 187; and modern critics, 145,
    149, 160. *See also* "Banner of Beauman-
    oir, The"; *Behind a Mask*
Serrano, Marcela: *Hasta siempre, mujer-
    citas,* 143
Seven Little Australians (Turner), 33, 58, 60
Shakespeare, William, 28, 142
Shannon (Kudlinski), 256n216
Shannon, Jacqueline: *Big Guy, Little
    Women,* 178
Shatner, William, 157
Shealy, Daniel, 149, 208n100, 214n8,
    256n219; *The Selected Letters of Louisa
    May Alcott,* 103
Sheltered Life, The (Glasgow), 181
Shepard, Odell, 104, 113, 114
Short Course in Literature, A (Hart), 30
Short Studies of American Authors (Hig-
    ginson), 31–32
Showalter, Elaine, 148, 205n39, 234n34
Sicherman, Barbara, 4, 14, 18, 210n123,
    242n11
Sidney, Margaret. *See* Lothrop, Harriett
Silber, Nina, 65
Simons, Judy, 161
Simpsons, The (TV series), 198
Sisters (Steel), 182
Sisters Three (de Horne Vaizey), 60–61
Six Little New Zealanders (Glen), 219n98
Skilton, David, 192–93
Smedley, Constance, 15
Smiley, Jane: *Moo,* 256n216
Smith, Frederick James, 95
Smith, Jessie Willcox, 54–56, 92, 145,
    186, 197
Smith, Nora Archibald: *Boys and Girls of
    Bookland,* 54, 56

Smith, Patti, 107
Smythe, R. R.: *Heart Murmurs,* 176
Sohoni, Neera Kuckreja, 108
Solt, Andrew, 129
Sontag, Susan, 107
Sorelline (Sagna), 143
Speicher, Allison, 181
Spencer, Charles, 142
Spencer, Sara, 118, 237n96
Spiller, Robert E.: *The Cycle of American
    Literature,* 103; *Literary History of the
    United States,* 103
Split Britches: *Little Women: The Tragedy,*
    176
Spofford, Harriet Prescott, 28
Stahl, P.-J., 16
Stearns, Frank Preston, 10, 35
Steedman, Carolyn, 4
Steel, Danielle: *Sisters,* 182
Steig, Michael, 191
Stein, Gertrude, 205n39
Steinem, Gloria, 107
Stephens, Alice Barber, 45, 55, 56, 82, 197
Stephens, John, 177
Stern, Madeleine B., 145; *Louisa May
    Alcott,* 104, 105, 114, 173
Stimpson, Catharine R., 148
Story of a Bad Boy, The (Aldrich), 37
Story of Louisa M. Alcott (Bush), 218n80
Story of Louisa May Alcott, The (Howard),
    116
Stowe, Harriet Beecher, 14, 254n193;
    Uncle Tom's Cabin, 44, 135
Strachey, Lytton, 53
Strand, The, 43
Suhre, John (John Sulie), 175
Sutherland, John, 141
Sweet, Blanche, 227n252
Swicord, Robin, 159, 250n116
Swinnerton, Frank, 15

Taggart, Marion Ames: *The Little Women
    Club,* 60, 61, 176
Tarrant, Percy, 55
Tassin, Algernon, 43–44
Taylor, Elizabeth, 131–32, 133, 241n172
Taylor, Maureen, 82, 87
Teasdale, Sara, 15

Temple, Shirley, 107
Terman, Lewis, 50–51
Terrell, Mary Church, 15
Terry, Ellen, 15
Thaner, Anna, 14
Thiede, Adolf, 55
Thomas, M. Carey, 14
Thoreau, Henry David, 97, 151
Thoreau-Alcott house, 97
Three Little Maids (Turner), 219n98
Three Little Women (Jackson), 62–67
Three Little Women as Wives (Jackson), 65, 68–69
Three Little Women at Work (Jackson), 63, 65, 68
Three Little Women series (Jackson), 60, 62–69, 101
Three Little Women's Success (Jackson), 63–64, 66–68
3LW (music group), 145
Time Garden, The (Eager), 177
Tiné, Mae, 94
Tompkins, Jane: *Sensational Designs*, 147
Toronto Public Library: *Books for Boys and Girls*, 52
Touchstones (Nodelman), 140
Tracy, Virginia, 94–95, 230n300
Tran, Tram-Anh, 141
Transcendentalism, 26, 38, 82–83, 87, 100, 136
Trans-sister Radio (Bohjalian), 256n216
Tribunella, Eric L.: *Reading Children's Literature*, 141
Trites, Roberta Seelinger, 139
Trubek, Anne, 12, 98
Tudor, Tasha, 145, 188–90
Turner, Ethel: *Seven Little Australians*, 33, 58, 60; *Three Little Maids*, 219n98
Twain, Mark, 32; *Adventures of Huckleberry Finn*, 103–4, 105, 212n160; *The Adventures of Tom Sawyer*, 37, 104, 212n160
Two Little Women series (Wells), 219n98

Uncapher, Robin, 245n23
Uncle Tom's Cabin (Stowe), 44, 135
Under the Lilacs (Alcott), 12, 203n16, 203n17

UNESCO, Index Translationum, 142, 246n41
U.S. Information Library, 108

Van Abbé, S., 117
Van Dyne, Edith, 219n98
Van Nattan, Mary, 244n4
van Stockum, Hilda, 116
Vellucci, Sabrina, 146
Venable, W. H.: *The School Stage*, 70
Very Little Women (Lip Service), 152
Vicinus, Martha, 173, 213n188
Villella, Edward, 158
Vitzizzai, Elisabetta Chicco: *Piccole donne in cucina*, 143
Voilley, Pascale, 172; *Louisa May Alcott*, 147

Wadsworth, Sarah, 109
Wagenknecht, Edward, 103
Wagoner, Jean Brown: *Louisa Alcott*, 115
Wakakusa-monogatari (translation), 235n50
Walsh, John, 141
Warner, Charles Dudley: *Being a Boy*, 37; *Library of the World's Best Literature*, 41
Warner, Susan: *The Wide, Wide World*, 44
Warren, Austin, 111
Warren, Sarah, 132
Washington Post, 50, 127
Watters, David, 100
We Alcotts (Fisher and Rabe), 174
Weber, Katherine: *The Little Women*, 183–85
Weldon, Fay: *Big Women* (*Big Girls Don't Cry* in U.S.), 256n216
Wells, Carolyn: Two Little Women series, 219n98
Wells, Ida B., 15, 205n40
Wendell, Barrett, 65
West, Dorothy: *The Living Is Easy*, 181
West, Patricia, 99–100
Wharton, Edith, 14, 65, 192
What Middletown Read (website), 12
Wheeler, Roger, 118
Wheelhouse, M. V., 55
Whitman Publishing Company, 1
Wickes, Mary, 215n31
Wide, Wide World, The (Warner), 44

Wilhelm, Julie, 136
Wilson, Jacqueline, 107
Wisniewski, Ladislas, 114, 115, 174
Within the Law (play), 76
Woman's Congress (Syracuse), 18
Woman without Experiences, The (Dienst-
  frey), 256n216
Wonder Years, The (TV series), 156
Woodward, Joanne, 158
Woollcott, Alexander, 15, 108
Work (Alcott), 35
World Film Corporation, 86–87

World of Louisa May Alcott, The (Ander-
  son), 144
Worthington, Marjorie: *Miss Alcott of
  Concord*, 115

Yezierska, Anzia: *The Bread Givers*,
  256n212
Yolen, Jane, 107
Yonge, Charlotte M., 15
Young, Robert, 157

Zehr, Janet, 39